"Lucky War"
Third Army in Desert Storm

Richard M. Swain

U.S. Army Command and General Staff College Press
Fort Leavenworth, Kansas

TO THE SOLDIERS  OF THIRD ARMY

Contents

Illustrations	vii
Preface	xi
Acknowledgments	xix
Introduction	xxiii
1. Prologue to Operation Desert Shield	1
2. Executing a Contingency	17
3. Planning a Ground Offensive I: The CINC's Study Group	71
4. Planning a Ground Offensive II: The ARCENT Process	103
5. Build-up to Attack	139
6. Desert Storm: Air Power and Final Issues	175
7. Desert Storm: Battle	225
8. Battle's End	279
9. Conclusions: "A Famous Victory?"	319

Appendixes

A. Command and Control, ARCENT, February 1991	349
B. Task Organization, Operation Desert Shield, 5 March 1991	350
C. Warfighting Command and Control, XVIII Airborne Corps	351
D. The XVIII Airborne Corps' Task Organization, 5 March 1991	352
E. Warfighting Command and Control, VII Corps	353
F. The VII Corps' Task Organization, 5 March 1991	354
G. Current Combat Capability, 24 February 1991	355
H. Chronology	356

Glossary 361
Bibliography 365

Illustrations
Figures

Figure 1.	Third Army is three armies	26
Figure 2.	CENTCOM command and control	28
Figure 3.	One-corps concept of operations	30
Figure 4.	ARCENT's headquarter's capabilities	34
Figure 5.	Third Army force generation rate	36
Figure 6.	Force generation—Desert Shield versus Vietnam	38
Figure 7.	Minimum essential force development	41
Figure 8.	Reserve Component support to ARCENT HQ	44
Figure 9.	Operation Desert Shield, command and control	47
Figure 10.	ARCENT Support Command, Operation Desert Shield	48
Figure 11.	Coalition coordination structure in Operation Desert Shield	57
Figure 12.	The status of deployment D-1, 16 January 1991	107
Figure 13.	G-day logistics posture	109
Figure 14.	Asset availability versus commitments	111
Figure 15.	Routes and distances between major locations	119
Figure 16.	The plan and timing of the attack	122
Figure 17.	Force generation in relation to the air campaign	125
Figure 18.	The commander's assessment, 9 February 1991	126
Figure 19.	Attack positions	130
Figure 20.	Phase II: Developing the offensive option, 9 November (C+94)—16 January (C+162)	141
Figure 21.	Liaison teams	148

Figure 22.	A comparison of Europe and Kuwait theater of operations	158
Figure 23.	Allied deployments the day prior to start of air operations	166
Figure 24.	Movement of two corps	178
Figure 25.	Patriot air defense	179
Figure 26.	G-9, 15 February 1991	200
Figure 27.	G-8, 16 February 1991	202
Figure 28.	G-7, 17 February 1991	203
Figure 29.	Threat locations	212
Figure 30.	Battle damage assessment, 24 February 1991	226
Figure 31.	Timing of the attack execution	231
Figure 32.	Third Army's final synchronization matrix	233
Figure 33.	Another comparison (concerning size of operational area)	249
Figure 34.	Demarcation line	320
Figure 35.	Planning is not fighting	339

Maps

Map 1.	Saudi Arabia	5
Map 2.	KTO: Comparison to Eastern United States	24
Map 3.	Desert Dragon III—September 1990: CENTCOM defends in sector	51
Map 4.	One-corps concept of operations	80
Map 5.	AO Eagle (and the hunt for Scuds)	86
Map 6.	Two-corps concept of operations	94
Map 7.	G-day, Sunday, 24 February 1991: Opening situation	208
Map 8.	Ground operations—G+1, Monday, 25 February, 0800	235

Map 9.	Ground operations—G+1, Monday, 25 February, 2400	242
Map 10.	Ground operations—G+2, Tuesday, 26 February, 2400	251
Map 11.	Ground operations—G+3, Wednesday, 27 February, 2400	253
Map 12.	The 101st Airborne move to FOB Viper and attack on EA Thomas	257
Map 13.	Ground operations—G+4, Thursday, 28 February, 2000	283
Map 14.	Basrah	294

Note: A photo essay appears after page 223.

Preface

There is a crossroads near Safwan in southeastern Iraq. Nearby, there is a small hill and an airstrip. After the Gulf War, Safwan became a gathering point for refugees fleeing the Iraqi Army as it reestablished control of Basrah. Prior to that, the airstrip was the site of the dictation of armistice terms to that army by the victorious coalition's military high command. Still earlier, at the end of the coalition attack, the absence of American forces on the airstrip and at the road junction was the source of the most serious command crisis of the U.S. expeditionary forces. Its resolution put at risk American soldiers and threatened the reputations of the very commanders who had just conducted the greatest offensive of concentrated armored forces in the history of the United States Army. In many ways, events at Safwan in late February and early March are emblematic of the Gulf War. It is to explain how U.S. forces arrived at Safwan, what they did and did not do there, and what this all meant, that this book is written.

The Gulf War was an undoubted success. It was also a war of clear, sharp contrasts. Saddam Hussein's rape of Kuwait was an obvious wrong that begged for setting right. Saddam's stranglehold on much of the world's proven oil reserves presented a clear and present danger to Western interests, and his wanton attack on Kuwait posed a clear threat to his Arab brothers. Moreover, Saddam's own ineptness in dealing with the crisis ensured the unity of the global community against him unless the diplomatic effort to resolve the situation was seriously mishandled. It was altogether a war of the old comfortable sort—good against evil, a wrong to be righted—a crusade.

It was for all that a difficult strategic and operational challenge for the American armed forces, which at first found themselves badly out of position. Though freed of the Soviet threat, U.S. forces were still deployed along the inter-German border and, half a world away, in the continental United States. Saddam was able to snap up Kuwait before Western military forces could intervene. In early August 1990, there was much to be done and precious little time in which to do it. It was a long road to the greatly unbalanced victory on the last day of February in 1991.

The purpose of this book is to provide an account, from the point of view of the U.S. Army forces employed, of the 1990-91 Persian Gulf War, from the Iraqi invasion of Kuwait to the withdrawal of coalition forces from southeastern Iraq. Like all contemporary history, this is written in one respect to provide work for revisionists. That is to say, it is written from the evidence at hand and from the author's observations as the Third Army historian. Much evidence remains unavailable. The Army is very bad at collecting the documentary record of its activities in any sort of systematic way. It certainly is not expeditious about it. The principal actors are only beginning to tell their stories. General Schwarzkopf's account, flawed by much unsupported special pleading, remains to be answered by those he indicts. Moreover, we know very little of the enemy's intentions and the reasons and details surrounding Saddam Hussein's actions. Perhaps we may never know much more.

So in many ways this history, like all history, is necessarily imperfect. Yet it must be written to form a part of what shall eventually become the historic view of these events. This work also offers an accounting to the American people for the employment of their resources and the conscious imperiling of their sons and daughters in the cause of liberating Kuwait. It is hoped that it will also provide a useful institutional record that can be called upon in the future when policy makes similar demands upon the Army. Most important, this work reminds the reader that the decisions and actions that took place in Operations Desert Shield and Desert Storm occurred in a larger and quite specific context, one often beyond the influence of the people on the ground who so often were portrayed as able to control events and their own destinies far more than was the case. In the end, no completely free agents existed in Saudi Arabia. The story of this and all wars depends on how commanders adapted to circumstances as they found them and how they turned existing conditions to their benefit.

This book's focus is on the Army's part in this war, particularly the activities of the Headquarters, Third Army, and the Army Forces Central Command (ARCENT). It looks especially at the activities of the VII Corps, which executed ARCENT's main effort in the theater ground force *schwerpunkt*—General Schwarzkopf's "Great Wheel." The book is titled "Lucky War" after the affectation of Third Army, whose telephone switch, as far back as General George Patton's World War II headquarters, has been named "Lucky." In the same fashion, the Third Army's tactical operations center in Desert Storm was referred to as "Lucky TOC." Its forward command post was "Lucky Wheels," and so on. "Lucky" is a talisman to Third Army as, incidentally, are "Jay Hawk" to VII Corps, and "Danger" to the 1st Infantry Division. It is for that reason alone that "Lucky" is incorporated in the title.

The author has made only limited use of oral interviews concerning tactical operations. Others in the field have more than adequately tapped the memories of participants at the ground level as well as in the high command. This work is based primarily on documentary evidence, clarified by interviews with participants, rather than the other way around.

This book does not presume to be an official history. The author speaks in his own voice and makes his own judgments and evaluations based upon available evidence. Thus, this is public history, written at public expense for public purposes: the education of Army officers and an accounting to the public of its Army in the operations in Southwest Asia as viewed from a military technical point of view.

The distinction between public and official history was laid down by Immanuel Kant almost two hundred years ago when he distinguished between the public and private use of reason. Kant allowed that those employed in the government's business might often be required to support the government's actions contrary to their own views. "One certainly must not argue," Kant says, "instead one must obey."[1] Such obedience is a hallmark of military discipline, particularly during a war.

Yet the Army has an institutional need for honesty and frankness in order to learn from its experiences. This requires not just a recording of events and actions but a critique that sets decisions and actions in context and evaluates them in light of available alternatives. Kant pointed out that, notwithstanding their official status, officials did not cease to surrender their membership in the wider community. He argued that in this broader persona, the official might address the public "in the role of the scholar . . . , without harming the affairs for which as a passive member he is partly responsible."[2] One of Kant's examples of someone divided in personal responsibility, interestingly enough, was a soldier, who, he noted, must obey any order he receives. "But as a scholar," Kant maintains, "he cannot be justly constrained from making comments about errors in military service, or from placing them before the public for its judgment."[3] This spirit animates this book.

This work was written against a deadline—or what the Army calls a "suspense." That constraint imposed limits on mastering even the incomplete materials available. But while this limitation will offend historical purists, haste was both necessary and justifiable. It was necessary because the information is perishable. Sometimes by the time an entirely "scientific history" is written, the practical need for it may be past. One is reminded that the Israeli Army's history of its 1967 war was not in the hands of that army when the 1973 war broke out. But facts alone are not the only interest of historians, who deal in interpretations of evidence that are, to a degree, merely approximations or imperfect representations of past reality. The reader can judge whether or not the evidence cited here is adequate to support the conclusions drawn.

In his magisterial work *Peace and War: A Theory of International Relations*, Raymond Aron chose three lines of inquiry—theoretical, sociological, and historical—as a way of understanding international relations. This book will attempt to take the same approach, though perhaps applying Aron's method in different proportions. This work is first of all a history, a narrative account disciplined by evidence. But war is essentially a social activity, not only because it occurs within political societies but because armies are themselves social organizations. To understand why and how decisions were made and actions were taken, one must understand the social milieu in which the actors existed. The story that follows does not ignore interpersonal relations in telling what really happened, for the history of the war would be distorted by the omission of discussion of this very human problem. That would be wrong indeed. As for theory, it will be used from time to time for its explanatory value.

Some judgments are necessary on the performance of the leaders who directed the successful effort to eject Saddam Hussein from Kuwait. This is done not from any mean-spirited belief that the author himself could have done it better had he the opportunity. There is a wide difference between knowing and doing, and commanders depend far more on the latter than the former. Clausewitz pointed out years ago that flanking maneuvers and concentration and maintenance of aim are not complex ideas, but their achievement is very difficult, indeed. "... let a general try to imitate Frederick!" he wrote, and that requires great reserves of "boldness, resolution and strength of will."[4]

One prejudice and two criteria undergird the judgments found in this book. The prejudice is simple: that killing in war is a means to an end, not an end in itself. What distinguishes the U.S. Army from many others is its recognition that there is a point, defined by diminishing utility to attainment of the goal sought, where simply killing the enemy ceases to be acceptable. Though one could not claim that this prejudice is a universal value in the Army, the capstone document for American armed forces doctrine, Joint Chiefs of Staff Publication 1,

Joint Warfare of the U.S. Armed Forces, carries with it a categorical imperative and a warning that seems to underscore the point:

> We also must have the courage to wield military power in a scrupulously moral fashion. We respect human rights. We observe the Geneva Conventions not only as a matter of legality but from conscience. This behavior is integral to our status as American fighting men and women. Acting with conscience reinforces the links among the Services and between the U.S. Armed forces and the American people, and these linkages are basic sources of our strength.[5]

The repeated willingness of American soldiers to comfort their captured adversaries in the field and the concern of the entire chain of command to avoid unnecessary loss of life or destruction would seem to indicate that this view of moral conduct is widespread in the U.S. Army.

One of my criteria for judgment came from the vice chief of staff of the Army, General Gordon Sullivan, on a trip to Saudi Arabia shortly after the war. Sullivan spoke to a Third Army staff, perhaps too full of themselves after their still recent success, and he took any tendency for swagger out of them with a simple observation. "The American people," he said, "expect only one thing from us: That we will win! What you have done is no more than they expect. You have won." We must now ask, therefore, whether the actions in question contributed to the ultimate success of the war. And to this, I would add, whether the accomplishment of the goals set by the coalition and national political executive were *economical.*

The second criterion was set by General Schwarzkopf himself, and it has to do with character. As Schwarzkopf told television interviewer David Frost: "I admire men of character and I judge character not by how men deal with their superiors, but mostly how they deal with their subordinates. And that, to me, is where you find out what the character of the man is."[6] The author will leave judgments of character to the reader, but he will not ignore events that seem to reflect upon this aspect of the American high command. The U.S. Army claims to invest great effort in the development and evaluation of this human attribute. To ignore its influence would be to suppress a vital part of the story of Operation Desert Storm.

Finally, a number of themes are evident in the account of Third Army's part in the Gulf War. The first is the success of the U.S. Central Command in anticipating the contingency that occurred. When Iraq occupied Kuwait, Central Command had planned for just such a contingency and was, therefore, able to respond much more promptly than would have been possible otherwise.

Central Command's anticipation notwithstanding, the threat posed by Iraq was not the one the U.S. Army of 1990 had been fashioned to meet. The Army had been organized, trained, and equipped to meet a Soviet invasion of Europe. A number of consequences for the Gulf War grew out of that salient fact. The Army and, indeed, the entire military panoply were equipped with the finest fighting equipment in the world. It lacked, however, the means for offensive operational maneuver because the European mission did not require them. Further, the Army had no doctrine and only a skeletal organization for echelons of command above the corps, like Third Army. The mobilization of an army-level headquarters and support structure had to be effected as events unfolded. How this was done is the second major theme of this book, and the story contains lessons about force building and deployment that should be useful for an Army that must increasingly respond to global contingencies in distant locales.

A third theme has to do with the corporate nature of the operational planning for Operation Desert Storm. Military doctrine and most historical accounts would suggest that military operations normally take place in response to a sequential and hierarchical planning sequence—from top to bottom. In Desert Storm, the process was multilevel, interactive, and simultaneous—as well as horizontal and vertical. The story of how the plan took form over a period of months and the assumptions that fashioned and shaped it in the theater of war are a central part of the story told in these pages.

The central role of logistics in operational war fighting, the power of personality in war, the unchanging features of war—friction, chance, and contingency—all are subordinate themes in the story of Third Army in Operation Desert Storm. The practice of command itself, the ability of a leader to make decisions and cause other men to both understand and obey him—in short, the role of the commander at the theater, operational, and tactical levels of war in an era of global tactical satellite communications—is the ultimate theme of this account. At the end of the day, it is the author's hope that the story told here will not be totally unfamiliar to those named in these pages.

Notes

1. Immanuel Kant, "An Answer to the Question: What Is Enlightenment," in Immanuel Kant, *Perpetual Peace and Other Essays on Politics, History, and Morals*, trans. Ted Humphrey (Indianapolis, IN: Hackett, 1983), 42–43.

2. Ibid.

3. Ibid.

4. Carl von Clausewitz, *On War*, trans. Peter Paret and Michael Howard (Princeton, NJ: Princeton University Press, 1976, 1984), 179–80.

5. Joint Chiefs of Staff, Joint Publication 1, *Joint Warfare of the US Armed Forces*, 11 November 1991, 9.

6. General H. Norman Schwarzkopf, quoted in transcript ". . . talking with David Frost," 22 March 1991, 28. Transcript in possession of the author.

Acknowledgments

During the Gulf War, I had the matchless opportunity to be assigned as theater army historian on the staff of the Third Army in Saudi Arabia. Though one would not necessarily draw such a conclusion from most published accounts of the Gulf War, Third Army was the senior operational headquarters of the United States Army in the Persian Gulf. Third Army was commanded by Lieutenant General John Yeosock, who was on Operations Desert Shield and Desert Storm from the start. Indeed, the Desert Storm army was largely his creation. But Yeosock had earlier served in an Army whose attitudes had been formed over the years by NATO scenarios in which the largest national formation was to be a corps. The U.S. Army had not foreseen a requirement to deploy a multicorps army. The interposition of an army headquarters between the corps and the theater commander was not without difficulties and gave rise to a certain cognitive dissonance at times. Yeosock himself is a man who shies from public exposure and who does not do particularly well before the camera. Criticism of the conduct of the war has tended to ignore the intervening headquarters between the two Army corps commanders and the very visible commander in chief, H. ("Stormin'") Norman Schwarzkopf. This picture is very wrong, and among other reasons, it is to correct this impression that this account is written.

This book would never have been completed without the material assistance of a number of people to whom the author owes a considerable debt. First, there is Bill Stacy, the historian of U.S. Army Forces Command, who made it possible for the author to go to Saudi Arabia as Third Army historian. Bill also has been a source of assistance and encouragement since then. He is everything an Army historian must be and so few are. His principal assistant, Mrs. Tammy C. Howle, must also be acknowledged for her assistance while the author was assigned to Fort McPherson, Georgia. I should also express appreciation to Lieutenant General Leonard Wishart, commandant of the U.S. Army Command and General Staff College (CGSC), and then-Brigadier General John Miller, the deputy commandant in 1990–91, for permitting me to go.

The commander and staff officers of Third Army made it possible for me to watch much of what took place and to collect the documents necessary to write this account. The army staff officers, busy with the conduct of the war, accepted the historian as a fellow professional, even though they often failed to understand why the headquarters needed a historian. Nonetheless, they always took the time to answer questions and to explain why various perceptions might be incomplete. Lieutenant Colonels Dave Mock, Mike Kendall, and the G3 planners were particularly helpful and supportive. The 44th Military History Detachment, commanded by Major Larry Heysteck, laid the foundation for the army history office, and Sergeant Bonnie Gray and Major Guy Sanderson helped run it. All were enthusiastic and great professionals, and the successes I enjoyed in Saudi Arabia are largely due to their efforts. The chief of military history, Brigadier General Hal Nelson, provided me with the opportunity to spend a year researching the records and writing the first draft of this account, sometimes in the face of opposition from his organization. Hal provided me with the time and resources to set up a research office in the Combined Arms Research Library (CARL) at Fort Leavenworth. There, I was assisted by three great confederates who, in truth, did most of the hard work. These were Dr. Pat Swann and Captains Russel Santala and Mark Traylor. Without them, nothing would have been accomplished. Pat is a geographer whom the Staff College could not figure out how to employ properly. She has now left the college for other government work. Russ Santala and Mark Traylor, both exceptionally gifted officers and veterans of the war, were invaluable in tracking down records, finding evidence, and criticizing the author's flights of fancy. Mrs. Elaine Hoinacki, the team typist, spent many long days listening to recorded interviews and transcribed faithfully all that was intelligible therein. Thanks are also owed the librarians of CARL's third floor, who made room and welcomed three intruders and their various file cabinets and safes into an already overcrowded attic.

I enjoyed the advice, too, of an excellent board of editors: Dr. Pete Maslowski, Dr. Larry Yates, Colonels Jim McDonough and Greg Fontinot, Major Mark Blum, and Don Gilmore. Professor Edward M. ("Mac") Coffman also read the draft and provided wise counsel. Their advice was always thoughtful, and I followed most of it. I likely should have followed it all, but old colonels are fixed in their views. The errors that remain are, thus, entirely my own. Mrs. Sharon Torres, my secretary and administrative assistant during my years in the Combat Studies Institute at CGSC, has been a great help, particularly in mediating between my Luddite ignorance and the world of computers and word processors. I also wish to thank D. M. Giangreco, design editor of the *Military Review*, and Byron G. McCary, visual information specialist at the Training Support Center (TSC), for their generous offer of photos to be used in this work. I am also indebted to Edward J. Carr and Robin Inojos, visual information specialists, and Alfred Dulin, graphics supervisor, for their coordination and layout of the manuscript. In addition, Carolyn D. Conway, editorial assistant,

Combat Studies Institute, deserves credit for her diligence and skill in inputting, correcting, and formatting the manuscript.

Finally, this book would have died in the hold box of the Center of Military History (CMH) but for the determination of the George C. Marshall Professor of Military History at CGSC, Dr. Roger Spiller, that it be published. Dr. Spiller recovered it from CMH, set up an editorial board, and encouraged, prodded, and otherwise motivated the author to take it up again and push it through to completion. Spiller has been chief editor and principal source of energy for seeing the project through to publication. Whatever errors remain are simply indications that no editor can do everything to correct the accumulated flaws of an author. Roger Spiller has been my intellectual mentor for seven years, and I owe him a great debt. That I am all too aware of the price he has paid, in terms of much time he might otherwise have turned to far more valuable projects of his own, only increases my sense of obligation.

Introduction

For a description of the human and material wreckage left in the aftermath of the Persian Gulf War, Richard Swain reaches back to the classical world. It was, he writes, " 'a hecatomb'—a gruesome sacrifice of hapless victims on a terrifying scale, meant to propitiate the ancient gods."[1]

Hapless, note, not helpless. Saddam Hussein's soldiers did not begin their war meaning to be victims. That role was meant for the people of Kuwait. Saddam's soldiers were made that way by their own leaders and by the combined forces of an international military expedition.

But the outcome of this war was not inevitable. The human and mechanical scale of the war, its geographical scope, its technical complexities, and its highly lethal effects posed choices for all the combatants that only rarely were self-evident or obvious. If the allied victory was not foreordained, neither was the process by which that victory was achieved. That depended upon a war fought as professionally and precisely as possible, with as strict attention to military and technical detail as the allies could muster. How this professional and technical process unfolded, as it was viewed from the United States Third Army headquarters and in the military formations whose operations that headquarters controlled, is the subject of Richard Swain's book, "*Lucky War.*"

History may never be able to learn just why Saddam Hussein decided to invade Kuwait in the summer of 1990. Seeing only a future that he preferred to see, Saddam may have been encouraged by the West's compliant policies toward Iraq during its long war with Iran. Perhaps he believed he had stored up credits of favor with the West by spending so much in that war. Or he may have misled himself with a spurious view of Iraq's brief national history; once in possession of Kuwait, supposedly a former Iraqi province, he may have planned to create a new pan-Islamic union in the region. Or, perhaps, there was only the oil: emboldened by the prospect of controlling a major part of the world's supply, he may have convinced himself that the rest of the world would countenance his fait accompli.[2]

But for any or all of Saddam's imaginings to yield success, it was imperative that he be allowed to keep what he had taken. This, he was not allowed to do. Once in Kuwait, Saddam's army could not leave, and the United Nations could not leave it there.

Modern military history records few examples of such a grossly miscalculated adventure as this one. It was a gamble, foolishly taken, badly played from the outset. The revolution in the Soviet Union had relaxed superpower tensions, but not so much that Western armies had irrevocably demobilized. Large, highly trained, and well-equipped standing armies were still in place in Europe and America and not lately used. If he thought about such matters at all, Saddam may have believed that, after so many years of cold war, the major powers would not so soon recommit themselves to a serious military enterprise.

In this, as in so much else, Saddam was mistaken. As a superpower and leader of the free world during the cold war, the United States looked forward to exercising its leadership in an atmosphere free of long-standing international antagonisms. The invasion of Kuwait challenged America's still optimistic ambitions for a post-cold war peace, a "new world order." When President Bush announced, shortly after the invasion, "This will not stand," his fervor seemed to arise at least partly from disappointment that there would be no respite from the demands of international leadership. The president's announcement marked the effective beginning of the Persian Gulf War.

As we now know, the president's decision was all his.[3] Some months were to pass, however, before the true dimensions of the military commitment by the United States and its allies would reveal themselves, and that was chiefly the business of the military professionals and the military policy makers. As Swain shows here, that business was marked by decisions taken, as usual, in an ambiguous and contingent atmosphere: the allied effort looked far different in late October than a month later, when it was finally agreed that only a military offensive against occupying Iraqi forces would suffice to meet the policy objectives set forth in United Nations Resolution 678.

Although some military pedants still dream of planning and conducting a war immune from the intrusions of policy, the course of military planning from Operation Desert Shield to the execution of Operation Desert Storm that Swain describes was a thoroughly modern war, bounded on all sides and shaped daily by the demands of policy. In recent years, presidents and their commanders have indulged in the conceit that they have not gotten in each other's way, but the history of recent military operations tells a different story entirely. Nearly instantaneous global and public telecommunications make certain that modern wars can no longer be fought as though they are quarantined from public view. Analysts now use the term "crisis transparency" to describe a diplomatic environment in which statesmen communicate with one another more by public than official means.[4] The effects of these technical advancements meant that policy could reach deeply into the allies' military machinery, affecting time-honored professional habits and behavior. When a field commander can tune in to his commander in chief's latest news conference, and then watch as his immediate superiors translate that news into military intent, we can see that, while the game may be the same in its essentials, the playing field has been dramatically changed.[5] If it has ever been so, it is no longer so that policy falls silent when the first guns are fired. It was not so in the Persian Gulf War.

The success of coalition-making in war depends upon all parties finding agreement on the war's purposes, shapes, and ends. The sturdiest coalition is one that does not bind its members too tightly to precise objectives that may be dear to one party but not to another. What is more important is that all parties to a coalition can agree in like measure and commitment, even if the resources each invests are disproportionate. These principles were followed in this war, and they manifested themselves as limitations on national operations.

For the Americans, this meant that there would be no overt campaign to dethrone Saddam, although, perhaps, accidents of war would not have been unwelcome. This meant, further, that no ground forces would cross the Euphrates River and make for Baghdad. The air war did not suffer this particular constraint, but allied airmen worked under their own unique limitations all the same. No terror bombings this time; no Dresdens or Tokyos were ever in the offing.

Those limitations extended not only to actions against the enemy but to the way in which allied operations were framed and conducted. Allied military objectives were to be met by commanders who husbanded the lives of their soldiers more strictly than in any other major conflict. And as the time drew closer for the ground offensive to begin, these commanders subordinated their operational plans and established tactical measures of control to prevent casualties from "friendly fire." One brigade commander has been frank to admit that the threat of friendly fire in tactical zones dense with soldiers and weapons, not the enemy, governed his tactical dispositions, and higher-ranking officers have not been reluctant to express the depth of their concern over this age-old problem of military operations.

These concerns, it must be said, did not arise so much from high-minded humanitarianism. American commanders were willing to surrender certain tactical advantages because of the possibility that casualties by misadventure might somehow erode popular confidence back home. Indeed, a curious agreement existed on this issue between Saddam and the commanders who fought against him. Paul Wolfowitz, who served as the undersecretary of defense for policy during the war, has written that Saddam "seemed to have concluded, from observing both the Vietnam war and the U.S. withdrawal from Beirut, that the United States lacked staying power . . . ."[6] The human costs of the coming war on the ground, whether by friendly or enemy fire, posed a dramatic and unresolved question that, for the Americans especially, reached back to those earlier conflicts.

From the president downward through the chain of command, the ghost of the Vietnam War hovered over every proceeding.[7] All that was necessary to ignite calls for U.S. withdrawal, Saddam seemed to have thought, was the prospect of high casualties, and these he bluntly forecasted on several occasions. If Saddam had been watching carefully, however, he would have seen that the tempo and pace of the allied build-up showed no signs of slacking, even after American casualty forecasts as high as 30,000 were made in public.[8] No evidence has yet come to light suggesting that casualty projections impeded the operations of the allied expedition in any way.

All of which is not to say that these anxieties had no effect on official views or behavior. Instead of shrinking from the prospect of the war, those anxieties seem to have moved the Americans in precisely the opposite way, toward an unstinting commitment of force of arms. Policy might dictate operational limitations, but there were to be no half-measures. Having himself thoroughly imbibed the "lessons" of Vietnam, the chairman of the Joint Chiefs of Staff, General Colin Powell, told the Saudi Prince Bandar in the early days of the crisis, "If we have to [fight], I'll do it, but we're going to do it with everything we have."[9]

In this sense, the Persian Gulf War was to be a redemptive war: commanders were intent on avoiding what they regarded as the mistakes of the past. Quite apart from immediate policy objectives, this war had institutional goals as well: it would be fought so as to reclaim for the U.S. Army preeminence in the world of professional soldiering. The actions of the American commanders suggested that they were not about to design another war so susceptible to the uncertainties of an American national will they viewed as fragile. They would design a war that would not, insofar as possible, again test the strength of that will. This war was to be planned from the outset as a short, violent, massive, and decisive victory whose conduct capitalized upon material abundance and professional and technological acumen as the means of reducing the human costs of the war. This war would be everything the Vietnam War had not been. And when the war was over, it would be the president himself who framed its larger significance. The victory celebrations were an opportunity for the nation to "kick the Vietnam syndrome" by affording returning troops a proper welcome of thanks.[10]

Within the shifting context of domestic experience and reaction, international diplomacy and strategy, there remained the fact of the war itself: the necessity that armed force was required to decide the issues at hand. The distance between conceiving and executing this decision entailed the mobilization, deployment, sustainment, and direction of a huge multinational force toward politically and militarily achievable goals thousands of miles from its points of origin.

The result, as we now know, was by no means the "near-run thing" so dear to the hearts of military romantics. It was a victory as complete as was wanted or could reasonably be had. In its fundamental character, it was a thoroughly American kind of war. Russell Weigley, the dean of American military historians, has written of the "American way of war," a national style of warfare, defined by its attritional impulse even in those instances when a more strictly modulated application of violence may have been more appropriate.[11] Erstwhile strategists will find no exquisite, stylish innovations in this conflict. Perhaps the most arresting, and telling, of Richard Swain's images in the pages that follow is his depiction of the coalition's ground attack as that of a "drill bit," boring remorselessly into a rock face. In its design, in its conduct, and perhaps even in it ending, the Persian Gulf War bore an unmistakably American stamp.

If materiel could be made to fight this war, then materiel could win it by sheer mountainous weight. The character of the American side of the war was, as Swain's metaphor suggests, relentlessly industrial. The humblest subjects—ones that do not ordinarily arrest the attention of strategists, "operational artists," or even tacticians—played critical parts in the war's design. That design required above all moving what amounted to a small city thousands of miles around the world and keeping it in good running order until the time came to close the assembly line and shut down the factory once more. No shortages of soldiers beset the generals, and because the work of most soldiers in this war had to do with the servicing of machines in one way or another, the older problem of numbers in war was replaced by one of distribution. Witness Swain's discussion of HETs, the heavy equipment transporters whose shortage occupied the time and energy of the Third Army's commanding general as did few other subjects.

HETs, how many available, where and when, the strength and state of their crews—indeed, where to get more? These were questions of substance, the assembling and organizing of assets, that called upon the true métier of the Americans—organization.

And organized the war certainly was, so thoroughly organized that the actual fighting seemed almost anticlimactic—except, of course as always, for those who actually had to fight. At one point, the force-to-space ratio very nearly squeezed an entire division between two others. No adroit maneuvering permitted or desired here: any dispersion or movements that would have elicited sighs of approval from the audience would have dissipated the concentrated power of the attack that had been planned from the beginning.

The Persian Gulf War was a professionals' war, and so Swain's book is by and large a professionals' book. "*Lucky War*" was conceived and written for military officers and other serious students of the military art. It is particularly meant to illuminate and explain the technical complexities of the war, matters that general war literature so often takes for granted or merely ignores. As an operational history of the war, it does not neglect to show how even the finest details of military planning and violent execution are subjected to the dynamic interactions of an event with so many moving parts. It is written from the vantage point of the U.S. Third Army, the headquarters placed between the fighting corps and the unified command of the war. From this vantage point, a clear view of both the highest and lowliest aspects of the war was available. From this position, Swain scouted in all directions for the sources of this history, from briefing rooms in Riyadh to the front-line traces. "*Lucky War*" is thus a book by both an informed observer and a participant.

When Iraq invaded Kuwait, Richard Swain was a colonel, serving on the faculty of the U.S. Army Command and General Staff College as the director of the Combat Studies Institute. A graduate of West Point, a field artillery officer, and veteran of Vietnam, Swain had also won a doctorate in history from Duke University. Between command and staff assignments, he had taught at West Point and at the Staff College's School of Advanced Military Studies. Along the way, he had made of himself one of the Army's most disciplined and productive students of the history of the military art.

Shortly after the invasion, Swain was asked for a forecast of the strategic end state of the crisis, whose barest outlines were only beginning to be revealed. He was not confident that the United States would intervene militarily, and he hoped that economic sanctions would resolve the trouble. But as the crisis grew more serious, Swain was quick to see that the U.S. Army was on the verge of another limited war, and one of significant proportions. A historic event of some magnitude was in the making. As the Army mobilized for the conflict, Swain was convinced that history should mobilize with it.

Armies preparing for war are rarely if ever sympathetic to the presence of historians. Historians and their work have to do with matters that seem remote to commanders and staff officers consumed by events at hand. The work of history seems all too easily postponed. Once the war is concluded, however, the reverse seems to be true. Armies at once become interested in commemorating and celebrating their victories, if indeed a victory has been recorded. They want to know, too, what lessons may be learned from their recent experience, the theory being that those lessons might be applied in future operations. In practice, however, these efforts seldom produce insights that alter professional behavior. Soon enough, armies revert to the routines of the garrison.

Swain was fully aware of these problems. He knew that armies in the past had paid for ignoring their own experience. He knew as well that commemorating an experience was no substitute for understanding it. And he knew that the discipline and patience demanded by close historical study would not permit the instant production of a book. If the war was serious enough to be fought, he believed, its history deserved a serious and deliberate effort.

Finally, Swain was moved by concerns that transcended his professional interest in the war and its history. As an *American* soldier, Swain believed that his nation deserved an accounting of its army's performance, that his fellow citizens had a right to demand a means of understanding how the energy of their sons and daughters and the fruits of their labors had been spent in a war that had been fought in their interests. Swain meant his history as a contribution to that understanding.

In late November 1991, Swain was finally notified of his appointment as the theater army historian. He was ordered to deploy to Third Army headquarters in Riyadh, Saudi Arabia, there to oversee the operations of several official military history detachments then operating with major unit formations and to record and eventually to write the history of the war. He arrived in Saudi Arabia in January 1991, just before the beginning of the ground offensive. He returned to the United States in May and for the next two years continued his research and writing.

"*Lucky War*" is Swain's fulfillment of his assignment. It is "official military history," a variety of history that the British military historian, B. H. Liddell Hart, once condemned as a contradiction in terms. Jaundiced by his relations with the British Army's official historians from World War I, Liddell Hart denied that serving officers, or anyone with intimate official relations, could produce a military history that a reader might approach with confidence. The shadow of Liddell Hart's opinion has darkened official history for decades. Swain was guided in his own research and writing by the ambition to prove Liddell Hart wrong once again. This, he has done in full measure.

ROGER J. SPILLER
Fort Leavenworth, Kansas

Notes

1. See, for instance, Michael Kelly's description of the "highway of death" in Martyrs' Day: Chronicle of a Small War (New York: Vintage Books, 1994), 233-44.

2. For a discussion of the effect of modern telecommunications upon crisis diplomacy, see Lawrence Freedman and Efraim Karsh, The Gulf Conflict: Diplomacy and War in the New World Order (Princeton, NJ: Princeton University Press, 1993), xxxiii-xxxiv, 78, 260.

3. Bob Woodward, The Commanders (New York: Simon and Schuster, 1991), 260.

4. See Freedman and Karsh, The Gulf Conflict: Diplomacy and War in the New World Order, 42-50.

5. For all the complications inherent in the technical improvements in global public communications, an equally complex set of problems inheres in modern military communications. One indicator of the scope of these problems combined can be found in what might be called the "electronic history" of the Persian Gulf War, where public communications consumed twice as much communications satellite band width reporting the war as the military did in fighting it. See Alan D. Campen, "Information, Truth and War," in The First Information War (Fairfax, VA: AFCEA International Press, 1992), 87.

6. Paul Wolfowitz, "Victory Came Too Easily," The National Interest, n. 35 (Spring 1994): 91.

7. The ghost warned against the dangers of confused national purpose, the corrosive effects of military gradualism upon popular support for a limited war, and of surrendering initiative to the enemy. Above all, the ghost insisted upon the prompt achievement of decisive victory by virtue of highly concentrated, overwhelming force. These precepts had already been codified by Caspar Weinberger while secretary of defense. The so-called Weinberger Doctrine set conditions for the employment of American force in future expeditions. Notwithstanding the dubious constitutionality of the exercise—American armed forces are instruments, not arbiters, of policy—the doctrine did resonate within the defense establishment: it conformed wonderfully to dearly held prejudices about the use of American military power that had been formed since the Vietnam War. See Caspar Weinberger's Fighting for Peace: Seven Critical Years in the Pentagon (New York: Warner Books, 1990), 400-402 and 433-45, for the secretary's discussion of the context in which his ideas were conceived, as well as the text of his speech before the National Press Club in which he first publicly enunciated his doctrine.

8. See James Blackwell, Thunder in the Desert: The Strategy and Tactics of the Persian Gulf War (New York: Bantam Books, 1991), 106-7.

9. Bob Woodward, The Commanders, 324.

10. President George Bush, "Remarks at a Meeting of Veterans Service Organizations," 4 March 1991, reprinted in Weekly Compilation of Presidential Documents 27, nos. 1-14 (Washington, D.C.: Government Printing Office, 1991), 248. Virtually every serious study of the Persian Gulf War employs the Vietnam War as an invidious comparison. Indeed, the story of the U.S. Army's recovery from defeat in Vietnam

forms the theme of the opening chapter in the Army's own first attempt to capture the history of the Persian Gulf War. See Brigadier General Robert H. Scales, Jr., et al., Certain Victory: *The U.S. Army in the Gulf War* (Washington, D.C.: Office of the Chief of Staff of the Army, 1993), 1–38.

11. See Russell F. Weigley, The American Way of War: A History of United States Military Strategy and Policy (New York: Macmillan, 1973), ix–xv and passim, for a complete exposition of this idea.

1
Prologue to Operation Desert Shield

In the first two months of 1991, the armed forces of an unprecedented global coalition attacked and destroyed the core of Iraq's military forces, thus freeing the small but oil-rich state of Kuwait from Iraqi occupation. Although the United States contributed almost half the friendly military forces engaged, the coalition based its international authority on a large majority vote of the United Nations Security Council.[1] Military contributions came from thirty-seven separate states and financial and material donations from others.[2] The regional legitimacy conferred on the endeavor by the U.S. partnership with the Saudi government and the participation, under Saudi sponsorship, of other Gulf States and major Arab powers was equally important.

Because the Gulf War was a coalition war, it remained a war of limited objectives. At no time was the destruction of Iraq a serious consideration. The strategists seem always to have had a keen eye on what the postwar regional balance of power would look like, not wishing to exchange one destabilizing imbalance for another.

The war occurred in a "new world" context. The old post-World War II framework of Soviet-American confrontation had been supplanted by a multipolar global community. Within this new global political environment, former members of the Warsaw Pact contributed contingents and materiel to serve in a variety of symbolic ways.

The fundamental causes of this war reach back a thousand years or more to the birth of Islam and its spread throughout the world. Certainly they extend to the breakup of the last great Islamic empire at the end of World War I. And they include the stresses operating since that time throughout the developing world as traditional societies have coped with the twin pressures of modernization and competing foreign (Western) ideologies. These causes, however, are largely beyond the scope of this study. Iraq's violation of the sovereignty of a weak brother Arab state was the sufficient cause of the 1990–91 Gulf War. This action alone—which threatened Saudi Arabia, the minor Gulf States, and the regional and global economic balance of power—called the anti-Iraq coalition into existence. With the collapse of the old world order, a clear precedent was called for in the form of united military action that would punish this wanton act by a mighty nation against a weak one and place it beyond the pale of legitimate international behavior. These are the circumstances that led to war.

Since World War II, the United States Department of Defense has divided the world into a number of geographic regions. Joint service military headquarters have been assigned responsibility for these regions, and they are responsible for conducting necessary military operations and forestalling trouble. Following the fiasco of Operation Desert One, the aborted attempt to rescue U.S. hostages in revolutionary Iran, a new theater, U.S. Central Command (CENTCOM), was carved out in the Persian Gulf, Arabian Sea, and eastern Indian Ocean area. CENTCOM's headquarters were located at MacDill Air Force Base in Tampa, Florida. The commander in chief of CENTCOM in 1990, General H. Norman Schwarzkopf, directed all U.S. military operations in the Gulf War. His headquarters and those of his subordinate service components, Army, Navy, Marine Corps, and Air Force, actually began to prepare for hostilities with Iraq long before fighting broke out.

Army units participated in the operations in Southwest Asia as part of a joint military response to Iraqi aggression. The contributions of other U.S. military services were at least as vital to the outcome as those of the Army. Each service contributed its own unique capabilities. Indeed, the Air Force can claim, with some justification, to have been the predominant service in this desert war. While this book will focus on the Army's contribution—particularly those of Third Army, its two assigned corps, and support command—the Army was but one service among five (counting the Coast Guard) in a coalition in which the armed services of many nations contributed to the final outcome, each in accordance with its own capabilities.

The military actions of August 1990 to January 1991 (Operation Desert Shield) and those of January and February 1991 (Operation Desert Storm) were only a part of the strategic response by the United States, Saudi Arabia, and their coalition allies to the Iraqi aggression. The total effort against Iraq combined economic, political, and military instruments of interstate power. Establishing the necessary political framework for military action often set the pace at which military preparations could be made. Many opportunities were available for any of the parties to have gone another way—except, perhaps, the government-in-exile of Kuwait. None of what actually happened was preordained.

Only the choices of the various players led to the resolution that came to pass. For many weeks, it appeared that a military standoff of undetermined duration had developed and that, behind the scenes, economic and political forces would have to be given time to impose a resolution. Only that prospect accounts for the discussion concerning transition of Third Army from a contingency headquarters to the status of a more permanent major army command and the simultaneous planning for the rotation of ground forces in and out of theater. These discussions went on in the fall of 1990 even as planning went forward for possible offensive actions in Southwest Asia.[3] Each succeeding step toward war was contingent on earlier measures, and nothing was very certain—except the determination of Saddam Hussein to remain in Kuwait and the equal determination of the coalition to have him out, one way or the other.

President George Bush did not announce development of an offensive military option until 8 November. Not until early January did the United States Congress—and not by an overwhelming mandate—follow the United Nations Security Council in authorizing the use of military force to break the deadlock in the desert.[4] The importance of the president's political strategy to the final outcome cannot be overstated, nor the skill with which he and his secretary of state, James Baker, orchestrated their actions. The secretary of state's ability to challenge the United States Senate on 5 December 1990—to demonstrate the same resolve already shown by the United Nations Security Council on 29 November—is indicative of the Bush administration's political skill.[5]

Finally, it is vitally important to understand that the ability to complete various military actions during the war's offensive phase, Desert Storm, was contingent on the need to compensate for earlier decisions made in response to a quite different set of assigned tasks and assumptions in effect during the earlier protective (defensive) phase, Operation Desert Shield. Decisions taken for good reasons in August and September, both at the political and theater level, had significant implications for how business could be done in December and January, as military forces in Saudi Arabia prepared for an offensive. Simply put, a force built for attack has different communications, logistics, intelligence, and force structure requirements than one created for deterrence and defense and under political guidance to deploy only "minimum essential forces." Over and above all these short-term influences lay another reality: the armed forces committed to the Arabian Peninsula had been designed and structured originally for a very different war—a forward defense of

NATO on the Central Front in Europe. This accounts for such anomalies as the Army's shortage of line-haul trucks, particularly heavy equipment transporters (HETs), the large flat-bed trucks used to transport heavy armored vehicles to the front.[6]

Strictly speaking, Operation Desert Shield began on C-day, 7 August 1990, when the president ordered U.S. military forces to the Arabian Peninsula to defend the Kingdom of Saudi Arabia from the threat of Iraqi aggression following Saddam Hussein's 2 August (0140Z) invasion of Kuwait.[7] (See map 1.) In fact, the operation was anticipated by several months of Central Command planning actions that placed Army forces, particularly Third Army and XVIII Airborne Corps, in an especially favorable position for the accomplishment of their assigned missions. Any account of this operation, then, must start by considering events that began in November 1989, when some critics considered Iraqi aggression against Kuwait scarcely creditable.

In the fall of 1989, the postwar global power structure had broken down. The Soviet Union was undergoing dramatic internal stresses, while its European empire was falling away rapidly. As Soviet interest turned inward, military planners everywhere responded by considering the emerging multipolar world as the strategic environment of the 1990s. U.S. estimates examined the restructuring of the American military in light of new threat assessments.

For Central Command, that meant shifting its focus from opposing a Soviet attack through Iran, the principal threat envisioned from 1983 to 1989, to a more regional threat, a hypothetical Iraqi attack against its weak but oil rich neighbors to the south. In November 1989, General Schwarzkopf directed that the theater operations plan that addressed an Iraqi threat to Saudi Arabia (Operations Plan [OPLAN] 1002-90) be made the priority for Central Command planning and that the plan be revised as quickly as possible.[8] In December, Schwarzkopf requested and was granted permission to shift the focus of a forthcoming Joint Chiefs of Staff war game from the disappearing Soviet threat (OPLAN 1021) to the defense of the Arabian Peninsula. In January 1990, Central Command called for the preparation of war plans against an Iraqi threat to the Arabian Peninsula. These were to be the basis of the exercise, Internal Look, scheduled for July 1990.[9]

Baghdad emerged from its eight-year war with Iran still strong enough to attack Saudi Arabia. Indeed, while recommending that the United States "continue to develop its contacts with Iraq by building selectively on existing political and economic relationships," General

Map 1. Saudi Arabia

Schwarzkopf told the Senate Armed Forces Committee in January 1990 that "Iraq is now the preeminent military power in the Gulf, and It is assuming a broader leadership role throughout the Arab world. Iraq has the capability to militarily coerce its neighboring states should diplomatic efforts fail to produce the desired results."[10] Critics of this view argued that Iraq lacked the intent or economic capability to move against its neighbors. Some suggested the CENTCOM analysis was no more than an attempt to justify the command's existence.[11]

As Saddam Hussein increased tensions in the region throughout the spring, U.S. assistance to Iraq (which dated back to the Iran-Iraq War) would become a political issue. In April, CENTCOM planners were directed to drop the country's identifications in their planning documents and to substitute the less politically sensitive color codes of RED (Iraq), ORANGE (Iran), and YELLOW (People's Democratic Republic of Yemen).[12]

Third Army, as the Central Command's Army component, was also reevaluating the regional threat. The principal Army war plan in the fall of 1989 assumed a Soviet attack through Iran to the Persian Gulf. The plan called for five and two-thirds U.S. divisions in the defense, mostly light and heavy forces at something less than full strength (apportioned to it by the Joint Strategic Capability Plan [JSCAP]). Less than two divisions were apportioned to the separate plan then in place for the defense of the Arabian Peninsula.[13]

Even before Schwarzkopf changed Central Command's planning priorities, ARCENT began adjusting to the idea that Iraq constituted the major regional threat. Third Army also held that any U.S. response to the potential danger would require a significantly larger and heavier force than had been anticipated. As early as March 1989, Third Army began to coordinate with the Army Concepts and Analysis Agency (CAA) in Bethesda, Maryland, to conduct a war game simulation of the existing war plan for the Arabian Peninsula to examine this hypothesis.

CAA ran Wargame Persian Tiger 89 in February 1990, as planning for a revised defensive concept got under way. Persian Tiger posited a defensive force of three Army light brigades (one airborne, two airmobile), a battalion of the Ranger regiment, an air defense artillery brigade, corps aviation, and artillery. Two Marine expeditionary brigades and aviation forces allocated under the existing plan were also portrayed. The findings of the game, which began to emerge in February but which were not published until August 1990, were that U.S. forces could not arrive in theater in time to resist an Iraqi invasion if deployment were ordered only upon outbreak of hostilities. It was learned also that the allocated U.S. force structure was too light to do what was required of it, in any event.[14]

By the time the results of Persian Tiger were published, Central Command's own planners had arrived at many of the same conclusions. The exercise provided a mechanism that supported ongoing Third Army planning in the spring of 1990 and offered an opportunity for Third Army and subordinate XVIII Corps planners to begin gaining practical experience in the problems they would actually face in August.

Between January and July 1990, Central Command, Third Army, and XVIII Corps planners prepared draft operation plans for the new contingency, and in July, United States Forces Command (FORSCOM), the headquarters commanding all continental U.S. Army combat forces, began selecting units to meet Army Forces Central Command's requirements.[15] The deputy commanding general of Third Army, Major General William Riley, began visiting various headquarters with a briefing on Third Army's view of the changing regional threat.[16] Back at Fort McPherson, Georgia, Riley and the Third Army staff conducted a functional analysis of the forces required for the new plan. This was the first step toward development of Desert Shield time-phased force development data (TPFDD), a troop list to support the new plan.

A number of features of the draft Third Army plan (1002-90), published in July 1990, show how prewar planning guided Third Army's actions during Operation Desert Shield. The plan was intended to direct the Army's contribution to Central Command's broader-objective regional plan "designed to counter an intraregional conflict on the ARABIAN PENINSULA to protect UNITED STATES (U.S.) and allied access to ARABIAN PENINSULA oil."[17] Central Command's strategy for a regional contingency spelled out its strategy this way:

> The USCENTCOM regional contingency strategy to counter an intraregional threat initially seeks to [secure] U.S. and allied interests through deterrence. Should deterrence fail, the strategy is to rapidly deploy additional U.S. combat forces to assist friendly states in defending critical ports and oil facilities on the ARABIAN PENINSULA. Once sufficient combat power has been generated and the enemy has been sufficiently attrited, the strategy is to mass forces and conduct a counteroffensive to recapture critical port and oil facilities which may have been seized by enemy forces in earlier stages of conflict.

Notably, as a precondition of execution, the plan indicated that "the scope of operations requires that this plan be executed independently of other major contingencies."[18]

The plan portrayed an Iraqi attack through Kuwait and into Saudi Arabia. The attack force consisted of sixty brigades, supported by 640 fighter/ground-attack aircraft and a minimum of 3,200 tanks. The plan assumed four days would be needed to take Kuwait and another five to reach the port of Al Jubayl. It credited Iraq with an operational reach no longer than Al Hufuf—enough grasp to occupy the main Persian Gulf ports and key oil facilities. The plan also assumed three to six months' increased regional tension and up to thirty days' strategic warning.

The corresponding Third Army plan assumed a deployment decision at least nineteen days prior to hostilities, an immediate 200,000-man selected Reserve call-up, and availability of assigned National Guard roundout brigades and necessary combat service support units.[19] In the pre-Desert Storm Army force structure, roundout brigades were National Guard formations that were expected to fill out incomplete Regular Army divisions and deploy with them to war. In the event, Third Army would enjoy neither the advanced warning nor have the benefit of an early selected Reserve call-up. The absence of both would influence significantly how Third Army went to war.

The Third Army plan was designed for the defense of critical port and oil facilities in the vicinity of Al Jubayl and Abqaiq, the operation of common-user seaports, and the provision of combat support and combat service support (logistics) to Central Command forces in theater.[20] The concept of operations called for a three-phase deployment.[21] Phase one addressed the introduction of "deterrent forces," the Third Army and XVIII Corps' forward headquarters, an aviation brigade task force, and troops from the 82d Airborne Division. These forces, along with Marine units, were to establish a deterrent force north of Al Jubayl to secure the points of debarkation at Jubayl, Ad Dammam, and Dhahran and, upon arrival of the Marines, to establish a defense of the Abqaiq oil facilities. The deterrent effect of ground forces would be greatly enhanced, of course, by the simultaneous arrival of air and naval forces. Indeed, in the first month of any deployment, the U.S. and Saudi air threat to extended Iraqi lines of communication *was* the deterrent.

Phase two of the Third Army deployment was to involve the 101st Airborne Division (Air Assault), the 24th Infantry Division (Mechanized) and the 5th Infantry Division (Mechanized) with their reserve component "roundout" brigades, a brigade of the 9th Infantry Division (Motorized) (then undergoing deactivation), and the 197th Separate Infantry Brigade (Mechanized). Arrival of these heavier forces would permit the establishment of a defense in depth behind Saudi and Gulf Cooperation Council forces to the north along the Saudi border and forward of the ports and oil facilities. Should the enemy attack at this point, the Air Force component (principally Central Command Air Forces [CENTAF]) was assigned to contest the offensive. The Army aviation task force of attack helicopters would link the ground forces with the theater air interdiction program. The brigade of the 9th Division (Motorized) was to be held in theater reserve. Phase three called for a coordinated counteroffensive involving Saudi, U.S. Army, and Marine forces to restore lost territory and facilities.[22]

In mid-July, Third Army and the other CENTCOM component planners went to Eglin Air Force Base, Florida, to test their plans in Exercise Internal Look.[23] Third Army's Internal Look concept of operations also called for a three-phased operation: building up a corps-sized force, defense of critical facilities, and a counteroffensive. Tactical command was to be the province of the commander, XVIII Airborne Corps. Third Army would assemble and sustain the force as the Army component of Central Command. A key assumption was that sustainment in an environment with no developed or prepositioned United States military forces would require maximum host-nation support to succeed. Country RED was portrayed as possessing significant armored forces (around 4,000 tanks), theater ballistic missiles, a strong air force, and a chemical and biological capability.[24]

Like the Third Army plan, the Internal Look scenario called for an Army force consisting of an attack helicopter brigade task force, the 82d Airborne Division, the 101st Air Assault Division, the 24th Infantry Division (Mechanized) (two brigades), the 197th Separate Infantry Brigade (Mechanized), the brigade from the 9th Division (Motorized), and the 5th Infantry Division (Mechanized) (two brigades). It also assumed the presence, late in the sequence of arriving units, of the 48th Infantry Brigade (Mechanized) and the 256th Infantry Brigade (Mechanized)—both National Guard roundout brigades—to complete the 24th and 5th Divisions. This was a total of seven light brigades (three airborne, three air assault, one motorized) and seven heavy brigades. The scenario assumed prior warning. D-day, the date of attack, was C-day plus 18 (C-day is the date upon which the force would be ordered to deploy). This assumption, in turn, permitted a further assumption, perhaps more tenuous, of the presence in theater on D-day of the corps headquarters, the aviation brigade task force, the airborne division, the 11th Air Defense Brigade, elements of the 1st Marine Expeditionary Force, and the ARCENT headquarters.[25]

The Marine Corps forces of Central Command were expected to land and move into a defensive sector along the coast protecting the port of Al Jubayl. Third Army was to defend inland, forward of Ad Dammam, Dhahran, and Abqaiq. The component boundary was located east of An Nuayriyah. The scenario, like the earlier plans, assumed participation of Gulf Cooperation Council members and Royal Saudi Land Forces in their own defense.

During planning, it had become clear to Third Army staff officers that their force was inadequate. The Third Army commander, Lieutenant General John Yeosock, used Exercise Internal Look as an opportunity to make a case with General Schwarzkopf that additional heavy forces and Patriot air defense systems were required to execute the assigned missions. Third Army believed that, although the currently assumed force could get to the theater rapidly and thus provide a credible deterrent (depending on the depth of the intent of the aggressor), it had inadequate armor to deal with the anticipated threat, an inappropriate covering force, and a lack of a counteroffensive capability required to restore any territory lost. Third Army also believed the motorized brigade provided was an inadequate theater reserve.[26]

While Internal Look took place, General Yeosock had his staff prepare alternative force lists. Option 1 called for a force of ten heavy brigades (three and one-third divisions). It eliminated the airborne and air assault divisions and the separate brigades and portrayed a force of an armored cavalry regiment, three heavy divisions (two mechanized and one armored), and included reserve component roundout brigades. The helicopter brigade task force, now the 6th Cavalry (Air Combat) Brigade, and the air defense brigade were the only Army units in the C+12 force. Such a force would double the armor capability. It would provide an armored cavalry regiment for the covering force and a counteroffensive capability. But it would not allow for rapid deployment and thus would not, by itself, form a strong deterrent in the early days of any crisis.[27]

A second alternative retained the air assault division as a C+12 force, along with the air defense brigade, to accomplish the deterrence mission. This called for a C+50 force of an armored cavalry regiment, two mechanized divisions, and one armored division—that is, ten heavy and three light brigades. This was the favored option, although it was recognized that sealift would be exceeded at C+40.[28] In addition, the Third Army commander used Internal Look to argue for the addition of more Patriot missile units.[29] All options required additional fast sealift to accommodate the heavier forces.[30] For Schwarzkopf, who was faced with a fixed resource in strategic transport, any increase in the Army's requirements would have to be met by a reduction in some other force's arrival time or a longer period of deployment. In the early hours of a crisis, the premium on the combat potential of tactical air forces would militate against any shift in priorities. Third Army briefers took the results of this exercise to the Department of the Army and briefed the plan only hours before Iraq invaded Kuwait.[31]

All this effort was not so much evidence of prescience as it was of professional military planners doing their job. It is the business of planning headquarters to anticipate possible threats to national security within their areas of responsibility and to plan to deal with them. Iraq was the greatest potential threat in the region once the Soviets were eliminated as a possible attacker. U.S. interests were genuine and of long standing. It can be argued that the threat of Iraq was always present and had just been countenanced because of the overriding global nature of the U.S.-Soviet rivalry and residual U.S. hostility with Iran.

For six months prior to commitment, the Third Army and XVIII Airborne Corps staffs had thought through the problems involved in the operation they were about to undertake. As a consequence, the Third Army commander had succeeded in convincing the chief of Central Command and the Department of the Army of the requirement for heavier, more lethal, forces and the need to employ the Patriot missile as a theater antitactical ballistic missile system. These decisions were to be justified in the following weeks and months. The studies also pointed out, as the deployment itself would confirm, that available strategic sealift was a significant weakness in the security of the United States' vital interests in the Persian Gulf area.

Notes

1. United Nations, Security Council, Resolution 678, 29 November 1990. The resolution demanded Iraq's unconditional withdrawal from Kuwait by 15 January 1991 and authorized the use of all necessary means by UN members to bring about Iraqi withdrawal thereafter. The Security Council vote was twelve for, two against (Yemen and Cuba). China abstained. "UN Resolutions," *Military Review* 71 (September 1991): 79. The text of the resolution is in "Text of U.N. Resolution on Using Force in the Gulf," *The New York Times*, 30 November 1990, A10; and "Resolution Sets Jan. 15 Deadline For Withdrawal," The *Washington Post*, 30 November 1990, A23.

2. United States Central Command, Executive Summary, Operations Desert Shield/Desert Storm, Exercise Internal Look '90 After-Action Reports, 17 July 1991, 1.

3. HQ, Forces Command, FCJ5-PP, Memorandum for Commander, ARCENT Rear, AFRD-XO (Colonel Edwards), Subject: ARCENT Organization and Functions to Support Operation Desert Shield, dated 8 November 1990. HQ, ARCENT, Command Group, ARCENT Update Briefing C+61, given to Chief of Staff, Army, on 7 October, slide titled, "Force Rotation Tour Considerations." This briefing is scripted, which makes it particularly useful as a status report.

4. "Congressional Resolution," *Military Review*, 91–92. The resolution was passed on 12 January by a vote of 52-47 in the Senate and 250-183 in the House.

5. Baker testimony in, United States Senate, Hearings Before the Committee on Foreign Relations, One Hundred First Congress, Second Session, 4 and 5 December 1990, U.S. Policy in the Persian Gulf (S. Hrg. 101-1128, Pr. 1), 140. Speaking to Senator Dodd, Secretary Baker said: "But Senator, surely you are not suggesting that we go over there [Iraq] and negotiate something short of the U.N. resolutions?"

6. See the comments in Lieutenant Colonel David Evans, USMC, Retired, "Desert Shield: From the Gulf," *U.S. Naval Institute Proceedings* 117, no. 1 (January 1991): 77–80.

7. U.S. Army, *Center of Military History*, Draft Chronology: Operation Desert Shield/Storm, 2. (Attributed to Iraq-Kuwait Chronology, by AP [1990].)

8. United States Central Command, Executive Summary, Operations Desert Shield/Desert Storm, Exercise Internal Look '90 After-Action Reports, 17 July 1991, 2. HQ, Third Army, AFRD-DTP, Memorandum for Desert Storm Study Group, Subject: OPLAN 1002, Desert Shield and Desert Storm Planning, dated 4 June 1991, 1–6. This memorandum was prepared by Major Steve Holley, the planning officer most involved with 1002-90, and signed by Colonel Harold E. Holloway, ARCENT chief of plans. It is the most comprehensive document available on the pre-August planning process. General Schwarzkopf fixes his decision to shift the focus on CENTCOM planning in July 1989, noting it was a decision that had evolved over a period of time. General H. Norman Schwarzkopf, *General H. Norman Schwarzkopf, The Autobiography: It Doesn't Take a Hero* (New York: Linda Grey Bantam Books, 1992), 273–87 (hereafter referred to as Schwarzkopf, *Doesn't Take a Hero*).

9. HQ, Third Army, AFRD-DTP, Memorandum for Desert Storm Study Group, Subject: OPLAN 1002, Desert Shield and Desert Storm Planning, dated 4 June 1991, 4.

10. "Statement of General H. Norman Schwarzkopf, Commander in Chief, United States Central Command," in United States Senate, Hearings Before the Committee on Armed Services, One Hundred First Congress, Second Session, 12 December 1989; 23, 24, 25, 26, 30 January; 2, 6, 7, 8, 21, 22 February; 7 March 1990 (S. Hrg. 101-70), 608, 626.

11. U.S. Army, Center of Military History, "Interview with General G. Sullivan, USA, Vice Chief of Staff, United States Army, 4 February 1991," 25. Major Steven Holley, the ARCENT planner for OPLAN 1001-90, told the author that the same point was raised by Department of State planners during the planning process at CENTCOM.

12. HQ, Third Army, AFRD-DTP, Memorandum for Desert Storm Study Group, Subject: OPLAN 1002, Desert Shield and Desert Storm Planning, dated 4 June 1991, 3.

13. Ibid., 1. See also HQ, ARCENT, Command Group, ARCENT Command Briefing; Preliminary Phase (Internal Look '90).

14. U.S. Army, Concepts and Analysis Agency, Wargame Persian Tiger 89, Study Report CAA-SR-90-5, August 1990.

15. HQ, Third Army, AFRD-DTP, Memorandum for Desert Storm Study Group, Subject: OPLAN 1002, Desert Shield and Desert Storm Planning, dated 4 June 1991, 3.

16. Major General William Riley, "New Realities Briefing."

17. HQ, ARCENT, COMUSARCENT OPLAN 1002-90 (Draft), 16 July 1990, 4.

18. Ibid., 5.

19. Ibid., 27–28.

20. Ibid., 20–21.

21. Ibid., 30–34.

22. Ibid., 34.

23. HQ, Third Army, AFRD-DTP, Memorandum for Desert Storm Study Group, Subject: OPLAN 1002, Desert Shield and Desert Storm Planning, dated 4 June 1991, 3. United States Central Command, Executive Summary, Operations Desert Shield/Desert Storm, Exercise Internal Look '90 After-Action Reports, 17 July 1991.

24. HQ, ARCENT, Command Group, ARCENT Command Briefing: Preliminary Phase (Internal Look '90). HQ, ARCENT, Command Group, briefing titled, "USARCENT OPLAN 1002-90 Force Structure," presented to USCINCCENT, 27 July 1990. HQ, ARCENT, Command Group, briefing titled, "USARCENT OPLAN 1002-90 Concept of Support," presented to USCINCCENT, 27 July 1990.

25. HQ, ARCENT, Command Group, briefing titled, "USARCENT OPLAN 1002-90 Force Structure," presented to USCINCCENT, 27 July 1990. Base Case. HQ, ARCENT, Command Group, briefing titled, "USARCENT OPLAN 1002-90 Concept of Support," presented to USCINCCENT, 27 July 1990.

26. HQ, ARCENT, Command Group, briefing titled, "USARCENT OPLAN 1002-90 Force Structure," presented to USCINCCENT, 27 July 1990.

27. Ibid., Option 1.

28. Ibid., Option 2.

29. HQ, 11th ADA Brigade, briefing titled, "Initial Patriot Battalion Incremental ATBM Capability," Internal Look '90, undated. HQ, 11th ADA Brigade, briefing titled, "Initial Assessment of USCINCCENT Patriot Requirement," Internal Look '90, dated July 1990. See also the remarks of General Charles Horner, USAF, "Offensive Air Operations: Lessons for the Future," *RUSI Journal* 138, No. 6 (December 1993): 22.

30. HQ, ARCENT, Command Group, briefing titled, "USARCENT OPLAN 1002-90 Concept of Support," presented to USCINCCENT, 27 July 1990. HQ, ARCENT, Command Group, briefing titled, "ARCENT Update," presented to the 1990 Army Leadership Seminar on 6 August 1990. The latter briefing showed the preferred force would take seventy-five deployment days vice fifty-five for base case. The requirement for either was fifty days. The ARCENT conclusion—"Need 6 more fast sealift ships."

31. HQ, ARCENT, Command Group, briefing titled, "USARCENT OPLAN 1002-90 Concept of Operations," presented to the vice chief of staff and Army Staff on 1 August 1990.

2
Executing a Contingency

Neither Central Command nor Third Army had operational forces assigned to them during normal times. Both operated on reduced establishment, which meant that both were confronted with the need to create expanded headquarters at the same time major forces were being deployed to the theater of operations under their command. Because of the distance from American and European bases and limits on strategic lift, U.S. forces were dependent upon host-nation support from the outset. Arrangements for provision of such support had to be made as troops flowed in. On top of this, because no doctrine existed for Third Army's role, much of what was done had to be made up as the process unfolded. The focus of this chapter is on the actions taken by Third Army to establish itself in theater in the late summer of 1990—the beginning of Operation Desert Shield, the defense of the Arabian Peninsula.

This chapter also assesses the personalities of the men selected to lead the Army's land effort. If the unwritten cultural values or prejudices of the Army are correct, the highly successful war in Southwest Asia was directed by the wrong generals. For the Army, the Gulf War was a tanker's war. Although he had commanded a mechanized division in the United States, General Norman Schwarzkopf was not ordinarily thought of as an authority on armored warfare.[1] The commander in chief (CINC) was a light infantryman, respected as an aggressive, indeed, combative leader. He was also known as a boss who "shot messengers," a big man whose leadership style was that of a classic bully, a commander who employed his size as a weapon of intimidation and tolerated neither fools nor honest disagreement gladly. Yet Schwarzkopf was also a leader known for the genuine affection he felt for his soldiers, and there are those who maintain that, in spite of his sometimes brutal treatment of subordinates, in the long run he rarely followed through on threats made in bad temper.

Schwarzkopf was said by retired Air Force General Charles E. ("Chuck") Yeager to have admitted to being put out to pasture when he was sent to CENTCOM as commander in chief.[2] That is not an entirely inapt assessment, for whatever planning was done in the 1980s for Persian Gulf contingencies, it would have been hard to find many Army officers who believed a major land war in that area likely. Deployment time for heavy forces was considered an insurmountable problem, although significant efforts were made to address this shortcoming.³ The Army's premier tanker, General Crosbie Saint, a former commander of III Corps at Fort Hood, Texas, had been sent to Europe to command U.S. Army Europe and NATO's Central Army Group in the event of mechanized war breaking out across the Iron Curtain. But that was before the sudden arrival of a "new world order."

Schwarzkopf had been an assistant division commander of the 8th Infantry Division (Mechanized) in Europe and had commanded the 24th Infantry Division (Mechanized) in Georgia, but he had never commanded a large armored force in the field. In 1985, he became the deputy chief of staff for operations (DCSOPS) at the Department of the Army and, thereafter, the commander of I Corps at Fort Lewis. The position of DCSOPS doubtless prepared him for his role as a joint-service commander, but it would have contributed nothing to his practical knowledge of mechanized warfare on a large scale. The I Corps commander commanded a headquarters and various light and Reserve Component forces focused largely on Korea and other Pacific theater contingencies. While commanding the 24th Division, Schwarzkopf had been appointed deputy to the Commander in Chief, Atlantic, during Operation Urgent Fury, the 1983 U.S. invasion of Grenada. No doubt his experiences in that operation instructed many of his decisions as Commander in Chief, Central Command.

In his memoir, Schwarzkopf portrays himself as something of a regional expert at the time he assumed command because he had lived in the region as a boy. It must be remembered, however, that he had last seen the Middle East as a 14-year-old on holidays from school. While he seems to have retained an emotional attraction to the region, one suspects whatever expertise he possessed in 1990 came from hard work done as commander in chief far more than from any earlier practical experience in the area.⁴

Lieutenant General John Yeosock, the Third Army commander, brought to his job a number of experiences that would be directly relevant to the tasks he would have to perform during the Gulf War. Yeosock was a career armored cavalryman.⁵ He commanded a squadron of the 3d Armored Cavalry at Fort Bliss, Texas, and the 194th Armored Brigade at Fort Knox. Later, he had been chief of staff, assistant division commander (ADC), and commander of the 1st Cavalry Division at Fort Hood. The division participated in Reforger (Return of Forces to Europe) exercises while he was both ADC and division commander. Yeosock commanded the division at the time General Saint was III Corps commander, and he took part in one of the most ambitious of the Reforger exercises, one in which the III Corps exercised its role as a reinforcing corps to Allied Forces Central Europe. Yeosock's association with Major General William G. Pagonis, Forces Command's J4, whom he would select to be his support command commander, went back to a Reforger exercise in which both officers moved the 1st Cavalry Division to Europe and back. Pagonis was then deputy commander of the 21st Support Command in U.S. Army Europe.

Equally important, Yeosock had served as assistant deputy chief of staff for operations when Schwarzkopf was the DCSOPS. He understood the commander in chief's personality and guided his behavior accordingly. More to the point, he was generally able to interpret the CINC's temperamental outbursts and able to extract from them the necessary information to get on with the business at hand.

Yeosock, in fact, was an uneasy complement to Schwarzkopf. Where Schwarzkopf was mercurial, forceful, and dynamic, Yeosock was thoughtful, thorough, and circumspect. The commander in chief was sensitive to his prerogatives, a characteristic that assumes clear definition of responsibility and a positivist view of bureaucracy. Yeosock thrived on ambiguity and the indirect approach. He was laconic by nature and his guidance could sometimes be cryptic. However, by not concerning himself with gaining credit, which might have appeared as an infringement on the CINC's business, Yeosock often succeeded in influencing or expanding his operating environment. He also seems to have made it a cardinal rule to disagree with Schwarzkopf only in private and to use his staff officers as stalking horses (what he called, "recon by fire") to feel out the theater commander's views on sensitive issues. This method of dealing with the theater commander was generally successful, perhaps even necessary, given the personalities involved. It may have sometimes disappointed subordinate commanders and staff officers, who would have preferred a more confrontational advocate with the CINC—especially since they would not have to carry the hod.

Although Yeosock, as a lieutenant general, was selected to be deputy Forces Command's commander and commander of Third Army, rather than being given command of a corps, he had other qualifications that especially suited him to his Desert Shield-Desert Storm responsibilities. As a former program manager for the Saudi Arabian National Guard (PMSANG), he knew the country, he knew the Saudi armed forces, and, most important, he knew the Saudi civilian and military leadership. Yeosock had experience in desert operations, not just from his tour in Saudi Arabia but also from his period as a squadron commander in the 3d Armored Cavalry Regiment at Fort Bliss; as commander of the 1st Cavalry Division, learning from unit experience at the National Training Center; and as the Third Army commander taking part in various exercises and consultations with regional leaders.[6] As deputy commander in chief of Forces Command, Yeosock had a thorough grasp of the capabilities of the Reserve Components and their place in contingency plans, and he knew how the FORSCOM staff itself would respond to the mission to deploy his forces. Finally, Yeosock had conducted the Army's analysis of the Department of Defense plan to downsize the armed forces (The Defense Management Review). Consequently, he probably had more knowledge about Army force structure than most of his peers, knowledge that would be vital to creating a theater-level command and support structure in Saudi Arabia.

Interestingly enough, Yeosock was almost entirely innocent of Army professional schooling. He had attended the Marine Corps Amphibious Warfare School, the Armed Forces Staff College, and the National War College. But if he had missed the Army's institutional fascination with abstract theory and doctrine during the 1980s, he had mastered thoroughly two traditional doctrinal concepts: the commander's estimate by evaluation of METT-T (mission, enemy, terrain and weather, and troops and time available) and the application of the complementary principles of war—mass (concentration) and economy of force. He would use the estimate process throughout Desert Shield and Desert Storm to balance short- and long-term risks involved in the various trade-offs required by political circumstances, changing missions, and the exigencies involved in operating at the end of a long strategic line of communications. He would employ the principle of mass to focus combat power against the enemy's most vital forces. These simple theoretical guides, combined with his practical experience in moving heavy forces, would be more than adequate to the task at hand.

For all that, the cultural value system of the Army held that the plum assignments for lieutenant generals were the two heavy corps in Europe (V and VII), and the III Corps at Fort Hood, Texas. For light soldiers, there were the XVIII Airborne Corps at Fort Bragg and the I Corps at Fort Lewis. Moreover, in 1990, the U.S. Army had no coherent doctrine addressing the roles and missions of an army-level of command. Since Vietnam, the Army had been structured physically and intellectually to go to war as part of a NATO organization in which member nations would contribute national corps to coalition army groups. The corps was the largest national tactical organization. The irony that the Third Army commander had never commanded at the corps level did not escape his principal tactical subordinates, fellow Lieutenant Generals Gary Luck of XVIII Corps and Frederick Franks of VII Corps.

These cultural norms were not eased at all by the nature of Third Army. Third Army, in normal circumstances, was a small planning headquarters of 222 active-duty officers. It was located at Fort McPherson, Georgia, and assigned responsibility for performing the Army planning and exercise duties pertaining to Central Command.[7] Sixty-five percent of Third Army's go-to-war logistics structure was in the Reserve Component. A significant part of its internal staff manning consisted of Army Reservists assigned to a local Army Reserve Troop Program Unit located in Atlanta. In fact, of the anticipated wartime headquarters strength of 894 officers and enlisted spaces (it actually reached over 1,000), 376 were Reserve Component, and 167 were not even provided for prior to mobilization.[8]

The detailed work of running Third Army fell upon the deputy commander, a major general. A colonel served as chief of staff, and fellow colonels as division chiefs. In many cases these were officers at the end of their careers. This contrasted sharply with the staff of XVIII Airborne Corps, which tended to attract hard chargers on their way up.[9] Staff officers at XVIII Corps, not infrequently and with no little arrogance, were accustomed to looking down on Third Army as "sleepy hollow," a view that did not facilitate interstaff coordination for going to war.

Third Army often appeared to be an appendix to the larger Forces Command headquarters. Indeed, the army commander served as the deputy commander of Forces Command, and the duties associated with the latter title often took precedence over those of the former. In fact, General Yeosock maintained two offices, and he spent more time in that associated with Forces Command than he did in the one down the street associated with Third Army. FORSCOM commands all continental-U.S.-based tactical forces, including XVIII Airborne Corps and all Reserve Component units. The XVIII Airborne Corps, which quite properly considered itself the Army's premier intervention force, ordinarily dealt directly with Forces Command, and only the preceding December, the corps had acted as a joint task force (JTF) and, for a time, as the JTF's Army Forces headquarters as well during Operation Just Cause in Panama.

On 2 August 1990, what had been a speculative exercise two weeks before became a real-life contingency. Saddam Hussein invaded Kuwait. That same day, the United Nations Security Council passed Resolution 660, condemning the invasion and calling for the immediate and unconditional withdrawal of Iraqi forces from Kuwait.

That day, President George Bush delivered a speech to the Aspen Institute in Colorado.[10] His address concerned the need to restructure U.S. military forces in response to changes in the global environment, specifically the rapid decline of Soviet power. The president's proposal called for an orderly reduction of U.S. military forces over five years. That plan was about to suffer a temporary interruption. On the 2d, the United States imposed an embargo on Iraq, and the Joint Chiefs of Staff issued an order for deployment of Air Force tanker squadrons and the movement of the USS *Independence* Carrier Battle Group into the North Arabian Sea.[11]

On the evening of 4 August, around 1900, John Yeosock was eating dinner at a neighbor's home when he received a telephone call from General Schwarzkopf at MacDill Air Force Base, Florida.[12] Schwarzkopf, who had briefed the president at Camp David earlier that day, instructed Yeosock to report to MacDill immediately and indicated that if there were no flights, a plane would be dispatched to pick him up. Yeosock had a few words with General Edwin Burba, commander in chief of Forces Command, followed by a brief meeting with his immediate staff. He then flew to MacDill. He took General Pagonis in tow to help him identify logistic requirements, especially for host-nation support.[13] Yeosock expected his absence from Atlanta to be brief. Instead, it would last almost a year and involve assembling an army and fighting a war half the world away. That same day, the European community imposed a trade embargo on Iraq.

The following morning, Schwarzkopf; his J4 (joint logistics staff officer), Major General Dane Starling; J5 (joint operations officer), Rear Admiral Grant A. Sharp; Yeosock; and Lieutenant Colonel Larry Gresham, chief of Third Army's G4 plans, flew to Washington, D.C.[14] There, they joined Lieutenant General Charles A. Horner, commander of Central Command Air Forces, CENTAF, and Colonel William Rider, his deputy chief of staff for logistics (DCSLOG). Horner had been called to Washington the previous day to participate in Schwarzkopf's briefing to the president at Camp David.[15] Following quick meetings in the Pentagon, these seven officers flew to Saudi Arabia with Secretary of Defense Richard Cheney. They were to be the first contingent of Operation Desert Shield.

On the 5th, global reaction to the invasion of Kuwait continued to grow. Japan suspended oil imports from Iraq. The same day, Forces Command ordered the Army Reserve's 1185th Transportation Terminal Unit (TTU) to the Port of Savannah, where, for the 1185th's annual active duty training exercise, the unit would outload the 24th Infantry Division. It was to be a longer than normal summer camp for members of the 1185th and many other Reserve Component soldiers.[16]

The secretary of defense and his party arrived in the Kingdom of Saudi Arabia on 6 August. Following historic nighttime meetings with the Saudi king in Jedda, during which King Faid requested U.S. assistance in the defense of Saudi Arabia, the secretary and CINC returned to the United States. The six military officers who had accompanied them traveled to Riyadh to begin Operation Desert Shield. That day, the UN Security Council passed Resolution 661, calling for an international embargo on Iraq and occupied Kuwait.

On 7 August, responding to the king's request, President Bush directed the commitment of U.S. military forces to the defense of Saudi Arabia (see map 2). The Joint Staff issued the initial deployment orders for operation Desert Shield. The president announced his decision to the public the following day.[17]

Conducting a military operation in Saudi Arabia is no simple task. The Arabian Peninsula is a large area, approximately the size of the United States east of the Mississippi. It has almost no modern road or rail network. The countryside consists almost entirely of a variety of desert terrains. There are no continuous rivers. Climatic conditions are extreme, especially in the high summer months during which the Kuwait crisis developed. On the other hand, the country's few urban areas possess a modern commercial infrastructure from which U.S. forces could and would draw support. There were a large number of modern airfields around the country, modern port facilities, especially at Dammam and Jubayl, and a developed system of basic services. Food, fuel, water, a modern (if limited) phone system, and shelter were all available if they could be tapped. Notwithstanding the absence of a developed road network, buses and trucks—particularly line-haul (long-distance tractor-trailer) trucks—were present in abundance. Because of the heavy investment of oil revenues in modernization and the annual need to accommodate the influx of pilgrims to the Islamic holy sites, the Saudi commercial structure was already heavily dependent upon contracting as a way of doing business. This would facilitate the acquisition of large-scale support to sustain U.S. and coalition forces.

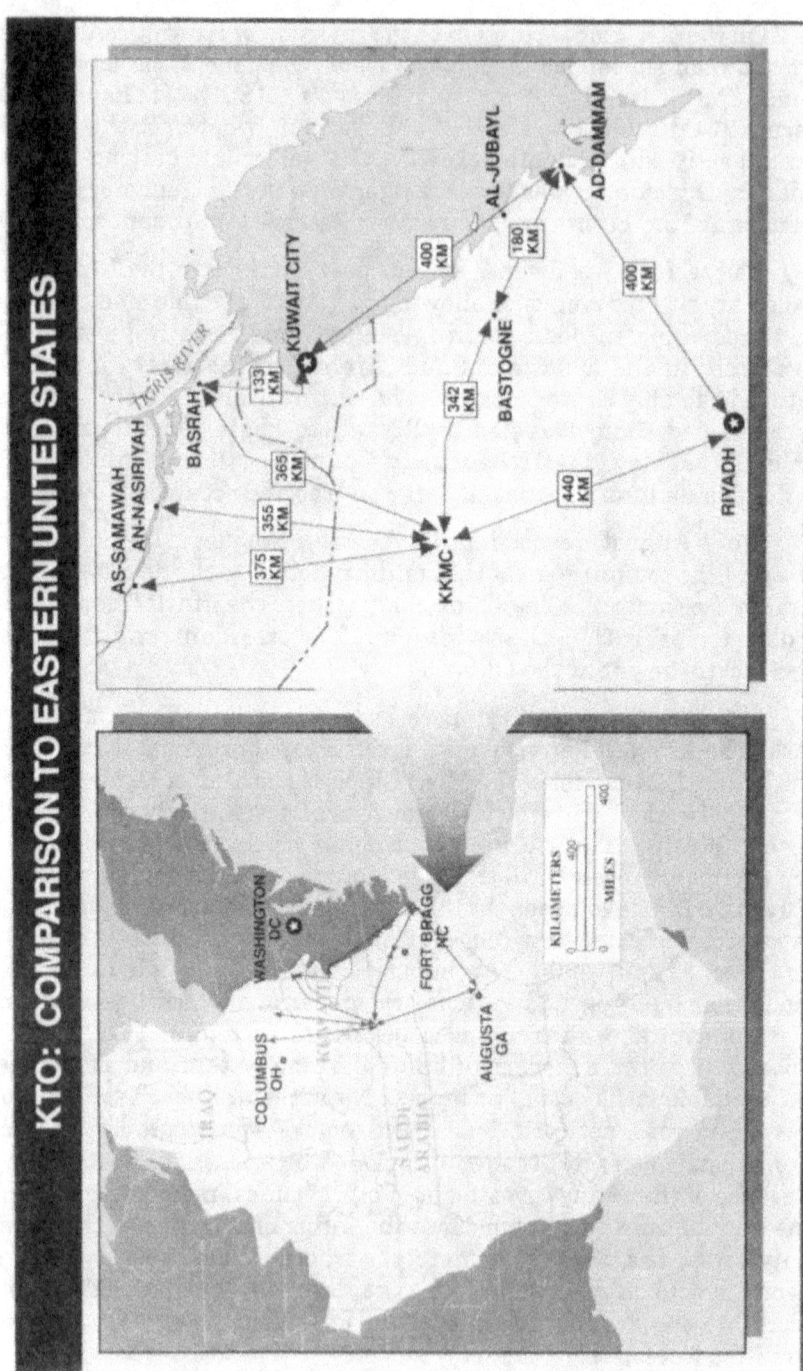

Map 2.

The U.S. military, however, possessed no operational infrastructure in the peninsula other than a Military Training Mission (USMTM) and the Office of the Program Manager, Saudi Arabian National Guard, both of which normally trained various parts of the Saudi military. These two groups, at least, provided some additional hands with which the Army and Air Force commanders could begin to build a U.S. military force in theater. As a former program manager for the Saudi National Guard, Yeosock leaned heavily on that office, using Brigadier General James B. Taylor, the incumbent program manager, as his initial interim chief of staff.

Yeosock's concept of Third Army, once deployed, was summed up in his idea that "Third Army is three armies."[18] (See figure 1.) As ARCENT (Army, Central Command), it was a service component headquarters for a unified commander. As such, it accomplished coordination with sister services and allied ground forces as the principal U.S. land force. The ARCENT commander exercised command over all Army forces assigned (less operational command for certain specified special operations forces) and advised the theater commander on Army matters. As Third Army, it was a "theater army," the major Department of the Army headquarters in theater. The theater army developed an echeloned force structure to support army and theater requirements for various technical capabilities in accordance with Department of Defense directives and the CINC's guidance. Among these were intelligence, communications, transportation, air defense, logistics, civil affairs, military police, and engineering. Finally, the theater army provided the linkage between Army units in the field, other major Army commands, and the Department of the Army.

The duties of service component and theater army are implicit, that is, they always obtain. In addition, the headquarters had to be able to assume a third role, that of a numbered field army. As a field army, Third Army planned operations, allocated combat power and sustainment resources, synchronized theater-level operating systems, and directed execution within the operational span of control assigned by the theater commander.

This division of these three complementary responsibilities is essentially heuristic; that is, it provides a means to address the various duties assigned to the army commander in such a way as to reflect the differing lines of accountability in terms of the army's several functions. It is important to note, however, that all functions were performed by the same staff under the authority of the army commander, often without any clear idea which "army" was

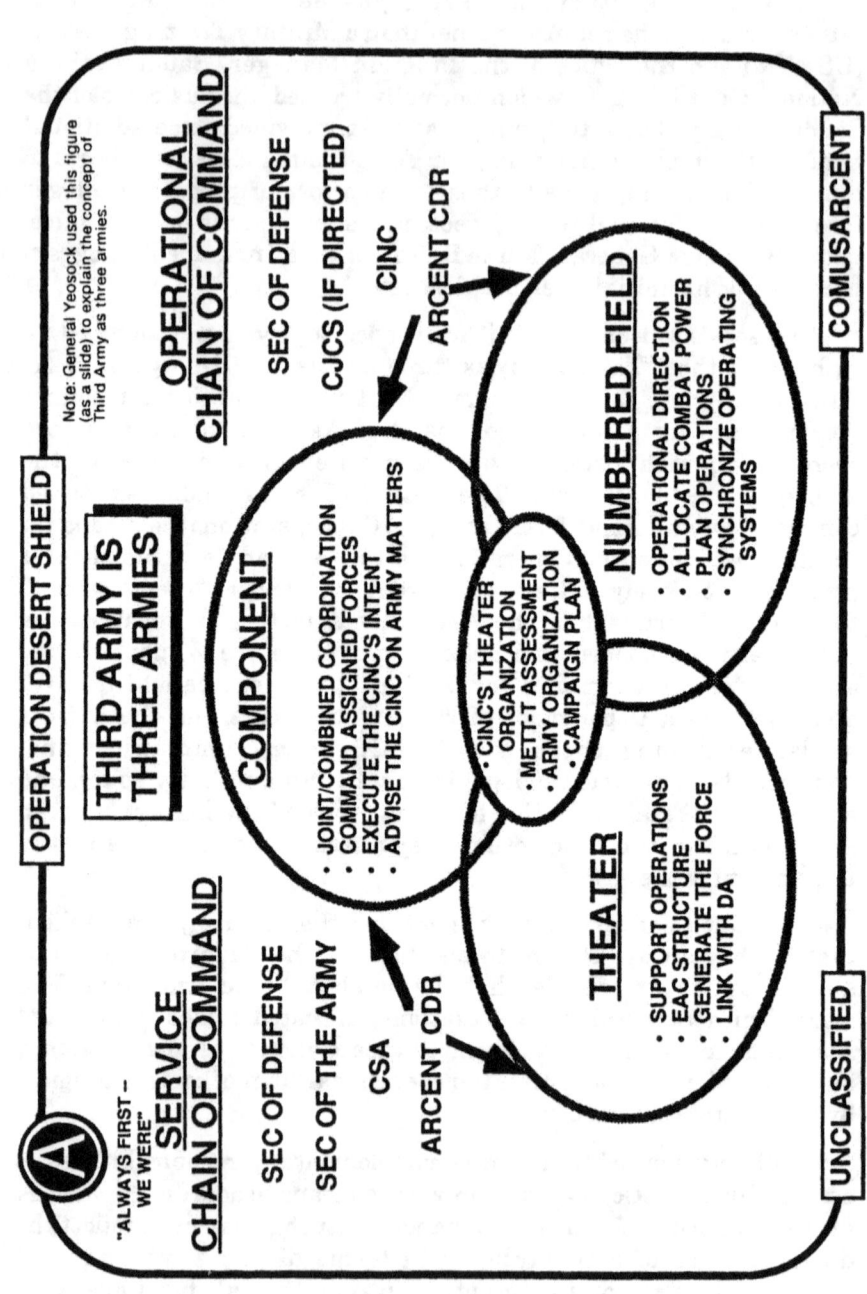

Figure 1.

performing at a given time. The army headquarters structure had to be flexible enough to reconfigure according to the functions it was expected to perform. In the case of Third Army, a major staff restructuring took place in November and December 1990 when the headquarters' functions were expanded consequent to the president's decision to create an offensive option.

The tripartite scheme reflected the division of responsibility within the Department of Defense.[19] The various defense reorganization acts since 1947 have retained separate service departments within a unified Defense Department. Service departments have been assigned responsibility for providing organized and equipped forces to theater commanders, whose operational chain of command runs directly to the secretary of defense.[20] Service departments have been responsible for the sustainment of their forces in theater, except where otherwise provided for. Service chiefs of staff answer to a service secretary on departmental matters and simultaneously sit as members of the Joint Chiefs of Staff, a collective body headed by a chairman who is subordinate to the secretary of defense and president.[21]

The Goldwater-Nichols Act (Defense Reorganization Act of 1986) transferred to the chairman of the Joint Chiefs of Staff responsibility and authority formerly vested in the corporate Joint Chiefs. It also provided for a greater role by theater commanders in determining the adequacy and direction of departmental budgeting and wartime theater sustainment. It left intact the departmental structure within the Department of Defense, however, and provided that any disputes that might arise between a theater commander and service departments would be forwarded by the CINC, through the chairman, for resolution by the secretary of defense.[22]

A major purpose of the Goldwater-Nichols Act was to provide theater commanders full latitude to organize their commands to achieve assigned national objectives. One method that has been used since World War II to respond to small contingencies with limited purposes has been the formation of a joint task force, generally commanded by an officer of the predominant service within a unified command and charged with the conduct of necessary operations. The Just Cause, XVIII Airborne Corps example has already been mentioned. General Schwarzkopf, however, chose to organize his forces generally as service components (see figure 2). That is, his major subordinate commands were Army Central Command, Central Command Air Forces, Marine Central Command (MARCENT), and Navy Central Command (NAVCENT). The exception to this

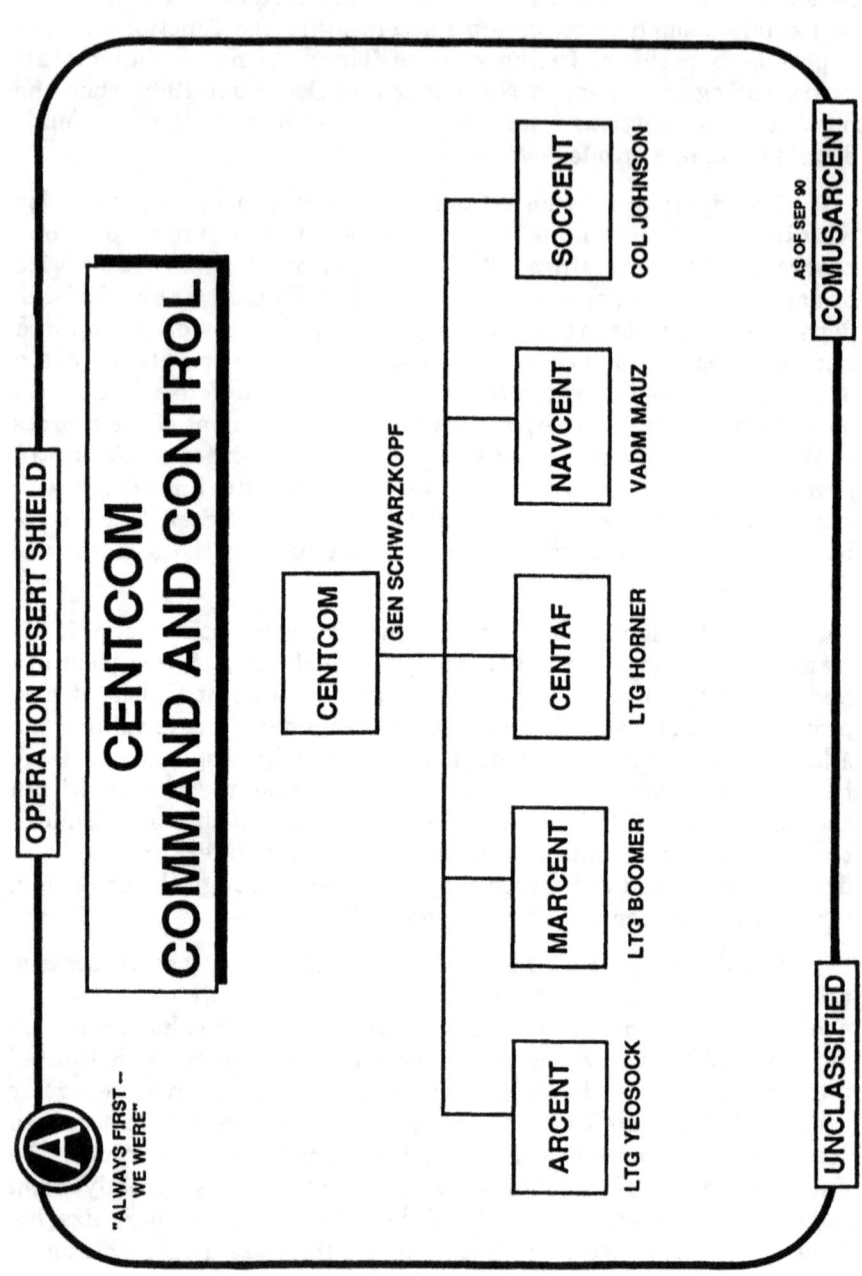

Figure 2.

organization was a fifth component, Special Operations Command, Central Command (SOCCENT), which held operational command of selected special operations forces from the separate services.

Within this general structure, the theater commander might assign executive agency or authority to a single component commander for performance of particular tasks. In this way, the commander of CENTAF was appointed Joint Forces Air Component commander to provide centralized direction to the theater air campaign.[23] The Army commander was given responsibility, among other things, to operate common-user seaports during Desert Shield and to exercise directive authority over rear-area terrain management and main supply route (MSR) priorities in the combat zone during Desert Storm.[24] The Army commander, in turn, assigned these responsibilities to one of his major subordinate commands, the 22d Support Command. Various grants of authority, or limits thereto, ordinarily went along with this sort of joint service responsibility. Also, within the general framework, forces from one component might be placed under the command of another, as the "Tiger Brigade" (the 1st Brigade of the 2d Armored Division deployed as the third ground maneuver brigade of the 1st Cavalry Division) was placed under operational command of the MARCENT commander for Operation Desert Storm.

The first phase of Operation Desert Shield, which lasted from 7 August 1990 until 8 November, consisted of the deployment of a joint military force to defend American and allied interests against Iraqi aggression, a force of sufficient strength adequate to enforce UN sanctions while defending the Arabian base (see figure 3). The Army's role consisted of building a viable ground combat force and a support structure sufficient to sustain, to various degrees, committed forces of all services. Both the Army combat contingent and theater support structure had to be built from scratch using forces from halfway around the world.

Schwarzkopf returned to Tampa in order to supervise personally the joint deployment. Such actions, however, are inherently decentralized. Senior officers managing each service's deployment are used to acting on their own, and Schwarzkopf found himself losing control. The Air Force, for example, deployed twice the number of F-15 and F-16 squadrons expected at the end of the first week. Thus, wrote Schwarzkopf, the requirements to bring in related support forces "tied up dozens of flights we had allocated for other units."[25] The XVIII Airborne Corps, to Schwarzkopf's irritation, led its deployment with

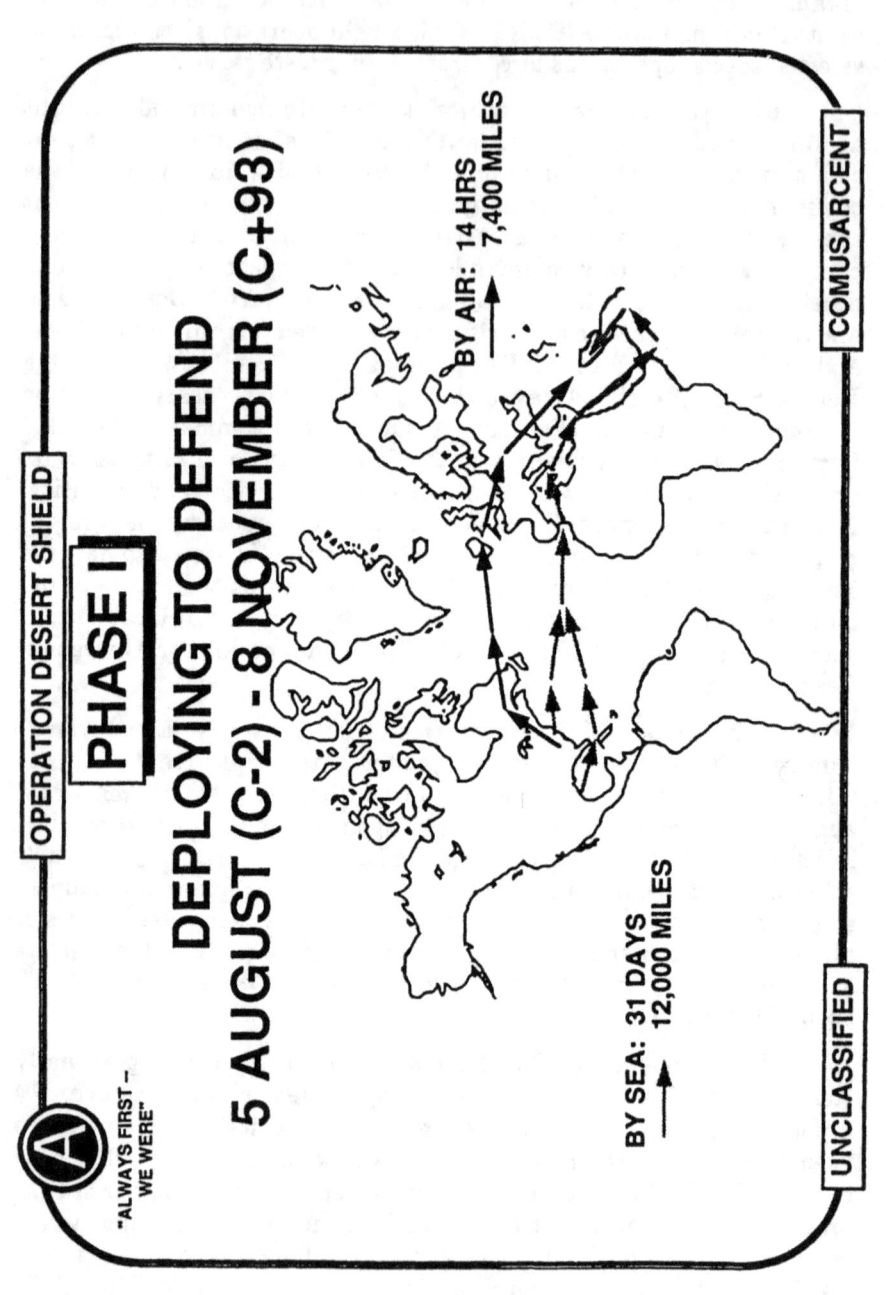

Figure 3.

an advance corps headquarters at the expense of paratroopers from the corps' 82d Airborne Division.

Army forces had to be deployed and sustained in a hostile and comparatively undeveloped environment. They were to deter aggression and to defend and restore Saudi territory should the Iraqis attack. This entailed, at the start, creating a crisis action time-phased force deployment list (TPFDL)—a list of units prioritized for movement—to ship the XVIII Airborne Corps' force of four and two-thirds division-force equivalents: 82d Airborne Division; 101st Airborne Division (Air Assault) plus the 12th Aviation Brigade from Europe; 24th Infantry Division (2 brigades) plus the 197th Infantry Brigade (Separate); 1st Cavalry Division (2 brigades) plus the 1st Brigade, 2d Armored Division (the "Tiger Brigade"); and the 3d Armored Cavalry Regiment, with supporting corps combat support and combat service support elements.[26] The commitment of forces also involved designing and deploying an army echelon-above-corps headquarters and the theater support structure appropriate for the conditions obtaining in Southwest Asia.

To complicate the task further, the deployed force in the beginning would have to be built solely from available units of the Regular Army. It would take some time for the president to mobilize the necessary political support to call up and retain the Reserve forces that had always been assumed to make up a major part of Third Army and XVIII Airborne Corps. This political mobilization, which is a remarkable story in itself, took place simultaneously with the initial deployment of Army forces. Yet even when Reserve units were fully manned and equipped, they still required time to be brought into active federal service and prepared for overseas deployment. This further delayed getting them into the theater.

Meanwhile, the force build-up had to proceed. Some deployment requirements could be and were met by Reserve Component units that volunteered or were assigned annual training in support of the active force deployment (like the 1185th TTU). Some Reservists even deployed as individual volunteers to Saudi Arabia. As a consequence, the governing assumptions for the Third Army staff were in a constant state of flux for some time, and essential personnel arrived in theater under a wide variety of legal provisions and service obligations.[27]

One very positive characteristic of the U.S. military operations in Southwest Asia was the extent to which the Bush administration consistently maintained a clear understanding of both political and military objectives. On 8 August, the president announced the initial deployment of U.S. forces to the Persian Gulf. At that time, he declared four national objectives: (1) to achieve the withdrawal of Iraqi forces from Kuwait, (2) to restore the legitimate government of Kuwait, (3) to defend Saudi Arabia, and (4) to protect American citizens abroad.[28] These political goals were translated that same day into three more limited military objectives by Secretary of Defense Cheney and by the chairman of the Joint Chiefs of Staff, General Colin Powell. These were (1) to deter further Iraqi aggression, (2) to improve Saudi Arabian military and defensive capabilities, and (3) to defend Saudi Arabia.[29] The difference between the two lists reflected the initial reliance on a variety of nonmilitary means to achieve the declared national goals. This pattern of formulating military objectives on the basis of policy announcements was maintained consistently through February 1991. Because such announcements were covered live by television's Cable News Network (CNN), the senior military chain of command could receive the commander in chief's guidance from the president himself, thus enhancing the coherence of the vision shared by all major commanders in the field.

By the time the initial policy directives had been issued, Yeosock and his small band of Army officers in Saudi Arabia had identified three immediate tasks for Third Army.[30] These were (1) to arrange for reception and onward movement of Army, Air Force, and Marine Corps forces (as yet *without a host-nation agreement or plan*), (2) to get the Kingdom of Saudi Arabia to change its traditional way of doing business in order to respond to the urgency of the moment, and (3) to this end, to establish a national-level, integrated warfighting command and staff.[31] The first task involved preparing to receive Army and Marine forces and Air Force heavy equipment through sea and aerial ports at Al Jubayl, Dhahran, and Ad Dammam. The last two tasks led Yeosock to create the Coalition Coordination Communication and Integration Center (C3IC) (to be discussed hereafter).

On 8 August, the ARCENT staff was practically doubled, to fifty-two, with the arrival of an advanced command and control element. ARCENT established itself in the Royal Saudi Land Forces Building, while the CENTCOM staff moved into the Saudi Ministry of Defense. Four more key figures arrived on the 11th: the deputy commanding generals, Brigadier General (later Major General) Robert Frix (Operations) and Major General (later Lieutenant General) William G. ("Gus") Pagonis (Support); Brigadier General James W. Monroe, Army G4; and Colonel Gene Holloway, the G3 plans. Like Pagonis, Frix and Monroe had previous connections with Yeosock. Frix had been

Yeosock's chief of staff in the 1st Cavalry Division. Monroe, who like Yeosock had served in Saudi Arabia before (with USMTM), had been G4 of the Third Army before his promotion to brigadier general. Indeed, his family had not yet moved to his new post in Detroit. He simply moved back into his old job at a higher grade.

Jim Monroe, the Third Army logistic staff officer, presented an interesting contrast to Pagonis, the army's logistic executive. Pagonis is short, peripatetic, dynamic, a Greek fighting cock, albeit with a sense of humor that can remind an onlooker of the antihero on the television series "M*A*S*H," Corporal Klinger. Monroe, on the other hand, was a tall, handsome African-American, sober and deliberate, patient and soft-spoken—an excellent counterbalance to his more dynamic opposite number.

Another key member arrived at army headquarters on the 11th, Major General Paul Schwartz. Schwartz, then serving as deputy commander of I Corps at Fort Lewis, Washington, was another former PMSANG. He had been brought in to build the U.S. side of the C3IC, which he would direct, first, for Third Army, then, for Central Command.[32] He, like Pagonis, Monroe, and Frix, had been selected by Yeosock almost immediately upon receipt of his own alert. Yeosock knew Schwartz from Fort Hood, where both had been chiefs of staff for neighboring heavy divisions. Schwartz was also the officer who had become PMSANG when, within months of Yeosock's departure from the desert kingdom, his immediate successor did not work out with the Saudis. Schwartz, a tanker, was by disposition and sympathies an ideal choice to work the interalliance staff. He was a patient, low-key and humane man with a perpetual sheepish grin and the patience of Solomon. Most important, he had long experience working in Saudi Arabia and a great respect for Saudi culture. Frix, Pagonis, and Schwartz were Yeosock's principal deputies from the early days of Desert Shield.

The Third Army's forward CP arrived in two echelons on 14 and 23 August, bringing the headquarters to 266 officers and men (see figure 4). These men and women would undertake the twin tasks of creating the instrumentalities of coalition cooperation, organization, procedures, and host-nation support agreements, while performing more traditional echelon-above-corps functions of force generation, sustainment, and coordination with higher and adjacent headquarters.

A new Third Army G3, Brigadier General (later Major General) Steven Arnold, arrived on 7 September direct from Korea where he had been assistant division commander of the 2d Infantry Division. A

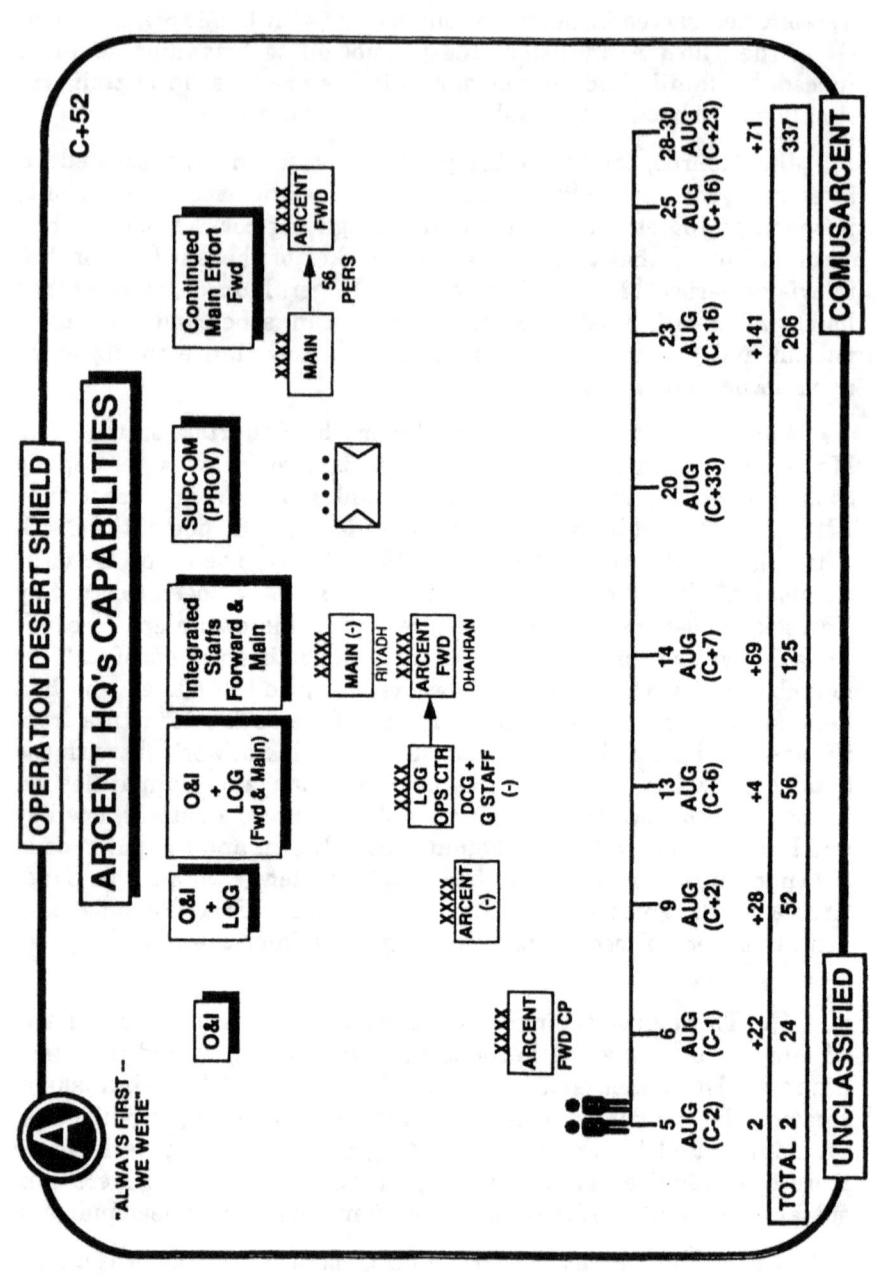

Figure 4.

general officer G2, Brigadier General John Stewart, was assigned in December.³³ These two key officers were not known to Yeosock before their arrival, though each, in his own field, would be essential to the success ultimately enjoyed by ARCENT. The fact that Yeosock was prepared to allow the Army to assign him a G3 and G2 while he took particular care who would serve his logistics and coalition needs probably says a good deal about where the army commander saw the headquarters' immediate problems and how he saw his own role in the developing theater command structure. In the end, he was most fortunate all around in his command team.

In August and September, the immediate tasks at hand included developing an Army component force capable of achieving the assigned military objectives in concert with sister services and alliance forces. Third Army would have to build and deploy a force that could fight on arrival and sustain long-term operations in an environment of strategic lift constraints, as yet limited host-nation support, changing requirements, and acceptance of prudent risk.

The first and obvious decision, given the immediacy of the threat, was to bow to necessity and deploy combat forces early—especially critical combat multipliers such as aviation units, air defense systems, and antiarmor weapons—in order to buy time should hostilities commence. The experience of Internal Look was useful if not completely satisfying. Internal Look had addressed only combat force requirements. Much of the postexercise work of designing the necessary support structure and identifying specific forces remained to be done. Furthermore, much of the work had to be accomplished manually, as predeployment data had not been entered into the necessary computer data bases.³⁴

The decision to bring in combat forces first was not without cost. It meant that forces in theater would have to maintain themselves under austere conditions for some time and that host-nation support, both donated and contracted, was a sine qua non to sustain the force for the immediate future. This decision was only possible because of the availability of supplies—particularly tentage, food, and ammunition—prepositioned on ships in the Indian Ocean. These prepositioned assets bought the time required to begin the flow of supplies from the host nation and the United States.³⁵ (See figure 5.)

The overall concept for the deployment of U.S. armed forces, of which Army forces were but a part, was characterized by General Powell on 11 September as consisting of three phases.³⁶ The phasing was designed to integrate the complementary capabilities of each arm,

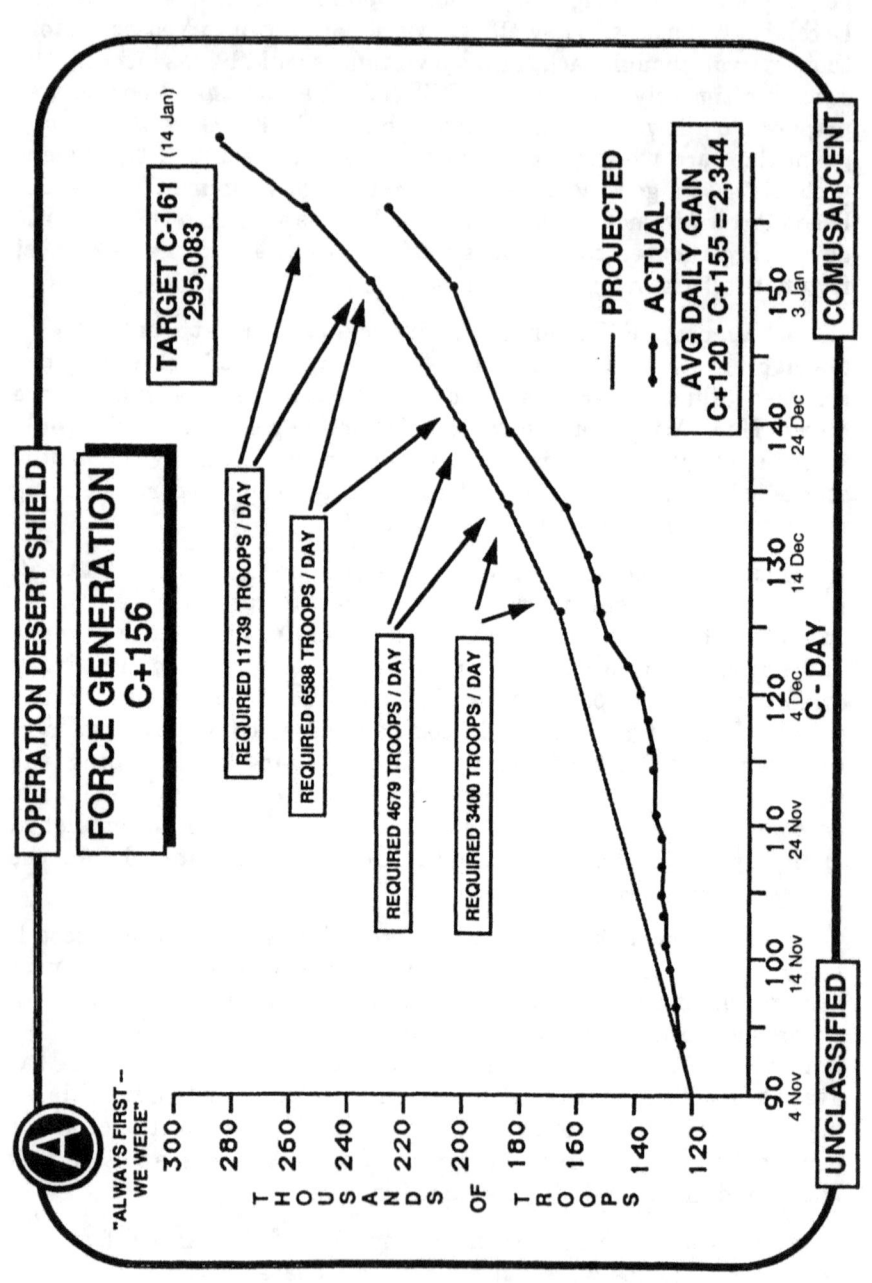

Figure 5.

balancing great strategic mobility with staying power. Phase one, intended to provide an immediate deterrent force, consisted of the concentration of deployed naval forces organized around two carrier battle groups, the USS *Eisenhower* and USS *Independence* groups, off the Arabian Peninsula; deployment of Air Force air-superiority forces from the 1st Tactical Fighter Wing in the United States; and dispatch of light ground forces.[37] As early as 12 August, on the strength of these forces, President Bush directed the Navy to enforce an embargo on Iraqi oil shipments and most imports. On 25 August, the UN Security Council approved the use of force to enforce UN sanctions (Resolution 665). The first U.S. shots had been fired enforcing the naval blockade on 18 August.[38] It is important to remember that, throughout Desert Shield and Desert Storm, indeed long after, a naval conflict, separate but related to actions on the ground, was going on in the Persian Gulf and the Red Sea approaches to Iraq and Jordan.

The second phase of the U.S. deployment, which commenced within days, brought in ground-attack aircraft, additional air-superiority fighters, and various maritime forces, specifically the 7th Marine Expeditionary Brigade (MEB) and, later, the 1st MEB, for which maritime prepositioning ships (MPS), with their heavy equipment and thirty days' supplies, were available in Diego Garcia and Guam.[39] The Marines prepositioned M60 main battle tanks—old but still highly effective models—provided the first true U.S. armored ground capability.

The two Marine Corps MPS completed off-loading on 2 and 5 September. The 82d Airborne finished its deployment on 9 September. It was joined by elements of the lead brigade task force of the 101st Airborne Division with its attack helicopters and elements of the 12th Aviation Brigade from Europe. The 101st Aviation Task Force arrived by strategic airlift, notwithstanding the high cost in airframes. This added the potent antiarmor combat power of the AH-64 attack helicopters to the deployed light forces. About the same time, the USS *Saratoga* Carrier Battle Group replaced the USS *Eisenhower*, and the USS *Kennedy* deployed to the Mediterranean with a third carrier battle group to support Central Command operations as required.

Finally, in phase three, the heavy ground, air, maritime, and sustainment forces required to ensure a successful defense of Saudi Arabia followed. Fast sealift ships (FSS) carrying the 24th Infantry Division (Mechanized), the Army's first heavy division to deploy, departed Savannah, Georgia, starting on 13 August, a week after the U.S. commitment. The first ship arrived in theater on the 27th.[40] (For a comparison between force generation in Desert Shield versus that in

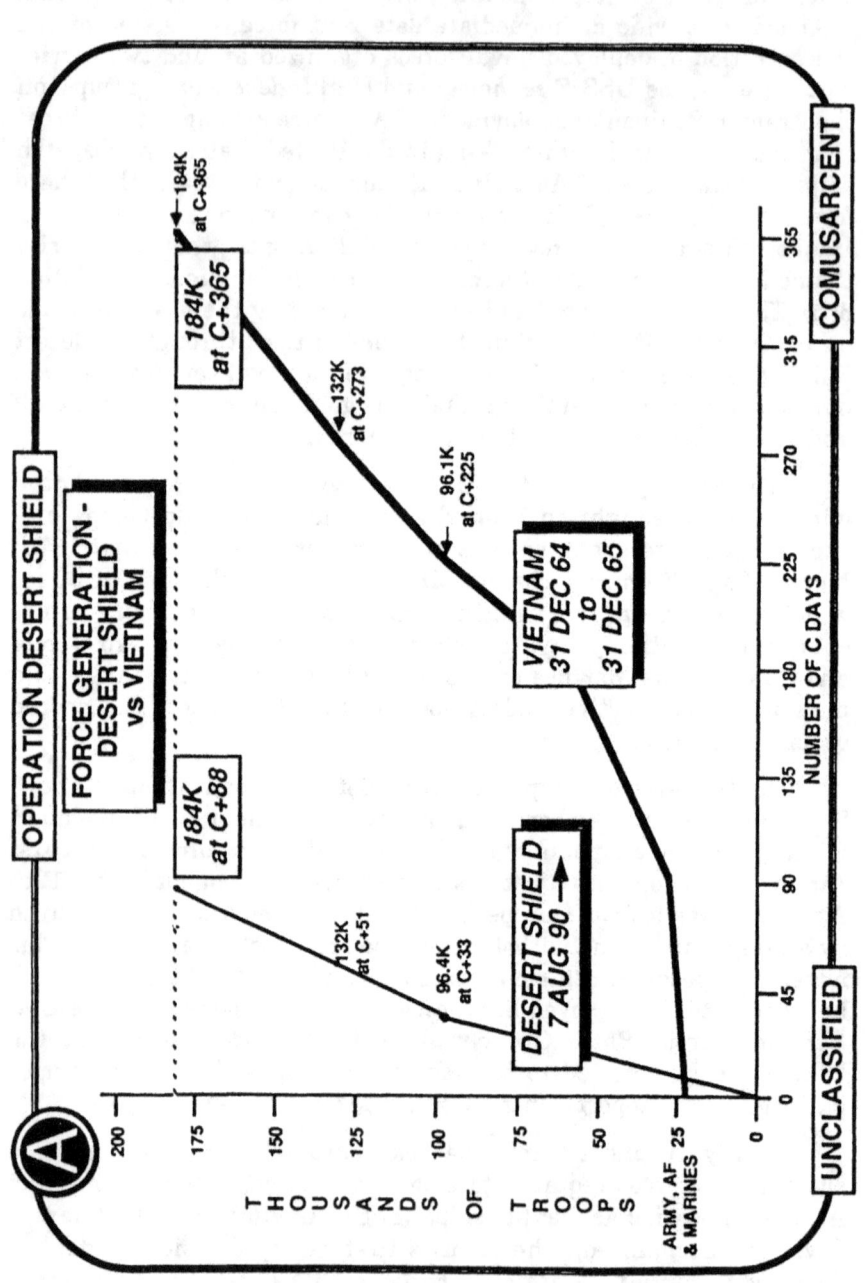

Figure 6.

Vietnam, see figure 6.) The 4th MEB deployed from Camp Lejeune as a self-contained amphibious force the same day the 24th left Savannah. It arrived by 16 September and presented a continuous amphibious threat to the Iraqi seaward flank. The 24th Division completed its deployment on 25 September with the arrival of the attached 197th Infantry Brigade (Separate).[41] The 101st Airborne Division (Air Assault) completed its movement on 7 October; the 3d Armored Cavalry Regiment, on 14 October; and the 1st Cavalry Division closed on 25 October.[42] These heavy forces provided the theater commander with the capability not only to defend but to counterattack in the increasingly less likely event of an Iraqi offensive against Saudi Arabia.

The Army's deployment actions had been begun upon President Bush's decision to commit U.S. forces. Staff officers used the Draft ARCENT OPLAN 1002-90 TPFDD (time-phased force and deployment data) created in conjunction with the Internal Look exercise as a starting point (four and two-thirds division force equivalents [DFE] or 253,000 personnel). The task of developing a revised force list was assumed by the Forces Command staff headed by its chief of staff, Major General Pete Taylor. Taylor was the pivotal figure in the force deployment "negotiations," acting as deputy commander in chief of Forces Command when dealing with Central Command, and as ARCENT's deputy commander (Rear) when responding to Third Army.[43] As Forces Command's chief of staff, he had visibility over all available U.S. Army active and Reserve Component units. He drove the Forces Command staff and the U.S. Transportation Command (TRANSCOM) to draft various force design alternatives against available transportation assets in order to achieve a reasonably balanced, if austere, C+90 deployed force.[44]

The assumptions that governed the force design process initially were that the force would have to be capable of fighting on arrival and also of conducting long-term sustained operations.[45] This meant the Army package would contain not only combat elements addressed in Internal Look but also a supporting force capable of meeting the specific needs of a mature theater in Southwest Asia. These assumptions had to be modified almost immediately to accommodate delays and limitations on Reserve Component mobilization, limits in strategic lift, and guidance that only minimum-essential forces were to be deployed.

General Powell was quoted as stating, with regard to Reserve Component mobilization, that the principle of minimum-essential force would be exceeded when one soldier got on CNN to complain of not being usefully employed.⁴⁶ (See figure 7.) This Army concern for the public perception of the legitimacy of any need to mobilize was indicative of the tentative nature of the initial U.S. commitment to military action. It also was clear evidence of the pervasive presence of Ted Turner's revolutionary all-news network. Meanwhile, the political leadership worked to build a positive response on the part of the American people.

Third Army had long based its war plans on the assumption that Reserve Component forces would be available immediately for any large-scale deployment. This was the basis of the Total Force Concept, a plan, attributed to General Creighton Abrams following the Vietnam War, to avoid commitment of active forces without some sort of mobilization of the public.⁴⁷ The concept was politically attractive, not just to the post-Vietnam-era Army but to a Congress concerned about "Imperial Presidencies." What the plan failed to take into account was the likely delay in mobilization in any case short of outright attack on American forces or territory. Such a delay would be the result of policy makers' proper concern with the full consideration of the available alternatives and public response, as well as the variable readiness of various Reserve (and Regular) Component units. The flaw in the concept was that events might not wait upon the convenience of defense decision makers.

Such was the case in August 1990. Deployment of Regular units was well under way before the president called up the first increment of Reserve Component forces. Had it been politically desirable, deployment of the two affected roundout brigades for the 24th Division and 1st Cavalry Division might have been delayed to the end of the XVIII Corps deployment as anticipated in the Internal Look planning. However, the Department of Defense decided to forgo calling any Army combat units in the first increment of Reserve Component activations.⁴⁸ It was decided, instead, to use two Regular units more immediately available, and not subject to loss in 90 days (or 180 with an extension), to roundout the two two-brigade divisions. Even in the case of combat support and combat service support units that were called, the need for immediate deployment also affected how Third Army structured its own echelon-above-corps forces, particularly the army headquarters and its theater support organization.

On 15 August, the secretary of defense requested that the president employ his authority to call up the selected Reserves.⁴⁹ The following day, Pentagon planners prepared advice for the president about the exercise of his authority to activate Reserve forces. Internal Look assumptions had presumed immediate use of the full 200,000-

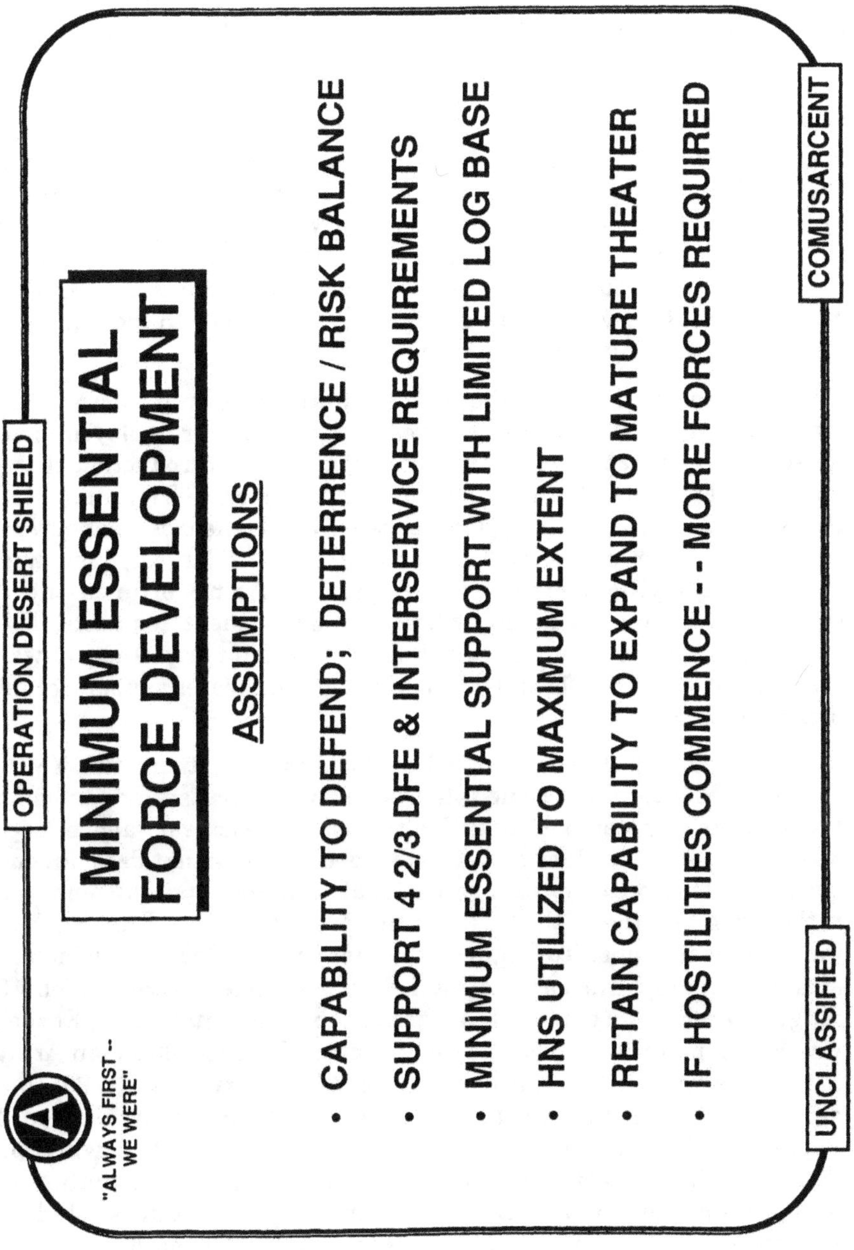

OPERATION DESERT SHIELD

MINIMUM ESSENTIAL FORCE DEVELOPMENT

ASSUMPTIONS

- CAPABILITY TO DEFEND; DETERRENCE / RISK BALANCE
- SUPPORT 4 2/3 DFE & INTERSERVICE REQUIREMENTS
- MINIMUM ESSENTIAL SUPPORT WITH LIMITED LOG BASE
- HNS UTILIZED TO MAXIMUM EXTENT
- RETAIN CAPABILITY TO EXPAND TO MATURE THEATER
- IF HOSTILITIES COMMENCE -- MORE FORCES REQUIRED

"ALWAYS FIRST -- WE WERE"

UNCLASSIFIED

COMUSARCENT

Figure 7.

man presidential call-up authority under Title 10, United States Code, Section 673b. The Department of the Army estimated a requirement for 33,772 Reservists by 31 August, assuming combat operations had not begun, and 88,000 if hostilities commenced.[50] On 22 August, the president informed the leaders of Congress that he had authorized the secretary of defense to exercise his authority under 673b. On the 23d, Secretary Cheney authorized the Army to order to active duty no more than 25,000 members of the Army Selected Reserve for the purpose of providing combat support and combat service support.[51] The other services were also limited in their authority, although these limits may have had as much to do with the rate at which the active services could absorb Reserve soldiers as with any reluctance to mobilize the Reserves in the long term.

In October, concern about "minimum essential force" was ultimately translated into a requirement that theater-deployed force levels not exceed 250,000 (a limit abandoned with introduction of the offensive capability of a second corps in November).[52] This limit was borne primarily by the Army, first, because it was the most manpower-intensive service; and second, because it was the largest, last, and slowest deploying component. Thus, the Army offered more opportunities for modification within the deployment sequence. The Army also benefited more from host-nation support, since it was responsible otherwise for providing much of the theater support for all deployed forces.

Initial Army deployment efforts focused on getting the XVIII Corps forces lined up to come into theater. Once that seemed to be on track in early September, attention turned to the echelon-above-corps structure. Some decisions had already been made by that date, among them the decision to form a provisional theater support command rather than to bring in the theater army area command (TAAC) called for in prewar plans. To begin with, there was a lack of sufficient strategic lift to transport the total doctrinal force.[53] Starting on 15 August and reporting out on the 26th, Headquarters, Forces Command, produced a revised force structure for a 151,000-man Army force. This was still too large an increment to arrive by C+90, so a second force structure design was forwarded to Saudi Arabia on 4 September. This force called for a ceiling of 142,000, down from 220,000. The creation of this force rested upon a number of assumptions, one being that the new numbers represented "a minimum essential force that hedges toward combat multipliers and accepts risk in selected support functions."[54] Heavy combat multipliers, field artillery, air defense artillery, chemical, and combat engineers were retained because of the time involved in their deployment. It was assumed lighter elements, for example intelligence units, could be called forward with dispatch. The corps support command was reduced in this plan to 12,500 from 20,000 and the theater support command to 10,400 from 25,000. Much of the balance was to be made up by host-nation support, the remainder by risk and a less than desirable sustainment and transportation capability. Troops would bear part of the cost involved in an austere desert environment.

General Edwin Burba's personal assessment was that this structure was "a prudent course with acceptable risk." "All must understand though," he continued, "at the first major indicator of an enemy offensive, we must quickly pile on combat service support with air and fast sealift."[55] In his reply, General Schwarzkopf seemed to agree. He pointed to the theater's dependence on host-nation support that permitted economies during the deterrent phase but noted that these economies might rapidly disappear should hostilities break out—especially given the Saudi dependence on third nation workers and contractors.[56]

Whatever his fears, Schwarzkopf in early October established a ceiling on Army end strength at 140,000.[57] Certain shortcomings, which became evident after the November build-up decision, and which were criticized after the fact, are understandable only when considered under the terms of reference in which the original trade-offs were made. In August and September, the mission assigned Third Army was to create a force capable of deterrence and defense and to do so with the minimum essential forces under a ceiling fixed largely by limits on strategic transport capability. A defensive force requires a comparatively small logistic base and, in particular, shorter logistic land legs than a mechanized and aerial force designed for offensive operations. It also requires a less robust intelligence structure, since most of the ground to be fought over is in one's own hands.

In early October, General Yeosock reported to General Carl Vuono, Army Chief of Staff, and Michael Stone, Secretary of the Army, that Third Army headquarters had only 346 of the anticipated 825 officers and enlisted personnel called for by the table of organization and equipment. (See figure 8.) The Army force had been reduced to 141,000 troops to be deployed, with 49,000 on call against contingencies. The formations-above-division to division force ratio was 1:1, compared to a design ratio of 2:1 in a mature theater. All this had been done by a combination of accepting prudent risk, by trading off housekeeping and base support activities (thus increasing soldier austerity), and by using direct and contracted host-nation support—

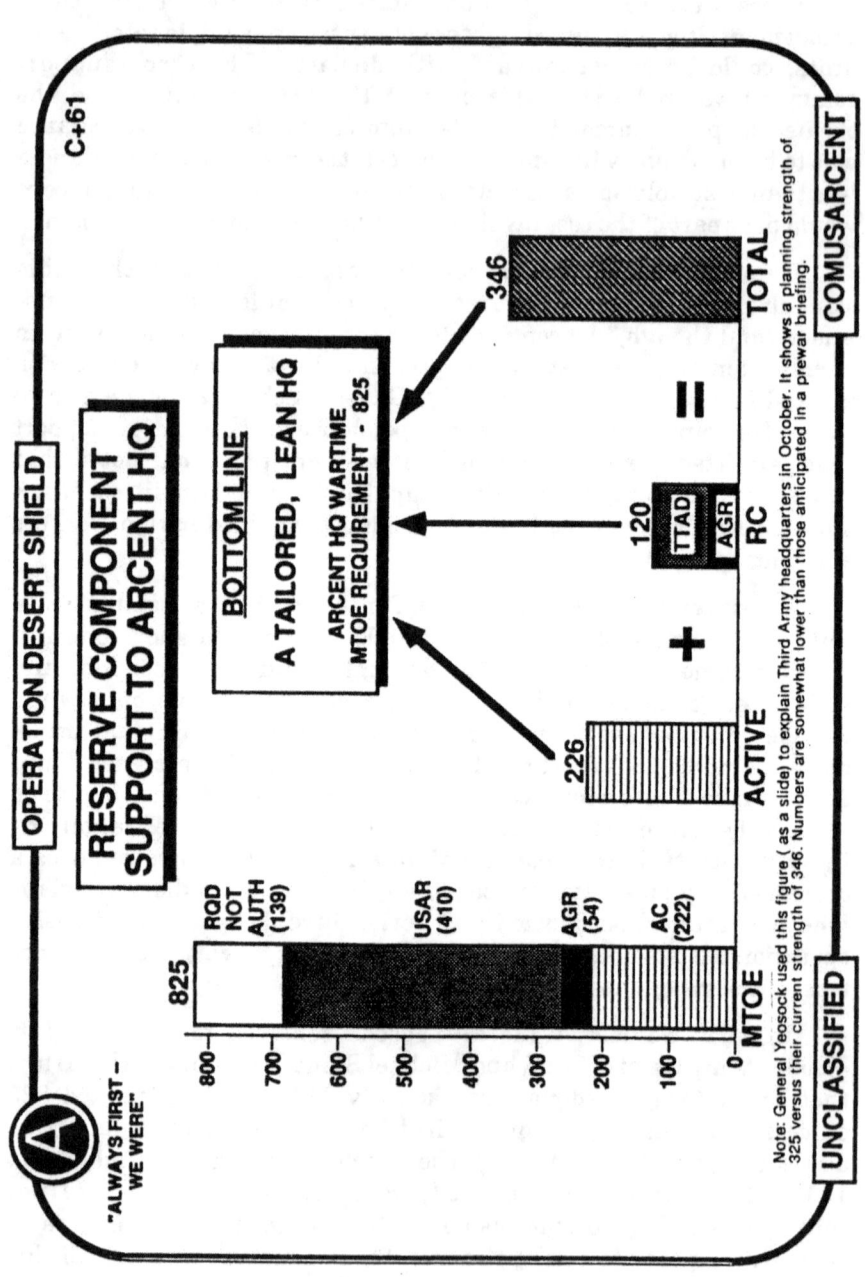

Figure 8.

particularly for water, fuel, and transportation—and other "work arounds" like reliance on out-of-theater depot maintenance support.[58] Among the limitations thus accepted was a force that was essentially not deployable out of its coastal sector—a condition acceptable so long as the mission was deterrence and defense but one that would defer a transportation and infrastructure cost if higher powers wanted to use the forces already deployed to do something else.

In November, Third Army would be called upon not only to bring on a second corps but to make up for legitimate economies accepted in the fall for quite understandable reasons. Third Army also had to create a significantly different type of echelon-above-corps structure, one for which the Army as a whole had not had to prepare when the principal design contingency was a NATO or Korean defense. It had to re-create itself into an army designed for an operational and strategic offensive.

Meanwhile, the army-level logistic organization designed to back up the corps support command and sustain echelon-above-corps units could be, and was, reduced to some extent by charging many of its duties to the already austere corps support command.[59] Some theater support structure was still required to operate ports of debarkation and to perform the theater army functions of operating the theater communications zone, integrating host-nation support, and supporting other services according to various Department of Defense directives. Third Army headquarters bore much of the burden of coordinating directly with the host government for host-nation support. The idea that XVIII Corps could have simply picked up the echelon-above-corps functions and dispensed with the army-level headquarters while giving full attention to operational matters does not seem realistic, even in the circumstances of Desert Shield.[60]

Most of the structural cuts accepted in the fall were borne in the sustainment area by limitations on the introduction of intermediate headquarters for echelons-above-corps functional commands and by combining theater-level and corps functions where possible.[61] From 15 August until 9 October, the ARCENT force structure was in a constant state of flux as guidance on minimum essential force deployment, authority to mobilize Reserve Components, and strategic lift constraints were all balanced against a notional C+90 force.

It was known at the outset that much of the absent support structure could be compensated for by host-nation support, but the ability of the host nation to supply support, or perhaps more important, the limits on this ability, was by no means immediately apparent to either Third Army planners or the host-nation government. No structure existed to tap it. This meant that such assumptions, cast into the force design process, carried a certain amount of risk, particularly given lead times required to acquire and deploy various specialist units.

General Yeosock designed his own echelon of command according to some basic principles.[62] First, he recognized the need to emphasize the early introduction of combat forces. Accepting implicitly the risk of diminished capacity, he brought in army-level units only at the last minute in order to ensure they were present when he absolutely required them and not a minute sooner. Second, he decided to minimize the creation of army-level functional commands (with their resultant layering of staffs) by providing that, so long as possible, army-level units would be commanded by his deputy commanding generals, using the Third Army staff. Functional commands would be established only when the task at hand exceeded in complexity the ability of the DCGs to perform this function. Even then, Yeosock would resist introducing general officer commanders and their associated staffs unless absolutely necessary. He recognized that those functions that were for the most part internal to the army echelon could often be performed adequately by incumbents already on the ground. For example, Colonel Chuck Sutten, commander of the 11th Signal Brigade, was given a much reduced functional command staff—part of the normal 6th Signal Command—and made its commander. A similar arrangement was made with the Medical Command (MEDCOM), with Colonel (Dr.) D. G. Tsoulos serving as both ARCENT surgeon and MEDCOM commander. (See figure 9.)

General Pagonis, as deputy commanding general (logistics), established an ARCENT forward headquarters at Dhahran. Initially, the executive functions of theater sustainment were performed under Pagonis' direction by the 7th Transportation Group, commanded by Colonel Dave Whaley, and a Provisional Area Support Group established in Dhahran.[63] Pagonis remained a deputy commanding general and assumed command of a provisional, later, the 22d Support Command, on 19 August, when the logistic structure grew beyond that capable of direction by the combined organization. Upon giving up command of his group, Whaley moved to the Support Command (Provisional) staff as an assistant commander, there to perform the role doctrinally assigned to a commander of a theater transportation command. (See figure 10.)

There was another reason to operate this way. In the absence of a Status of Forces Agreement and facilities utilization agreements,

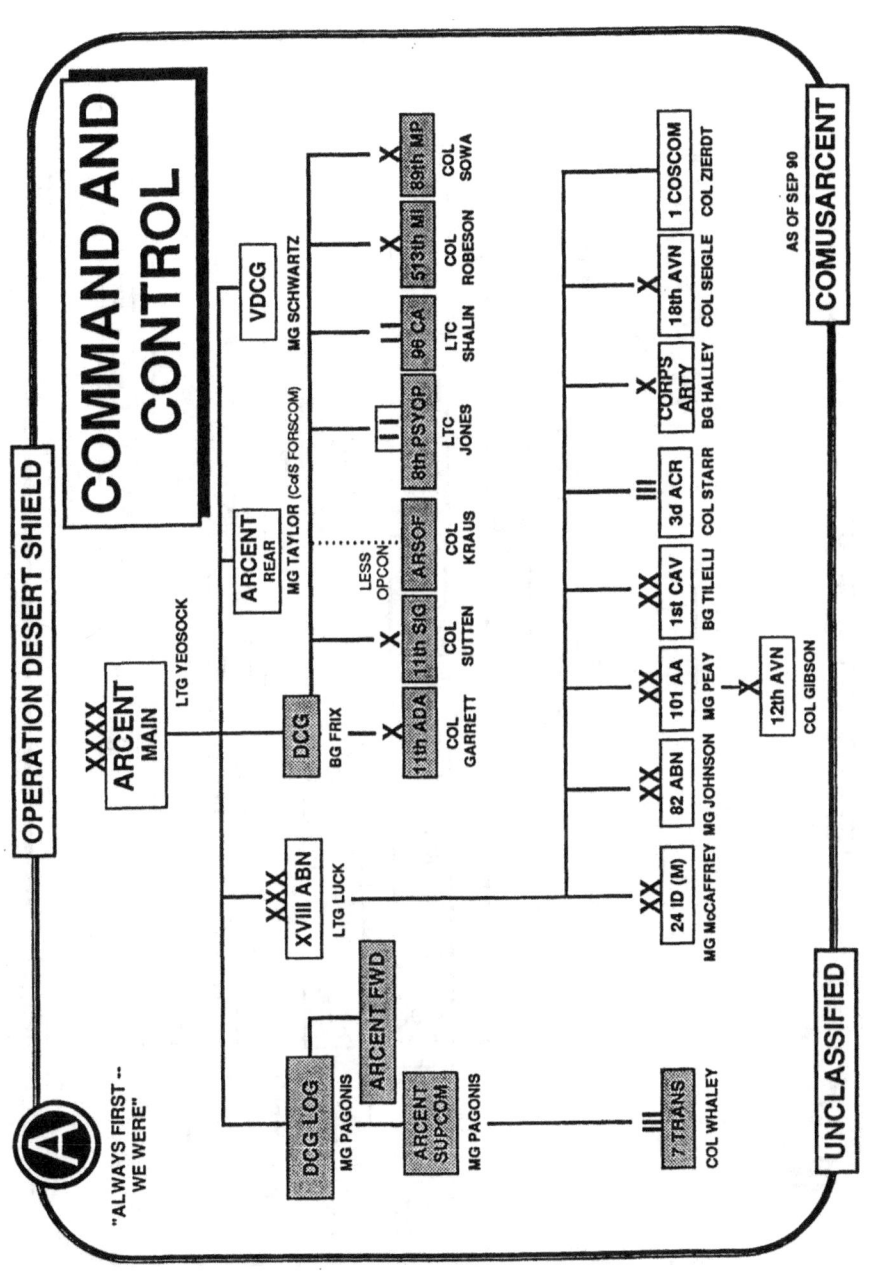

Figure 9.

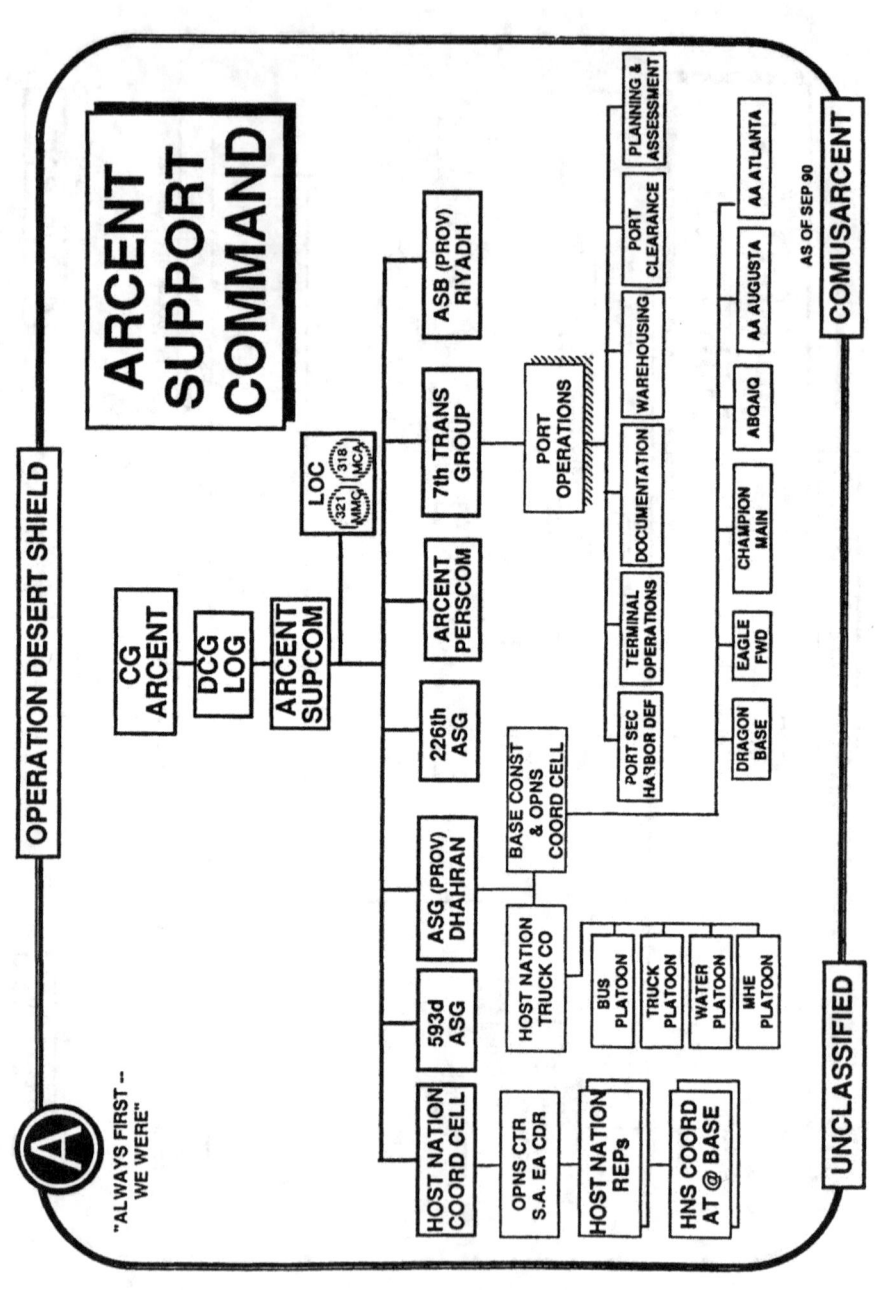

Figure 10.

numerous individual understandings had to be achieved immediately with the host-nation authorities and local contractors just to introduce U.S. forces. Most agreements were made on-site and as personal undertakings. It was not until 17 October that the Department of Defense dispatched a team to negotiate a variety of host-nation support agreements, principally for fuel, water, food, transportation, and shelter.[64] Officers of the Support Command had been making agreements and receiving extensive support almost since arrival. Meanwhile, it was essential that personnel changes be kept to a minimum to ensure the continuity of these agreements. A theater-support agency had been necessary as soon as forces began to enter the theater, and one was put together on an ad hoc basis under the pressures of the moment. By the time limited authority existed to call up Reservists, a nascent theater support structure was already in place.[65]

The first Central Command operations order was issued on 10 August.[66] The order identified a ground threat of five Iraqi divisions in Kuwait. The mission statement provided that "USCENTCOM forces will deploy to the area of operations and take actions in concert with host-nation forces, friendly regional forces, and other allies to defend against an Iraqi attack into Saudi Arabia and be prepared to conduct other operations as directed."[67] The plan called for a three-phase operation. Phase I called for deployment to deter an Iraqi attack, the conduct of combined training, preparations for defense, and exercises with allied forces in theater. Phase II, which would occur if deterrence failed, involved the defense of the Arabian Peninsula against Iraqi attack, with particular regard to the critical air and sea ports at Al Jubayl, Ad Dammam, and Dhahran. Phase III provided for a counterattack to restore the integrity of the Saudi border. The order indicated that Central Command forces would remain organized as components, the single major exception being SOCCENT, under whose operational control the service components would place certain of their special warfare forces. This reservation of operational command of special operations forces (SOF) to theater level was a normal doctrinal practice reflecting the strategic nature of many SOF actions.

The Central Command Army component was to deploy designated subordinate forces in order to support or implement deterrent measures as required, to be prepared to defend the critical oil and port facilities in the vicinity of Dhahran, to attrit and delay advanced enemy forces as far forward as possible, and when directed, to redeploy and defend in sector to protect the critical petroleum facilities in the vicinity of Abqaiq.[68] Other selected taskings involved commanding (less operational control) selected Army special operations forces (psychological operations and civil affairs forces excepted); conducting psychological and civil affairs operations; acting as Central Command executive agent for civil affairs and as coordinating authority for military psychological operations to include joint planning; operating common user seaports; providing combat support and combat service support in accordance with interservice agreements; conducting enemy prisoner of war operations; and supporting noncombatant evacuation operations as required. ARCENT was also to provide a brigade-sized theater reserve by C+55 and be prepared to conduct counteroffensive operations to restore the integrity of Saudi Arabian territory.

ARCENT Operations Order (OPORD) 001 was issued on 22 August and generally followed the CENTCOM order and the Internal Look concept of operations.[69] Two more Desert Shield operations orders would be issued by ARCENT: 002 in October and 003 in December.[70] Each reflected a new stage in the development of U.S. capabilities. The first was directed at covering the initial force deployment and reflected the paucity of forces that would exist for some time. The October order reflected a more robust force after the deployment of the XVIII Airborne Corps. OPORD 003 incorporated VII Corps into the defensive scheme following the president's 8 November announcement of the corps deployment.

OPORD 001 envisioned an enclave defense behind the Saudi and Gulf Cooperation Council forces that were securing key port facilities. The main purpose of the defense was deterrence. OPORD 002 provided for a defense-in-depth as heavy forces arrived. ARCENT would assume a zone alongside a MARCENT force, in a position behind the Arab-Islamic Forces and forward of the ports and oil facilities at Abqaiq. The XVIII Airborne Corps was to screen forward with the 101st Air Assault Division and the 3d Armored Cavalry Regiment and defend in-depth with the 24th Infantry Division and 1st Cavalry Divisions abreast, while the 82d Airborne Division secured the port and oil facilities.[71] (See map 3.) Contingency plans for the defense of Riyadh were added to the base plan. The VII Corps Desert Shield Order (003) called for a defense by two corps abreast and referred only vaguely to follow-on operations. (Desert Storm planning was taking place separately but simultaneously.)

All the while, the U.S. build-up had progressed steadily. Army forces had begun to deploy to Saudi Arabia on 8 August. The first troops to arrive had been the forward command post of the XVIII Airborne Corps, which arrived at Dhahran on the 9th, with troops

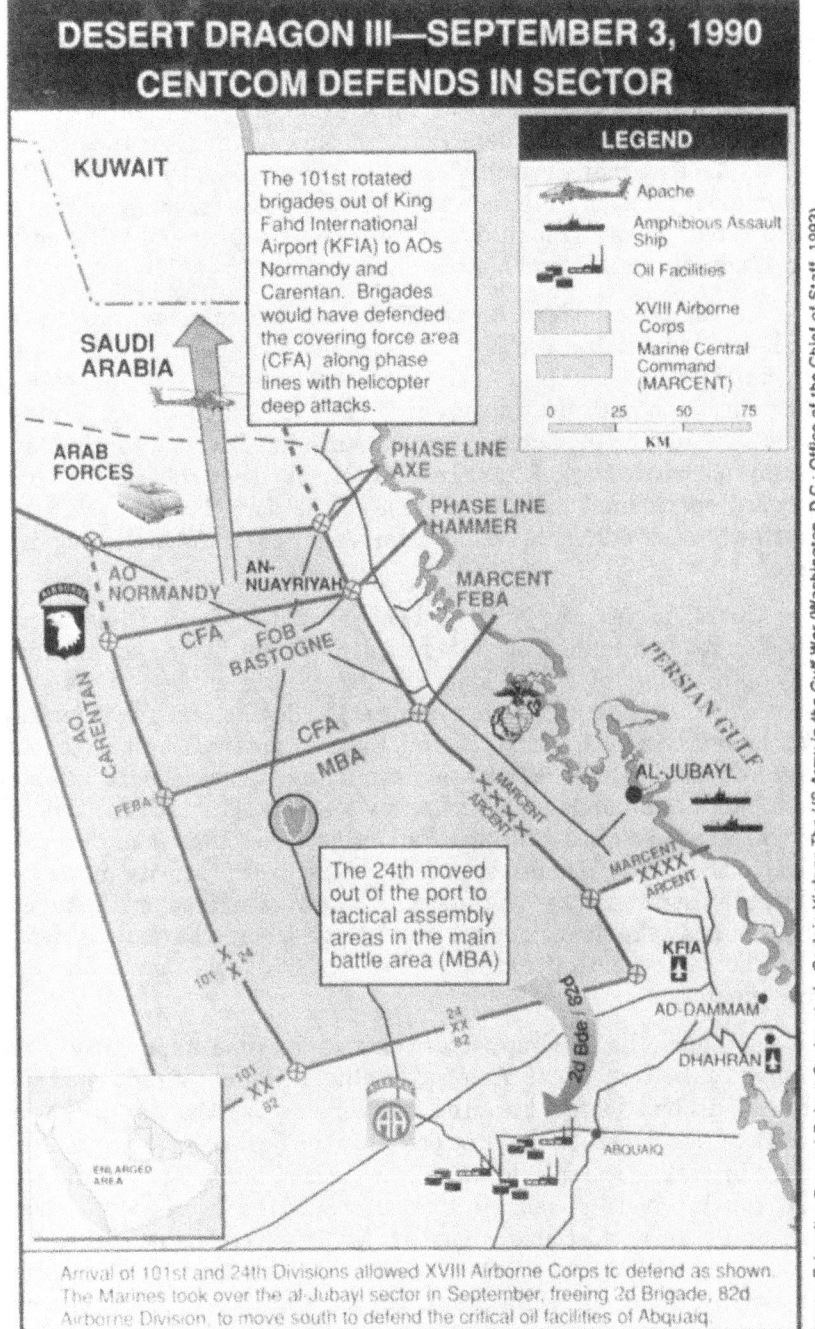

Map 3.

from the division ready brigade of the 82d Airborne Division.[72] The rapid deployment of these lightly armed troops, while risky in terms of effective fighting power against a heavily armored force, enabled the United States to make a clear demonstration of national intent in the hope that Iraq would be deterred from any further advance to the south. The first plane was guided to its parking slot by the ARCENT commander himself, as there was no existing base structure to receive them. These Army ground forces were accompanied and followed by significant air, naval, and Marine forces.

In August, all Third Army efforts had been directed toward the build-up of a viable combat force under command of the XVIII Airborne Corps. The Third Army commander saw his principal task as the generation and sustainment of forces with which the corps would fight any subsequent battle. The 82d Airborne Division continued to deploy forces through Dhahran and, on 12 August, established a forward operational base at Al Jubayl, the port through which the Marine forces would enter the theater. Army-level units also began to arrive.

On 14 August, the 2d Brigade of the 82d Airborne Division (the division ready brigade) completed its deployment. It was accompanied by one battalion of AH-64 attack helicopters from the 82d Aviation Brigade, which had become operational the day before. The same day, the commander of the 11th Signal Brigade entered the theater and began to establish a theater army communications network utilizing both Saudi commercial nets and Army systems. The 11th Air Defense Brigade began to introduce the Patriot batteries that would prove so vital to theater air defense or at least to a sense of security in the face of Iraqi missile attacks. The first two batteries arrived on 17 August, the same day the first elements of a 101st Airborne Division Aviation Task Force and the 24th Infantry Division's advanced elements came into theater.

Although the build-up seemed slow at the time, apparently it was not without effect. On 19 August, intelligence sources remarked that the Iraqis had begun building barriers across the Saudi-Kuwait border.[73] In retrospect, this was probably the first clear indication that Iraq's intention was to hold what it had seized rather than continue to the south. (A less-clear indicator would have been the Iraqi preoccupation with securing Kuwait City in early August rather than proceeding directly into Saudi Arabia.) On the 22d, President Bush authorized a call-up of Reserves. On 24 August, the Third Army's nightly situation report (SITREP) contained its most optimistic assessment to date, reporting: "ARCENT NOW HAS A POTENT

COMBAT FORCE WITH ALMOST A FULL ABN DIV, TWO BNS OF ATK AND THEIR SLICE OF CS AND CSS. . . . SITUATION IMPROVES SLIGHTLY EACH DAY. . . . AS OF TODAY, WE ARE CONFIDENT IN OUR ABILITY TO DETECT AND PUNISH A MAJOR ARMORED ATTACK."[74]

The following day, MARCENT was able to assume the security mission for Al Jubayl. By 28 August, the first heavy equipment of the 24th Infantry Division had begun to arrive. (The sea voyage could last from fourteen to twenty-five days.) On the 30th, the commander's SITREP reported, as it would more or less until the beginning of Desert Storm: "COMMANDER'S INTENT IS TO BE PREPARED TO FIGHT A COMBINED/JOINT BATTLE AT NIGHT WITH GIVEN FORCES, TRANSITION FROM ENCLAVE DEFENSE TO DEFENSE IN SECTOR, BUILD COMBAT POWER, IDENTIFY, SECURE, AND ESTABLISH BASES AND MSRS TO SUPPORT FUTURE OPERATIONS AND MAXIMIZE SECURITY AND SAFETY OF THE FORCE."[75]

By 31 August (C+24), the Iraqi force was estimated to be fifteen heavy and nine light brigades.[76] These forces were confronted along the Saudi border by a growing Arab force backed up by an American force of three infantry brigades, two attack helicopter battalions, elements of a Sheridan battalion (Sheridans are tracked, light-armored vehicles, not considered to be tanks), and division artillery. Two M1 tank battalions and one mechanized infantry battalion were in-country but not yet ready for action. When the Marine forces were included, 602 (land) antiarmor systems were available to Schwarzkopf. U.S. aircraft strength in theater was 106 air-to-air, 204 air-to-ground, and 214 dual-role aircraft, for a total of 524 combat aircraft.[77] These air assets obviously formed the main deterrent against land attack until the arrival of substantial heavy land forces.

It would be 30 October before XVIII Corps could report its entire force list assembled in theater, but the intervening time was busy. In early September, Schwarzkopf issued guidance for combined training with Saudi allies.[78] On 10 September, the Third Army commander acknowledged three missions: force generation, defense, and training. As a consequence, on the 13th, ARCENT began to look at expansion of its headquarters staff to an organization more closely resembling a major army command, which it was rapidly becoming in light of administrative and training tasks not envisioned by the peacetime TOE. These discussions were highly academic in light of force ceilings then being developed.

On 14 September, Schwarzkopf instructed Third Army, whose defensive sector had heretofore run east of Riyadh, to develop a contingency plan for the capital's defense. On the 24th, the 24th Infantry Division's equipment had all arrived, followed soon after by the 3d Armored Cavalry Regiment's. The First Cavalry Division's equipment began to arrive on 5 October.

Divisions moved through the ports and began to take up positions in the army defensive zone. They were confronted with the triple tasks of acclimatization—learning to live in 120 degree (or hotter) temperatures in the harsh desert environment, building a base structure, albeit austere, and training for the coming clash, be it defensive or offensive. In so doing, they had to confront a number of challenges, not all environmental. Early on, there was little or no training ammunition, and it would not do to fire up the basic load. As a sea line of communication was established, it was possible to get training ammunition, but units found that in recent years, ammunition sections of unit staffs had become part of the installation structure in the United States. The positions had been civilianized to save military force structure, as had range activities. Consequently, units had to learn not only how to obtain range areas in Saudi Arabia but how to run them.[79]

Simultaneously with creating the Army component of a viable deterrent, then defensive force, it was necessary to develop the instrumentalities of a coalition command, both to achieve unity of effort in any ground combat and, of more immediate importance, to provide points of access through which to address issues such as host-nation support. Doing this, largely without instructions or authority, may well constitute General Yeosock's principal contribution to Desert Shield, along with his detailed work creating the Army force structure.[80] Yeosock undertook the task almost at once, creating the Coalition Coordination Communication Integration Center (C3IC).

Why did the Army create the C3IC rather than headquarters Central Command? It did so largely because Yeosock realized that during operations in an allied state, ground forces bear a unique burden. They must occupy, train, and operate on land that belongs to another nation. They must do so without undermining the legitimacy of the host government whose continued security is the reason for their presence in the first place. For that reason and because ground forces are the most socially and culturally intrusive, the predominant land force commander, normally the Army component commander, must expect to be responsible for much of the practical U.S.-host-nation military intercourse. This is especially true where no system of allied agreements preexists at the onset of military operations.

Yeosock did not believe the Army component was relieved of this inherent responsibility by the presence of a theater commander. The problem is simply overwhelming in its detail and magnitude and must be accomplished within general theater guidelines by those executive agents who know the scope and detail of what must be done. In early August, Schwarzkopf was in Tampa. Yeosock was on the ground trying to get his forces established in the peninsula, as was General Horner who, incidently, was the deputy commander in chief, forward. Yeosock could not wait for the CENTCOM staff to begin building a coalition command structure when he had troops in the air almost immediately. He saw what needed doing, he did it, and it worked. Schwarzkopf underwrote it, once it was done, and ultimately took the organization into his own headquarters.

Unlike NATO or even Korea, this new coalition was starting from scratch to develop those organizations and procedures, not to mention provision for essential host-nation logistic support, that would guarantee unity of effort. As an old Saudi hand, Yeosock was aware of the difficulties involved in obtaining a quick decision in a society governed by a monarch, where the power of decision was highly centralized and family-based, and inaction was often the key to political survival. Yeosock was aware that U.S. forces would be heavily dependent on a responsive host-nation support system just to get ashore and survive and that the traditional methods would not be responsive enough to meet the demands soon to be placed upon them. However, whatever instrumentalities were established, it was essential that Saudi authority not be undermined by an appearance of U.S. domination. Respect for the authority of the host nation had to remain a central element of any solution.

In the same way, as a former PMSANG, Yeosock was aware of the professional strengths and limitations of the Saudi land forces, a dual military (the Royal Saudi Land Forces and Saudi National Guard) consisting of brigade-sized units distributed geographically. He recognized the need to improve the Saudis' professional competence without slighting their political and cultural sensitivities. To this end, he devoted considerable effort to the development of the C3IC. This combined body was established on 13 August under the authority of the Joint Military Committee, the organ created to achieve unity of effort between the Saudi and American militaries while maintaining the independence of both.[81] (See figure 11.)

On the Saudi side, the C3IC was headed by Lieutenant General Khalid, the son of the minister of defense and a member of the royal family. Each of the Saudi and American principals had a deputy. The first Saudi deputy was Major General Abdul Aziz Al Sheik, who played a particularly important role in negotiating host-nation support. As the responsibilities of these officers increased with the growth of the Arab-Islamic Coalition Joint Forces Command, the Saudis appointed a succession of general officers to represent the Joint Forces Command in the C3IC. As indicated previously, Yeosock's deputy in C3IC was Major General Paul Schwartz. Schwartz was appointed vice deputy commanding general of Third Army, a title selected by Yeosock so that, on the one hand, no one on the American side would be quite sure what he did and, on the other, because the Saudis particularly respected the title qualifier "Vice."[82]

The C3IC was the principal interface organization between the Americans and Saudis. In December, Central Command assumed direct control of C3IC, taking Schwartz along with it. The C3IC was successful in becoming a forum through which the U.S. side could work a variety of coalition issues more rapidly than they could have done otherwise. By placing the Third Army planning staff in the C3IC (until its transfer in December), it also served as a model, by example, for the Saudi staff officers and, through "leadership by question," got the Saudis to do a sort of combined planning they might not have done otherwise. For Schwartz, the most important function of the C3IC was to act as a "reduction gear," to prevent "type A" American hard chargers from overwhelming the less compulsive Saudis.[83]

The location of the Third Army plans section in the Ministry of Defense building with the C3IC organization had mixed results. Aside from facilitating communication and coordination among coalition ground forces and stimulating and guiding much of the Saudi planning, it also permitted close coordination with the Central Command planners who were likewise located in the Ministry of Defense.[84] On the negative side, it separated the G3 Plans Section from the Third Army G3, who was located with the army headquarters in the Royal Saudi Land Forces headquarters some distance away. Since the G3, General Arnold, was new and had not learned to look for Colonel Gene Holloway as his principal planner, and since Holloway was effectively General Schwartz's chief of staff at C3IC, some internal stresses and delays in decision making resulted.

C3IC did not become an integrated headquarters as, perhaps, the U.S. side would have preferred, but it did allow combined staffing of issues of mutual interest, most particularly combined fire support and

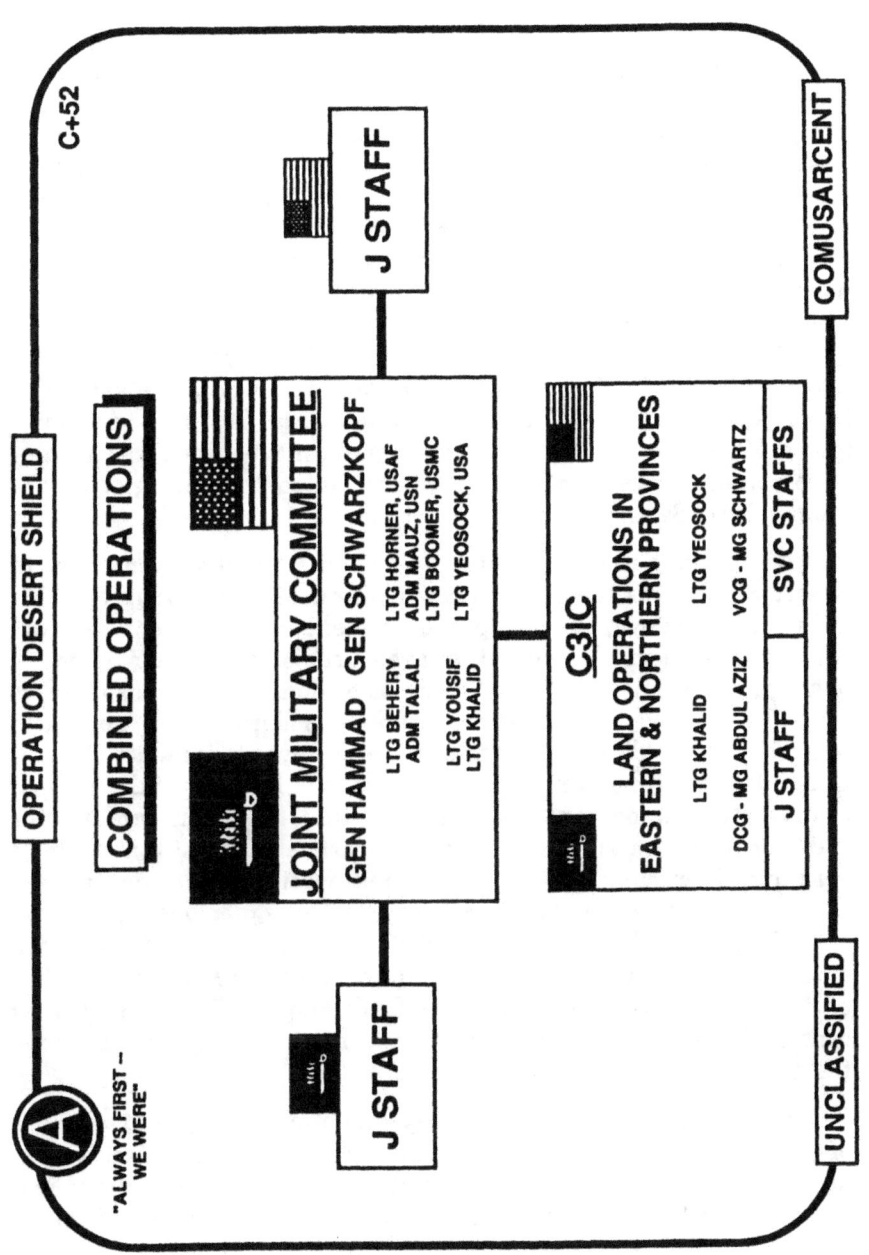

Figure 11. Coalition coordination structure in Operation Desert Shield

joint recognition procedures. It also provided a point of entry to develop host-nation support agreements.

In November 1990, Schwartz summarized the C3IC's accomplishments.[85] As its greatest achievement, he singled out orienting the Saudi staff to the operational processes used by U.S. forces. He noted that U.S. members brought to the task at hand a knowledge of multicorps operations. The Saudis could provide information about local terrain and operating constraints. Moreover, he observed that the process of professional interaction had a value in itself, referring to the C3IC as a "24 hour a day model classroom on how to establish and maintain an operations center."[86] The C3IC served as a conduit to the Saudi Joint Staff and spawned such vital forums as the Joint Forces Support Committee, where the army G4, Brigadier General James Monroe, could address host-nation support issues. If the organization did not meet staff college principles for unity of command, it was particularly well adapted to dealing with the complexity of Saudi politics and society.

Also among the most important activities undertaken early in Desert Shield was the force modernization of selected units. This complex procedure, involving replacement of older, less capable equipment with more modern, improved models, or introducing wholly new equipment into the force, could not be done without ensuring its costs did not exceed its benefits. Force modernization normally requires that soldiers be retrained to use new equipment; thus, it demands some time during which the unit is less than fully combat ready. More important in this case was the requirement for transportation, both intertheater and intratheater, a cost that could be very high in circumstances where transportation assets were always at a premium. In a theater where every HET was precious, as many as forty-four could be required each day to transfer modernization equipment. The whole process had to be managed closely. The commander's intent was to "field fully employable systems that contribute substantially to combat capabilities and require a minimal train-up."[87]

Interestingly enough, the first system brought in proved to be one of the least difficult to move or assimilate, and its contribution was decisive. Indeed, Yeosock was to call its introduction one of three keys to success.[88] The system was the small lightweight global positioning system receiver, a hand-held or vehicular-mounted device that tells the user where he is in the featureless desert. It was these devices and other comparable global positioning systems (GPSs) that made possible the decisive and simultaneous maneuver in formation of five armored divisions and an armored cavalry regiment during Desert Storm. Global positioning systems were also absolutely essential to maintaining accurate indirect fire in the fast-moving mechanized attack.

SLUGR and similar but less expensive (and less capable) long-range, very-low-frequency navigation systems (LORAN) were purchased "off the shelf." Introduction of SLUGR was requested by Lieutenant General Gary Luck, the commander of XVIII Airborne Corps, who had used the devices during Operation Just Cause.[89] Purchase of a limited supply of GPSs for contingency operations had been discussed at the Department of the Army as recently as 1 August. The first Desert Shield-Desert Storm purchase was authorized by Major General Jerome Granrud, the ADCSOPS for force development, as early as 24 August 1990. Consequently, 7,509 GPSs were issued in theater, down to maneuver platoons and artillery batteries.

In addition to GPSs, by the beginning of the ground attack in February, seventeen battalions/squadrons had been reequipped with new M1A1 tanks, the first taken from European stocks on 24 October for delivery to XVIII Corps units in November. The first major item of equipment issued in theater was the AH-1F helicopter, which arrived for the 3d ACR on 22 October. Prior to Desert Storm, thirteen battalion sets of countermine equipment were issued along with forty-three combat engineer vehicles (CEVs) mine rakes (eight were loaned to the Egyptians). Eleven battalions/squadrons received M2A2/M3A2 Bradley fighting vehicles. Ninty-nine M9 Armored Engineer vehicles also were issued. In addition, 1,802 M939A2 five-ton trucks, 2,642 HMMWVs (including 50 or so "borrowed" by the Marines at Dhahran), sixty-one AH-1Fs, and thirty-two UH-60Ls were brought into the force.[90]

Aside from improving troop confidence and effectiveness, force modernization also introduced greater mechanical reliability, a major contributor to operational success. That these systems came from throughout the Army, from all theaters, indicates the support the entire Army gave to Operation Desert Shield-Desert Storm.

Sometimes, the introduction of new systems also contributed to global efforts not immediately associated with actions in the Persian Gulf. Introduction of the M1A1 tanks is a case in point. The introduction of M1A1s involved Army Materiel Command project managers, Europe's 7th Army Training Command New Equipment Training Teams, and much departmental and ARCENT staff coordination.[91] Since the tanks came from Europe, their arrival enhanced the rate of mutual disarmament on the NATO Central Front while contributing to combat effectiveness in Saudi Arabia. The ARCENT commander's ability to tap into Army equipment stocks around the world is perhaps the most vivid example of what a component commander can do for the theater commander in his "departmental" as opposed to "joint" role.

As C+90 approached, Army forces in Saudi Arabia were completing their deployment. The naval embargo was in place, and Saddam Hussein was digging in in Kuwait. Toward the end of October, unmistakable signs appeared that the American administration had no intention of allowing a long-term stalemate to take hold.

Notes

1. HQ, Department of the Army, Army Public Affairs, Department of the Army Pamphlet 360-11, *Army General Officer Resumes* (18 March 1991), "Resume of Service Career of H. Norman Schwarzkopf, General." Schwarzkopf considers himself an experienced commander of both mechanized and light forces. He acknowledges, however, that his first experience with heavy forces came as a brigadier general. Schwarzkopf, *Doesn't Take a Hero*, 223, 240.

2. David Lamb, "Schwarzkopf Tries Not to Wear Out Hero's Welcome," *Los Angeles Times*, 20 October 1991, 1. Schwarzkopf's memoir indicates he saw the posting as one where he could "make history," but he acknowledges it was not viewed that way by his sponsor, Army Chief of Staff Carl Vuono. Schwarzkopf, *Doesn't Take a Hero*, 270–72.

3. Efforts are summarized in Andrew E. Gibson and Commander Jacob L. Shuford, "Desert Shield and Strategic Sealift," *The Naval War College Review* (Spring 1991): 6–11. Ronald O'Rourke, *Sealift and Operation Desert Shield* (Washington, D.C.: Library of Congress, Congressional Research Service, 17 September 1990), CRS 9–10.

4. Schwarzkopf, *Doesn't Take a Hero*, 273–74, 277–80.

5. HQ, Department of the Army, Army Public Affairs, Department of the Army Pamphlet 360-11, *Army General Officer Resumes* (18 March 1991), "Resume of Service Career of John Yeosock, Lieutenant General." Yeosock considered his former associations with Saudi political leaders his greatest strength in light of the magnitude of the host-nation support problem. In negotiating Saudi support for arriving American units, it was necessary to know who to ask, who had authority to decide, and develop a personal relationship of mutual trust.

6. Lieutenant General Yeosock to author.

7. HQ, Third Army, slide titled, "Third US Army HQ," New Realities Briefing, given by Major General Riley to the commander in chief, Forces Command, in July 1990.

8. Ibid.

9. For example, the corps chief of staff and G3 were both promotable colonels; none of the ARCENT staff were.

10. President George Bush, "Reshaping our Forces," a speech delivered at the Aspen Institute, Aspen, Colorado, 2 August 1990, reprinted in *Vital Speeches of the Day* 56, no. 22 (1 September 1990): 676–79.

11. "Chronology of Events, 1 August 1990 to 27 March 1991," Annex E to U.S. Army, Concepts and Analysis Agency Study Report, CAA-SR-91-18, Headquarters, Department of the Army Desert Shield/Desert Storm After-Action Report, vol. 1, Main Report (September 1991), E-Chronology-1. In late July, responding to concerns of the United Arab Emirates about Saddam's threatening position, the United States deployed aerial tankers and established a naval radar picket across the Persian Gulf to provide warning of air attack. Schwarzkopf, *Doesn't Take a Hero*, 292–93.

12. Interview with Lieutenant General John Yeosock at the Royal Saudi Land Forces Building, 26 September 1990, 7.

13. Chronology—22d Support Command, Operation Desert Shield/Desert Storm, HQ, 22d Support Command (TAA) Memorandum, Subject: Update Desert Storm, dated 6 June 1991. This report is part of the Desert Storm after-action report collection process. According to General Yeosock, the first request he made to General Burba, following the summons to go to MacDill AFB, on 4 August 1990, was for the services of General Pagonis to be his DCG logistics. Schwarzkopf had been involved in hectic activity to inform the president and his inner circle of available U.S. military responses since the detection of the Iraqi deployment. Schwarzkopf, *Doesn't Take a Hero*, 294–302. General Pagonis describes the predeployment atmosphere at Fort McPherson in Lieutenant General William G. Pagonis with Jeffery L. Cruishank, *Moving Mountains: Lessons in Leadership and Logistics for the Gulf War* (Boston: Harvard Business School Press, 1992), 63–72. According to Pagonis, his initial contract extended only to host-nation support and expanded under the pressures of the deployment. Ibid., 90.

14. Interview with Lieutenant General John Yeosock at the Royal Saudi Land Forces Building, 26 September 1990, 8. Interview with Lieutenant Colonel Larry Gresham, n.d.

15. Horner, "Offensive Air Operations: Lessons for the Future," 19.

16. "Chronology of Events, 1 August 1990 to 27 March 1991," Annex E to U.S. Army, Concepts and Analysis Agency Study Report, CAA-SR-91-18, Headquarters, Department of the Army Desert Shield/Desert Storm After-Action Report, vol. 1, Main Report (September 1991), E-Chronology-2, 8.

17. President George Bush, "The Defense of Saudi Arabia," delivered at the White House, Washington, D.C., 8 August 1990, reprinted in *Vital Speeches of the Day*, vol. 56 (1 September 1990): 674–75. The president's statement is followed by that of King Fahd Bin Abdel Aziz. *The New York Times* reported the deployments on 7 August, *The New York Times*, 8 August 1990, A1. Schwarzkopf describes negotiations with the king in Schwarzkopf, *Doesn't Take a Hero*, 304–5.

18. Yeosock, "Army Operations in the Gulf Theater," *Military Review* 71 (September 1991): 2–15. "H+100: An Army Comes of Age in the Persian Gulf," *Army* 41, no. 10 (October 1991): 44–58. Slide titled, "Third Army Is Three Armies," from the Third Army Operation Desert Storm command briefing dated 15 August 1991.

19. Department of Defense, Joint Chiefs of Staff, Armed Forces Staff College, Armed Forces Staff College Publication 1, *The Joint Staff Officer's Guide, 1991*, paragraph 201, "Organization for National Security," 2-2 to 2-7.

20. Ibid., paragraph 204e, "The Joint Chiefs Today, Chairman," 2-11 to 2-12.

21. Ibid., paragraph 204, "The Joint Chiefs Today," 2-9 et seq.

22. Ibid., paragraph 206d, "Unified and Specified Commands, Authority," 2-21 to 2-22.

23. Message, 101100Z August 90, FM USCINCCENT, MACDILL AFB FL, MSGID/ORDER/USCINCCENT, NARR/ THIS OPORD FORMS USCINCCENT ORDER FOR OPERATION DESERT SHIELD, 32.

24. Ibid., 31. HQ, USCENTCOM, USCINCCENT OPLAN for Operation Desert Storm, 16 December 1990. The term "communications zone" seems to have been avoided

throughout. To all intents and purposes, ARCENT, through the 22d Support Command, operated the theater communications zone.

25. Schwarzkopf, *It Doesn't Take a Hero*, 311–12.

26. There is a difference in the way division force equivalents were counted by ARCENT in Internal Look and Desert Shield. In Desert Shield, to arrive at four and two-thirds division force equivalents, you have to count the aviation brigade as a one-third division force equivalent. This was not done in the case of Internal Look, where only ground maneuver units (brigades and regiments) were counted. The continued use of four and two-thirds probably reflects the force of habit on the part of the slide makers. See HQ, Third Army, ARCENT Update briefing, C+52 (presented to the Secretary of the Army) 28 September 1990, slide titled, "Minimum Essential Force Development," dated 28 September 1990.

27. Ibid., slide titled, "Reserve Component Support to ARCENT HQ," dated 28 September 1990, shows the headquarters had 226 Active Component personnel against the authorization of 222; 120 Reserve Component personnel, the bulk of whom were TTAD (temporary tour of active duty UP AR 135-210), the remainder Active Guard and Reserve (AGR) soldiers, for a total of 346 against the wartime MTOE requirement of 825.

28. President George Bush, "The Defense of Saudi Arabia," delivered at the White House, Washington, D.C., 8 August 1990, reprinted in *Vital Speeches of the Day* 56 (1 September 1990): 674. The ARCENT "Phase I" Command Briefing listed as its fourth objective "Protect the Persian Gulf" in lieu of "Protect American Citizens Abroad." That objective was stated in the president's speech as well as the four enumerated.

29. Department of Defense, Office of the Assistant Secretary of Defense (Public Affairs), DOD New Briefing, Tuesday, 8 August 1990, 1:00 P.M. Secretary of Defense Richard Cheney, chairman, Joint Chiefs of Staff, General Colin Powell, USA, 1–8.

30. HQ, Third Army, ARCENT Update briefing, C+19, 26 August 1990, slide titled, "ARCENT HQ's Capability" shows twenty: Yeosock, Gresham, five from PMSANG, and thirteen from USMTM. This slide was corrected by C+27 (3 September) to show nine from PMSANG for a total of twenty-four.

31. HQ, Third Army, ARCENT Update briefing, C+19, 26 August 1990, slide titled, "ARCENT Major Tasks, First 72 Hours (6–8 August)." This was among the longer-lived slides in the army command briefing.

32. Interview with Major General Paul Schwartz at Fort Lewis, Washington, 18 April 1991, 5–7.

33. Interview with General Steven Arnold, Eskan Village, Riyadh, S.A., 15 March 1991, 2. Interview with Brigadier General John Stewart, Eskan Village, Riyadh, Saudi Arabia, 30 March 1990, 2.

34. HQ, Third Army (AFRD-DTP), Memorandum for Desert Storm Study Group, Subject: OPLAN 1002, Desert Shield and Desert Storm Planning, dated 4 June 1991, paragraph 3a, 5–6. The memorandum was prepared for Colonel Holloway, chief of plans for ARCENT by Major Steve Holley, the 1002 plans officer. HQ, Third Army (AFRD-DT), Memorandum thru Chief, G3 Program Division, Subject: Joint Operations Planning and Execution System (JOPES) Branch Historical Report Input, dated 21 February 1991. This memorandum, prepared for the army historian,

points out that the normal joint planning cycle lasts from eighteen to twenty-four months. In this case, 1002-90 was seven months into that cycle. Schwarzkopf, *Doesn't Take a Hero*, 310–11.

35. The conclusion is taken from the logistics overview briefing given by ARCENT to the Secretary of the Army on 14 March 1990. There were two kinds of preposition ships in the CENTCOM area of interest. MPS ships (Maritime Prepositioning Ships) carry Marine Corps expeditionary brigade sets, to include fighting systems, the concept being that Marines are flown into theater and join their equipment in the port, much like POMCUS stocks in Europe. The Army and Air Force have APS (Afloat Prepositioned Ships) that carry sustainment (ammunition, food, fuel, water, tentage) and port-operating supplies—the assumption being that fighting systems will come by air or ship. O'Rourke, *Sealift and Operation Desert Shield* (Washington, D.C.: Library of Congress, Congressional Research Service, 17 September 1990), CRS 15–18. United States Congress, House of Representatives, *Hearings Before the Subcommittee on Merchant Marine of the Committee on Merchant Marine and Fisheries on Our Nation's Capabilities to Meet Sealift Requirements Caused by American Deployment to the Persian Gulf, September 18 & 25*, 1990, Serial No. 101-120, Statement of Vice Admiral Francis R. Donovan, USN, Commander Military Sealift Command before the House Merchant Marine and Fisheries Committee Subcommittee on Merchant Marine Oversight Hearing on Sealift Requirements for the Persian Gulf Crisis, 18 September 1990, 103–5. For an account of what this looked like on the receiving end, see Pagonis, *Moving Mountains*, 84–130. On prepositioned shipping, see Ibid., 70.

36. Statement of General Colin L. Powell, USA, chairman of the Joint Chiefs of Staff to the Senate Armed Services Committee, 11 September 1990, reprinted in U.S. Department of Defense, Office of the Assistant Secretary of Defense (Public Affairs), American Forces Information Service, *Defense Issues* 5, no. 39. The chairman did not match the deployments with the phases. The phases given obviously overlapped. For the discussion of force deployments against these phases identified by the chairman, the author has drawn heavily upon the explanation given by Colonel Paul Tiberi and James C. Wendt in *Gathering the Storm: Contingency Planning and Force Projection*, Association of the United States Army, The Institute of Land Warfare, *The Land Warfare Papers*, no. 7 (September 1991). This author has diverged in small details from the Tiberi and Wendt explanation. (I place the deployment of the 7th MEB in Phase II rather than Phase I, and I disagree somewhat with their characterization of phases. By titling the third phase "coercion," the authors of this paper read rather more into the third phase than the chairman said or the force structure seemed to warrant in October 1990 when laid down against the simultaneous Iraqi deployment into Kuwait. During Desert Shield, coercion came first from the sea and then in the air but not on the land. That must be understood to understand the import of the 8 November creation of an offensive option. Those issues aside, the study is an excellent overview of the Desert Shield deployment.)

37. Tiberi and Wendt, *Gathering the Storm*, 9; and Schwarzkopf, *Doesn't Take a Hero*, 321–23.

38. Michael R. Gordon, "Bush Orders Navy to Halt All Shipments of Iraq's Oil and Almost All Its Imports: Some Food to Pass, Word 'Blockade' Avoided to Sidestep Question of New U.N. Vote," *The New York Times*, 13 August 1990, A1 and A8; "U.S. Ships Fire in Warning When Iraqis Refuse to Halt," *The New York Times*, 19 August 1990, A11.

39. Tiberi and Wendt, *Gathering the Storm*, 9-12. U.S. Department of Defense, *Conduct of the Persian Gulf War; Final Report to Congress Pursuant to Title V of The Persian Gulf Conflict Supplemental Authorization and Personnel Benefits Act of 1991 (Public Law 102-25)* (April 1992), Appendix E, "Deployment," E-20.

40. Ibid. Arrival is confirmed by the ARCENT SITREP, C+21 (28 AUG 90), AFRD-CS (282330 AUG 90), Memorandum for All Major Subordinate Commands and Staff, Subject: ARCENT Command SITREP #12 as of COB 28 August (C+21). (During the early days of the deployment, ARCENT headquarters sent out two SITREPS each day—one a message, one a memorandum. By the end of the month, both were combined into a single message.) The fast sealift ships carry about one brigade in two ships, a mechanized division in eight, or two divisions' equipment sets in eight. O'Rourke, *Sealift and Operation Desert Shield*, CRS 18-19.

41. Tiberi and Wendt, *Gathering the Storm*, 9-12.

42. The ARCENT SITREP reports closure of the 101st on 7 October, Message, 072359ZOCT 90, FM COMUSARCENT MAIN//AFRD-DCG//, MSGID/SITREP/USARCENT MAIN G3//; Tiberi and Wendt, the 4th. The 3d ACR is reported closing 14 October by ARCENT, Message, 142359 OCT 90, FM COMUSARCENT MAIN//AFRD-DCG//, MSGID/SITREP/USARCENT MAIN G3//, by Tiberi and Wendt, the 13th. The difference probably depends on what is counted for arrival and whether U.S. or Saudi time is used.

43. HQ, ARCENT, Command Group, Force Generation Briefing (as of 7 November 1990), slide titled, "DS 90 TPFDD Chronology." HQ, ARCENT, Command Group, ARCENT Update C+52 (28 September 1990), slide titled, "Command and Control." HQ, Third Army (AFRD-DT), Memorandum thru Chief, G3 Program Division, Subject: Joint Operations Planning and Execution System (JOPES) Branch Historical Report Input, dated 21 February 1991.

44. See EYES ONLY Message, 051830Z SEP 90, FROM SSO FORSCOM TO SSO CINCCENT (FOR MAJ GEN JOHNSTON, C/S, CENTCOM, MAIN DHAHRAN, FROM MG TAYLOR, DCINCFOR), Subject: Minimum Essential Support for Desert Shield, which summarizes process to date and indicates principal constraint was transportation.

45. HQ, ARCENT, Command Group, ARCENT Update C+52 (28 September 1990), slides titled, "Minimum Essential Force Development."

46. Crisis Action Team (CAT) Tasking Form, CAT No. 8302, Suspense: 171000 August 1990, Subject: Minimum Selective Reserve Call-Up Requirements.

47. Harry G. Summers, Jr., *On Strategy II: A Critical Analysis of the Gulf War* (New York: Dell Books, 1992), 72-73.

48. General Schwarzkopf found himself at loggerheads with his mentor, General Carl Vuono, the army chief of staff, over the issue of the roundout brigades. Vuono wanted to deploy the units; Schwarzkopf did not because of the 180-day limit on their mobilizations. Schwarzkopf, *Doesn't Take a Hero*, 323.

49. CAT Tasking Form, CAT No. 8241, Suspense: 161100 August, Subject: Service Estimates for Selective Reserve Call-up. Attached to the form is a memo from J4 of the Joint Staff that indicates the 15 August date.

50. Department of Defense, Joint Staff, JS Form 137L Feb 90, Joint Action Processing Form, Subject: Selective Reserve Call-up Requirements by Service.

51. Department of Defense, Office of the Secretary of Defense, Memorandum for the Secretaries of the Military Departments, Chairman of the Joint Chiefs of Staff, Subject: Call of Selected Reserve Units and Personnel to Active Duty, dated 23 August 1990.

52. Message, 041700C OCT 90, FM USCINCCENT TO RHIUFAA/USCENTAF FWD HQS ELEMENT, et al., PERSONAL FOR GENERALS HORNER, YEOSOCK, BOOMER, ADMIRAL MAUZ AND COLONEL JOHNSON FROM GENERAL SCHWARZKOPF, Subject: Force End-Strength Ceiling. The British forces deployed in the fall of 1990 also operated under strict minimum-essential force guidance, called more colorfully the "arm in the mangle" policy, after Margaret Thatchers' comment that, "The Government was anxious 'not to get its arm caught in the mangle'—not to be dragged into a conflict which would demand ever-increasing commitment of men and resources." General Sir Peter de la Billiere, *Storm Command: A Personal Account of the Gulf War* (London: Harper Collins, 1992), 17, 77, 129.

53. EYES ONLY Message, 051830Z SEP 90, FROM SSO FORSCOM TO SSO CINCCENT (FOR MAJ GEN JOHNSTON, C/S, CENTCOM, MAIN DHAHRAN, FROM MG TAYLOR, DCINCFOR), Subject: Minimum Essential Support for Desert Shield.

54. Ibid.

55. Message, 060111Z SEP 90, FM SSO USCINCCENT REAR TO USCINCCENT O511800Z SEP 90 ZYH, FROM SSO FORSCOM TO SSO CINCCENT, EYES ONLY FOR GEN SCHWARZKOPF, CINCCENT, FROM GEN BURBA, CINCFOR, Subject: Minimum Essential Face [sic] for Desert Shield, 2.

56. EYES ONLY Message, 190500Z SEP 90, FROM GENERAL SCHWARZKOPF TO GENERAL BURBA, Subject: Minimum Essential Force for Desert Shield.

57. Message, 091501Z OCT 90 FROM USCINCCENT TO RHIPAAA/COMUSARCENT MAIN, PERSONAL FOR LTG YEOSOCK FROM GENERAL SCHWARZKOPF, MSGID/SYS.RMM/USCINCCENT/CCCC//RMKS 1. The message approved an ARCENT CAP of 140,000.

58. HQ, ARCENT, Command Group, ARCENT UPDATE Briefing C+52 (presented to Secretary of the Army) and, HQ, ARCENT, Command Group, ARCENT Update Briefing C+61 (presented to the chief of staff, Army).

59. For example, the XVIII Finance Group assumed responsibility for EAC finance support as well as that of the corps. HQ, Third Army, AFRD-RM, Memorandum for ARCENT History Office (Colonel Swain), Subject: Command Report Operation Desert Shield, dated 8 March 1991, 3.

60. At a seminar at Fort Leavenworth, Kansas, Lieutenant General Luck, Commander XVIII Corps, and Major General Funk, Desert Storm commander of the 3d Armored Division, were paraphrased as having taken the position that Third Army was an unnecessary headquarters. HQ, Combined Arms Command and Fort Leavenworth, ATZL-CG, Memorandum for Record, Subject: AirLand Operations Seminar with

Desert Storm Commanders, dated 27 June 1991, 2. The note taker was Lieutenant General Leonard Wishart, the Combined Arms Command commander.

61. HQ, Third Army, Command Group, Force Generation Briefing. Briefing titled, "SWA Force Comparison," located in Lieutenant General Yeosock's AAR files.

62. Notes from interview with Lieutenant General Yeosock on 31 May 1991. HQ, ARCENT, briefing titled, "SWA Force Comparison." This briefing, found in the commander's papers, its origins unknown, compares ARCENT force structure to that called for by Army of excellence (AOE) requirements. See also, HQ, ARCENT, Command Group, ARCENT Update C+52 (28 September 1990), slides titled, "Reserve Component Support to ARCENT HQ" and "Minimum Essential Force Development (2)."

63. Notes from interview with Lieutenant General Yeosock on 31 May 1991. HQ, ARCENT, Command Group, ARCENT UPDATE C+52 (28 September 1990), slides titled, "Theater Logistics Chain of Command" and "ARCENT Support Command (Provisional)." HQ, 22d Support Command, AFSC-MHD, Memorandum for Commanding General, ARCENT, Attn: AFRD-CS-MH, Subject: Command Report Operation Desert Shield, 22d Support Command, dated 23 March 1991. To those who had to execute, it looked much more drastic. Pagonis, *Moving Mountains*, 89–95, 97–104.

64. The agreement, effective 1 November 1990, is reproduced as Annex F to HQ, 22d Support Command, AFSC-RM, Memorandum for ARCENT Historian, Subject: Command Report for Operation Desert Shield, dated 23 February 1991. Pagonis, *Moving Mountains*, 107–18.

65. Notes from interview with Lieutenant General Yeosock on 31 May 1991. See also note by General Robert Frix, ARCENT chief of staff, on cover sheet to ARCENT Command SITREP, C+26 (2 SEP 90), Memorandum for Major General Taylor, ARCENT Rear; Info Major General Riley, Subject: ARCENT Command SITREP #16 as of COB 2 SEP (C+26). The memorandum gives the position of COMUSARCENT on 377th TAACOM. See also HQ, 22d Support Command, AFSC-MHD, Memorandum for Commanding General, ARCENT, Attn: AFRD-CS-MH, Subject: Command Report Operation Desert Shield, 22d Support Command, dated 23 March 1991.

66. Message, 101100Z August 90, FM USCINCCENT, MACDILL AFB FL, MSGID/ORDER/USCINCCENT, NARR/ THIS OPORD FORMS USCINCCENT ORDER FOR OPERATION DESERT SHIELD.

67. Ibid., 13.

68. Ibid., 30–32.

69. Message, 220900Z August 90, FROM CDRUSARCENT RIYADH SA, Subject: Desert Shield Operations.

70. HQ, ARCENT, G3 AFRD-DTP, Memorandum for USARCENT Historian, Colonel Swain, Subject: HQ, USARCENT, G3 Plans, Historical Narrative of Desert Shield, Desert Storm, Defense and Restoration of Kuwait, and Redeployment. This memorandum, prepared by Major Steve Holley for signature by Colonel Harold E. Holloway, summarizes the role of the ARCENT G3 plans in Desert Shield-Desert Storm. It is the most comprehensive historical document prepared by the ARCENT staff for the Gulf War. Because the plans shop was central to Yeosock's way of doing

business, this twenty-three-volume documentary set is invaluable to anyone who would understand what ARCENT did during the war. All ARCENT orders are included in the set.

71. Enclosure 2 to HQ, ARCENT, G3 AFRD-DTP, Memorandum for USARCENT Historian, Colonel Swain, Subject: HQ, USARCENT, G3 Plans, Historical Narrative of Desert Shield, Desert Storm, Defense and Restoration of Kuwait, and Redeployment. These concept slides appear in the daily ARCENT Update briefings for August as well.

72. HQ, XVIII Airborne Corps, Initial After-Action Report Operation Desert Shield/Desert Storm, Operation Desert Shield Chronology, 1–2.

73. Message, 192300Z AUG 90, FROM COMUSARCENT FT MCPHERSON GA//AFRD-DSO//MSGID/SITREP/USARCENT AFRO-DTD//PERID/182400Z/ TO: 192400Z/ AS OF: 192400Z, 6–8.

74. Message, 242300Z AUG 90, FROM COMUSARCENT FT MCPHERSON GA//AFRD-DSO//MSGID/SITREP/USARCENT AFRD-DSO//PERID/232400Z/ TO: 242400Z// AS OF: 242400Z, 7.

75. Message, 302359Z AUG 90, FROM COMUSARCENT MAIN RIYADH SA//AFRD-DCG, MSGID/SITREP/USARCENT MAIN G3, 9.

76. HQ, ARCENT, Command Group, ARCENT Update Briefing C+24 (31 August 1990), slides titled, "Current Situation 31 Aug" and "Threat Summary 31 Aug." These early estimates were highly subjective. The ARCENT situation report for 31 August listed eight to ten Iraqi divisions with eleven heavy and nine light brigades. Whatever the count, the Iraqis were vastly superior in heavy ground combat forces.

77. HQ, ARCENT, Command Group, ARCENT Update Briefing C+24 (31 August 1990), slide titled, "If We Have to Fight Tonight." Message, 012115Z SEP 90, FM USCINCCENT, MSGID/SITREP/USCINCCENT/023/SEP//, 8.

78. Message, 062359Z SEP 90, FM COMUSARCENT//AFRD-DCG, MSGID/SITREP/USARCENT MAIN G3, 12–13.

79. HQ, ARCENT, G3 Training (AFRD-DT), Memorandum for COMUSARCENT, Attn: History Office, Subject: Training, Command Report Operation Desert Shield, dated 25 February 1991. Notes from interview with Lieutenant Colonel Pat Lamar, G3, 24th ID.

80. Schwarzkopf's memoir would seem to indicate he discussed the general principles for combined command with Horner and Yeosock around the 8th. Schwarzkopf, *Doesn't Take a Hero*, 313. C3IC was the embodiment of that guidance.

81. HQ, USCENTCOM, C3IC, Memorandum for Deputy CINC, USCENTCOM, Subject: C3IC Support to the Saudi Military Staff, dated 26 November 1990. This memorandum, prepared by Major General Paul Schwartz, summarizes C3IC while under ARCENT. General Schwartz has contributed a lengthy interview on the role of C3IC as well.

82. Stories provided to author by Yeosock and Schwartz. See also interview with Lieutenant General John Yeosock, Royal Saudi Land Forces Building, Riyadh, S.A., 26 September 1990, 11. Interview with Major General Paul Schwartz at Fort Lewis, Washington, 2 May 1991, 3.

83. Comment about "reduction gear" was made by General Schwartz to author. See also interview with Major General Paul Schwartz at Fort Lewis, Washington, 2 May 1991, 57–58.
84. HQ, ARCENT, G3 AFRD-DTP, Memorandum for USARCENT Historian, Colonel Swain, Subject: HQ, USARCENT, G3 Plans, Historical Narrative of Desert Shield, Desert Storm, Defense and Restoration of Kuwait, and Redeployment, 2.
85. HQ, USCENTCOM, C3IC, Memorandum for Deputy CINC, USCENTCOM, Subject: C3IC Support to the Saudi Military Staff, dated 26 November 1990.
86. Ibid.
87. The mission is taken from ARCENT Force Modernization Briefing given the Secretary of the Army on 14 March 1991 at Riyadh, slide titled, "Commander's Intent." More contemporary slides are two briefings given by ARCENT G3 to CG on 10 and 11 October 1990 concerning M1 upgrade program.
88. HQ, ARCENT, Command Group, ARCENT Update Briefing for Chief of Staff, Army, 20 April 1991, slide titled, "Commander's Keys to Success."
89. HQ, Department of the Army, DAMO-FDC, Memorandum for Chief, Center of Military History, Washington, D.C., Subject: Procurement of Small Lightweight Global Positioning System Receivers (SLUGR) for Operations Desert Shield/Storm.
90. ARCENT Force Modernization Briefing given the secretary of the Army on 14 March 1991.
91. A complete report of materiel fielding efforts is to be found in Program Executive Office, Armored Systems Modernization, Operation Desert Shield/Desert Storm (Saudi Arabia) Material Fielding Team Historical Report, 2 July 1991.

3
Planning a Ground Offensive I: The CINC's Study Group

The popular view of the Persian Gulf War, at least in the Army, is that it was a war of maneuver. It was nothing of the sort, at least not if "maneuver" is viewed as the psychological undermining of an enemy by movement alone. Viewed from the theater level, Desert Storm was a war of attrition based upon air power. Coalition air forces disrupted the Iraqi national command and control structure, won air supremacy (unopposed freedom of action in the air) early, and then prepared the theater of operations through a program of continuous bombing. Some still believe air power worked so well that the ground operation only reaped the effects achieved from the air, effects which, given a week or two more, would have led to an Iraqi withdrawal without a ground attack at all.[1]

The ground attack was ultimately a necessary but clearly dependent and contingent part of the theater campaign plan. Time was running out. As the holy month of Ramadan approached (starting 15 March), to be followed by the end of the cool season and the heat of the Arabian summer, the impasse with Iraq had to be broken.[2] Looking ahead, it was becoming increasingly impossible to gamble that air power would compel Saddam's withdrawal without ground action to force the pace.

Nonetheless, the ground offensive was seen to depend absolutely upon the air arm's success in achieving air supremacy. This dominance would free the ground forces to reposition to the west, build up the massive supply bases required for mechanized warfare, and concentrate for attack without interference. Ground commanders from General Schwarzkopf to the lowest armored battalion commander believed that success on the ground depended on the Air Force inflicting significant destruction upon enemy ground forces, particularly the artillery and armored reserves who were believed to outnumber coalition forces greatly and to be well armed and capable of tough resistance. Most analysts assumed Iraq would employ chemical weapons, particularly once threatened with defeat.

Army commanders did not doubt that the execution of a ground attack would be necessary at some point, first, to drive dug-in enemy formations above ground so that they would be subject to destruction by both ground and air attack; second, because liberation of Kuwait ultimately required taking possession of territory—Kuwait itself, as the primary mission, and southeastern Iraq, to ensure negotiations. The ground offensive was planned and conducted in accordance with the Army's AirLand Battle doctrine. Developed during the decade following the U.S. defeat in Vietnam, AirLand Battle doctrine is an application of classic twentieth-century maneuver theory for mechanized forces.

Since the attack on the Somme in World War I, ground maneuver commanders have tended to discount the disruptive effects of fire, even though it forms the basis of any army's minor tactics. They prefer to think of operational maneuver, in which fire plays a subordinate and supporting role as the key to unlocking enemy defenses. Indeed, two competing views of modern mechanized warfare might be characterized loosely as the romantic and the realist. The romantic view is often associated with B. H. Liddell Hart and his concept of the indirect approach. This view emphasizes dislocation of the enemy as the objective of maneuver. Indirection and speed of execution are the means. These hold out the ideal of so upsetting the enemy by operational movement that no tactical engagement at all is required to bring about the foe's destruction.[3] For Liddell Hart, the characteristic maneuver of the indirect approach in ground warfare was the turning movement, with the hope that seizure of position alone might cause the enemy to surrender or at least force him to battle where the operational attacker had the advantage of the tactical defense.

The realist's view of armored warfare was based upon the more Jominian tradition of achieving victory by the successive destruction of fractions of the enemy's force by masses of one's own. Best articulated in the works of J. F. C. Fuller, the benefit of mechanization had to do largely with the ability of mechanical transport to concentrate forces rapidly against more vulnerable *and more decisive* rear areas before an enemy could react to the traditional rear attack.[4] For Fuller, battle, albeit on favorable terms, was the necessary end of maneuver; dislocation was but a means to a tactical end. In Fuller's view, speed of execution is a more relational concept because it is measured against the enemy's ability to respond before decision is reached, rather than on the psychological effect achieved. For Fuller, the envelopment was the more productive maneuver.

The Army's AirLand Battle doctrine, as articulated in FM 100-5, *Operations* (May 1986), reflected *both* views. The defining passage maintained that

> The object of all operations is to impose our will upon the enemy. . . . To do this we must throw the enemy off balance with a powerful blow from an unexpected direction, follow-up rapidly to prevent his recovery and continue operations aggressively to achieve the higher commander's goals. The best results are obtained when powerful blows are struck against critical units or areas whose loss will degrade the coherence of enemy operations in depth.[5]

AirLand Battle doctrine assumed the synergistic employment of Air Force ground-attack systems both in support of the close (direct-fire) battle and in depth, interdicting enemy forces not yet engaged by ground forces or withdrawing beyond their reach. The doctrine assumed, implicitly, possession of air superiority.

These ideas formed the theoretical context within which plans were drawn up for the ground portion of Operation Desert Storm. Although the aerial isolation of the operational area south of the Euphrates, and the deep envelopment of the Iraqi front-line forces through the Iraqi desert, employed elements of indirection, Schwarzkopf placed himself ultimately in the realist camp by his selection of the Iraqi operational reserves, particularly the Republican Guard, as the focus of his attentions. Destruction of the Iraqi armored forces was part of his strategic and operational program. In fact, his analysis of his mission required it.[6] His hopes for the success of the attrition-ground preparation phase of the air campaign—to "open the window for initiating ground offensive operations by *confusing and terrorizing* Iraqi forces in the KTO and shifting combat force ratios in favor of friendly forces"[7]—indicate he was also no stranger to the value of dislocation, though his faith rested in fire more than maneuver.

A most important feature of planning for Desert Storm ground operations was the extent to which commanders themselves were involved in all key decisions. The plan itself had a hundred fathers, but no decision of consequence was taken except by the senior commanders. Therefore, some key events in the evolution of the plan must be set forth at the outset. The first was the theater commander's briefing to his commanders on 14 November. From that time on, what had been a closely controlled planning process grew horizontally and vertically in an environment in which each commander, from division level and above, had heard the general concept of operations from Schwarzkopf himself.

From the November briefing to early January, there were a number of key back-briefings—from the corps to Third Army, from Third Army to the theater commander, and on 20 December, to the secretary of defense and chairman of the Joint Chiefs of Staff—on the status of theater preparations for offensive action.

During the last week of December, Third Army held a map exercise (MAPEX) in Eskan Village, near Riyadh, attended by senior Army commanders and representatives of the other U.S. service components. This event provided the opportunity for the senior Army commanders and their staffs to work out the details of their plans. The staffs addressed those details that could be resolved and identified those that could not. After the formal sessions, the two corps commanders, the Support Command commander, and the Third Army commander retired to a conference room alone. There, closing discussions took place on the ARCENT concept of operations.

The MAPEX was followed by briefings to Schwarzkopf on 4 and 8 January. Schwarzkopf seemed to have misgivings but then renewed his confidence in the plan of attack. A final "commanders' huddle" was held by the Third Army commander on 1 February, then the secretary of defense and chairman were briefed again on the 9th. Subsequently, only decisions involving matters of detail and execution remained to be made, most contingent on the outcome of initial combat actions. These conferences and briefings constituted the major turning points in the planning process. Each marked a new advance in the evolution of the plan that led to the victory in Desert Storm.

The planning process for ground operations began in mid-September 1990. Central Command campaign planning had begun even earlier while the deployment of U.S. forces was still in its first days. Because the allied air forces (reinforced by U.S. Navy and Marine air wings) provided the first offensive capability available to the alliance high command, an offensive air campaign was planned almost at once and largely independent of consideration of any specific ground operations that might follow. Much of this planning was done by the U.S. Air Force staff in Washington and then adapted by CENTAF.[8] The theater campaign plan ultimately grafted a ground operation plan onto the existing air plan because the latter continued to be an appropriate—indeed necessary—way to proceed with the employment of available coalition air power. Targeting in the Kuwaiti Theater of Operations (KTO), to be sure, would be affected at some point by the details of the ground operation, but the air component's "major muscle movements" remained constant.

According to his memoir, Schwarzkopf came under pressure from Washington to develop a concept for a ground offensive to free Kuwait almost upon initiation of the Desert Shield defensive deployment.[9] He resisted the pressure because he was convinced that the force he had just begun to deploy was both inadequate to the task and configured only for defense. The pressure continued intermittently, though Schwarzkopf seems to have done nothing substantive until he relocated to the theater of operations in late August.

To develop a ground offensive plan, the CINC requested and was assigned four recent graduates of the Army's bastion of the operational art, the School of Advanced Military Studies (SAMS), located in the Command and General Staff College, Fort Leavenworth, Kansas. The officers were reassigned from joint posts and other duties in Army units not yet alerted for movement to the Gulf. They were Lieutenant Colonel (later colonel) Joe Purvis, at the time assigned to the U.S. Pacific Command staff in Hawaii; Major Greg Eckert, G3 training, 4th Infantry Division, at Fort Carson, Colorado; Major Dan Roh, executive officer, 708th Main Support Battalion, 8th Infantry Division, in Germany; and Major Bill Pennypacker, executive officer, 1st Brigade, 1st Infantry Division, at Fort Riley, Kansas.

However these officers were chosen, fortune favored Schwarzkopf in the choice of team chief. Purvis was an officer of medium height, slender, and quiet in demeanor, but he concealed in his taciturn nature a highly disciplined and most perceptive intellect not easily swayed by bluster and bravado. When he said something was so, you could bank on it, for the simple reason that Purvis would not say he knew until he was sure he did. He also had a wry sense of humor and the ability to laugh at his own discomfort, no small talent in the high-pressure world he entered in September 1990.

These officers formed a small planning cell for consideration of ground operations. They would be at the center of planning for Operation Desert Storm. The life of this group was instructive about how Central Command and Third Army worked together, how Schwarzkopf exercised his command, and about the role played by General Yeosock and ARCENT in achieving U.S. and coalition goals in Southwest Asia.

Planning was evolutionary.[10] While the Third Army staff focused on deploying its forces and developing the defensive plans for Operation Desert Shield, Purvis and his planners began to explore the possibility of a U.S. ground offensive by examining what could be done with forces available in the fall of 1990. Planning soon expanded to look at options that would be feasible only with the addition of more U.S. forces, forces that were allocated in November. All of this went on while the XVIII Airborne Corps was still arriving and during a period when there was no commitment to remove Saddam Hussein from Kuwait by force of arms—when, in fact, decisions were being made that were contrary to the needs of a major operational offensive.

Responsibility for planning, although limited at first to a small group at theater headquarters, eventually involved both Yeosock and his G3, General Arnold. Once Schwarzkopf was satisfied he knew what he wanted his components to do, planning for Army operations was transferred to the Third Army staff and transformed over several weeks into a process of simultaneous and iterative dialogue between commanders and staffs from division to theater, with each command echelon having a part in the process in accordance with its immediate and legitimate interests. These officers were assisted in their adaptation to the new requirements by the knowledge they had acquired exploring various counterattack options.

ARCENT offensive planning continued until 8 January, when Schwarzkopf approved the ground operational plan in its essentials. Incremental adjustments were made up to the eve of the attack. The principal linkage between Third Army's planning and Schwarzkopf's work at Central Command was the CENTCOM planning cell itself. Once Schwarzkopf's concept was formulated, Purvis and his team continued to work in the Central Command headquarters in the basement of the Saudi Ministry of Defense Building. However, they were placed under the supervision of Yeosock and Arnold, who were given responsibility for further development of a theater ground attack plan. The Central Command operational concept was gradually worked into a more detailed, all-component and coalition ground offensive plan. Eventually, as planning spread outward to encompass all participating units, the Purvis Group planners resumed duties as a cell within the theater staff dealing with all components alike.[11]

Ground operational planning involved a process of iterative negotiation from bottom to top. This established a single concept in the minds of all commanders, an essential element of successful synchronization of their disparate activities. However, it is now clear that certain divergences of view and philosophy also began to appear, particularly about Iraqi abilities to absorb the Air Force preparation fires. Though little remarked at the time, these divergences would lead to painful misunderstandings during and after the offensive.

The "gang of four," as the Purvis Group became known, reported to Headquarters, Central Command, in Riyadh on 16 September 1990.[12] On the 18th, Schwarzkopf charged them to plan an offensive ground campaign using the forces available in theater at the time—

one corps of two heavy, one light (airborne), and one medium (air assault) divisions; an armored cavalry regiment; a combat aviation brigade; a Marine amphibious force of one division; and the various coalition forces then arriving.[13] The CINC's initial comments made clear that he was looking for an indirect approach, not a frontal attack into enemy strength.

At the outset, only ten or so CENTCOM personnel were to have knowledge of the Purvis Group's activities and plans. For the group, that meant that getting information was often difficult, as it was not possible to tell the source exactly why a piece of information was required. In this, the network of SAMS graduates assigned throughout the theater proved most useful. Many occupied key operational and planning positions at all levels of Army command. These officers knew each other and were willing to study questions and respond to their caller without spending a great deal of time asking why he needed to know.[14] Within Central Command headquarters, on the other hand, inquiries often required a great deal of creativity to make the request plausible without giving away the game.

The Purvis Group was enlarged by the addition of a naval rating, Petty Officer First Class (IS1) Michael Archer, who would be the team's intelligence specialist. In early November, Brigadier Tim Sullivan, a British Guards officer, joined as well. From time to time, experts from various agencies were called in as semipermanent members or for consultation. Among these were Major James Mudd from the Central Command Combat Analysis Office and Lieutenant Colonel (later colonel) John Carr from the ARCENT Provisional (later 22d) Support Command. As the concept took form, the Commander, MARCENT, whose headquarters was not located in Riyadh (as were Headquarters, ARCENT and CENTAF), was kept informed through briefings to his liaison officer to CENTCOM.

The planning group developed and refined various concepts in light of the CINC's guidance, briefed the CINC periodically, received new guidance based on whatever the commander's current concerns happened to be, then went back to the drawing board for another iteration. In a real sense, the group served as Schwarzkopf's alter ego as he clarified his own thinking. Their product was a broad, general outline that would have to be filled in, in ever greater detail, by the components and their major commands. The process, best characterized as a series of "negotiations," was more important than the written products, for it was the process that ultimately produced not just direction but the detailed understanding at every level of how the battle would be fought. The written orders, like interstate treaties, simply provided a reference to the resolution of issues already decided. There certainly were flaws in the understanding achieved, but these had to do with style, not substance.

By 25 September, Purvis and his group had developed a set of operational considerations for review by the CENTCOM J5, Rear Admiral Grant A. Sharp.[15] First for consideration was the principle that CENTCOM forces should seek to fight only a minimum number of the enemy's formations; they would bypass others. The second and perhaps key assumption was that the air offensive would have to reduce enemy forces about 50 percent in aggregate if acceptable friendly-to-enemy force ratios were to be realized prior to beginning any ground attack. This assumption, which quickly became an article of faith at all levels of the Desert Shield-Desert Storm command, made the acceptability of ground offensive operations explicitly dependent on the success of air operations in the Kuwait theater of operations. Third, with mechanized trafficability in the theater being what it was, it was apparent that rapid intelligence acquisition, reporting, and targeting would be essential to success.

Finally, the whole issue of sustainability became an early and long-lived concern.[16] Operational reach of mechanized ground forces is bought by wheeled vehicles. The Army, which had been designed for defensive war in Europe, was short of wheeled vehicles in general and heavy equipment transporters (HETs) in particular. It was also short of line-haul fuel trucks, especially fuel trucks capable of long-distance off-road movement. HETs provide the ability to concentrate armored forces operationally without undue wear and tear on tracks and power trains. Fuel trucks make it possible to keep the armored columns moving forward in the attack. These shortages of wheeled vehicles had been aggravated by decisions having to do with achieving minimum essential forces for the Desert Shield deployment. A great deal would depend upon the ability of the host nation and allied nations to make up the deficit in all categories.

In addition to stated U.S. national goals, Central Command planners assumed as implied objectives the destruction of an Iraqi offensive capability and a consequent restoration of a regional balance of military power.[17] They assumed that the allied coalition would support a combined offensive to free Kuwait, that Iraq would use chemical weapons in its defense, and that alliance forces would not employ nuclear weapons. It was assumed that any offensive operation must ensure, in its movements, the continued security of ports and critical oil facilities. Obviously, any plan should *minimize friendly casualties* and collateral damage to civilian populations. The primary risks recognized at the outset were the dependence of any attack on extended lines of communication over unimproved roads, the possibility of terrorist attacks in the coalition's rear areas, and the difficulty of judging with any accuracy residual Iraqi capabilities as enemy forces came under sustained air attack. The theater planning mission was simply stated: "On order, friendly forces conduct offensive operations to eject Iraqi forces from Kuwait; be prepared to secure and defend Kuwait."[18]

By mid-September, intelligence analysts knew the Iraqis in Kuwait were laying out a multiechelon, deliberate defense in depth.[19] Regular Iraqi infantry and growing numbers of conscript units occupied fixed positions facing south and east (to sea) in increasingly better-prepared defensive belts. Mobile tactical and operational reserves and regular army mechanized forces were positioned to react to any allied penetration. The Republican Guard Forces Command, pulled back from Kuwait to southeastern Iraq, constituted a theater reserve to conduct the decisive counterattack once the coalition forces were tied down in the forward defenses.

It became clear from their open western flank that the Iraqis believed their defensive array was secured by the empty, featureless Iraqi desert beyond the Wadi al Batin. Aside from some token forces securing the few roads in that area, Saddam continued to pour his defensive forces into Kuwait, trying to build a defensive "nut" too tough to crack. The Iraqi leader failed to consider several things that would negate his assumptions: the cumulative effect on his soldiers of a coordinated air campaign by the world's leading air power; the aggregate technological advantages enjoyed by his enemy, not to mention the skill of the men and women employing them; the specific navigational capability that inexpensive global positioning systems (devices for which civilian analogs exist in any Radio Shack store) might give allied ground forces; the immediate and hostile response of the Arab world to his initial incursion into Kuwait; and the determination of President George Herbert Walker Bush to have him out of that country.

The planning cell briefed their recommended courses of action to Schwarzkopf and selected members of his primary staff on 6 October. In response, Schwarzkopf directed the development of a concept of operations that would place the coalition main ground attack west of the elbow or panhandle of Kuwait, penetrate the Iraqi defenses, exploit to seize an objective cutting the north-south line of communication (the Basrah-Kuwait City highway) sixty kilometers north of Kuwait City, and, on order, continue the attack to seize the

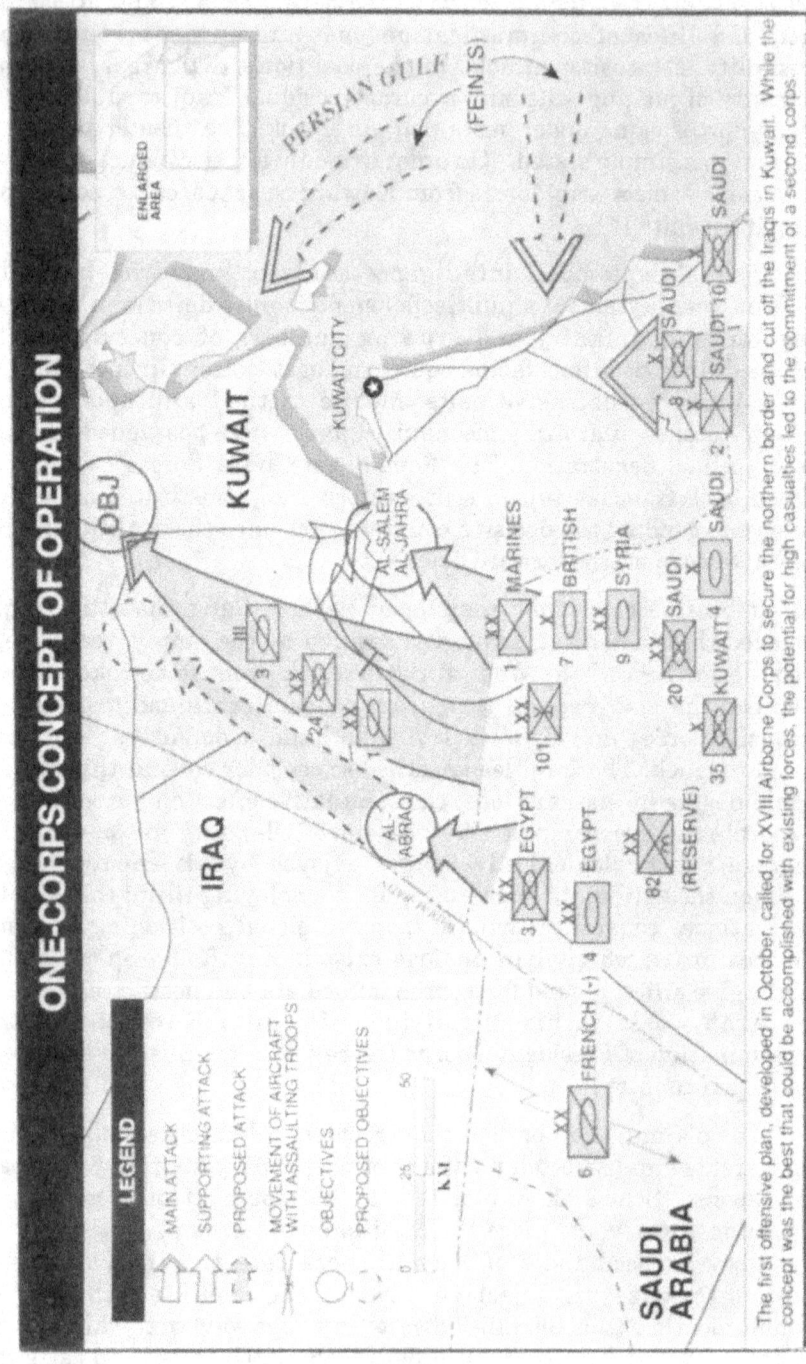

Map 4.

Rawdatayn oil fields and secure the northern Iraqi-Kuwaiti border (see map 4). It was Schwarzkopf's judgment that, although such an attack risked failure in light of the unfavorable force ratios, the force itself would not be at risk of catastrophic loss.[20]

This plan and the air offensive plan were taken to Washington on 9 October by Major General Robert B. Johnston, the CENTCOM chief of staff, Brigadier General Buster C. Glossen, a CENTAF planner, Lieutenant Colonel Joe Purvis, and Major Richard F. Francona from the CENTCOM intelligence staff (J2). The plan was presented to the Joint Staff and then, on the 11th, to the president and his advisers.[21] Concerns were expressed that the ground offensive plan attacked into the enemy strength and that barrier-breaching operations would be extremely difficult. Schwarzkopf's view was that, while this might be true, the command lacked sufficient forces and logistics support, particularly cross-country tankers, to attack farther west, avoiding enemy strength entirely.

Schwarzkopf told David Frost in March 1991 that he had told the president the Saturday after Iraq's invasion of Kuwait that, if the national policy were to escalate to require a ground offensive to remove Iraqi forces from Kuwait, he (Schwarzkopf) would require a force larger than that allocated for Desert Shield.[22] At an October briefing, he had General Johnston state that the plan for the one-corps offensive was submitted under some duress; indeed, the briefing itself was followed by the disclaimer: "That is not what the Commander in Chief of Central Command is recommending. It is a weak plan and it is not the plan that we are recommending. . . . if we are serious about ejecting them [Iraq] from Kuwait what we need is more forces to be able to execute a proper campaign."[23]

Colonel Purvis, who was present in Washington during the October discussions, made some important observations about these exchanges. He believed the real value of the meetings was that they established a dialogue between the nation's civilian political leaders, the Joint Staff, and the theater commander. Whatever disagreement existed was, in his view, by no means arbitrary. The president's civilian advisers apparently believed Schwarzkopf had not considered adequately an "Inchon-like" envelopment. Central Command did not agree, and the dialogue continued.[24]

Following the Washington briefing, Schwarzkopf, who had remained in Riyadh, directed that the planning group examine some new questions. What could he do with a new corps? What should it look like? When would it be available? Still, the group's focus remained on the one-corps option. The J2 was asked to identify Iraqi logistical vulnerabilities that the allied forces might exploit. The real chore, however, was to try and project a future threat, since Saddam had already begun what was to be a long-term process of reinforcement of the occupation forces in Kuwait, an action that proved to be his undoing.[25]

On 17 October, the United Kingdom's theater commander and General Yeosock were brought into the planning process in two separate briefings. Sir Peter de la Billiere, the British commander in chief, had arrived in Saudi Arabia on 6 October. Like Yeosock, Sir Peter had a long association with desert operations, in his case with the British Special Air Services, the famous SAS. At this time, the British land commitment was a single armored brigade, the 7th. This was increased to a balanced two-brigade division shortly after the United States announced its commitment of a second heavy corps in November.

During the briefings they received, Yeosock and de la Billiere raised a number of issues. Among these were questions of allied capabilities and the willingness to participate in an offensive, the need to keep forces concentrated in the face of unfavorable force ratios, the trafficability of terrain north of the Saudi border, the desirability of a deception plan, the difficulty of staging adequate logistic support in a timely fashion given the distances involved and the lack of good supply routes, and the need to keep the east covered adequately while forces were concentrated for an attack in the west.[26]

Yeosock also received a briefing from the Third Army's Support Command concerning sustainment issues associated with a one-corps offensive plan. The plan at issue provided for the movement of the XVIII Airborne Corps' heavy forces (3 ACR, 24th Infantry Division, 1st Cavalry) to the Saudi border area with western Kuwait, east of Hafar al Batin. Support Command's planners calculated that it would take nine to thirteen days to complete the movement at night. The principal constraint was the number of trucks available. The briefing noted that by 25 November there would be no more than 112 U.S. military HETs in theater (on 10 October there were none) and that it would take up to nineteen days, using all military and known host-nation capabilities, to move the one-corps force to attack east of Wadi al Batin.[27] Prestockage of forward logistic bases would take from three to sixteen days depending on when the execution date came and whether or not both day and night movement could be used.[28] It was quite evident that, for any offensive concentration inland, the force would have to use a combination of commercial, host-nation, and military HETs. Consequently, the acquisition and allocation of HETs would be the Third Army commander's biggest concern in December and January.

On the 18th, Admiral Sharp was briefed on three courses of action for a two (U.S.) corps attack. The favored alternative called for two corps to attack abreast west of the Kuwaiti border, with a follow-on mission to destroy the Republican Guard Forces Command. Later that same day, the group briefed Brigadier General James Monroe, the Third Army G4. Monroe was perceived to be very receptive and helpful, which was important, as he would play a key role in the sustainment of any operation. At this time, logistic prepositioning and unit repositioning to forward assembly areas were the major conundrums involved in any two-corps plan.

Schwarzkopf was briefed on 21 October. He approved the idea of a ground offensive plan with a main effort consisting of two U.S. Army corps attacking west of the Kuwaiti border to get behind the principal Iraqi forces. He personally set the operational objective of the attack as the *physical* destruction of the Republican Guard, which he recognized as a strategic center of gravity in the KTO.[29] Pointing to a map, he said,

> With these two corps there [pointing at the US corps] . . .
> I've got forces here [pointing into Kuwait].
> I sit on Highway 8.
> I've defeated him in his mind.
> I've threatened his Republican Guard;
> Now, I'll destroy it.[30]

Schwarzkopf identified as issues outstanding the question of trafficability and supportability (Yeosock estimated that the concept was supportable), the proper role for coalition forces given their varied capabilities and the absolute political as well as military necessity for their active participation, and the need to find a proper role for MARCENT in light of the corps' short logistic legs, sea-based close air support, and proximity to forces afloat.[31]

The following two days, the Central Command staff in Riyadh briefed the chairman of the Joint Chiefs of Staff on both the one- and two-corps options, with emphasis on the possibilities of the former. Powell apparently believed that a one-corps offensive could succeed. It took two and one-half hours on Friday, 22 October, and two more on Saturday, to convince him that a one-corps attack was a gamble, not just a risk. The chairman's guidance to Schwarzkopf was straightforward and entirely supportive: "Tell me what you need for assets. We will not do this halfway. The United States military is available to support this operation."32

The conclusion was that a second U.S. Army corps (at that time, two divisions and an armored cavalry regiment; later, a third division was added at the request of the Third Army commander) would provide the necessary forces to permit maneuver to the west, around the Iraqi main deployments. Air Force resources would increase proportionally, as would deployed naval forces. Obviously, Third Army would have to build a substantial theater and host-nation logistic support structure simultaneously with arrival of the new corps if there were to be sufficient means to project the offensive force the distances required to bring it into contact with the Republican Guard troops and to sustain it in battle once joined. Most of the theater logistic forces would have to be drawn from the Reserve Components.

Through the vicissitudes of international politics, Southwest Asia, heretofore a secondary theater where the rule had always been one of economy of force, was now within days of becoming the main effort for the United States' armed forces. The chairman took the two-corps graphics back to Washington with him.33

On 24 October, the planning cell was placed under operational control of the Third Army commander to develop further the concepts for ground operations. The group continued to be located at Central Command to maintain its security. Yeosock and Arnold would work to flesh out the theater ground offensive plan and, at the same time, begin preparing for the main ground effort within that plan.

For the time being, however, focus remained on one-corps options, the principal case at this time, with a U.S. Army corps west of the Kuwait border (considered to be possible, if risky, with the then-current threat), the MARCENT and United Kingdom (U.K.) brigade just inside the border protecting the XVIII Corps' eastern flank, and the Egyptian and Syrian corps farther to the east by the "elbow" of Kuwait. Amphibious operations were planned only as demonstrations and feints. No Inchons seemed likely.34

Colonel Purvis observed that, the one-corps focus notwithstanding, his group believed the two-corps option would be selected because of the chairman's reaction. Schwarzkopf, however, was not yet ready to allow them to brief the two-corps option to the components. ARCENT and the Department of the Army were still discussing rotation policies for forces already in theater. But confirmation of the Purvis Group's hunch was not hard to find. On 25 October, immediately following the chairman's return to the United

States, the secretary of defense appeared on the morning news programs of all four major TV networks and announced a pending increase of U.S. ground forces. He hinted broadly that the number could reach 100,000 and involve units from Europe.[35]

As planners anticipated approval of the two-corps option, a question was raised on 27 October about U.S. attacks on airfields and surrounding SCUD sites located in western Iraq within missile range of Israel. Concern about Iraq's ability to disrupt the U.S.-Arab coalition by prompting an Israeli intervention had begun to grow in Washington. In response, ARCENT set up another special planning group staffed with representatives of the ARCENT and XVIII Airborne Corps. Its members were Lieutenant Colonel Bob Butto, from the 513th Military Intelligence Brigade; Lieutenant Colonels Bob Westholm and Matt Kriwanek, from the commanding general's personal staff; Major Bob Dement, ARCENT's G4 plans; and Lieutenant Colonel Dave Huntoon and Major Teri Peck from XVIII Airborne Corps' G3. Major Matt Smith, the 1st Cavalry Division liaison officer to ARCENT, rounded out the group and looked out for the interests of III Corps' headquarters should it be deployed.[36]

The ARCENT and corps planners evaluated options for attacking these targets, particularly the airfields, called H2 and H3, but saw such efforts by conventional ground forces as both a significant logistical risk and an unproductive diversion of forces from the main effort.[37] Further inquiries elicited the same response. Ultimately, special operations forces from the United States and Special Air Service forces from the United Kingdom were committed to the SCUD hunt in western Iraq (see map 5). SCUD hunting also caused a significant diversion of air support during the conduct of air operations after 16 January.

On 6 November, two days prior to the president's announcement of further deployments, Secretary of State James Baker and King Fahd agreed to an allied command plan that essentially blessed the existing structure of dual command, with Saudi preeminence in decisions involving defense of the kingdom itself and American freedom of action for U.S. forces for contingencies beyond the Saudi borders, with the caveat that offensive action would require advance agreement by both heads of state. Baker was quoted as saying that " 'a new phase' had begun in the Persian Gulf crisis in which the global community is prepared to 'resort to force' if a peaceful solution is not found."[38] By the end of the month, there would be agreement in the United Nations Security Council to just that. The agreement on

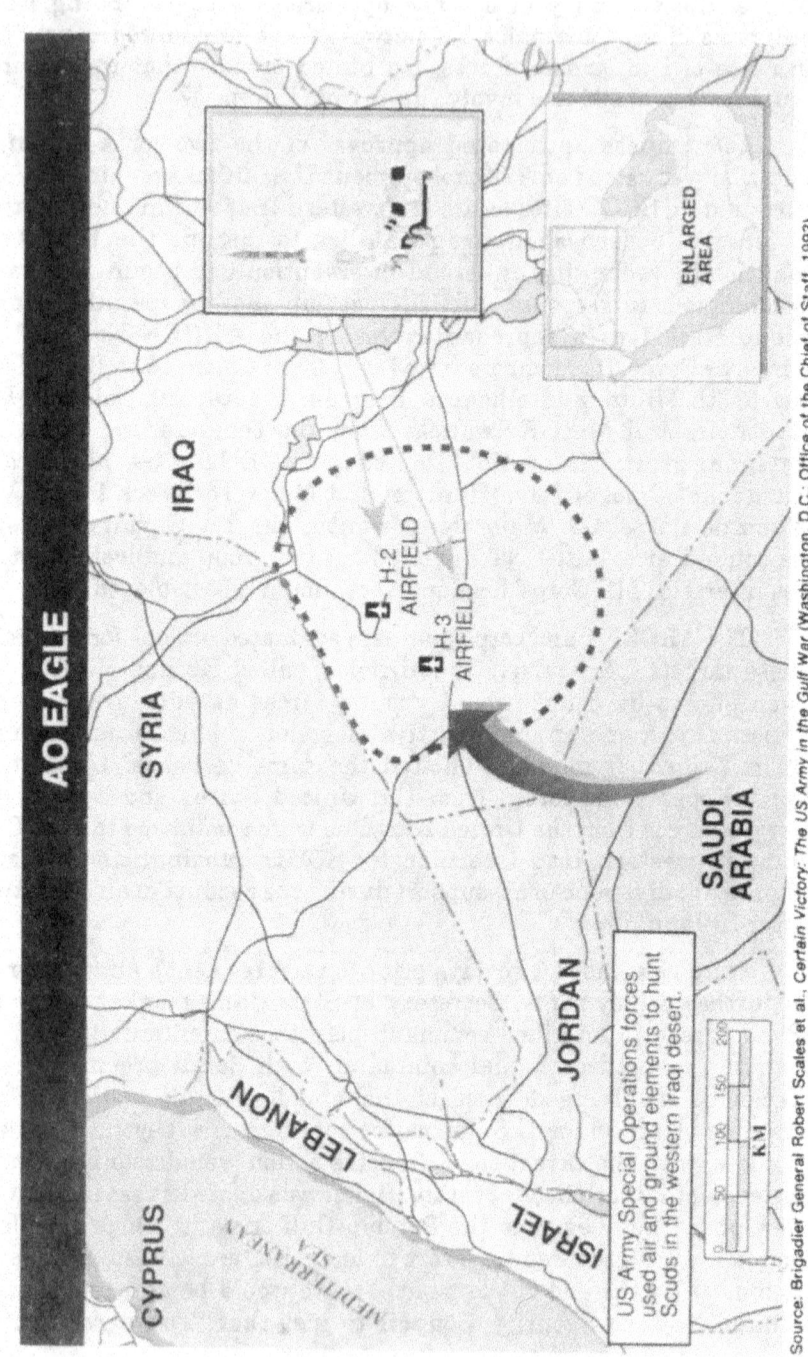

Map 5.

coalition command, it was reported, did not bind other nations, who would be brought in by separate bilateral agreements.

For a time, the focus of the planning process remained in the Ministry of Defense basement. Lieutenant Colonels Westholm and Kriwanek acted as Third Army points of contact as required, as did Lieutenant Colonel Huntoon and Major Peck at XVIII Airborne Corps. The ad hoc solution at Third Army was called for, not only because of security considerations, but because, as previously noted, the regular Third Army planners had been used to set up the C3IC organization in August. They simply were not readily available, and presumably there would have been concern about possible compromise of the plan to the Saudis before the proper diplomatic preparation had been accomplished.

Planning continued on the one- and two-corps options and the H2-H3 airfield excursion. Schwarzkopf was briefed on H2-H3. He objected to the operation as being too risky because of the distance the airfield attack force would be from any sustaining base and the main effort. His guidance was to focus planning on the two-corps concept. On 31 October, forces available for planning included five U.S. heavy divisions, two armored cavalry regiments, the airborne and air assault divisions, six field artillery brigades, two aviation brigades, the French light armored division(-), a British armored division(-), four Saudi heavy brigades, a Kuwaiti heavy brigade, two Egyptian heavy divisions, a Syrian heavy division(-), two U.S. Marine divisions, and two Marine expeditionary brigades. Objectives as far west as Samawah on the Euphrates were considered for a secondary attack. Although Baghdad was mentioned, the conclusion was that it was too far away to hold even if it could be captured and, more to the point, that its capture would exceed the UN charter for coalition forces, which limited their objective to the liberation of Kuwait.[39]

On 1 November, a number of sustainment issues were raised by a representative from 22d Support Command, Colonel John B. Trier. Trier followed the earlier work done by Colonel Carr and became the point of linkage with the support command for development of the sustainment concept for Desert Storm. Concerns identified in November generally involved the burden of introducing a new corps package. Given the existing strains already accepted in the theater logistics structure and recognizing that the overriding need for haste that had governed the August deployment no longer obtained, the new corps' logistic elements would have to precede tactical units to provide necessary life support and transport. Because the ports lacked the infrastructure to support linkup and marshaling, incoming forces would have to pass through the ports rapidly and transition to the assembly areas to "stand up."[40]

A recommendation was made that the area around King Khalid Military City (KKMC), southwest of Hafar al Batin, serve as the logistics center for the concentration of the incoming corps. In December and January, VII Corps would concentrate in the desert, east and south of KKMC and west of XVIII Airborne Corps. This would require that the new corps pass through the area defended by XVIII Airborne Corps. Subsequently, this would also require XVIII Airborne Corps to pass in front of VII Corps for deployment for the attack. Though this sounds inconvenient, it allowed XVIII Airborne Corps to continue to perform its Desert Shield defensive mission while VII Corps deployed and formed in the desert. It became a major part of the deception operation for Operation Desert Storm. Third Army established KKMC as a major forward operating and logistics base, the pivot for the redeployment to attack positions west of Wadi al Batin that began on 17 January.

The planners were beginning to deal with the fact that the existing and anticipated operational areas between KKMC and the port of Ad Dammam were limited to a road net consisting of an irregular polygon of roads, mostly two lanes wide, often unimproved and full of Saudi civil traffic in ubiquitous white Toyota pickups. If one went on out to Rafha (as ARCENT would), that added another 168 miles of adequate-to-bad two-lane road. This created an extraordinary transportation problem, compounding the general shortage of HETs and line-haul trucks. The distances involved far exceeded those of the famous Red Ball Express of World War II.

On 2 November, the planners briefed Yeosock on their two-corps concept: an attack west of Wadi al Batin by a notional heavy corps that would drive north to the Euphrates, turn the Iraqi defenses, and destroy the Republican Guard in the area of Iraq just north and west of the Kuwaiti border.[41] At that time, it was envisioned that the Marines would attack and penetrate defenses just inside the Kuwaiti border. Two Royal Saudi Land Force brigades would attack on the Marines' left, up the Wadi some limited distance. The XVIII Corps would follow the Marines in sector, pass through and conduct a supporting attack eastward across northern Kuwait. The bulk of the Arab Islamic forces would attack and penetrate into Kuwait from the south. A variant showed XVIII Corps attacking toward An Nasiriyah to the northwest, while the notional heavy corps advanced on an axis of advance approximating the Kuwaiti border, northeast then east.

On 6 November, Schwarzkopf was briefed along with his principal staff and, finally, his component commanders. Schwarzkopf emphasized the need for a deception plan to avoid giving away the scheme of maneuver. The deception was intended to portray the threat of attack only through the Kuwaiti southern border area, with no intent to enter via Iraqi territory. No U.S. force or logistic prepositioning was to be allowed west of Wadi al Batin prior to the start of the air offensive. That, it was hoped, would blind the Iraqi defenders. American units, which would make the main attack, were to be kept behind Arab-Islamic forces and off the border until just before the attack itself.[42]

The deception plan had several implications. It meant that the massive logistic preparations for an offensive would have to take place simultaneously with the operational repositioning of maneuver forces, both using a very limited road net and a limited number of wheeled vehicles. It meant, as well, that intelligence collection and, consequently, air preparation of the battlefield would have to be from the top down, from theater and army level to corps and division, because of the resulting blindness of attacking tactical units. Tactical commanders and some ARCENT staff members found these considerations to be increasingly discomforting. The deception plan also meant that air preparations of the KTO would have to be conducted in such a way that those targets most important to Army commanders in the main attack would be attacked last, a consequence that tried the patience of all.

Schwarzkopf found the concept as briefed too detailed and indicated component commanders should be given greater flexibility in development of their own concepts. In fact, he also seems to have warned the component commanders to allow their subordinates to do their business without overcentralization at component level.[43]

Schwarzkopf directed the Marines to be employed in the east, both for reasons of logistic sustainment and in order to maintain the cover story of an attack through Kuwait. (As late as 20 February, Iraq continued to push forces into the "heel" of Kuwait, no doubt in part due to the highly visible Marine Corps presence ashore and afloat.) Schwarzkopf also set out his priorities for the air attack in support of ground operations, the disruption of command and control facilities and the logistics supporting the KTO, and the attrition of the Republican Guard. The operational goal remained the cutting off and destruction of the Republican Guard.[44] Finally, the theater commander identified three major issues for resolution: the shape of the new U.S. Army forces and the time needed to get them in position ready for use, the logistical supportability of the concept, and the matter of trafficability. Regarding the last issue, XVIII Corps was to do a good deal of desert driving on terrain similar to that in southeastern Iraq in order to develop some empirical data.

On 8 November, President Bush announced the deployment of the European-based VII Corps to Central Command in order to establish an offensive option for the resolution of the Kuwait crisis.[45] Talk of troop rotation plans were set aside and preparation for a possible offensive were taken in hand. Component plans continued to be fleshed out and back-briefed to Schwarzkopf until he was comfortable with them. The secretary of defense and chairman would make two trips to the theater, in December and in February, before they would be convinced that the details were sufficiently in hand for them to recommend to the president a date for the ground attack. Meanwhile, there was now a theater concept within which the components could begin their own considerable hard work.

On 14 November, Schwarzkopf held what was probably his most important briefing of the war from the standpoint of transmitting the commander's intent: he briefed his ground commanders, division level and above, in Dhahran. The commanders from deploying units were brought to Saudi Arabia from their U.S. and European bases for the meeting. Schwarzkopf laid down the primary objective: "to destroy the Republican Guard."[46] He also enjoined absolute security concerning the scheme of maneuver and indicated he expected the Iraqis to employ chemical weapons, though he seems to have drawn no particular operational conclusion from that fact. The one discordant note Schwarzkopf would later record was an observation by Lieutenant General Fred Franks, the commander of the VII Corps, Schwarzkopf's major maneuver force, that he would need additional forces, specifically the 1st Cavalry Division, to carry out his assignment.[47] In retrospect, this seems to have been the first of a series of events that would lead to various postwar recriminations. At the time, it did not seem a major issue.

Major General Tom Rhame, the commander of the 1st Infantry Division (Mechanized) from Fort Riley, Kansas, emphasized the importance of this briefing in an interview later televised by one of the cable TV networks.[48] Rhame pointed particularly to the CINC's clear articulation of the task at hand, "to destroy the Republican Guard," as a mission that even privates could understand and upon which they could concentrate their efforts. This briefing and subsequent conferences and briefings ensured an extraordinary degree of unity of effort in the U.S. offensive. The selection and clear articulation of the command's military objective may well have been Schwarzkopf's greatest contribution as theater commander, for it produced a harmony of action rare in complex operations. The harmony was, in part, enforced, as in the period following the briefing, the CINC would make it quite clear, sometimes with implicit threats, that tactical (corps and division) commanders would do well not to spend time second guessing his offensive concept,[49] a message that would prove to be counterproductive in the long run. Nonetheless, from the 14 November briefing onward, planning for the offensive proceeded at all levels with continuous discussion and negotiation.

Third Army and coalition planning continued for a while to be concentrated in the Purvis Group, working under Yeosock's guidance. After the commander's conference, there was additional guidance from Schwarzkopf that had to be accommodated.[50] The CINC demanded a heavy division as theater reserve. For obvious reasons, the division would have to come from ARCENT. The 1st Cavalry Division, less the "Tiger Brigade" (1st Brigade, 2d Armored Division), would ultimately fill this role. The XVIII Corps would be committed in the west in the area from As Salman to As Samawah. The U.K. forces, which were to be increased to a division, were to remain with the U.S. Marines. (Ultimately the British forces were reassigned to ARCENT in exchange for the "Tiger Brigade.")

The time from 15 to 23 November was a period of adjustment and revision. Schwarzkopf wanted a placement of coalition forces that would best utilize the different capabilities represented and that would take into account regional animosities and suspicions. Concern remained about the off-road trafficability of the area in which XVIII Corps would operate and about casualties at the breach site. These concerns would remain active to the point of execution.

On 23 November, Schwarzkopf was briefed again. He gave qualified approval to Third Army's draft plan, which was issued to the Army major subordinate commanders the following day.[51] The plan called for a four-stage operation: logistical build-up, prepositioning, ground offensive, and consolidation. It set a stockage level for forward bases of five days of supply in class III (fuel) and class V (ammunition), plus the necessary stocks to support the forces in their tactical assembly areas. The entire ground operation was expected to take up to eight weeks.

The plan called for VII Corps to be in a defensive position west of XVIII Corps no later than twenty-five days prior to the ground attack. Northern Area Command would pull its forces east of Wadi al Batin, and the French 6th Light Armored Division, which drew its support from the Red Sea, would screen the area west of the wadi. Redeployment of the two corps to their preattack tactical assembly areas was expected to take two weeks. The XVIII Corps was to be on the left, VII Corps on the right, both west of Hafar al Batin. Repositioning was to take place in conjunction with the initiation of air operations. The destruction of the Iraqi Air Force, together with any ground sensors likely to detect allied movement in time for the Iraqis to react, was essential if the ground attack was to achieve surprise and the ability to concentrate.

The ground attack itself was expected to take up to two weeks. The plan assumed that coalition fixing attacks would go in at daylight on D-day (later G-day to differentiate ground from theater [air] attack), with the main attack following twelve hours later (H+12), to "maneuver deep West of Kuwait to destroy the RGFC and cut off LOCs to Iraqi forces in the KTO."[52] For reasons that will be addressed later, this delay ultimately grew to twenty-four hours. The initial offensive was to be followed by a consolidation phase anticipated to last up to four more weeks during which Iraqi forces remaining in Kuwait would be defeated.

The four major coalition commands from east to west would be, starting on the right, the Eastern Area Command (Joint Forces Command East), which was to attack north along the Kuwaiti coast to deceive the enemy and fix his reserves, and MARCENT. MARCENT, then including the U.K. armored division, was to attack near the elbow of Kuwait to penetrate forward Iraqi defenses, fix tactical reserves south of the As Salem airfield, occupy a blocking position, link up with the Northern Area Command on the left, then, in conjunction with the Northern Area Command, isolate Kuwait City and conduct consolidation operations. In the center, the Northern Area Command (later Joint Forces Command North) containing the Egyptian and Syrian combat units, as well as Royal Saudi Land Forces and a SANG brigade, was to penetrate the enemy defenses, drive to the north of the As Salem airfield, join with Third Army, and occupy a blocking position north of Kuwait City on the north-south Kuwait City-Basrah highway. The two Arab-Islamic commands would liberate Kuwait City.

The VII Corps was to conduct the Third Army's main attack. It was to penetrate the enemy's forward defenses and attack in zone to defeat the Republican Guard. On the left of the ARCENT sector, the XVIII Corps would conduct a supporting attack to block the Highway 8 valley. The corps would be prepared to continue the attack to the east down the valley in order to assist VII Corps in destruction of the Republican Guard. Both corps would prepare plans for consolidation and occupation of sectors in western and northern Kuwait.

Schwarzkopf approved this outline for planning. He charged Yeosock to guarantee supportability of the concept or to modify it.[53] On 24 November, the Third Army commander briefed his subordinate commanders. On the 28th, there was a logistics conference at Dhahran to work out a concept of support. The next day, the regular ARCENT planning staff was brought into the process, and planning at Third Army gradually flowed back into normal component channels. The special planning group reverted to CENTCOM control on 18 December. The C3IC passed to Central Command at about the same time. This released the ARCENT planners back to the Third Army's G3. Major General Schwartz, who would have become Yeosock's principal deputy had he returned to Third Army, was retained as chief of the C3IC, working directly for Schwarzkopf.

On 30 November and 7 December, the XVIII Corps and the VII Corps, respectively, gave their initial briefings to the Third Army commander, at times offering significant modifications to the conceptual plan. For example, VII Corps proposed, among other alternatives, either moving the XVIII Corps to VII Corps' eastern flank (very much like the old two-corps option) in order to extend the maneuver area for Schwarzkopf's "Great Wheel," or having XVIII Corps penetrate and VII Corps pass through into the attack. The effect in either case would have been to force the lighter XVIII Corps troops into the breaching operations required ultimately of the 1st Infantry Division, a move neither Yeosock nor Schwarzkopf was likely to contemplate. The corps' passage of lines would have been prohibitively time consuming. In any event, General Rhame had volunteered his 1st Infantry Division to do the breaching operation because of the training it had completed prior to alert for Desert Shield. VII Corps thus remained the inner (U.S.) corps.[54]

Another point of contention concerned the proper employment of the French 6th Light Armored Division (ultimately placed under Tactical Control of the XVIII Corps on the far left flank) and the 1st U.K. Armored Division. Two different issues were involved. In the case of the French, the issue was political. In its simplest terms, French Minister of Defense Jean-Pierre Chevenement opposed subordination of the French to the U.S. commander. (The defense minister very likely opposed U.S. policy altogether.) This situation changed when Chevenement resigned in December and was replaced by Pierre Joxe. The British commander, General de la Billiere, was for his part

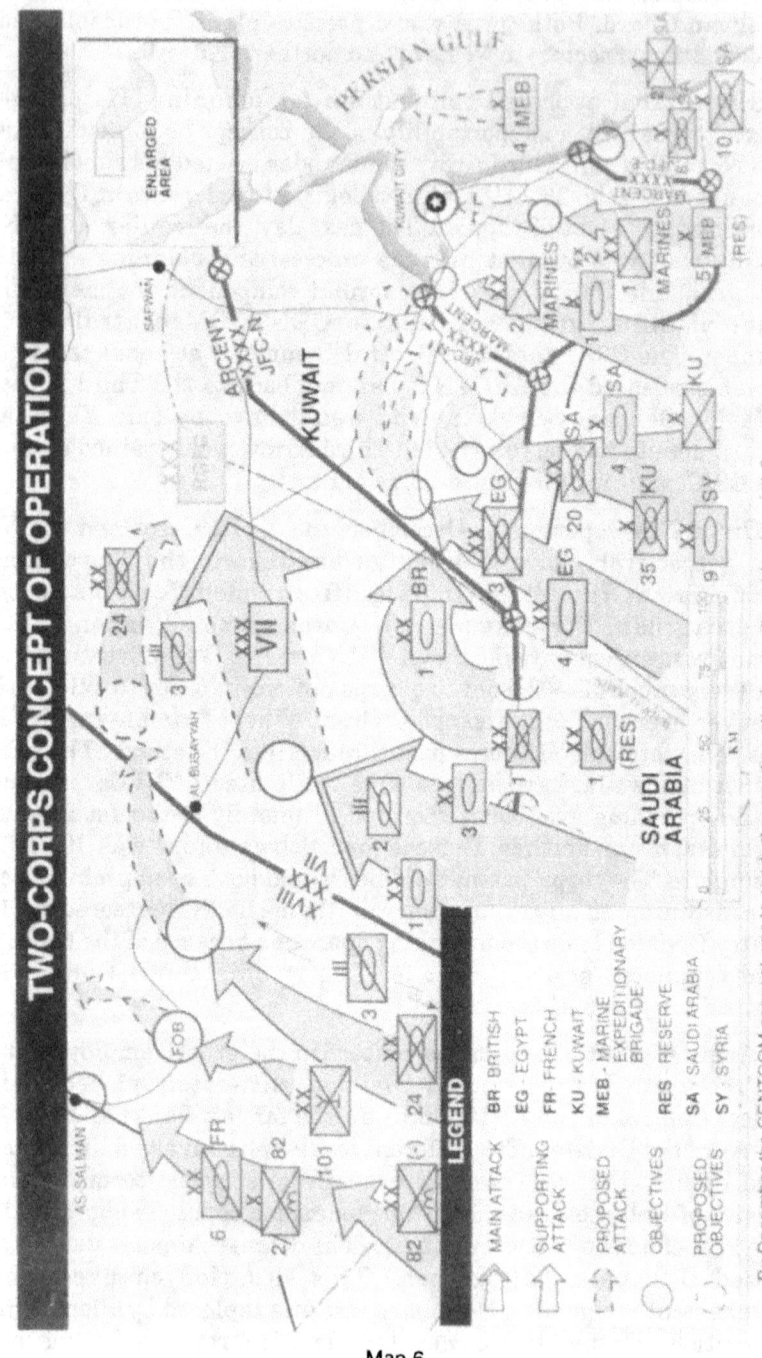

Map 6.

concerned about casualties if the British remained with the Marines in the fixing attack and wanted his force employed in the sort of open maneuver warfare for which it was trained. Schwarzkopf, with some misgivings, acceded to de la Billiere's request and replaced the British two-brigade division with the "Tiger Brigade." By the time Secretary of Defense Cheney was briefed on 20 December, ARCENT had already planned for the employment of the French division with the XVIII Corps on the extreme left and the British with the VII Corps.[55] (See map 6.)

As boundaries changed east or west, it became increasingly evident that there was going to be a significant transportation problem to be solved, one that involved both the general shortage of some types of critical vehicles and the rate at which transportation units could be brought into theater. The influx of transportation units had not only to respond to the needs of the new corps, but it also had to remedy cuts accepted when the force structure guidance had been based upon the concept of "minimum essential forces."[56]

The concept paper or draft plan passed by the CENTCOM planning group to the ARCENT G3 planners (and briefed to the commander in chief on 23 November) was neither a normal joint headquarters directive nor a coordinated operations plan, though it was formatted generally as the operations portion of the latter. The details of the actual actions of the two corps on the ground remained to be worked out, although the general parameters had been established and would be retained: the VII Corps would attack on the ARCENT right, west of Wadi al Batin, driving north and east and destroying the Republican Guard Forces Command; the XVIII Corps would conduct a secondary effort designed to distract the Iraqi high command with a putative or apparent threat to Baghdad. Meanwhile, the light corps would attack to As Samawah and, more important, cut the major axis of withdrawal along Highway 8 south of the Euphrates River. Ultimately, the corps could advance southeast along the river to secure the northern fringe of the pocket of southeastern Iraq, which the allied high command wished to hold at the end of the operations, and, simultaneously, assist VII Corps in the destruction of the Republican Guard.[57]

A Third Army planner, Major Steve Holley, was detailed from the plans section in the C3IC organization and, with Lieutenant Colonel George H. Del Carlo, another Third Army G3 staff member, established an office in a small room on the fifth floor of the Royal Saudi Land Forces headquarters (the location of ARCENT's headquarters in December) to prepare the draft Third Army operations plan for Desert Storm in conjunction with the Purvis Group in the Ministry of Defense. In mid-December, these two officers were joined by Major Dan Gilbert, a SAMS graduate assigned, like most new staff members, from a unit not identified for deployment to Desert Shield. Gilbert developed the ARCENT MAPEX that provided the formal venue for the major commands and commanders to discuss their concepts and begin hammering out the comprehensive plan for the Desert Storm main attack.

Notes

1. Richard Saltus, "Air Force Says It Might Have Won the War in 2 More Weeks," *The Boston Globe*, 5 April 1991, 10.

2. De la Billiere, *Storm Command*, 53.

3. B. H. Liddell Hart, *The Decisive Wars of History* (London: G. Bell & Son, Ltd., 1929), 141–58. Reprinted in a number of editions under the title *Strategy*. Colonel Boyd owes his fame to a briefing given widely but never to the author's knowledge disciplined by being produced in print. The key insight of Colonel Boyd's presentation has to do with "getting inside the enemy's decision cycle." For a summary of Liddell Hart's theories, see Brian Bond, *Liddell Hart and the Weight of History* (London: Cassell & Co., Ltd., 1977); and Brian Bond, *British Military Policy Between the Two World Wars* (Oxford: The Clarendon Press, 1980). See also John Mearsheimer, *Liddell Hart and the Weight of History* (Ithaca, NY: Cornell University Press, 1988). For a discussion of Boyd, see William S. Lind, *Maneuver Warfare Handbook* (Boulder, CO: Westview Press, 1985), 4–8.

4. Jomini maintains that "Employment of the forces should be regulated by two fundamental principles: The first being *to obtain by free and rapid movements the advantage of bringing the mass of the troops against fractions of the enemy*; the second, *to strike in the most decisive direction*." Baron de Jomini, *The Art of War*, trans. Captain G. H. Mendeil and Lieutenant W. P. Craighill (Philadelphia, PA: J. B. Lippincott & Co., 1862; Greenwood Press Reprint, n.d.), 299. Fuller says: "Grant's object was consistent; strategically it was to threaten his enemy's base of operations, and tactically to strike at the rear, or, failing the rear, at a flank of his enemy's army. This being so, the pivotal idea in his generalship was absolutely sound, and firmly based on economy of force." Major General J. F. C. Fuller, *The Generalship of Ulysses S. Grant* (Millwood, NY: Kraus Reprint, 1977), 194. For Fuller's thought, see Anthony John Trythall, *"Boney" Fuller: The Intellectual General* (London: Cassell & Co., Ltd., 1977); and Brian Holden Reid, *J. F. C. Fuller: Military Thinker* (New York: St. Martin's Press, 1987).

5. Department of the Army, Field Manual 100-5, *Operations* (May 1986), 14.

6. Schwarzkopf, *Doesn't Take a Hero*, 386–87. Note refers to draft strategic guidance Schwarzkopf submitted to JCS as evidence of how *he* analyzed his strategic mission.

7. HQ, U.S. Central Command, Riyadh, Saudi Arabia, USCINCCENT OPLAN Desert Storm, dated 16 December 1990, 13.

8. Schwarzkopf, *Doesn't Take a Hero*, 313, 318–21. The most comprehensive account of the air campaign planning available for the public at this time is in Department of Defense, Office of the Secretary of Defense, "Conduct of the Persian Gulf War: Final Report to Congress Pursuant to Title V of the Persian Gulf Conflict Supplemental Authorization and Personal Benefits Act of 1991" (Public Law 102-25), chapter 6, 83–92. An account for the general reader is presented by James P. Coyne, "Plan of Attack," *Air Force Magazine* 75, no. 4 (April 1992): 40–46. HQ, U.S. Central Command, Commander, Memorandum, Subject: Operations Desert Shield/Desert Storm, Exercise Internal Look 90 After-Action Report, dated 11 July 1991, 9.

9. Schwarzkopf, *Doesn't Take a Hero*, 314–15, 320–21, 326–27.

10. The primary document for the activities of the Purvis Group (planning) is a log kept by Major Eckert for the group. *Unless otherwise noted*, this is the source for the narrative of the planning cell actions that follows, hereinafter referred to as Purvis Group Diary.

11. Note from Colonel Purvis to author on manuscript draft.

12. Purvis Group Diary, 1.

13. These were the Desert Shield forces.

14. Comment by Colonel Purvis to author. See also interview with Major General Steven Arnold, Eskan Village, 15 March 1991, 15–16.

15. Purvis Group Diary, 1.

16. Note from Colonel Purvis to author on manuscript draft.

17. Briefing received from Colonel Purvis, Purpose: Provide a Briefing on the Development and Execution of Operation Desert Storm, slide titled, "NCA Objectives."

18. Ibid., slide titled, "Mission."

19. The Threat Summary on the ARCENT Update Briefing for 15 September, under "Major Trends," reads: Iraqi Forces continue to improve their defense in depth. Divisions in forward positions [sic] are deployed with infantry forward. Mech and armored units are deployed to permit rapid reinforcement and counterattack. Iraqi forces retain the capability to conduct offensive operations. HQ, ARCENT, Command Group, ARCENT Update Briefing, dated 15 September 1990, slide titled, "Threat Summary."

20. This appears to incorporate the concept Schwarzkopf sketched out for Chairman Powell in Washington in August. Schwarzkopf, *Doesn't Take a Hero*, 315, 356. Schwarzkopf's judgments are taken from the Purvis Group Diary, 1–2.

21. Schwarzkopf, *Doesn't Take a Hero*, 359–60.

22. Transcript of Frost interview dated 22 March 1991, in possession of author, 6. Schwarzkopf reiterates the same point in his memoir. Schwarzkopf, *Doesn't Take a Hero*, 301.

23. Transcript of Frost interview dated 22 March 1991, 8. Schwarzkopf, *Doesn't Take a Hero*, 359–60, reproduces CINC's assessment.

24. Notes from Colonel Purvis to author on manuscript draft. Purvis subsequently concluded that had the October briefing contained an indication that a second corps would be used in an envelopment west of Wadi al Batin, it might have assuaged some concerns in Washington, D.C., that Schwarzkopf was committed to a frontal attack.

25. Purvis Group Diary, 3. On 9 October 1990, ARCENT's Update Briefing reflected an Iraqi presence in the KTO of twenty-five divisions (thirty-six heavy, 3,700 tanks,

and forty-three light brigades). On 15 January 1991, the Update Briefing showed forty-five divisions (forty-five heavy, 4,280 tanks, and eighty-three light brigades).

26. Ibid., 3–4..

27. HQ, ARCENT Support Command (Prov), briefing titled, "CSS Sustainment"; slides titled, "Move the Force HETS (As of 10 October)" and "Move the Force, Number of Days." Briefing dated 17 October on General Yeosock's briefings-slide index. Pagonis, *Moving Mountains*, 118–25. General Pagonis writes that his planning effort reflected anticipation of future possibilities rather than an effort growing out of Schwarzkopf's planning cell.

28. Ibid., slide titled, "Prestockage Time Requirement."

29. Purvis Group Diary, 4.

30. Quoted by Major Dan Roh in interview of Purvis Group conducted by the author and Major Larry Heystek, commander, 44th Military History Detachment, at Riyadh on 7 March 1991, 33.

31. Note from Colonel Purvis to author on manuscript draft.

32. Quoted in Purvis Group Diary, 5. Notes from Colonel Purvis to author on manuscript draft. Schwarzkopf's account is in Schwarzkopf, *Doesn't Take a Hero*, 366–67.

33. Note from Colonel Purvis to author on manuscript draft.

34. Purvis Group Diary, 5. Note from Colonel Purvis to author on draft.

35. R. Jeffrey Smith and Patrick E. Tyler, "U.S. Considers Sending More Forces to Gulf: Goal Is to Maintain 'Credible' Offensive Power, "*The Washington Post*, 25 October 1990, A1. Patrick E. Tyler and Molly Moore, "U.S. Strength in Gulf May Rise by 100,000: Many Troops Would Be Shifted From Europe, "*The Washington Post*, 26 October 1990, A1, A32. Michael R. Gordon, "U.S. Decides to Add as Many as 100,000 to Its Gulf Forces; Cheney Statement; No Date for Deployment—Some Troops May Come From Europe," *The New York Times*, 26 October 1991, A1.

36. Lieutenant Colonel Matt Kriwanek provided membership of group to author and a note from Colonel Purvis to the author on the manuscript draft addressed concern that III Corps might rotate in and have to execute the plan. ARCENT had explored the possibility of III Corps replacing the XVIII Corps as early as August.

37. Purvis Group Diary, 6; and HQ, ARCENT (CENTCOM Planning Group), briefing titled, "ARCENT Contingency Operations (H2-H3 Brief)," dated 30 October on General Yeosock's briefings-slide index. Schwarzkopf is scathing about the "western excursion," which he sees as unwarranted interference in professional matters by civilian political leaders. Schwarzkopf, *Doesn't Take A Hero*, 368–69. See also de la Billiere, *The Storm Command*, 103.

38. David Hoffman, "Baker, Fahd Set Command Plan: Accord Helps Prepare for Possible Attack, "*The Washington Post*, 6 November 1990, A1, and A16.

39. Purvis Group Diary, 6.

40. Ibid.

41. Ibid., 7. General Yeosock's briefing files hold a briefing dated 5 November, titled, "2 Corps Option Packet by ARCENT Staff to CG." Either date is possible given CG's schedule but 2d looks more likely since CG went to visit 24th ID during day of 5th. Slides dated 5th may have been prepared after briefing to CG for presentation to the CINC.

42. Purvis Group Diary, 7. A complete history of the deception plan was prepared by Major Louis J. Ovnic, the ARCENT G3 planner who took responsibility for ARCENT deception planning. HQ, ARCENT, G3 AFRD-DTP, Memorandum for Record, Subject: Command Report Operation Desert Storm—Deception Operations, dated 14 March 1991.

43. Purvis Group Diary, 7. Handwritten notes by General Yeosock of CINC's briefing, copy in possession of author.

44. Purvis Group Diary, 7–8. Copy of handwritten notes taken by General Yeosock.

45. George Bush, "The Need for an Offensive Military Option," in *The Gulf War Reader: History, Documents, Opinions*, Michael L. Sifty and Christopher Cerf, eds. (New York: Times Books, 1991), 228–29. Department of Defense, Office of the Assistant Secretary of Defense (Public Affairs), News Briefing, Secretary of Defense Dick Cheney, Chairman of the Joint Chiefs of Staff, General Colin Powell, DOD News Briefing, Thursday, November 8, 1990–4:45 P.M. Ann Devroy, "Bush Orders 200,000 More Troops to Gulf," *The Washington Post*, 9 November 1990, A1, A32. Michael R. Gordon, "Bush Sends New Units to Gulf to Provide Offensive Option; U.S. Force Could Reach 380,000; Tank Buildup a Key; President Suggests New Troops May Persuade Iraq to Back Down," *The New York Times*, 9 November 1990, A1 and A12.

46. Schwarzkopf, *Doesn't Take a Hero*, 380–84, describes 14 November briefing from CINC's perspective.

47. Ibid., 383.

48. *Journals of War*, a VHS tape produced by Kurtis Productions, Ltd., in Association with Arts & Entertainment Network (1991). Tape in possession of author.

49. Both General Peay and General Luck had occasion to be reprimanded by the CINC for presuming to make suggestions concerning operational planning. General Peay told the author of his experience himself. General Luck's experience was related by one of his senior staff officers. In all likelihood, Schwarzkopf was touchy about people getting into his planning business because of all the help he was receiving from Washington.

50. Purvis Group Diary, 9–10.

51. Ibid., 10. Document titled, "COMUSARCENT Desert Shield Operations Plan 003, Operation to Conduct Offensive Operations Against Iraqi Forces," dated 1200 23 November 1990, enclosure 13 to HQ, ARCENT, G3 (Plans) AFRD-DTP, Memorandum thru Colonel Holloway, Chief, G3 Plans, for Colonel Swain, USARCENT Historian, Subject: Command Report on Operations Desert Shield and

Desert Storm, dated 20 March 1991. Following description of late November concept is taken from this document.

52. Ibid., 11.

53. Purvis Group Diary, 10.

54. Ibid., 11-13. For VII Corps alternative, see briefing, HQ, VII Corps, titled, "Planning Update," dated 5 December 1990, presented to General Yeosock. On General Rhame volunteering for mission of breach, see interview with Major General Thomas Rhame, Fort Riley, Kansas, 26 July 1991, 57-58; and interview with Colonel Stan Cherrie, Fort Leavenworth, Kansas, 29 August 1991, 3.

55. Purvis Group Diary, 12-13. The CENTCOM Desert Storm OPLAN, dated 16 December, allocated the two allied units for planning. For French, see award-winning staff of *U.S. News and World Reports, Triumph Without Victory: The Unreported History of the Persian Gulf War*, 314; de la Billiere, *Storm Command*, 50-51, 159-60; Schwarzkopf, *Doesn't Take a Hero*, 390. For British, see de la Billiere, *Storm Command*, 48, 92-95, 132-39, 150-52; and Schwarzkopf, *Doesn't Take a Hero*, 385-86.

56. Ibid. See also HQ, ARCENT, G3 (Plans), AFRD-DTP, Memorandum for USARCENT Historian, Colonel Swain, Subject: HQ, USARCENT, G3 Plans, Historical Narrative of Desert Shield, Desert Storm, Defense and Restoration of Kuwait, and Redeployment, dated 6 April 1991, 20-24.

57. HQ, ARCENT, G3 (Plans) AFRD-DTP, Memorandum for USARCENT Historian, Colonel Swain, Subject: HQ, USARCENT, G3 plans, Historical Narrative of Desert Shield, Desert Storm, Defense and Restoration of Kuwait, and Redeployment, dated 6 April 1991, 7-9.

4
Planning a Ground Offensive II: The ARCENT Process

The Third Army planning process was marked by continuous dialogue. Discussion took place horizontally, within the ARCENT staff, and vertically, between Central Command above and subordinate corps and support command staffs below. Major decisions were made, or in some cases deferred, at commanders' conferences.[1] Similar processes were going on in each corps. This sort of activity lasted into late January and up to the "commander's huddle," when the army commander and his principal subordinates gathered at King Khalid Military City on 1 February for a final meeting.

By the time General Schwarzkopf and his component, corps, and support command commanders briefed Secretary of Defense Cheney and General Powell in mid-December, the Third Army plan had taken a fairly clear form. The concept called for a two-corps attack on a broad front that would block the Iraqi routes of escape and destroy the Republican Guard Forces Command (RGFC).[2] The Air Force component was responsible for isolating the theater of operations south of the Euphrates River by keeping bridges down. The army commander's intent was to penetrate and envelop the defensive forces, fix and block forward-deployed heavy forces in order to secure the flanks and lines of communication, and continue the attack deep to destroy the Republican Guard.[3]

The VII Corps would be the coalition mass of maneuver. It would carry out the decisive part of the theater commander's ground attack plan as the Third Army's main effort. The 1st U.K. Armored Division, after December under tactical control of VII Corps, would pass through a 1st Infantry Division breach, turn east, and defeat the Iraqi tactical reserves. It would secure, thereby, the deep movement of the U.S. heavy "fist." The fist itself was to consist of the 2d Armored Cavalry Regiment, the 1st and 3d Armored Divisions, the 1st Infantry Division (once the breach was secure), and the 1st Cavalry Division(-), should the latter be released to Third Army by the theater commander. While VII Corps' mission was oriented toward force rather than terrain, it was assigned a zone of action within which to maneuver. The corps zone did not include the highway running northwest from Basrah south of the Euphrates River. That corridor belonged to the XVIII Airborne Corps and, ultimately, to the 24th Infantry Division.

Initially, the VII Corps plan called for the entire corps to pass through a breach to be made by the 1st Infantry Division in the Iraqi defensive line. As the corps grew familiar with the ground and identified the end of the Iraqi defenses—which terminated "in the air" (or simply petered out) about forty kilometers from an escarpment that dominated the right flank of XVIII Corps' zone—plans for the two armored divisions and armored cavalry regiment were gradually modified to move the core of the iron fist around the end of the Iraqi positions but still east of the escarpment. This idea was tested in a simulation conducted in January at King Khalid Military City by the team from the Battle Command Training Program (BCTP). In consultation with his division commanders and in the face of his staff's continuing doubts, Lieutenant General Frederick M. Franks, Jr., revised his plan. The modified version called for a maneuver around the enemy defenses by the 1st and 3d Armored Divisions (behind the 2d Armored Cavalry Regiment), with only the 1st U.K. Armored Division following the 1st Infantry Division through the breach.[4] The end run was to be a tight squeeze. It required the 3d Armored Division to move in a column of brigades with a fifteen-kilometer front. The 1st Armored Division, with a frontage of twenty-five kilometers on its left, was only marginally better off, but this maneuver avoided the necessity of passing successive divisions deployed in column through an obstacle belt.

Once beyond the breach, the corps' armored fist was to move north to the vicinity of Phase Line (PL) Smash, a lateral road about halfway to the Euphrates. It would then turn gradually to the right, looking for the RGFC, which it expected to encounter in Objective Collins, a large open expanse of desert just northeast of the point where the corps would turn eastward across PL Smash. In effect, the corps plan called for two successive, deliberate attacks: first, the breaching operations by the 1st Infantry Division and, second, the movement to contact by the armored fist. The weight of the corps' supporting forces, principally its artillery, would have to be shifted from right to left, from one effort to the other, while the corps moved north. Maintaining balance and concentration would require a good deal of the corps' energy as it moved to the battle.

XVIII Corps, on the extreme left of the coalition line, was to launch the 101st Airborne Division toward As Samawah, on the Euphrates, in the far northwestern corner of the corps sector, to block the Iraqi escape route down Highway 8. The 24th Infantry Division was to launch its three brigades into the empty desert to link up with the 101st and then turn down the same highway to attack enemy concentrations along the river. The French 6th Light Armored Division, under tactical control of the XVIII Airborne Corps and with the 82d Airborne Division in support, was to attack north on the Third Army's left flank toward the settlement and airfield at As Salman. The 3d Armored Cavalry Regiment was to attack on the corps' right flank, parallel to the VII Corps boundary (the plan called for the regiment to maintain contact with its neighbor).[5]

Planning was based on the assumption that forces and supplies, both of which depended upon a fixed and fairly predictable rate of arrival in theater, would be prepositioned in tactical assembly areas (TAAs) east of Wadi al Batin by 31 January and that the corps would have two weeks, during the preliminary air campaign, to move into attack positions west of the wadi. These assessments are important precisely because they were fixed. VII Corps' 3d Armored Division *could not* complete its arrival in Saudi Arabia until 31 January (in fact, it was late due to shipping delays and did not close in the TAA until 12 February).[6] The fact that the air attack began on 17 January in no way influenced the ground forces' arrival schedule. Indeed, ARCENT's principal task throughout the planning effort seems to have been to find ways, using computer graphics, to display the progressive build-up so that the higher decision makers could understand what forces they had to work with at any given moment. In resolving this problem, the Third Army commander was often his own action officer, supported by his small personal staff with their desk-top graphics. The success, or lack thereof, of any briefing to Schwarzkopf depended on the clarity of the display of information, thus making a staff officer's facility with computer graphics an essential skill at higher levels of command.

The critical constraint was strategic sealift, particularly roll-on and roll-off ships that carried unit equipment sets (soldiers were usually moved by air). There were not enough ships to establish a continuous arrival rate equal to the capability of available ports to receive units. The ground operation was subject, first of all, to the arrival of heavy forces and was constrained by limits on strategic sealift. Second, it was limited by capacity for operational ground movement, which was plagued by shortages in heavy wheeled vehicles, HETs, heavy expanded mobility tactical trucks (HEMTTs), fuelers, and so forth. The quantity of these unglamorous vehicles fluctuated, depending on the Army's ability to bring in, or even find, long-haul trucks of various types. The December briefing to Secretary of Defense Cheney showed a theater requirement for 1,295 HETs and a projected strength of only 788 available from all sources. Only 250

HETs were expected to arrive in the peninsula by 15 January.[7] These wheeled vehicles established the port throughput rate, which never equaled unloading capacity.

G-day, the date of the ground attack, depended on the ability of planners to get coalition forces to the start line. If VII Corps were to participate, that would not be possible at all before 31 January. Even then, the forces would still be incomplete. This was the real significance of the famous December interview with the newly arrived deputy commander in chief, General Calvin Waller. Waller told the press covering Cheney's December briefing that the Army would not be ready to attack by the UN deadline in January (see figure 12). This was correct, although there was certainly sufficient combat power in the peninsula to conduct an air offensive, a fact that appears to have escaped the journalists.[8]

The other key operational issue was the likely ratio of opposition to friendly forces. This calculation was, by necessity, purely Jominian. It was presented as such on a briefing slide that projected 50 percent attrition of the enemy by the air campaign. Given this assumption, VII Corps would have an advantage of 11.5:1 at the breach site, 3.8:1 en route to the Republican Guard, and 2:1 at the decisive point.[9] These figures are important because the overall force ratio expected in the VII Corps' sector (counting friendly and enemy brigades as roughly equivalent) was assumed to be no better than 1.3:1, far below any acceptable theoretical rule of thumb. VII Corps was seeking, in Jomini's words, "to obtain by free and rapid movements the advantage of bringing the mass of the troops against fractions of the enemy."[10] That these calculations may have been proved pessimistic by subsequent events in no way detracts from their influence on the planners and fighters who believed them at the time.

Between 23 and 28 December, a group directed by General Pagonis conducted a planning exercise in Dhahran to develop a final movement plan for repositioning Third Army west of Wadi al Batin. Pagonis and his staff had been developing movement plans to support various offensive options since September. The purpose of the December exercise was to fill in details for the execution of Schwarzkopf's concept, with particular regard to logistics—the provisioning of food, fuel, ammunition, medical support, and, always the critical issue, transportation. All this had to be laid out against a schedule.[11] Major Steve Holley from the Third Army G3 (plans) and Colonel Robert Kleimon, the ARCENT transportation officer, represented the ARCENT G3 and G4. The result was publication of a

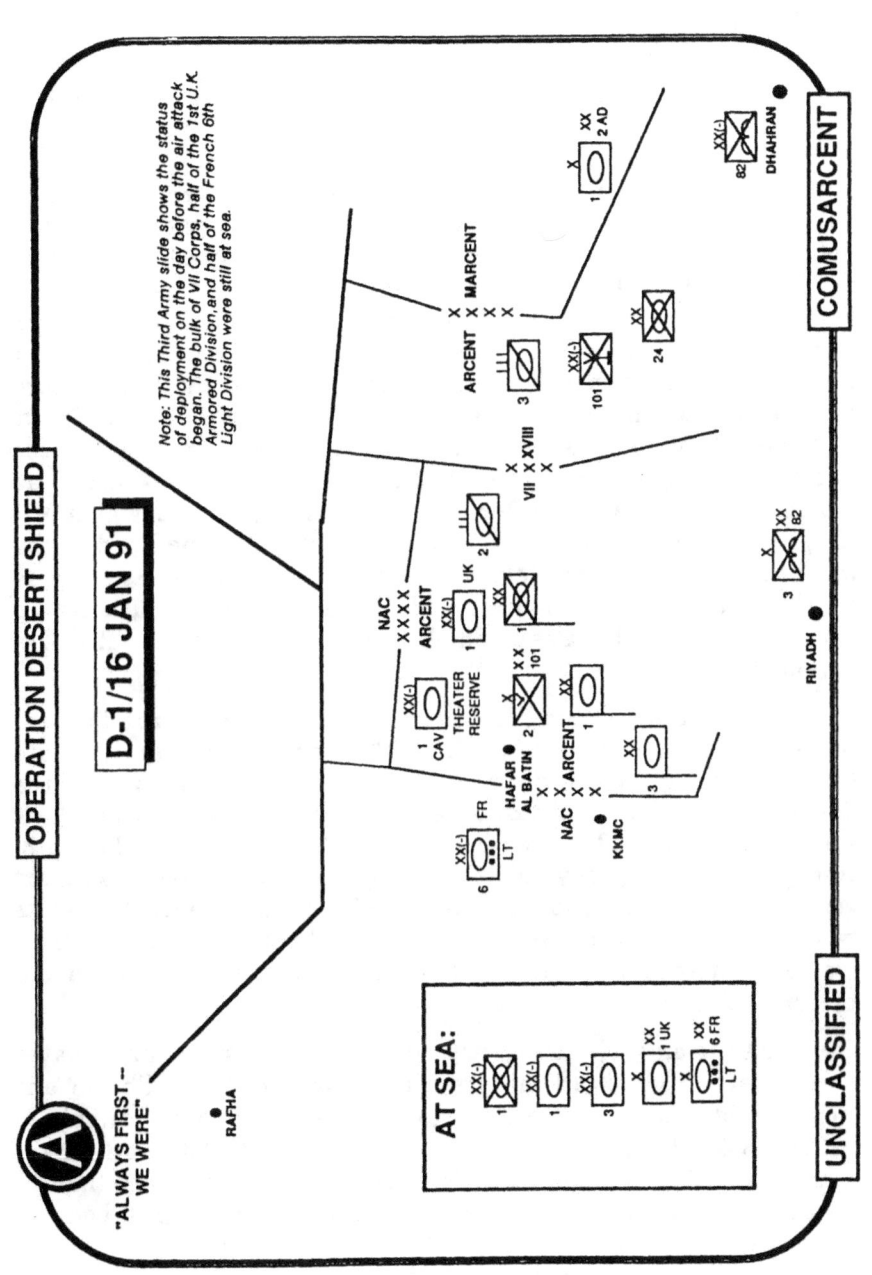

Figure 12.

transportation annex for the attack plan and a briefing for the commander in chief that was given on 28 December.[12]

Schwarzkopf's strict guidance in support of the deception effort was that no preparations for Desert Storm were to be made west of Wadi al Batin prior to initiation of the air campaign. Because of the distances involved in the operational redeployment and those anticipated during the offensive, it would be necessary to create two forward logistic bases (one for each corps) west of the wadi. This could not begin before D-day. The movement briefing assumed a D-day (air attack day) of 16 January and a G-day (ground attack day) of 1 February. Based upon these dates, the logistics plan provided for creation of two theater army logistic bases, Charlie and Echo, west of the wadi. Three intermediate bases—Alpha, Bravo, and Delta—were to be established in the east (see figure 13). These could be filled prior to D-day. They were essential, in any event, to support the forces deploying into tactical assembly areas, as well as serving as intermediate depots thereafter. Log Base Alpha, around which VII Corps was to form in the desert, was located on Tapline Road at the forward end of the corps' defensive (Desert Shield) zone. As early as October, Pagonis and his staff had planned to begin building up supplies forward in the Desert Shield zone to facilitate future offensive options.[13]

The two corps would plan subsequently to open corps forward bases (Oscar, Romeo, and "Nellingen") along Main Supply Route (MSR) Virginia, the lateral oiled road (also PL Smash) through the desert about halfway to the Euphrates. These bases would be one day's round trip along the Tapline Road from the theater bases to the south. A day's round trip beyond MSR Virginia, the division support commands would establish their forward bases, and the fighting units would operate about a day's drive beyond them. In short, the army would reach its operational (logistic) limit at about the point it ran out of terrain to clear.[14]

Based upon projected transportation resources and anticipated arrival dates, Pagonis and his group estimated Log Bases Charlie and Echo would reach their desired stockage levels (five-day supply of rations, 3.4 million gallons of fuel, and 15,000 to 45,000 short tons of ammunition for XVIII and VII Corps respectively) no sooner than 11 February.[15] The build-up of Army medical capacity, 11,280 beds (in Saudi Arabia or loaded on vehicles for movement), would be finished no sooner than 13 February.[16] Units were expected to be in attack positions by 7 February.[17]

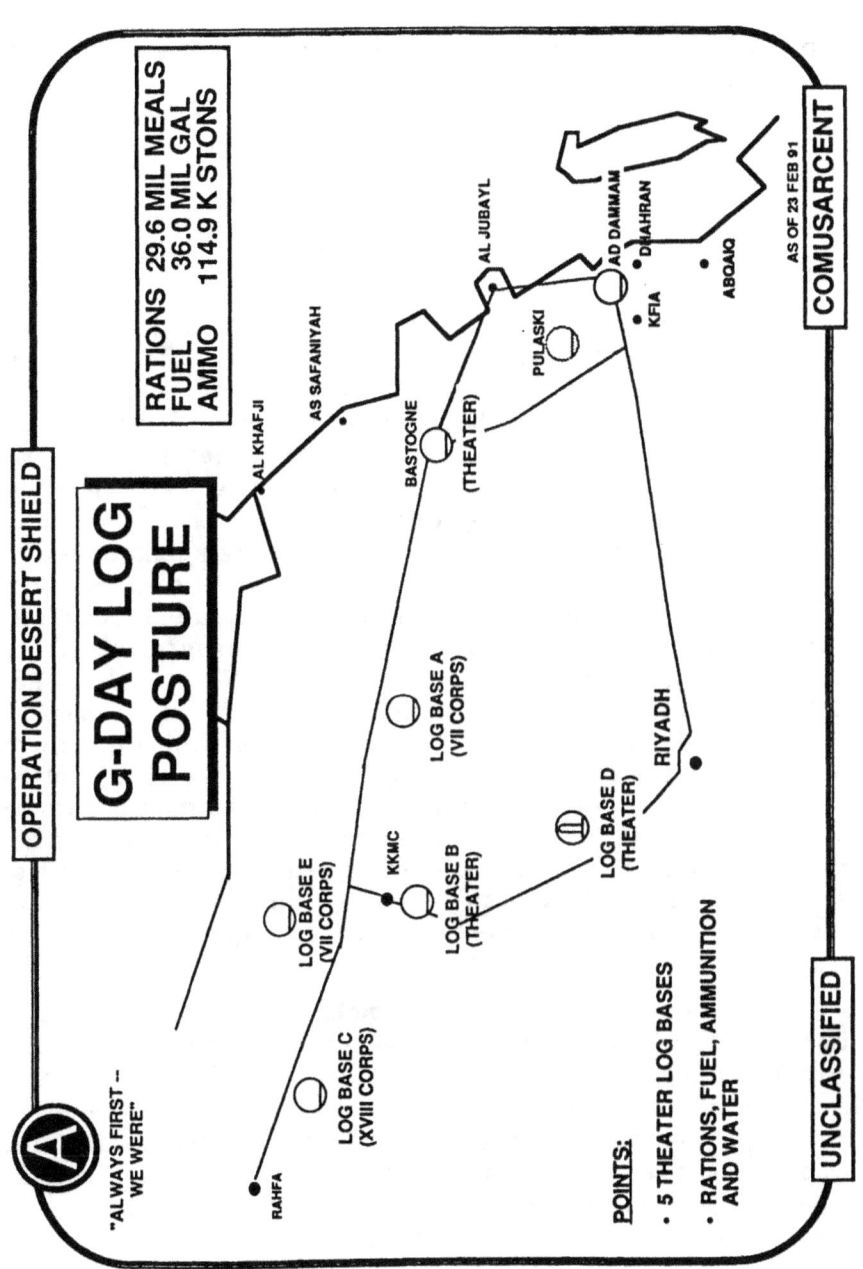

Figure 13.

Each briefing chart told the CINC where he would be on the road to completion on any possible G-day. Three large flow charts displaying transportation availability were created. These showed the daily requirement for line-haul trucks and a forecast of the number available. Interestingly enough, the transportation estimates showed a deficit of vehicles, which would have to be made up from some source if time lines were to be met (see figure 14). In short, success required significant acquisition of transport vehicles and movement of them on schedule. The CINC told Pagonis that these projections were his "contract."[18]

From 27 to 30 December, while the logistics study was being completed, the Third Army commanders and their staffs met at the new army headquarters for the MAPEX. Originally, General Arnold's intention was that this should be a war-gamed exercise, but this seems to have run afoul of the commanders' sense of their prerogatives or just the number of people involved.[19] Instead of a war game, this meeting was, in fact, a mutual briefing session in which questions could be asked by the commanders and principal staff officers (and the staffs then turned loose to resolve the issues raised) and issues requiring further work or decisions could be identified. The results were briefed back to the commanders on the 30th. Representatives from CENTCOM, CENTAF, MARCENT, and SOCCENT attended, and, indeed, one of the major long-term issues carried out of the exercise was a concern about the extent to which the Army would be able to influence the air preparation of the battlefield. Another issue involved the distribution of resources. This was generally accomplished to the detriment of the XVIII Airborne Corps, now a supporting actor rather than the only show in town. The evolving plan called for the corps to attack into an area that just did not have many enemy forces to overcome. General Luck appeared to find this experience somewhat frustrating.[20]

On 4 January, Yeosock and Arnold went again to Central Command headquarters to brief the theater commander on the ARCENT concept of operations. The object of the briefing was somewhat confused. Information had arrived that Syria would not agree to its troops participating in the offensive. At best, this required some readjustment of missions along the coalition front lines. At worst, it sowed suspicions that Syrian forces might go over to the Iraqis if the attack itself seemed unlikely to succeed.[21] Moreover, the Egyptians used the event to request substantial support from the United States as insurance against failure. Among other things, Egypt requested reinforcement by an American division and attachment of

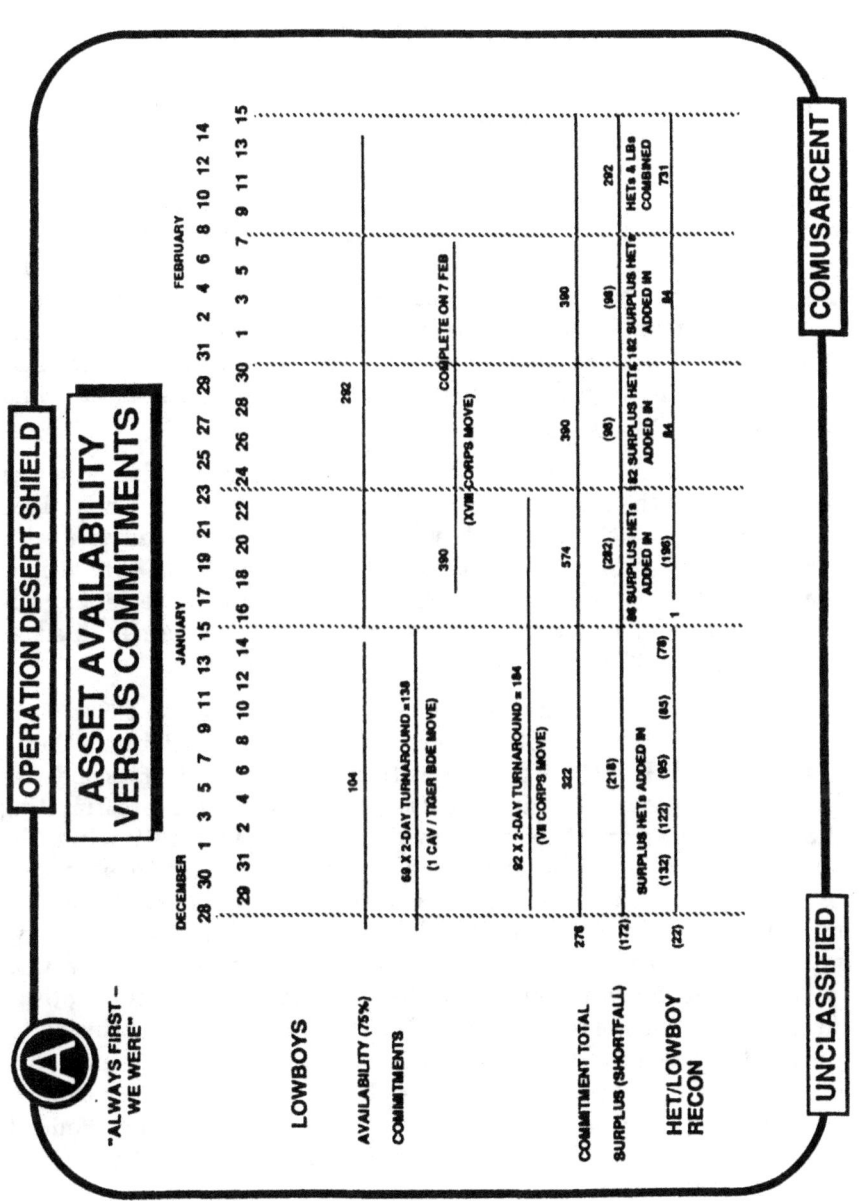

Figure 14.

U.S. attack helicopters. Yeosock was challenged to find alternatives to present to Schwarzkopf that would reassure the Egyptians without weakening the theater main effort.

The briefing seems to have been intended originally to address the adjustments that the Syrian decision might demand, but Yeosock also had another agenda. He had to "smoke out" from Schwarzkopf, now rather late in the day, clear indications of the limits of his own freedom of action as field army commander. Somewhat typically, he would do this by indirection, to no little discomfort on the part of Arnold, his G3, who in such cases served as the stationary target for the CINC. Schwarzkopf's patience was probably not improved by the frustrations that had led to the need for such a briefing: four days of high-level squabbling with his Arab allies, a report that a British staff officer in London might have compromised the plan, and the fact that he had spent the day of the briefing in the north, attending a grand review for the Saudi king.[22]

Yeosock and Arnold went to brief Schwarzkopf with a set of options rather than a single ARCENT concept of operations. This method frustrated Schwarzkopf, who dismissed his subordinates with some heat and ordered them to come back in four days with a new briefing.[23] Arnold was clearly crestfallen by this experience, but Yeosock left believing he now knew the rules of the game, albeit at some cost to his G3's self-esteem.[24]

Schwarzkopf had attacked his subordinates' plan on three main points.[25] The first was the decision to send the XVIII Airborne Corps' 101st and 24th Divisions northwest to As Samawah. The second was his belief that ARCENT and VII Corps were greatly overestimating the practical strength of the Iraqis, particularly following the anticipated 50 percent attrition of them by the air interdiction program. Finally, Schwarzkopf was extremely discomfited by the idea that, as the plan was presented to him, VII Corps intended to observe an operational pause, once the corps was through to the enemy tactical depths, to rearm and refuel in the vicinity of Objective Collins. According to the one non-general officer present (the "slide turner" at the briefing), Schwarzkopf expressed the view that if VII Corps halted along Phase Line Smash to rearm and refuel, it would miss the war that he predicted would be over in twenty-four to forty-eight hours.[26] Notably, in light of later developments, General Franks was not present at this briefing.

Schwarzkopf's "guidance" addressed a number of other issues for reexamination: the role of the 82d Airborne Division (as a follow-on force and in support of the French 6th Armored Division), the location of boundaries, the timing of attacks (synchronization of the corps), and the location of the XVIII Airborne Corps attack. Schwarzkopf directed that forces stay out of built-up areas and towns and that no force be put at risk to block Highway 8. Logistic support remained a further concern.[27]

There were substantive issues about which Schwarzkopf had good reason to be concerned. Leaving aside for the moment his objection to the XVIII Corps plan, the CINC's optimism about the Iraqis' powers of resistance seems to have been borne out by the events that followed. There is no evidence, however, that he ever convinced his subordinates that he was correct in this view, and ARCENT's assessments remained sober through G-day. Schwarzkopf seems to have been unwilling to impose his views on his Army commanders and unable to convince them. His concerns about the threat and the importance of maintaining momentum are important in light of subsequent events.

The idea of an operational pause was a concept that seems to have originated with staff planners. It was an idea that senior commanders were never able to kill. It was compounded by a confusion over the precise meaning of this quasi-doctrinal term. General Franks had decided as early as a pre-Desert Shield Battle Command Training Program exercise in Germany that accepting an operational pause, if by that one meant stopping the entire corps, would be to surrender the initiative.[28] At the MAPEX in December, he spoke of the importance of relentless attack.[29]

The ARCENT staff, nonetheless, had discussed such a pause along Phase Line Smash, the one east-west line of communications (MSR Virginia) in southeastern Iraq running through As Salman. But Yeosock ultimately rejected the idea for the same reason Franks did. Indeed, in a postwar discussion, Yeosock indicated that above the brigade level, the corps was always in motion. The reconnaissance line, he noted, advances at about five kilometers an hour, slow enough that the armored brigades, which are the fighting formations of a corps, can stop periodically to rest and refuel and still catch up by employing their power of acceleration, since they are traveling through a zone already cleared.[30] In Yeosock's mind, a pause was no more than an intellectual stocktaking. He clearly believed such stocktaking would be necessary before closing with the Republican Guard. The Guard was bound to react to VII Corps' initial penetration, and the final attack plan had to account for whatever the enemy did. It also appears that he intended to meet with the corps commanders to review the situation when the troops crossed PL Smash, but that would not, in itself, require stopping divisions, which advance pretty much on their own.³¹ Interestingly enough, given some of the postwar criticism, Franks remembered later that General Waller raised the matter of a pause with him just prior to G-day, at a time when Waller was acting as Third Army commander in Yeosock's absence.³² The idea of a "pause" seems to have been on a lot of minds.

Whatever the commanders thought, the staffs knew that the maneuver brigades (and divisions) would run out of fuel about the time they got to PL Smash, and they continued to address among themselves the necessary refueling halt in terms of a pause. The 2d Armored Cavalry Regiment assumed the need to stop for fuel on PL Smash in a late December staff exercise. The 1st Armored Division plan allowed for time to refuel and regain balance before attacking across PL Smash.³³ In the XVIII Corps area, the 24th Infantry Division foresaw a pause-refueling halt before advancing beyond PL Smash and again before its last attack southeast along Highway 8.

The fuel problem did not go away. The question boiled down to how much of the force would stop, at any time, to refuel and rearm before getting on with the war. Could refueling be accommodated by rippling it along the front, a brigade at a time? Because large units, divisions and corps, rarely exercise as complete units in the field, the problem of refueling a division, much less a corps on the move, is seldom confronted. Moreover, refueling in an offensive posture is harder to accomplish, than while in a delay or retrograde movement, because of the need to carry fuel forward to the moving forces rather than being able to preposition it along the way. It seems apparent that the term "pause" had different connotations for different officers depending on their immediate concerns and that much of the discussion that seemed to settle on the issue only sowed further confusion.

There remained the problems of the XVIII Corps plan to attack toward As Samawah on the Euphrates, in the northwest corner of the corps' sector, and Schwarzkopf's belief that the ARCENT commanders overestimated the enemy. Aside from the distance over which sustainment would have to be accomplished—down the road to Rafha and up to As Samawah—this objective would take the 24th Infantry Division and the 101st Airborne Division away from the main attack before they turned down the Euphrates valley along Highway 8. The force, attacking into a great empty area, would not be in supporting distance of VII Corps.

Why had the army commander not pulled the 24th Infantry Division in toward the main attack to begin with? Perhaps the first explanation to suggest itself is that the idea of going to As Samawah had originated with Schwarzkopf himself, and he had shown himself ready to react violently to any attempt to question his concept by providing alternatives. Indeed, at the MAPEX, General Luck stated quite clearly that the principal argument for the move was its origin.[34] The CINC said to do it that way! Second, Yeosock would seem to have been reluctant to interfere with the corps commander's judgment of how to do his business, perhaps as a result of an ambiguity still existing about the army commander's authority over operational questions between the CINC and the corps commanders. Luck had been given a mission and forces to accomplish it, and Yeosock was not disposed to interfere with his subordinates unless he perceived a risk to the whole operation.

Third, XVIII Corps had a real practical problem with the alternative to its planned route. A large area in the center of the corps' sector consisted of very rough, rocky terrain. If the corps sent its mobile forces east, they would have to move across this area, perhaps against resistance; they might also be pushed into a narrow sector of advance in order not to interfere with the VII Corps' maneuver space, essential for it in the main attack when it would send as large a force as possible around the enemy fortifications.[35] If there was resistance, the 24th Division might not arrive at the Euphrates in time to achieve its mission of blocking the enemy route of withdrawal.

Fourth, there were few potential lines of support available to XVIII Corps, but one ran from Rafha, through As Salman, to As Samawah. The 24th Division probably could have gotten to that point to link up with the 101st, but it would have become increasingly attenuated as it advanced down the Highway 8 corridor toward Basrah. Indeed, the plan provided only for a ground advance to Tallil (with a possible follow-on assault by the 101st toward An Nasiriyah). On the other hand, if the corps' heavy forces were to advance in the eastern sector, as they ultimately did, initial support would have to come through As Salman and turn east until a more direct route was created by engineers in the rear of the advancing heavy forces. Then, VII Corps would have to open a line of communication for them through its own rear area once they turned southeast. The VII Corps could not do that, however, until after its own maneuver forces had turned east, and no commander likes his MSR in someone else's territory. This, in fact, is what was done. XVIII Corps did try and fail to gain possession of the necessary strip of terrain by requesting a boundary change, a request pursued into Desert Storm. Consideration was given to attaching the 24th Division to VII Corps for that part of the operation, but the idea never gained support with either General Waller during his interregnum as Third Army commander or General Yeosock.[36]

In short, these questions came down to a subjective appreciation of relative risk and comparative gain. If the Third Army and XVIII Corps commanders elected to move the 24th Infantry and 101st Divisions east, there was the risk of the enemy reacting to the initial attack and confronting the turning force[37] in compartmented and generally rough terrain. There was also a risk inherent in a more complex sustainment problem and, perhaps most important, the risk of appearing to challenge Schwarzkopf in an area of command he felt was peculiarly his own. Nonetheless, it is difficult to argue with Schwarzkopf's final conclusion. If VII Corps required the assistance of XVIII Corps' heavy forces to destroy the Republican Guard, the "Victory Division" would have been too far away under the original XVIII Corps plan. If it turned out that they were not required for the destruction mission, any slowdown in their northward progress as a consequence of eastern sustainment problems would not matter much. The CINC might always call on air power to block the Highway 8 line of retreat until the ground forces could establish a blocking position. The 101st Airborne Division made it to the river first in any event! The advance to the Euphrates by the 24th Division was almost unimpeded except for the difficulties of terrain, and the division was on the river on G+2. The advance of the Victory Division demonstrated again B. H. Liddell Hart's assertion: "Natural hazards, however formidable, are less dangerous and less uncertain than fighting hazards. All conditions are more calculable, all obstacles more surmountable, than those of human resistance. By reasoned calculation and preparation they can be over-come almost to time-table."[38]

All this seems to have been Yeosock and Luck's conclusion as well, because when Schwarzkopf was briefed again on 8 January, the axis of advance for the 24th Division was moved to the general direction of An Nasiriyah to the northeast, with the 24th Division and 3d Armored Cavalry Regiment, in effect, becoming the outer wing of Schwarzkopf's great wheel.[39] At this briefing, the slides depicting the build-up were far clearer and more definitive. Not surprisingly, Schwarzkopf approved the plan. What should have been far more unsettling for the army commander was the theater commander's very optimistic views about the likely effect of the air effort on the Iraqis' ability to resist on the ground and the idea that ARCENT commanders were greatly overestimating the strength of the enemy.

Those who would actually be called upon to lead ground forces into battle would remain far less sanguine about the effect of the air campaign on enemy capabilities than the theater commander, and therein lay much mischief. Schwarzkopf may appear to have been vindicated by events, though the clear technological advantages enjoyed by ground forces in direct-fire engagements and artillery counterbattery fire may lead one to underestimate the resistance still remaining in the Republican Guard forces and the Iraqis' better regular army units.[40]

Before 28 February, none of that could be known for sure. General Franks, who would lead the coalition's main attack, argued consistently for what he believed were three essentials for success. These were relentless attack (no pauses once the operation was under way), maintenance of concentration—hitting with a closed fist rather than open fingers—and the absolute need for three heavy divisions at the point of impact with the RGFC, this based upon various means of analysis and simulation and, no less, on professional judgment.[41]

The need for concentration meant a tightly controlled advance and a corps attack that moved deliberately in a particular sequence. The fist, the 1st and 3d Armored Divisions and the 2d Armored Cavalry Regiment, would have to move under corps control to begin with, just to avoid having the units separated or intermingled—something to be avoided, not only to maintain concentration but also to avoid fratricide. The rate of march, like that of a fleet at sea (which the divisions so closely resembled on the desert floor), could not exceed the speed of the slowest vehicle, very likely the M109 howitzer, which moved no faster than fifteen miles per hour. Moreover, the whole body could not get so far ahead of the 1st U.K. Armored Division as to expose the "fist's" eastern flank to interruption by Iraqi tactical reserves. Moreover, since the 1st Cavalry Division(-) did not appear likely to be released in time to get into the VII Corps fight with the RGFC (as the division's release was increasingly tied to the success of the Egyptian attack), the 1st Infantry Division would have to be the third heavy division upon which the VII Corps commander believed success rested. That meant, again, that the wheeling divisions would have to retard their movement long enough for the 1st Infantry to breach the enemy line, pass the 1st U.K. through, then fall in on the "fist's" right or rear. This, too, called for a highly disciplined, closely controlled maneuver, not the "devil-take-the-hindmost" charge-of-the-light brigade rash and gallant dash the more romantic critics would seem to have anticipated.42

The difference in opinions about the situation comes back to differing degrees of confidence in the ability of the air operations to break the spirit of the only forces in the theater that mattered—the heavy forces of the Republican Guard and the regular Iraqi Army. Also worthy of much discussion were the implications of concentrating and maneuvering twenty-five armored battalions, sixteen mechanized battalions, and three regimental cavalry squadrons (8,508 tracked vehicles, 27,652 wheels) in a confined space. After 8 January, however, the broad outline of the ARCENT Desert Storm plan was set, and internal planning and negotiation turned to matters of force allocation and details of execution.

On 1 February, General Yeosock held his final commander's planning meeting at King Khalid Military City, site of his mobile command post and the support command forward headquarters. Attending were the corps and support command commanders, the ARCENT's primary staff, and the commander of the theater reserve, Major General John Tilelli, Jr. By 1 February, air operations were in their sixteenth day. Most of VII Corps had closed into the tactical assembly areas around King Khalid Military City, and XVIII Corps was well into its displacement to the west. G-day was approaching, but as yet, the estimated attrition of the Iraqi forces in Kuwait was disappointing to the Army commanders.43

The logistic build-up continued, and anyone driving south on either of the MSRs would have been overwhelmed by the number of heavy trucks of all sorts on the road north. The most important service member in theater was probably the military policeman at the intersection of the main highways at Hafar al Batin, who fed the traffic from east and south into the combined westward flow (see figure 15 for distances between major locations). No one driving south or east in the face of the endless convoys—containing everything from armored vehicles on carriers to fuel trucks, ammunition trucks, and flat-beds full of mail or, alternatively, prefab privies—could doubt a major attack was imminent.

The "commander's huddle" was held in the aftermath of the battle of Khafji. Khafji was the single Iraqi attempt, on 29 January, to conduct a spoiling attack against the Saudi Joint Forces Command East and the U.S. Marine forces. The defeat of this probe seems to have reinforced Schwarzkopf's confidence that the Iraqis would not be able to mount a coherent defense. If anything, Khafji had the opposite effect

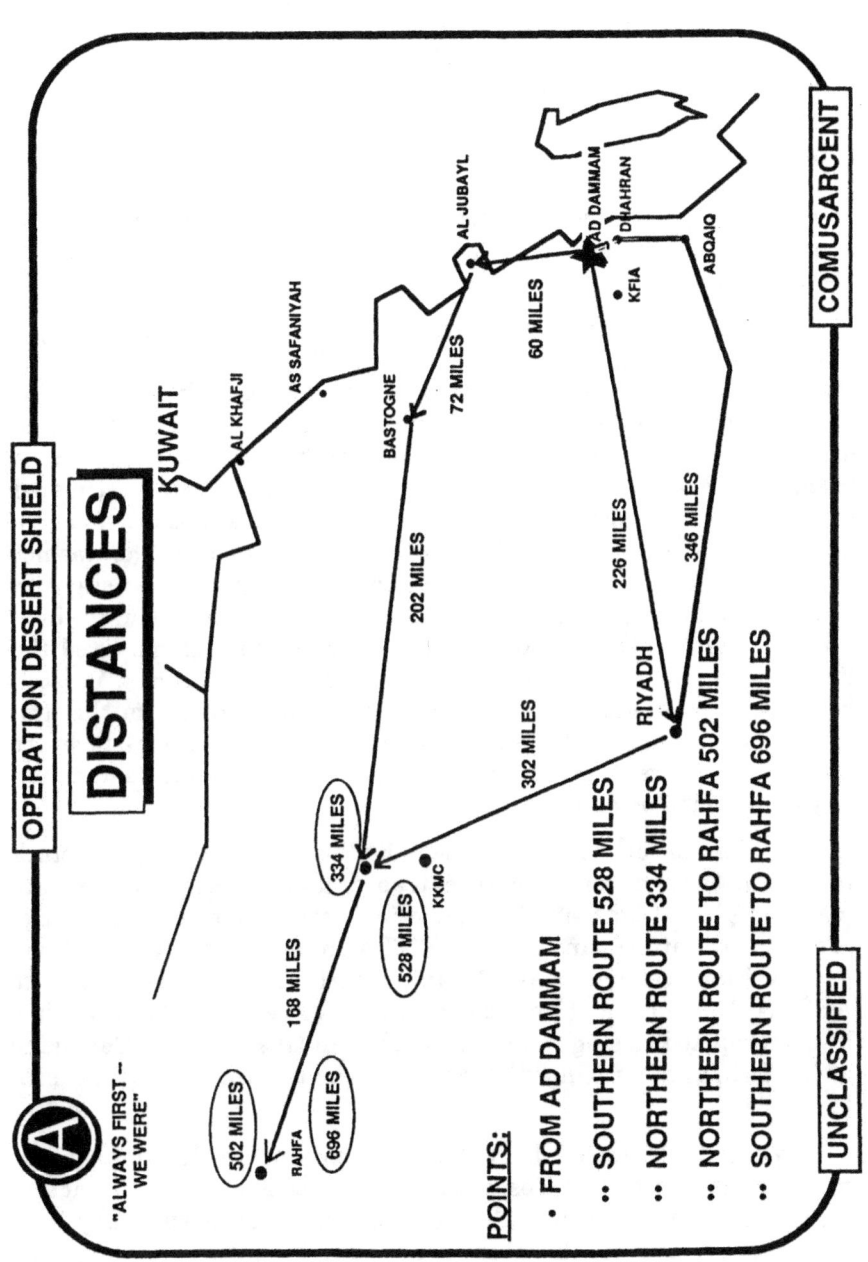

Figure 15.

on the ARCENT commanders.⁴⁴ This was no meeting of men confident that the enemy would not stand. These were men seriously intent on seeing to it that when they closed with an enemy, whom they fully expected to fight and fight hard, they would have every available means at hand. Emphasis was on achieving simultaneous employment of the total ARCENT heavy force (from both corps) when it came time to fight the Republican Guard. Concern was expressed about the potential use of gas by the Iraqis, a capability that was taken quite seriously by all concerned, through G-day and through the four-day battle that followed.

The G2, Major General John Stewart, laid out three major possibilities for employment of the Republican Guard. The first of these was to counterattack if the Iraqis sensed a possibility for success. The second was to fall back and defend Basrah and Kuwait City to drag out the war. A third possibility was another drive south to seize a bargaining chip in case of a stalemate.⁴⁵ General Yeosock estimated the Republican Guard would either "hunker down" at Basrah and give up Kuwait, or it would defend and stand fast. In any event he was not prepared, now or even on G-day, to decide before it was necessary on the particular plan for the destruction of the Republican Guard. Like the Elder Moltke, he would wait and see how the plan survived the first contact.⁴⁶ In response to a question from General Franks, Yeosock said the corps would likely receive its first order from him the first night, but it would be for execution seventy-two to ninety-six hours later.⁴⁷ In the event, however, the war would move much faster than anyone anticipated on 1 February.

By the time of the "commander's huddle," the Third Army attack had been thought through in extraordinary detail. Multivariate matrices plotted battlefield preparation actions for the eight days preceding the attack, and the ARCENT staff produced a twenty-three-page written scenario that examined various enemy responses to ARCENT's actions and possible reactions. A detailed planning time line anticipated closing with the Republican Guard Forces Command at $H+74$ in a scenario in which VII Corps did not begin its attack until $H+26$.⁴⁸

What the "huddle" did not do was produce a decision on the preferred option for the destruction of the RGFC or for the actual timing of the attack across the front. In part, these issues may have been deferred because they were not subject to final resolution at that time. That more was not accomplished may also have been because the meeting got badly off schedule and the anticipated executive session could not be held after the staff briefings because General Luck had to leave for another engagement.[49]

The split timing of the various attacks, particularly the synchronization of the attacks of the two corps, had been a point of contention with Schwarzkopf and continued to be a matter of discussion at the "commander's huddle" and after. According to the plan, the Marines and Joint Forces Command East were to attack on G-day. The VII Corps and Joint Forces Command North were to attack on the following day, on G+1, after Iraqi attention and reserves, it was hoped, had been fixed by the G-day attacks. The reasons for this were complex (see figure 16).

Because the engineers would have to establish a direct line of communication behind the 24th Infantry Division and 3d Armored Cavalry Regiment, and the road for this would not be immediately available on G-day, XVIII Corps wanted to attack with the French 6th Light Armored Division and 82d Airborne Division on the corps' left at least twenty-four hours (twice as long as originally planned) before the heavy forces in order to open an initial main supply route through As Salman. The 101st Airborne was to conduct an early morning air assault on G-day as well, to a forward operating base midway to the Euphrates River. Intending to synchronize the coalition's logistics flow with its maneuver, planners also argued that these attacks would pose a threat fixing Iraqi forces not yet deployed to the south. Of course, the attacks might also have drawn Iraqi mobile forces west, before the coalition's heavy forces attacked. That was not necessarily bad, since it would pull the Iraqis into the open for attack from the air and perhaps jeopardize their flank. By seizing As Salman, the corps would not only protect ARCENT's left flank but would allow supplies to flow north, then east, on the lateral oiled road (MSR Virginia). The corps would also build the coalition's first intermediate logistic base to the east of As Salman.[50]

For the most part, the ARCENT's planning effort was completed at the "commander's huddle." Questions of the roles of the two headquarters echelons (corps and army) also seem to have been resolved. On 9 February, the secretary of defense and chairman of the Joint Chiefs of Staff returned to Riyadh to receive a briefing from General Schwarzkopf and his commanders on preparations (and presumably the need) for a ground offensive. General Yeosock; General Franks; the commander of the 24th Infantry Division, Major General Barry McCaffrey; and the commander of the 1st Armored

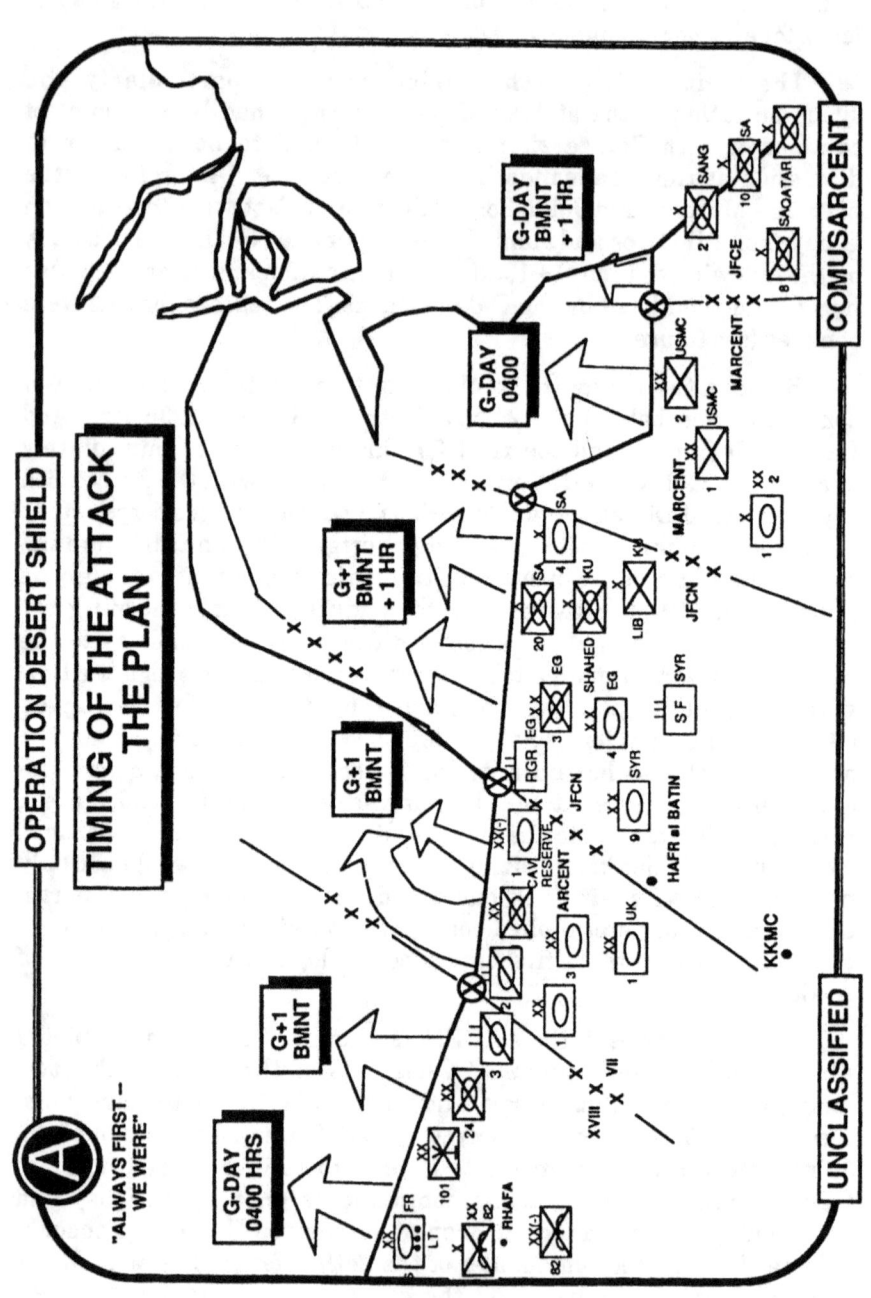

Figure 16.

Division, Major General Ronald H. Griffith, briefed their respective plans.

Prior to the briefing, Schwarzkopf expressed his concerns to Yeosock that the VII Corps attack might be overly cautious in light of the extent of the aerial preparation. "I want VII Corps to *slam* into the Republican Guard," he said, and warned against any pause for rearming and refueling in light of the chemical threat.[51] Yeosock explained Franks' concerns to the theater commander. Beyond that, it is not clear what else he was to do. First of all, he seems to have shared the general skepticism of the other ground commanders that the aerial preparation would be as effective as advertised.[52] Then, he was as aware as his corps commander that the initial challenge for the heavy corps would be winning the necessary maneuver room. This challenge would require, on the one hand, squeezing two heavy divisions into a narrow opening between the Iraqi defensive line and the escarpment to the west and, on the other, a deliberate breaching operation by the 1st Infantry Division. The breaching operation would be followed by a passage of lines by the 1st U.K. Armored Division (reinforced by the U.S. 142d Artillery Brigade, Army National Guard). The British were to turn to the east and attack the Iraqi tactical reserves in order to protect the corps' flank and to relieve the pressure on the Egyptian Corps, thus freeing the theater reserve for the main attack. To Yeosock and Franks, these deliberate preliminaries were essential if the Third Army and VII Corps' mass of maneuver—three armored divisions and an armored cavalry regiment—were to "slam into the Republican Guard," which had to be located and fixed. Having explained Franks' tactical concerns to Schwarzkopf and having acknowledged the CINC's operational intent, Yeosock kept his own counsel when discussing the issues with Franks, who continued to believe his plan had Schwarzkopf's confidence.

The ARCENT briefing on the 9th addressed the attrition of the enemy force, noting that it had not reached the 50 percent desired; moreover, it was proceeding at a rate one-half that required. General Stewart displayed a chart showing that, given an increase of 1 percent a day (to 2 percent) in the rate of attrition, the 50 percent point could be reached in two weeks.[53] This, of course, implied an increased investment of air assets in preparation for the ground attack.

Based upon this estimate, a graph was shown indicating to Secretary Cheney and General Powell that, if the decision were taken to begin the necessary preparation of the battlefield for the ground attack (G-13), movement into attack positions could begin in six days (G-7) as attrition mounted, and preparation for attack would follow from G-5 to G-day.54 (See figure 17.) No dates appeared on the slide, but as the date of the briefing was the 9th, the earliest date that would meet the schedule for the attack was the 23d. This chart was followed by a depiction of final ground preparations (G-8 to G-day), the timing of attack, and alternatives for achieving destruction of the Republican Guard based upon the enemy's response. Other charts demonstrated that after 21 February, the sustainment resources (particularly trucks) necessary for the operation would be in-country. Based upon a continuous monitoring of Iraqi maneuvers, or rather the complete failure to detect any in the Kuwait theater of operations, the ARCENT commander concluded that the enemy would not maneuver but that he would fight, that the corps were ready, and that there was sufficient fuel and ammunition on hand to support the plan.55 (See figure 18.)

General Franks briefed the ARCENT main attack. He was followed by General McCaffrey and General Griffith, who seemed to have been present to show the chairman that the tactical details of communications, movement, and sustainment had been worked to the last detail, as well as to give the high command a sense of the confidence of the leaders who would actually direct the coming battle. In his memoirs, Schwarzkopf adds gratuitously to his account of these briefings: "All very impressive, I thought, except Franks, whose plan was still too deliberate and who insisted on telling the secretary and the chairman that he was to need the reserves."56 If the theater commander felt that way at the time, there is no evidence he allowed his frustration to find voice, either in the presence of his superiors or after their departure.

At the end of the rehearsal briefing at ARCENT on the 8th, in response to an inquiry from Yeosock if anything else was on their minds, Franks observed that, while it was above his pay grade, he hoped someone had thought about how it all was supposed to look on the ground when it was over. He hoped someone had thought about a "war stopper."57 Later, Franks would observe that at the end of his briefing on the 9th, the secretary of defense raised the same question and asked how Franks thought the end of the ground battle would look.58 In the event, the complex problem of war termination would be the one detail not well thought out by the strategic leadership before the secretary's question was posed. Events on 28 February raised the question of whether it was adequately studied thereafter. Franks and McCaffrey would find themselves in no small difficulty as a consequence.

A World War I general, perhaps French Marshal Joffre or Field Marshal Hindenburg, was once asked who had won his greatest battle.

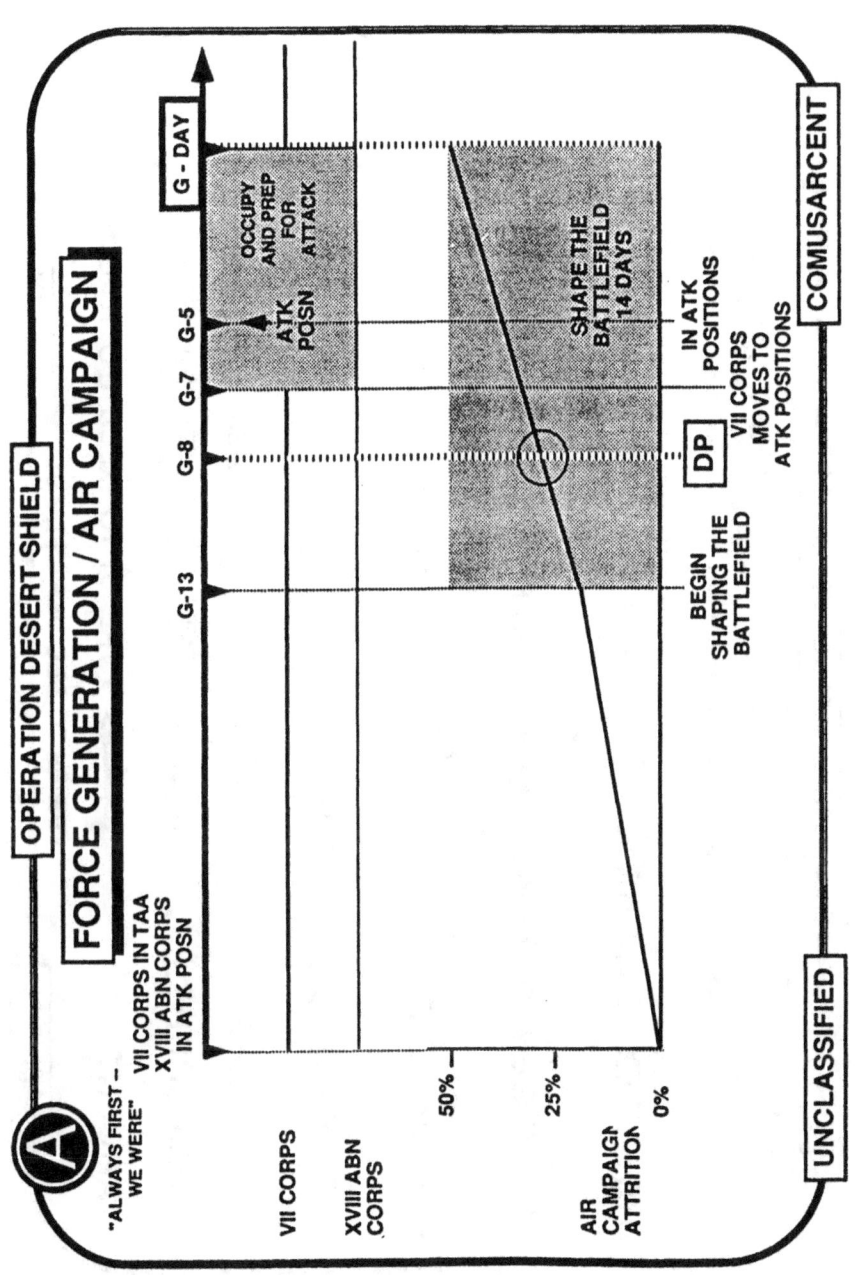

Figure 17.

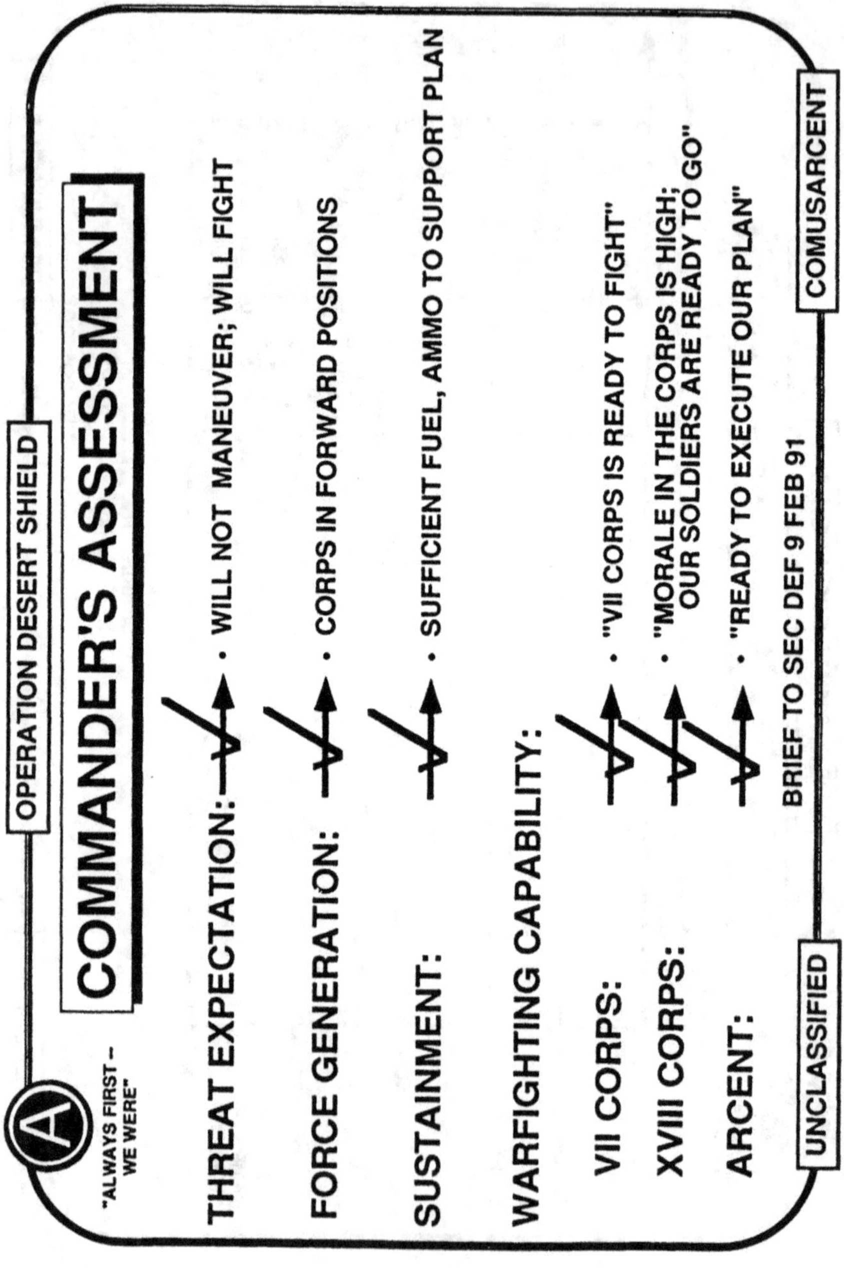

OPERATION DESERT SHIELD

COMMANDER'S ASSESSMENT

A "ALWAYS FIRST — WE WERE"

THREAT EXPECTATION: • WILL NOT MANEUVER; WILL FIGHT

FORCE GENERATION: • CORPS IN FORWARD POSITIONS

SUSTAINMENT: • SUFFICIENT FUEL, AMMO TO SUPPORT PLAN

WARFIGHTING CAPABILITY:

VII CORPS: • "VII CORPS IS READY TO FIGHT"

XVIII CORPS: • "MORALE IN THE CORPS IS HIGH; OUR SOLDIERS ARE READY TO GO"

ARCENT: • "READY TO EXECUTE OUR PLAN"

BRIEF TO SEC DEF 9 FEB 91

COMUSARCENT

UNCLASSIFIED

Figure 18.

It is said that he thought for a moment and replied: "I don't know who was responsible for the victory. But I know who would have been blamed for the defeat." The commander is always responsible, particularly for defeat. Victory, according to an old proverb, has many fathers; defeat is an orphan. Among the several things that stand out in the Desert Storm planning process, perhaps the most important is that the Desert Storm plan was the result of a process, not an event, not one man's brilliant or clever insight.

Perhaps all successful military operations are the product of the corporate skills of the institution, but this was particularly the case of Desert Storm. Colonel Joe Purvis and his team started the process with a good deal of personal direction (and sometimes abuse) from General Schwarzkopf. Certainly Schwarzkopf's forensic abilities counted heavily, both in convincing Colin Powell that two corps were required for an offensive and in articulating to his subordinates a clear vision of what they were about. General Steve Arnold's role was decisive in linking the efforts of ARCENT and the two corps with those of CENTCOM. Tireless and good humored, even under what at times was severe hammering from Schwarzkopf over issues like planning for the employment of the theater reserve, Arnold was the heart and soul of the ARCENT staff planning effort. His ability to draw in and combine harmoniously the efforts of multiple, independent, and often competing agencies and powerful personalities was matchless. General Pagonis was everywhere on the MSR in his command van with cellular phone in hand, but he was still able to oversee planning of the most difficult and dynamic logistic build-up since Korea, and he saw to it that the operators' goals were made possible. Many supporting agencies not addressed here, the CENTCOM Analysis Agency and BCTP representatives particularly, provided simulation analysis to support the commander's judgments and provide many bright ideas as well. Finally, the ability of the Third Army commanders to bury their differences and strong personalities to produce a comprehensive plan like that for Desert Storm is a tribute to the character of the men who have risen to command the Army of the nineties.

The plan itself had several points of interest. First of all, although the CENTCOM OPLAN spoke of a campaign of four phases (strategic air campaign, air supremacy in the KTO, battlefield preparation, and ground offensive plan), the coalition offensive would consist of two separable and distinct parts: (1) an air offensive of three parts (attacks to achieve air supremacy, strategic bombing in Iraq north of the KTO, and air operations in the KTO designed to reduce the Iraqi forces in occupation) and (2) an air-ground offensive *should it prove necessary*—all carried on within the ongoing naval interdiction effort. The logic of the strategic situation would not require a follow-on ground operation *if* Saddam Hussein bowed to the logic of his situation and agreed to withdraw and comply with the pertinent UN resolutions. Certainly, the air operations provided significant persuasion to that end. It is equally certain that the air operations were unsuccessful in convincing Saddam to retreat under circumstances acceptable to the president and the coalition leadership.

The requirement for subsequent political permission to undertake ground operations shows that the ground offensive was conceived to be an escalation, separable from the air attacks. The ground attack was contingent, not concomitant, to the air campaign, notwithstanding Schwarzkopf's complaints in his memoir that he was repeatedly pressured to initiate a ground attack before he was ready. Ultimately, the plan fit neither of the two patterns posited at the start of the last chapter: destruction by maneuver-induced psychological dislocation or rear attack. Rather, it was an amalgam, perhaps best characterized as *pragmatic*. The plan clearly hoped for psychological dislocation (albeit one achieved by aerial fires as well as maneuver). But the plan ultimately provided for physical destruction at all levels should that be required.[59] Indeed, the physical destruction of Iraqi armored forces became an important, if collateral, objective to ensure future regional stability—a strategic goal. At the end of the day, there is little so psychologically dislocating as daily subjection to a battering from which there is no relief and for which there is no reply.

This understanding of the theater campaign plan is important, because it accounts for the fact that commitment of air resources to prepare the ground *specifically* in support of the Army ground operation (as opposed to achieving attrition of the forces in the KTO as a part of the air campaign) was delayed until eight or nine days before the start of the ground attack. The campaign of attrition (the first part of Phase III) was directed by the joint forces Air component commander in accordance with the theater commander's guidance and priorities—a fact many Army ground tactical commanders found hard to accept, though it was entirely consistent with the nature of the campaign plan. Once the decision was taken to launch the ground attack (and final approval undoubtedly *followed* the visit of the secretary of defense and chairman on 9 February), air resources began to be employed to prepare for ground operations. At the same time, the Air Force continued the general process of air-ground attrition, strategic bombing, and maintenance of air superiority.

The allied ground forces were employed in ways that accorded with their capabilities and the needs of the coalition. The "piano key" deployment of the forces across the front—Joint Forces Command East, MARCENT, Joint Forces Command North, and ARCENT—ensured that the two Arab-Islamic commands could call on U.S. components for assistance, particularly for help obtaining and controlling air support (see figure 19). It also ensured that Arab forces were properly positioned to liberate Kuwait City. The Egyptian Corps, part of Joint Forces Command North but a force with which the U.S. Army had some experience through periodic Bright Star exercises, was aligned with VII Corps' eastern flank. The U.S. Army provided support on a bilateral basis to bolster the Egyptian effort, to include the loan of some required breaching equipment, positioning of the theater reserve, and the provision for on-call AH-64 support. Third Army sent a special liaison team to the Egyptian Corps as well as to Joint Forces Command North.

MARCENT was positioned near the coast in light of the short operational reach of Marine forces and appeared to be the landward part of an amphibious envelopment. The Marines were highly visible on CNN and in press reports, an unwitting contribution by the news media to misleading the Iraqis. The 1st U.K. Armored Division was employed with the NATO-based U.S. corps in accordance with the British desire to take part in more open, less costly maneuver operations. The French, whose thoroughly professional but light force was based on the Red Sea to the west, were placed on the ARCENT's left to seize As Salman and open the limited road net behind XVIII Corps, a task they accomplished in exemplary fashion in the time deemed necessary by the XVIII Corps before the fact.

The burden of the planned ground attack rested firmly on the VII Corps. All else could come a cropper and yet, if VII Corps succeeded in destroying the Republican Guard and Iraqi operational reserves, come right in the end. If VII Corps failed and the Republican Guard was able to counterattack, the offensive through the Iraqi defenses could become very bloody indeed, although the success of U.S. air power against the Iraqi armored forces at Khafji probably indicated that coalition success was inevitable once the Iraqi forces had to come above ground and concentrate to resist the attacking ground forces. That was not yet as clear in February 1991 as it is today. What was clear was that air supremacy was a sine qua non for the entire ground effort, as was the preattack concentration west of Wadi al Batin.

Ultimately, the ARCENT plan was Lieutenant General John Yeosock's. Not because he can be seen working any particular part of

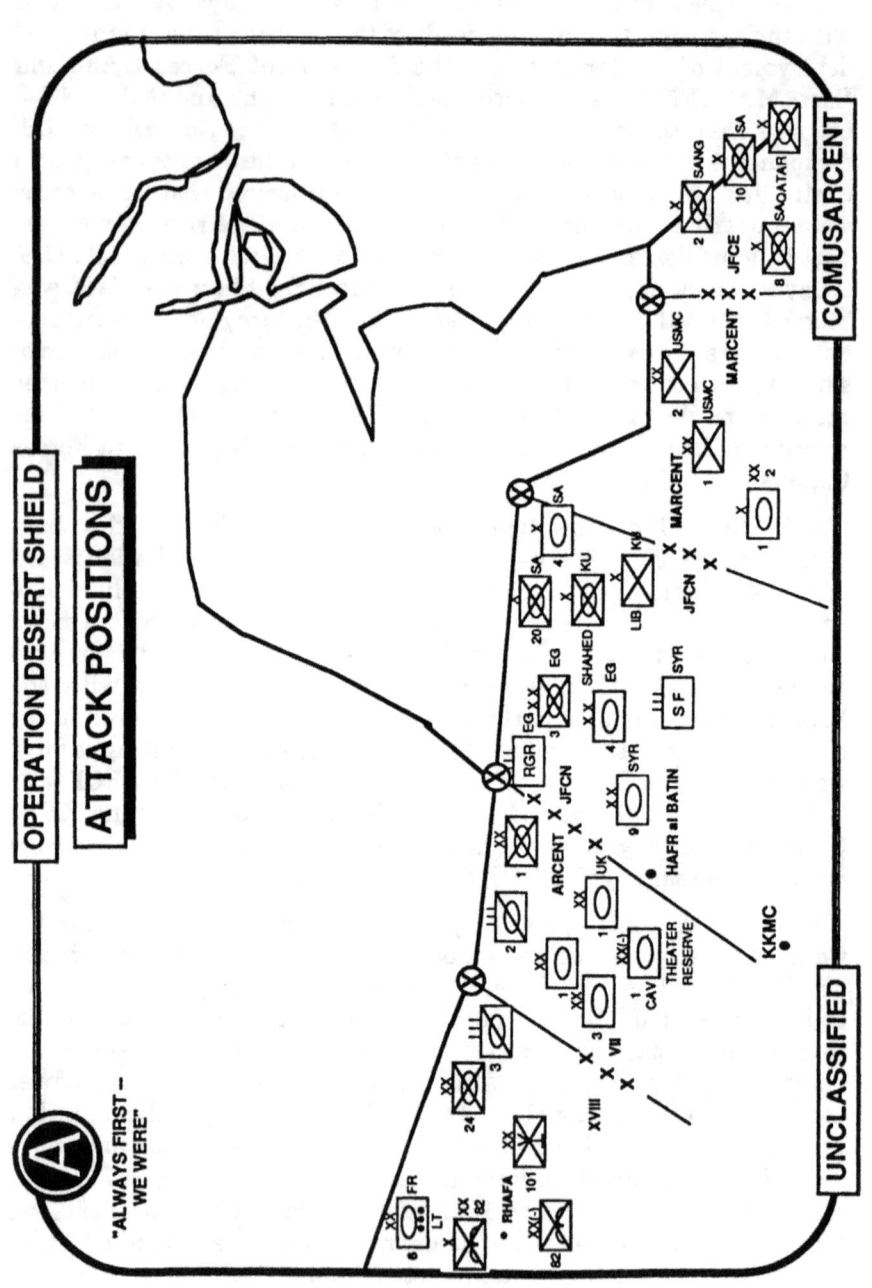

Figure 19.

it. Indeed, he seemed to have spent the greatest part of his time in the introduction of Army forces into the theater, provisioning of host-nation support, creation of an echelon-above-corps intelligence capability, and obtaining whatever he could beg, borrow, or steal from other major Army commands to make Desert Storm work. But it was Yeosock who married what was possible, largely General Pagonis' business, with what was thought to be required by his two corps. His life from November to February was a series of trade-offs and work arounds. He evaluated what was required and more often decided what could be done with what was available. At the same time, he balanced risks and generally strove to unencumber the corps so they could concentrate on the immediate problems of training, deploying/redeploying, and preparing for the anticipated offensive.

Notes

1. The CENTCOM OPLAN Desert Storm was published on 16 December. The ARCENT Plan, Desert Storm OPLAN 001, was published on 5 January. As the narrative will show, significant details remained to be resolved at each publication date. Their resolution would be documented by contingency plans and annexes published at dates later than the basic orders.

2. HQ, ARCENT, Command Group, briefing for the Secretary of Defense, dated 15 December 1990, slide titled, "ARCENT Concept of Operations." There are two briefings in the ARCENT Command Briefing set for the December visit of the secretary of defense. The first set, dated 15 December, appears to be the ARCENT set, the second dated 20 December, the date of the briefing itself, appears to be the CENTCOM set less the ARCENT and corps briefings.

3. HQ, ARCENT, Command Group, briefing for the Secretary of Defense, dated 15 December 1990, slide titled, "Commander's Intent."

4. HQ, ARCENT, G3 (Plans), AFRD-DTP, Memorandum for USARCENT Historian, Colonel Swain, Subject: HQ, USARCENT, G3 Plans, Historical Narrative of Desert Shield, Desert Storm, Defense and Restoration of Kuwait, and Redeployment, dated 6 April 1991, 15-16. Interview with General Frederick Franks at the Pentagon, by the Strategic Studies Institute, U.S. Army War College, Carlisle Barracks, Pennsylvania, on 31 October 1991, 19. Interview with Colonel Stan Cherrie, G3 VII Corps, at Fort Leavenworth, Kansas, 29 August 1991, 7-9 on staff resistance to CG's plan.

5. HQ, ARCENT, G3 (Plans) AFRD-DTP, Memorandum for USARCENT Historian, Colonel Swain, Subject: HQ, USARCENT, G3 Plans, Historical Narrative of Desert Shield, Desert Storm, Defense and Restoration of Kuwait, and Redeployment, dated 6 April 1991, 14-15.

6. Message, 120300Z FEB 91, COMUSARCENT MAIN//DT//, MSIG ID/SITREP/USARCENT/D+26/FEB, 9. ARCENT did have a contingency plan for an early attack by available forces after 31 January should it be required.

7. HQ, ARCENT, Command Group, briefing for the Secretary of Defense, dated 15 December 1990, slide titled, "HET Status." The fact the slide is present in the packet, of course, does not necessarily indicate the slide was briefed to the secretary or chairman. It is taken to indicate what the ARCENT commander believed to be the case on the date indicated. There were only 897 HETs in the Army inventory.

8. Eric Schmitt, "Forces Not Ready for January War, U.S. General Says: Candid Assessment: Gulf Deputy Commander Seen as Undermining Bush's Diplomacy," *The New York Times*, 20 December 1990, A1, A20. Schwarzkopf, *Doesn't Take a Hero*, 394-95.

9. HQ, ARCENT, Command Group, briefing for the Secretary of Defense, dated 15 December 1990, slide titled, "Ground Force Correlation (Assuming 50% Iraqi Attrition by Air)."

10. Baron de Jomini, *The Art of War*, trans. Captain G. H. Mendell and Lieutenant W. P. Craighill (Philadelphia, PA: J. B. Lippincott & Co., 1862, Greenwood Press Reprint, n.d.), 299.

11. HQ, ARCENT, G3 (Plans) AFRD-DTP, Memorandum for USARCENT Historian, Colonel Swain, Subject: HQ, USARCENT, G3 Plans, Historical Narrative of Desert Shield, Desert Storm, Defense and Restoration of Kuwait, and Redeployment, dated 6 April 1991, 6–7.

12. HQ, ARCENT, G3, Memorandum for Commander, 22d SUPCOM; Commander, VII Corps; Commander, XVIII Corps, Subject: Theater Movements Plan, dated 11 January 1991, and HQ, ARCENT, Command Group, untitled briefing, dated 27 December 1990. Documents are tabs 14 and 15 to vol. 2 of HQ, USARCENT, G3 Plans, Operation Desert Shield/Storm Historical Narrative and Input into Command Report.

13. HQ, ARCENT, Command Group, briefing titled, "USARCENT OPLAN 001 Desert Storm," dated 27 December 1990, section titled, "Theater Logistics Concept." General Pagonis' account in Pagonis, *Moving Mountains*, 118–22.

14. Pagonis, *Moving Mountains*, 135.

15. HQ, ARCENT, Command Group, untitled briefing, dated 27 December 1990, slides titled, "Log Base Alpha, Bravo, etc."

16. Ibid., slide titled, "Medical Beds."

17. Ibid., slide titled, "Unit Moves."

18. As to a contract comment, a story was told to author by Lieutenant Colonel Mike Kendall. Briefing slides (3) in Ibid., titled, "Asset Availability Versus Commitments." Pagonis' version in Pagonis, *Moving Mountains*, 136–40. Schwarzkopf's version is in Schwarzkopf, *Doesn't Take a Hero*, 400–401.

19. HQ, ARCENT, AFRD-DTP, Memorandum thru Colonel Holloway, Chief, G3 Plans, for Colonel Swain, USARCENT Historian, Subject: Command Report Operation Desert Storm, dated 16 March 1991, prepared by Major Daniel J. Gilbert, Tabs 1, 2, and 3. Interview with General Steven Arnold (in progress).

20. Note from Lieutenant Colonel Mike Kendall to author on early draft of the manuscript. See comments by General Luck in transcript of MAPEX, Eskan Village School House, Tape C (27 December 1990), 8. See also Tape A, 27.

21. The whole question of the Syrian adherence to the plan of attack has become controversial. Schwarzkopf is clear that the Syrians balked at participation in the offensive, for whatever reason. Schwarzkopf, *Doesn't Take a Hero*, 401–3. De la Billiere confirms this view, de la Billiere, *Storm Command*, 178. Prince Khalid disputes this, pointing out that the Syrians followed the Arab attack in support when the offensive took place. Khalid, of course, is correct but does not contradict directly Schwarzkopf or de la Billiere's versions, which was one understood at ARCENT. Khalid bin Sultan, "Schwarzkopf Falls Short in Writing History," *Army Times*, 2 November 1992, 21.

22. Comments made to author by General Yeosock after review of draft manuscript. General Yeosock indicated that this "recon by fire" was a technique he felt bound to use with the CINC. Similar comments were made by his executive officer, Lieutenant Colonel Kendall, in notes returned on a draft manuscript in possession of the author. See also the interview with Lieutenant General John Yeosock, Fort McPherson, Georgia, 29 June 1991, 5–6. For interalliance bickering, see Schwarzkopf, *Doesn't Take a Hero*, 401–5. De la Billiere addresses security lapse and data (4 January) of the Alliance Grand Review, de la Billiere, *Storm Command*, 179–81, 183.

23. Major Dan Gilbert was the slide turner for the 4 January briefing and described the "atmospherics" to the author. Lieutenant Colonel Gilbert has provided the author with some notes and recollections of the contretemps in response to reviewing an early draft of this chapter.

24. Lieutenant Colonel Kendall's handwritten comments on draft manuscript, 143–45. General Yeosock to author.

25. Lieutenant Colonel Gilbert's contemporary note reads: "Briefed CinC—Changed all. Said plan stinks/not doable. Ranted/raved. Now I understand 'Storming Norman' nickname." HQ, ARCENT, G3 (Plans) AFRD-DTP, Memorandum for USARCENT Historian, Colonel Swain, Subject: HQ, USARCENT, G3 (Plans), Historical Narrative of Desert Shield, Desert Storm, Defense and Restoration of Kuwait, and Redeployment, dated 6 April 1991, 15–16.

26. Letter to author from Lieutenant Colonel Dan Gilbert, dated 4 March 1992, with notes of 4 January briefing to CINC.

27. Ibid.; and Purvis Group Diary, 16.

28. Interview with Colonel Stan Cherrie, VII Corps G3, at Fort Leavenworth, Kansas, 29 August 1991, 21–22.

29. Transcript of the ARCENT MAPEX, Tape A, 27 December 1990 and Tape E, 27 December 1990.

30. Comments made to author by General Yeosock after review of draft manuscript.

31. Lieutenant Colonel Kendall's handwritten comments on draft manuscript, 155.

32. Interview with General Frederick Franks, Fort Leavenworth, Kansas, 6 March 1992, 40.

33. HQ, 2d Armored Cavalry Regiment, AETSAC-AT, Memorandum, Subject: 2ACR Staff Exercise After-Action Report, dated 27 December 1990, attached briefing shows a twelve to twenty-four-hour pause on PL Smash. HQ, 1st Armored Division, TAA Thompson (KTO) 141200C February 1991, Operations Order #6-91m (attack/movement to contact). Para 3B(C) reads: "Units will pause at Atk Python to consolidate, tactically rearm, refit, refuel, and posture for future operations."

34. Transcript of the ARCENT MAPEX, Tape B, 30 December 1990.

35. As indicated above, the trend was for the VII Corps to push its main attack as far west as possible.

36. General Waller turned down such a request while he was ARCENT commander from 13–23 February, and General Franks indicates that he thought of requesting such attachment the night of 27 February but felt the question would only lead to an argument with XVIII Corps and did not pursue it. Interview with General Calvin Waller by General Timothy J. Groggin, et al., on 2 May 1991, 93. Interview with General Frederick Franks at Fort Leavenworth, Kansas, 6 March 1992, 38–39. One can only speculate that there was resistance to taking the one heavy force assigned to XVIII Corps and attaching it to VII Corps at the climax of the battle, largely reducing the XVIII Airborne Corps to a mopping-up force with the exception of the plentiful AH-64 units that were conducting the ARCENT's deep battle.

37. The term "turning force" is used advisedly. The attack down the Euphrates valley to assist in destruction of the Republican Guard seems always to have been somewhat tentative; it remained an on-order mission. On the other hand, cutting Highway 8 is a clear initial mission. Cutting the LOC is a turning movement.

38. B. H. Liddell Hart, *Thoughts on War* (London: Faber and Faber, 1944), 63–64.

39. HQ, ARCENT, Command Group, briefing titled, "Purpose: To Back Brief ARCENT Scheme of Maneuver for Operation Desert Storm," dated 8 January 1991. Of great interest is the note that the plan was to be executable by 15 February with a contingency plan capable of execution by 25 January. HQ, ARCENT, G3 (Plans), AFRD-DTP, Memorandum for USARCENT Historian, Colonel Swain, Subject: HQ, USARCENT, G3 Plans, Historical Narrative of Desert Shield, Desert Storm, Defense and Restoration of Kuwait, and Redeployment, dated 6 April 1991, 15–16.

40. This difference of view about the anticipated enemy resistance continued through the briefing to the secretary of defense. The pessimistic view was generally agreed to in the author's hearing at the rehearsal briefing by ARCENT commanders at HQ, ARCENT, prior to the final briefing for the secretary of defense. Also, see Lieutenant Colonel Kendall's handwritten comments on draft manuscript, 158–59. Kendall notes that at a prebrief for the CINC that he attended with General Yeosock prior to the secretary of defense briefing, the CINC again blew up, first because General Arnold addressed an ARCENT employment of the 1st Cavalry Division(-), which by then was tied to the success of the Egyptian attack, and he (Arnold) used the words "operational pause." Kendall writes: "Again CinC signaled he didn't expect heavy opposition to the ground assault. It was obvious his commanders didn't agree but they were not about to raise the issue at the Sec Def brief."

41. The author heard General Franks make these points at briefings in Saudi Arabia and discusses them in interview with General Frederick Franks at Fort Leavenworth, Kansas, 6 March 1992.

42. After writing this chapter, one of the author's research assistants discovered a memorandum from Colonel Don Holder to General Franks that raised concerns about the complexity of coordinating the corps' advance in light of the sequential nature of the tasks to be accomplished in the breach. Colonel Holder was commander of the 2d Armored Cavalry Regiment. He is as sober a tactician as the Army owns and a former director of the School of Advanced Military Studies and principal author of the Army's AirLand Battle Doctrine. HQ, 2d Armored Cavalry

Regiment, AETSAC, Memorandum for VII Corps TAC (Attn: G3), Subject: Comments on VII Corps FRAGPLAN #7, dated 230900 February 1991.

43. HQ, ARCENT, Command Group, briefing titled, "Commander's Huddle," dated Friday, 1 February 1991 (D+15).

44. Transcript of Frost interview dated 22 March 1991 in possession of author, 16. HQ, ARCENT, Command Group, Memorandum for Record, Subject: Notes from Huddle Meeting, 1 February 1991, dated 1 February 1991.

45. HQ, ARCENT, Command Group, Memorandum for Record, Subject: Notes from Huddle Meeting, 1 February 1991, dated 1 February 1991.

46. Ibid. The ARCENT Desert Storm operation order did not contain a plan for destruction of the Republican Guard. That annex was not published, rather the G3 Plans section prepared a number of contingency plans one of which would be selected at some appropriate point for implementation to achieve the ARCENT mission in accordance with circumstances then obtaining. This will be discussed at some length hereafter. See HQ, ARCENT, AFRD-DTP, Memorandum thru Colonel Holloway, Chief, G3 Plans, for Colonel Swain, USARCENT Historian, Subject: Command Report Operation Desert Storm, dated 16 March 1991, prepared by Major Daniel J. Gilbert, 4–6.

47. HQ, ARCENT, Command Group, Memorandum for Record, Subject: Notes from Huddle Meeting, 1 February 1991, dated 1 February 1991.

48. HQ, ARCENT, Command Group, briefing titled, "Commander's Huddle," dated Friday, 1 February 1991 (D+15).

49. Lieutenant Colonel Kendall's handwritten comments on draft manuscript, 158–59.

50. The issue of the timing of the attack is discussed in HQ, ARCENT, AFRD-DTP, Memorandum thru Colonel Holloway, Chief, G3 Plans, for Colonel Swain, USARCENT Historian, Subject: Command Report Operation Desert Storm, dated 16 March 1991, prepared by Major Daniel J. Gilbert, 5, and enclosure 29. It was a matter of discussion at the "commander's huddle." HQ, ARCENT, Command Group, Memorandum for Record, Subject: Notes from Huddle Meeting, 1 February 1991, dated 1 February 1991. HQ, ARCENT, Command Group, briefing titled, "Commander's Huddle," dated Friday, 1 February 1991 (D+15).

51. Schwarzkopf, *Doesn't Take a Hero*, 433–34.

52. Sir Peter de la Billiere expresses the ambiguity felt by many, noting on the one hand anticipation of a costly battle and, on the other, a private optimism that the Iraqi Army would collapse under air attack before the ground attack went in. De la Billiere, *Storm Command*, 277.

53. HQ, ARCENT, Command Group, ARCENT Update, dated 8 February 1991, slide titled, "Battle Damage Estimate." The slide showed a BDA assessment of only 23 percent on 9 February.

54. Ibid., slide titled, "Force Generation/Air Campaign."

55. General Yeosock told the author that among the first things he told his G2 to track was the matter of whether or not the Iraqis in the KTO were conducting unit training. Absent evidence of such training for the period of occupation, Yeosock concluded, rightly it turned out, that the Iraqi armored forces were incapable of tactical maneuver as opposed to tactical movement. Assessments are in, HQ, ARCENT, Command Group, ARCENT Update, dated 8 February 1991, slide titled, "Commander's Assessment."

56. Schwarzkopf, *Doesn't Take a Hero*, 434.

57. The author was present at the briefing.

58. General Franks to the author.

59. This third category was suggested to me by Professor Jim Schneider, SAMS, USACGSC, Fort Leavenworth, Kansas.

5
Build-up to Attack

The president's 8 November announcement did not change General Yeosock's conception of his command. Third Army would continue to be *three armies:* service component, theater, and numbered field. It would expand its heretofore limited operational responsibilities. The new circumstances, with two assigned corps conducting an operational offensive instead of one corps defending in depth, required a dramatic restructuring of the headquarters and the army-level force structure. This had to be done while bringing VII Corps on line and seeing to it that the logistic build-up and operational redeployment were properly executed. New units arriving from Europe and the continental United States (CONUS) had to be fitted into the transportation sequence, so they did not arrive a day before they were required, but just in time to participate in the offensive.

Some environmental acclimation was desirable for combat units, though this was not always possible. Much of the 3d Armored Division became acclimated on the way to the line of departure. However, February weather in Saudi Arabia is nothing like the heat of the summer; rain can be heavy as a monsoon and accompanied, notwithstanding, by blowing sand. Temperatures range well into the thirties during the night while remaining cool throughout the day. (It was reported one morning at the ARCENT command briefing that, during the night, temperatures had reached 27 degrees Fahrenheit in the area occupied by the 24th Infantry Division.)[1] Adapting to desert conditions, of course, requires a good deal more than becoming accustomed to temperature. The sheer emptiness and unlimited vistas make orientation difficult and distort estimates of time and distance. For those more used to houses and trees, the desert can contribute to a sort of melancholy.

The process of concentrating an expanded Third Army in the Arabian Peninsula was not easy to manage. An unavoidable delay occurred between identification of a need and mobilization, shipment, arrival, and deployment in theater. Anything required in February had to be identified by the end of the previous November. The deficits left by the ceiling on the size of the initial army and corps organizations had to be corrected and a new corps force structure built. This was made easier after ARCENT's various force structure excursions, both to hold down the size of the force (minimum essential force guidance) and to examine the requirements involved in making

Third Army an Army MACOM (major army command). Much of the design work, too, had been ongoing in Europe for some time. The VII Corps and U.S. Army Europe had long anticipated possible calls for forces to reinforce the Persian Gulf army.

The new deployments involved bringing together in the theater of war, at the proper time, units from Europe and the United States. The new units had to be introduced quicker and in larger numbers than during the initial XVIII Corps deployment.[2] (See figure 20.) This, of course, implied the acquisition, through call-up or contract, of additional strategic transportation resources by the joint service transportation command. Often there were no good answers. Choices involved trade-offs, each possessing attendant risks.

The U.S. Army was not structured or trained for an operational offensive in open desert terrain such as that now confronting its commanders. Because it had been designed for war in Europe, it was seriously suboptimized and required significant augmentation. The operation required tactical and operational movement of large units that rarely had assembled in one place for training, let alone maneuvered tactically in formation. The means of operational transport, both vehicles and drivers, were not readily available and could not be assembled in time. A number of expedients had to be formulated in December and January, then coordinated with the Department of the Army as well as the host nation, to make up for the deficiencies.

Yeosock continued to define his task as "unencumbering" the two corps so that they could concentrate on training and fighting. In addition to bringing the VII Corps into the theater, it was also his job to project the gathering forces to the west and deploy them with all the means necessary to launch and sustain both corps for up to two weeks of intense combat. For the most part, accomplishing this would be the task of General Pagonis and the 22d Support Command. The ARCENT commander focused most of his efforts on solving problems, while his staff concentrated on planning and coordination. Meanwhile, subordinate maneuver units prepared for battle.

Before 8 November, Third Army's responsibilities for operational oversight of its single corps were minimal. It is probable that, had the Desert Shield defensive plan ever been executed, General Schwarzkopf would have taken direct operational command of the 1st Marine Expeditionary Force and XVIII Corps. Moreover, the defensive plan, which was limited in geographic scope, did not require a large echelon-above-corps structure. Logically, then, Third Army headquarters had

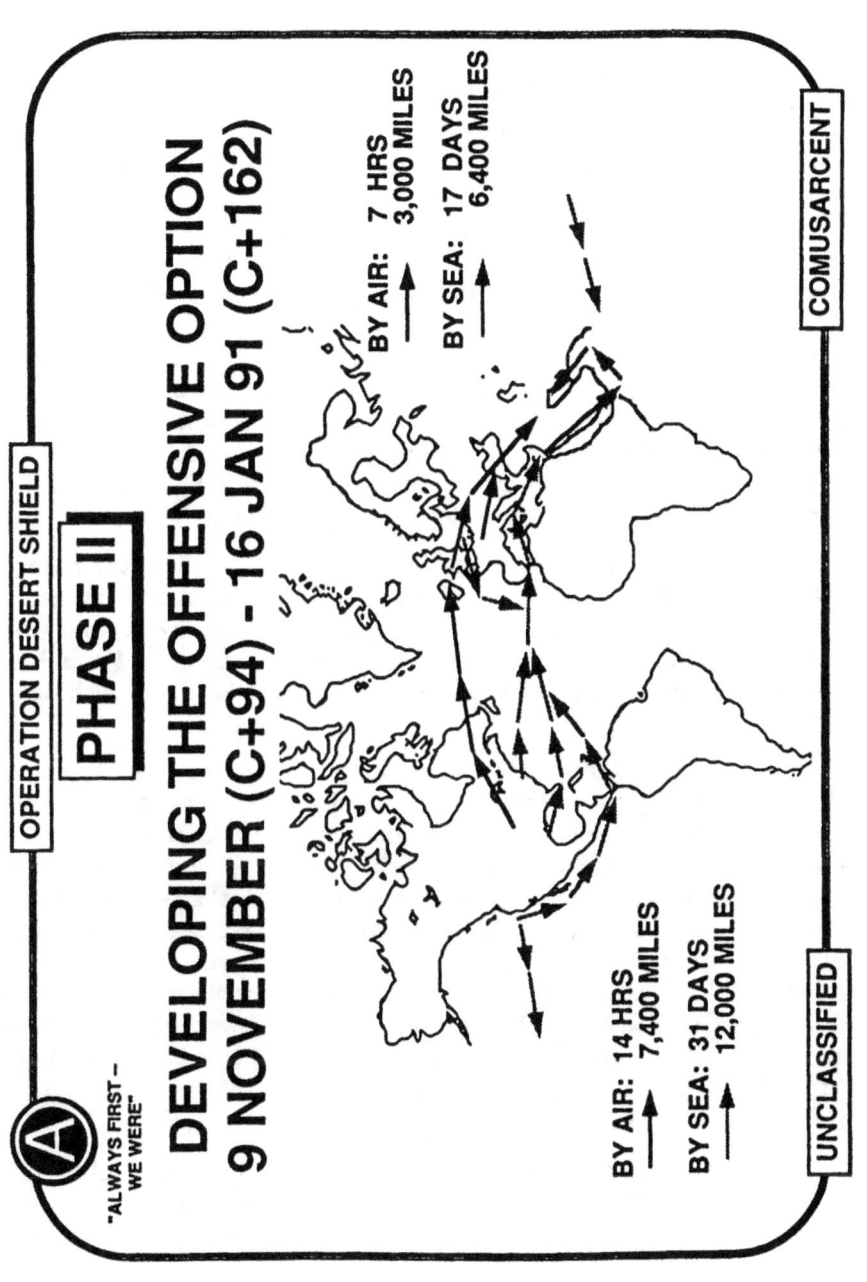

Figure 20.

been one of the biggest bill payers for the minimum essential force ceiling, retaining only, with limited exceptions, its peacetime premobilization size and structure and even providing the personnel to man the U.S.-Saudi C3IC staff.

Now that ARCENT would command two corps operationally and a substantially larger echelon-above-corps force, the headquarters structure, and even its way of thinking about itself, had to be changed in very short order. To assist in this change of orientation, the army commander developed a system of liaison teams, "directed telescopes," that were to be located in all key headquarters across the front and offer, not just to ARCENT but to CENTCOM, a quick, extra-bureaucratic source of immediate information on the situation of friendly forces. These teams provided one more vital bridge to cover the gaps in the allied command structure to compensate for the coalition's lack of true unity of command. Third Army also created an advanced mobile command post (CP) called "Lucky TAC," or "Lucky Wheels," since it was housed in wheeled expando-vans.

How all this was done and why provides insights into the nature of operational command and coalition and joint warfare. It is also a story that is only complete when various human aspects of what was done are examined; for the headquarters restructuring had social as well as organizational consequences that had to be dealt with on a daily basis.

In the fall of 1990, Colonel John Jorgenson, the ARCENT deputy chief of staff, expressed the view to General Yeosock that the army headquarters was, to its detriment, dominated by light infantrymen and field artillery officers, particularly in the operations staff.[3] The observation was partially correct. General Arnold, the G3, had been a brigade commander in the 82d Airborne Division, then an assistant division commander in the 2d Division in Korea. Colonel Bob Beddingfield, the deputy G3 (and displaced premobilization G3), and Colonel Glenn Lackey, the G3 operations chief, were field artillery officers. Colonel Gene Holloway, the G3 plans, was an aviator. Major Steve Holley, the principal staff planner for Desert Storm, was an air defense officer—and so on!

The Army, like any large organization, has its unofficial unions and organizational shibboleths. The issue raised by Jorgenson, that only heavy maneuver arms officers could understand large-unit heavy-force operations, is typical of these and, in the main, perhaps, quite valid—if not in the specific case of all the officers named above. It is worth pointing out that, although Arnold had commanded a light (airborne) infantry brigade, he had held a number of posts in the 8th Infantry Division in Germany, to include battalion command, so heavy forces were not entirely foreign to him. These general beliefs, however, are not unimportant. To the extent they are honored, they affect the legitimacy of an organization's members to do their business. It is also true that experience, if not the best, is ordinarily the most effective teacher.

So an effort was made to infuse the staff with what were called "long ball hitters." These were up-and-coming officers, drawn by the Army Personnel Command from throughout the Army on the basis of training, education, and experience to fill specific requirements in the Third Army headquarters. Their arrival supplemented and sometimes displaced the proprietary Third Army staff officers, while bringing in a good bit of talent. Among those selected were Lieutenant Colonel Dave Mock, Major Paul Hughes, Major Dan Gilbert, Major Rick Halblieb, and Major Clay Newman.

Dave Mock is a quiet, firm, and rock-solid cavalryman. He was the balance wheel in the army's forward operations cell, maintaining a modicum of order and rationality in an environment that could, on occasion, resemble a futures market. Paul Hughes is a tall, shy, but extraordinarily competent communicator. He played a vital role in establishing the communications network, linking the forward headquarters with army units in the forward area of operations. Dan Gilbert, a bright and studious infantryman, became a principal Desert Storm planner, while Rick Halblieb, an aggressive, articulate, and sometimes obsessive intelligence officer, became the principal targeting-battle damage assessment officer in General Stewart's G2 section. Indeed, when Stewart arrived to be G2 in late December, his "long ball hitters" all but marginalized the existing G2 organization. Clay Newman, a persistent logistician, served as a logistics expediter for the army staff, helping to locate lost or misdirected equipment during the build-up and redeployment. All but Newman were SAMS graduates.

Obviously, this rapid expansion produced some strains in the headquarters organization. Colonel Jorgenson himself was a victim of the process. Jorgenson was one of the most talented senior staff officers in Third Army. He was a former heavy maneuver brigade commander who had, in a previous assignment, served as Yeosock's squadron executive officer in the Third Armored Cavalry. Professionally frustrated by nonselection for general, Jorgenson was looking toward retirement when Desert Shield broke out. Faced with the need to fill his primary staff positions with general officer principals, Yeosock also had to find a general officer chief of staff. This was particularly the case since the G4, Brigadier General Jim Monroe, had served on the Third Army staff, under Jorgenson as "chief."4 Yeosock appointed his deputy commander, General Bob Frix, ARCENT chief of staff as well as deputy commanding general. Jorgenson became his deputy.

Had General Schwartz returned to ARCENT in December, when C3IC was absorbed by CENTCOM, he would have become Yeosock's principal deputy for operations, leaving Frix to act as a traditional chief of staff. But Schwartz did not return. Frix, as deputy commanding general, continued to work primarily as Yeosock's main troubleshooter and "outside man," ultimately moving forward in January with the advanced command post and then heading Task Force Freedom to reconstruct Kuwait after the war. Jorgenson did the work of running the staff through the staff section deputies (colonels) and acted as the principal mediator between the field grade staff and the commander. But he did not attend the daily general officer meetings where major decisions were made and command guidance was provided. Once General Frix moved forward, the chief of staff functions were picked up by the commander himself, his G3 General Arnold, Colonel Jorgenson, and the commander's executive officer, Lieutenant Colonel Michael Kendall.

Restructuring the army headquarters had to accord with a fundamental belief on the part of Yeosock that, as an army commander, he commanded two corps commanders, not two corps. He believed his principal role was ensuring the sustainment of the force and the allocation of force multipliers not otherwise accessible to the corps—especially logistics, air power, and intelligence. He was also charged with organization of such necessary but generally neglected functions as postal services, graves registration, enemy prisoner of war (EPW) operations, and medical support and evacuation. Yeosock recognized that corps commanders were men largely capable of synchronizing their own battles and that, in any event, corps were large organizations whose response to new orders was bound to take some time, given the number of echelons of command between the army and the level where orders are carried out, i.e., the platoon and squad. Yeosock was determined to deal only in major issues and only with large units. Moreover, he was disposed to take a somewhat Jeffersonian view of high command as something done best when done least. This view was probably necessary because of the compulsive-activist behavior of the CINC, not to mention a sense of lingering ambiguity about the extent to which Schwarzkopf might intend to deal directly with his corps commanders and their restiveness under a peer who had not commanded at their level.

So as long as ARCENT, as the operational headquarters, could assign missions, allocate forces, set objectives and boundaries, conduct deep fires, and monitor progress, it was, in Yeosock's view, synchronizing the operations of the two corps. That could be done from wherever the army commander had communications and a picture of what was going on in an operational level of detail. Unstated was a realization that there were two geographic and two "environmental" conditions requiring, in Yeosock's view, his presence in Riyadh.

The geographic considerations were the location of the theater intelligence apparatus and the proximity of General Pagonis in Dhahran, or at least his headquarters. Pagonis himself seemed to be in continuous motion all over the theater. Operational intelligence was critical to decision making, and the immediate linkages with strategic and operational systems were at Riyadh. Proximity to Support Command (SUPCOM) was important to the demands of keeping the movement process from the ports to the corps in order, a process in which Yeosock took a personal daily interest from December through February.

The first "environmental" condition was the need to stay close to the commander in chief. This was a consequence of the personality of the CINC himself. Schwarzkopf, an active, mercurial, highly emotional, and often impatient man, was best dealt with face to face and one on one.[5] In many ways, Schwarzkopf used Yeosock as Grant used Meade. In both cases, higher duties no doubt mandated such a solution, but such working relationships are seldom comfortable for either partner. Yeosock believed proximity was vital.

The second "environmental" requirement was the need to be able to work face to face with major coordinating commands, especially the Saudis and the CENTAF commander, General Horner, with whom Yeosock shared quarters. Yeosock knew from his experience as PMSANG that proximity to principal Saudi decision makers, often civilians, was essential to coordinate the fight and to address vital issues of host-nation support, particularly transportation, fuel supply, and prisoner of war support.[6] Circumventing the bureaucratic Army-Air Force interface by direct discussions with Horner permitted Yeosock to understand Schwarzkopf's view of the Air Force as a distinct operational instrument. Thus, Yeosock could work on a personal level for Army needs within the broader theater-strategic vision.

Yeosock was confident that army communications could give him a picture of the battlefield adequate to provide his forces the appropriate guidance and coordination while he remained in the capital. He had his communication system designed accordingly, and his G2 built a massive intelligence structure next door to his headquarters. In November and December, Yeosock also created two additional elements of the headquarters to ensure his concept could be realized—a mobile CP and seven liaison teams designed to be "shadow staffs," or "directed telescopes." The commander's intentions for the mobile CP seem always to have been largely misunderstood by key subordinates. Yeosock would call the liaison teams one of the three chief reasons for success in Operation Desert Storm.[7]

As early as 27 October, General Frix, as ARCENT chief of staff and deputy commanding general, alerted General Taylor at Forces Command (and deputy commander, ARCENT rear) that a great deal of attention was being given to the headquarters' ability to act as a field army, an operational headquarters. Taylor was told to expect requests for both "senior officers with experience in Armored/Mechanized Operations and Communications Equipment and signal personnel capable of communication over great distances."[8] About the same time, Colonel Glenn Lackey, G3 operations officer at ARCENT, was to build an Operations and Intelligence Center (war room) in the Eskan Village school house, from which the commander and his G3 could monitor operations and communicate with higher, lower, and adjacent headquarters. He was to create six, later seven, liaison teams to send to adjacent and subordinate headquarters. And he was to develop a mobile command post.

Lackey received his guidance from both Yeosock and Arnold. Colonel Chuck Sutten, the G6 (communications electronics and information management staff officer), provided technical advice and designed the communications system. Assistance in obtaining the equipment and manpower for the mobile CP and liaison teams was provided by Major General Jerry Granrud's Force Development Office at the DCSOPS in the Pentagon, and the two projects were tied together under the titles of Project 5 and 5A (liaison parties and mobile CP respectively). A related project to obtain a mobile armored CP for the XVIII Corps was undertaken at the same time.

Yeosock had a clear vision of what he wanted from the liaison parties. Arnold observed that his own first idea was simply provision of traditional two- or three-man teams whose purpose would have been limited largely to communications. Yeosock was thinking bigger, especially in the case of those teams assigned to the Arab-Islamic coalition's two commands. He wanted an organization "that could be a minicorps headquarters if it had to be."9

The broad concept was similar to that of the C3IC organization. The liaison party was not just to be a means of communication but an instrumentality to influence how the allies did business, even to assist them in complex staff work if necessary. This put a premium on the quality and seniority of the officers and men assigned. Team chiefs, with one exception, were colonels who were War College graduates. The one exception, Lieutenant Colonel Rick Gutwald, was a talented staff officer who became team chief when the colonel originally assigned clashed with corps staff and was reassigned to another team to promote harmony. Gutwald's team was assigned to XVIII Airborne Corps.

In the case of the Arab-Islamic allies, the liaison parties provided an ARCENT linkage with Special Operations Forces (SOF) assigned by Central Command to Arab tactical units to provide advice and training.10 By cooperating and combining ARCENT efforts with the SOF liaison parties, the U.S. command, in fact, had a communications and command information net in the Arab forces more reliable than that possessed by the Northern and Eastern Area Commands themselves. The ARCENT liaison teams assisted in planning and obtaining deep targeting support for the Arab forces from CENTAF, offered Arab tactical commanders intelligence not otherwise available, provided immediate "ground truth" to the ARCENT commander and, during the ground campaign, to the CENTCOM commander as well. A team was also provided to the Egyptian Corps, which was subordinate to Joint Forces Command North but closely associated diplomatically and militarily with the Americans. The presence of this team ensured both close cooperation with VII Corps' eastern neighbor and often ensured communication between the Egyptians and their own higher operational commander at Joint Forces Command North. (See figure 21.)

The liaison parties with U.S. coordinating forces facilitated the army commander's provision of various types of support to MARCENT. It allowed him to influence positioning of the CENTCOM reserve division, 1st Cavalry Division(-), prior to commitment, as well as to keep the reserve division commander informed about Third Army's current intentions. For principal subordinate forces (VII and XVIII Corps), the mission was more conventional but more substantial in light of the caliber of officers assigned and their ability to achieve immediate access to the army commander when necessary. On one occasion after the cease-fire, for example, a liaison team was able to

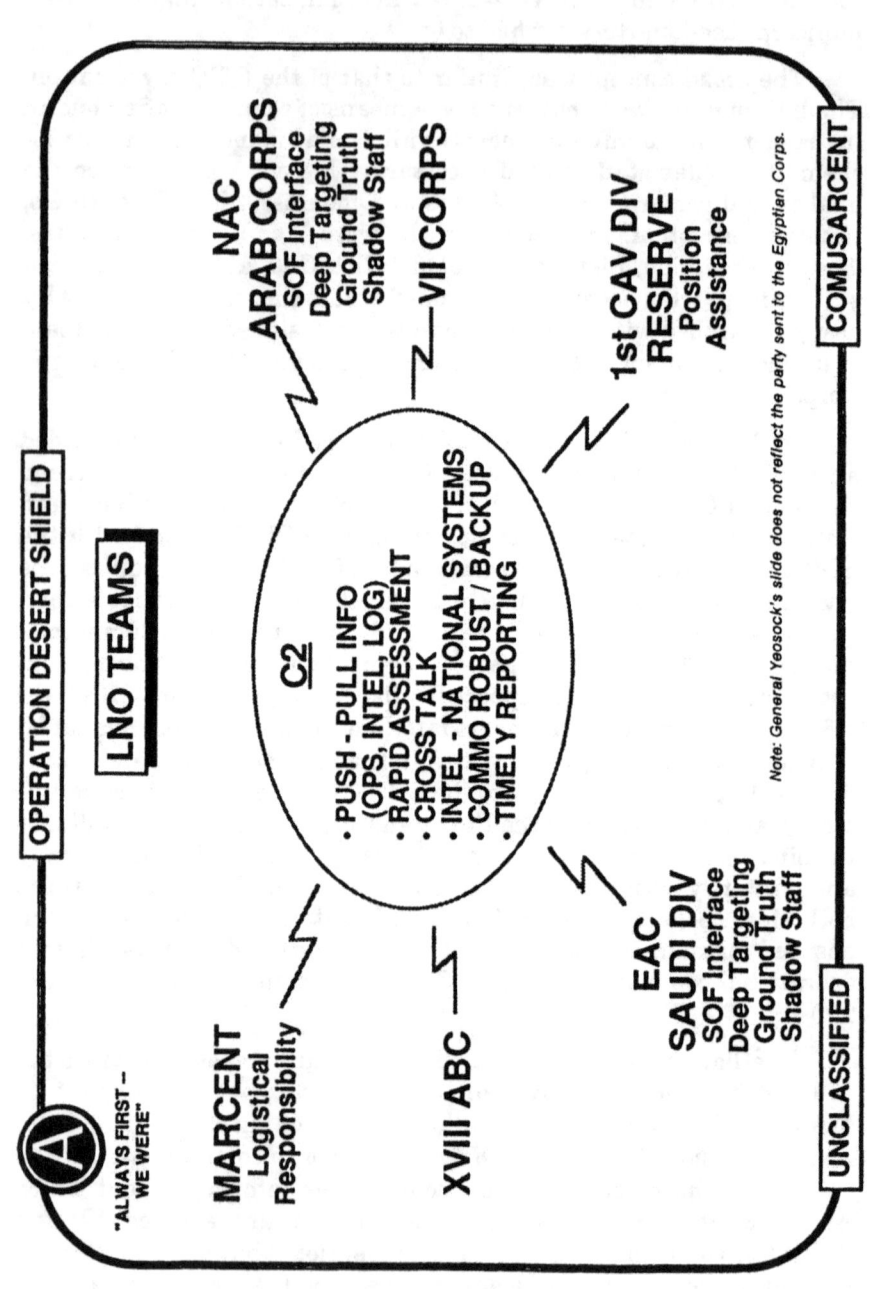

Figure 21. Liaison teams

report to the Third Army commander the premature withdrawal of occupation forces from Iraq by a senior subordinate commander understandably interested in getting his forces home.[11] Another team, in what must have been the loneliest job in the theater, acted as the permanent point of contact with Iraqi representatives after the cease-fire agreement in March.

These parties were to be large—up to thirty or so officers and enlisted soldiers—and multifaceted, to cover all staff functions. They were to have several vehicles and redundant robust communications, particularly multichannel TACSAT (tactical satellite) equipment.[12] Liaison officers (LNOs) were not just to pass on information but to evaluate it from the point of view of the army commander. They were, in fact, to provide information that distances and circumstances prevented the army commander from obtaining firsthand. The chief LNOs were to be "directed telescopes"—the eyes and ears of the commander. In Yeosock's words after the war, the key was "to bridge" the command and control functions of the land component commander (in the absence of such a figure). The solution was to use LNO teams that had capabilities in command, operations, logistics, plans, and communication. "For U.S. forces it was overkill, but for Arab-Islamic forces it became in many respects a shadow staff to make up for their inability to deal with planning at the level required."[13]

While these parties were created by ARCENT, those teams assigned to duty with the Marines and Joint Command East were virtually taken over by CENTCOM once operations were under way. Particularly with the Arab forces, the teams became a means of addressing a variety of coalition problems whose resolution was required to ensure the success of Desert Storm. During the conduct of the battle, the two parties with the American corps and those with the Egyptians and the Joint Forces Command North acted as an extension of the army commander's personal staff and reported not through the G3, though they kept him informed, but through the commander's executive officer. This allowed Yeosock to circumvent the bureaucratic delay imposed by a large general staff structure. All seven team chiefs reported to the army commander's executive officer at least twice daily to update the commander on the situation where they were located.

If the idea of large liaison staffs was the commanding general's, the mobile CP seems to have been General Arnold's. Arnold was thinking in terms of a division or corps tactical CP.[14] Indeed, he took the idea from his experiences as G3 in the 9th Division and, later, I Corps. For Yeosock, the facility was never to be more than an alternative command post that he could use if the main CP were destroyed or interfered with.15 In either case, the facility had to be mobile (the Department of the Army provided nine expando vans), have a sophisticated communications package approximating that of the main CP, and be manned with a talented staff to monitor ongoing operations.

After 12 January, Yeosock used the mobile CP as a base for his deputy, General Frix, and Frix's de facto deputy (actually a deputy G3 who had arrived in theater as director of the Army's Training and Doctrine Command [TRADOC] Battle Command Training Program), Colonel Carl Ernst. They could act as ARCENT expediters—that is, as informed representatives of the commander, who could go and see what was happening, interpret guidance, synchronize ongoing operations, and provide feedback to the commander. This was done in a situation where the corps headquarters maintained communications with the main CP and the army commander. Subordinate commanders could refer to either when the interpretation of the expediters did not fit their own notions.16

Third Army was working out its command and control structure and processes as it deployed two corps and re-created itself from a basic shell. The mobile CP was an entirely new creation with a scratch team, like the rest of ARCENT, and its place in the command and control structure was unclear. It had to be developed even as it coordinated a major operational redeployment. The difference of creative vision between the tactical CP and the mobile alternate, as well as the presence of so much talent forward, sometimes produced a sort of schizophrenia in the headquarters. Moreover, both Arnold and Stewart, back at the main CP, seemed to be convinced that army command should be conducted forward. Yeosock, however, had always maintained he needed to be in the capital.

The principals at the forward CP clearly did perform as the field army "tactical" headquarters—that is, the operational center of the command and control apparatus for near-term actions during the assembly of the army around King Khalid Military City and for its redeployment to the west. The forward CP, "Lucky TAC" (after Patton's forward headquarters in World War II), included cells from the Support Command's 318th Movement Control Agency and the 89th Military Police Brigade, which had responsibility for ensuring the one east-west MSR operated efficiently. A small plans element headed by Major Kevin Reynolds developed contingency plans and served as something of an alter ego to the Plans Cell at "Lucky Main" in Riyadh. The G3 argued that the tactical CPs (TACs) should talk to corps TACs, the main CP to the corps' main CP, that fragmentary orders (FRAGOs) should be issued by the TAC (this was granted, but approval still came from the main CP and, when time was scarce, was not always observed anyway), and that contingency planning should be the sole province of the TAC, while long-term plans would be drawn up in the main CP.[17]

What all this "structure" failed to comprehend was that command takes place where the commander is. Throughout, Yeosock, who did not believe operational command and tactical command are analogous, maintained limits on the initiative of the mobile CP, which frustrated its aspirations to operational control. In the end, the army's war was run largely by the commander, through his personal staff at Eskan Village and his liaison teams (with key subordinate and adjacent headquarters), while using his general staff for detail and longer-term work. The mobile CP, as Yeosock always intended, was an alternate command post, a base for expediters who could untangle immediate problems and a headquarters to oversee the operations of the various echelon-above-corps troops. It did oversee important actions leading up to the initiation of the ground attack, not only redeployment but prisoner of war camp construction, development of echelon-above-corps communications systems, the conduct of mass casualty drills (in anticipation of chemical warfare), and replacement system operations—thereby freeing the army commander and his G3 to focus on future operational issues. The mobile CP also served as an aggressive seeker of information, supplementing the work of the liaison officers and main CP. One mark of its capabilities was that General Waller, who served as interim commander from 17-23 February while Yeosock underwent surgery in Germany, indicated that he intended to command from the mobile CP rather than the main CP.[18]

Whether Waller's solution would have been more or less successful than Yeosock's is speculative. The communication net at the mobile CP was not as robust as that at the main CP, which had been designed as the center of a communications web. Moreover, selection of the commander's location depended upon the respective officer's assessment of his relationships, not just with subordinates but with his superior and coordinate commanders. To have made the mobile CP a TAC was more congenial with most officers' cultural values, but it seems to have implied a great deal more direct control of tactical events than Yeosock intended or thought necessary. Waller's view also reflected greater confidence in his personal ties to Schwarzkopf and less concern with maintenance of personal contact with the joint air component commander and Arab officials once the ground attack began.

The third of Colonel Lackey's projects, the war room, was the least novel, though perhaps the most important one, since it was from here and the commander's office adjacent to it that the ARCENT war was run. The war room, a large bay-like facility, was built in the courtyard of the Eskan Village school house. Staff officers and liaison officers were placed in parallel banks of desks, with secure phones, in front of a large operational map. It was a sort of field expedient version of the NASA operations rooms. The war room had an extraordinary communication network that allowed the commander or G3 to speak to anyone from the JCS to the divisional CPs. G2 and G3 operations were integrated. This was underpinned by Generals Arnold and Stewart having held corresponding positions in the 9th Division earlier in their careers. Thus, the physical layout was backed up on the more personal level.

One external influence on the expansion of the army staff (and those of the corps and Support Command) should be addressed. This had to do with the Battle Command Training Program (BCTP), of which Colonel Carl F. Ernst was the director prior to his seconding to Third Army. BCTP is important because its multilevel involvement in planning and organizational activities is indicative of the extent to which the entire Army immediately focused its energies on supporting the forces in theater, sometimes overwhelming the actors with good ideas but generally making a large and positive contribution.

The BCTP is an organization designed to exercise and stretch the capabilities of senior staffs by providing an evaluated, interactive, computer-based war game to division and corps headquarters. It is the headquarters' combat training center. The BCTP evaluators are a group of bright, skilled, and often aggressive staff officers who critique in detail the staff processes and applications of doctrine by the units that are required to contend with their unforgiving opponent. To the extent that Colonel Purvis and his colleagues from SAMS represent the intellectual legacy of General William E. DePuy's organization of TRADOC, BCTP represents the countervailing tendency to a technical and positivist view of war reflected in the Army Training and Evaluation Program (ARTEP) and the national training centers. Its creed is tough, evaluated, realistic training to standard.[19]

Upon the initiation of Desert Shield, Colonel Ernst immediately offered his services and those of his organization to XVIII Airborne Corps, and as the crisis developed, he supported both the corps and the army headquarters by running staff exercises, developing simulations to test different planning options and, perhaps most important, seeding the various staffs with BCTP evaluators who became full working members of the organization (while retaining their contact with Ernst).[20] Two of these, Lieutenant Colonel Bob Schmidt and Major Kevin Reynolds, played key roles in writing operations plans for both corps and ARCENT.

BCTP members also set the standards for staffs coming together under pressure, as a large number of new members flowed in, particularly at ARCENT but also at VII Corps. This was not always without friction with the proprietary staff members, but most of the BCTP people were able to provide instruction without appearing to be Field Marshal Montgomery coming to "save" the Americans at the Bulge.

Ernst was ultimately retained as deputy G3 at ARCENT. Colonel Mike Hawk, one of his team chiefs, was deputy chief of staff at VII Corps. Ernst kept three BCTP members, among them Major Reynolds, with him in the mobile CP as a sort of alternate plans cell. Lieutenant Colonel Schmidt became chief of plans at VII Corps. The BCTP network, whatever else it did, provided another channel for information to flow between headquarters, sometimes to get previously rejected ideas reconsidered, often to get new ideas on the table. It is a measure of the trust vested in Ernst and his team that XVIII Corps took liberties with security surrounding the war plan to allow the colonel to test various offensive options against simulation, thereby widening significantly the circle of those privy to the ground attack plan, to include stations in CONUS.[21] The secret was held and useful insights were developed that subsequently assisted the command in preparing for Operation Desert Storm.

With the late December-early January forward deployment of the liaison teams and mobile CP and the development of the war room, ARCENT-Third Army had become a warfighting headquarters. At the same time, ARCENT continued to be a theater army, the departmental command in theater. In addition to, and simultaneous with, introducing a new corps, ARCENT had to expand its echelon-above-corps force structure to provide for a significantly greater demand for operational (theater) transportation, intelligence information, and such practical functions as engineer construction, graves registration, enemy prisoner of war operations, and civil affairs—matters generally not addressed in Army schools or on peacetime exercises. The 416th Engineer Command, 352d Civil Affairs Command, and the 800th Military Police Brigade were Reserve

Component units. ARCENT also formed an echelon-above-corps personnel command.

At the same time, ARCENT had to continue, indeed expand, the force modernization programs already under way, work out a scheme for replacement operations in anticipation of heavy combat losses, and organize a vast medical support structure built almost entirely on Reserve Component hospitals.

The expansion of the intelligence capabilities was extraordinary. When the ARCENT mission had called for a defense fought only by a single corps, that corps' intelligence organization had been deemed adequate. The intermediate army intelligence structure had been limited, and the ARCENT G2, unlike the G3 and G4, was a colonel, Beauford W. Tuton. Tuton had planned for expansion of the intelligence structure but had not been able to bring the desired augmentees forward under the minimum essential force guidance. Then, in November, the mission changed.

On 1 November, the echelon-above-corps intelligence brigade (the 513th Military Intelligence Brigade) had only 453 personnel in country; by 1 December, only 647. On 21 December, General Stewart was appointed Third Army G2 upon the medical evacuation of Colonel Tuton. Stewart had been commander of the Army Intelligence Agency. On 15 January, 1,546 members of the 513th had arrived in theater, and by 14 February, there were 1,792.[22]

Stewart was not responsible for calling forward the remainder of the 513th, but he did bring to the problem of establishing a theater army intelligence structure the rank and authority of a general officer, a great deal of dynamic energy (he was a tireless promoter of intelligence systems), and a fund of personal knowledge of the wider Army intelligence community that allowed him to bring in a number of talented assistants and several developmental systems for managing and distributing intelligence information. He thoroughly integrated the 513th into the G2 organization until, to all intents and purposes, he headed a staff section of almost 2,000, housed in a high-rise apartment complex next to the "School House," surrounded by barbed wire, and marked by a large number of satellite antenna dishes, communication vans, people in civilian clothes, and other attributes of a little "Langley." In essence, Stewart assembled and energized the theater ground intelligence structure in the month prior to D-day.

Stewart has provided a massive classified history of intelligence in the desert war and a personal executive summary.[23] The major issues from the standpoint of Army operations would seem to be these. Intelligence, prior to G(day)-8, was, by virtue of the deception plan and the nature of tactical intelligence systems, largely top-down. Because the echelon-above-corps intelligence structure arrived only late in the day, a good deal of operational and necessary tactical intelligence was not available when VII Corps arrived. Indeed, General Franks has noted that he could get little intelligence upon which to base his offensive plans when he began responding to the CINC's initial briefing in November.[24]

The lack of photographic support was particularly troublesome for forces that would have to breach the enemy defenses. Engineer diagrams on maps did not give breaching units the same confidence that overhead photography might have. Photographic imagery would be a continuous and emotional issue with tactical commanders, a consequence of paying for sophisticated strategic satellite systems by retiring older, but more numerous, operational and tactical aviation and Air Force systems without adequate replacements. Satellite imagery was excellent in quality, but its capability was limited in the number of targets it could handle at any given time. Because priorities for strategic systems were set elsewhere and because system design has been based largely on strategic needs, there was a clear loss of the capability that most division and brigade commanders had known in Vietnam. They were not happy about it.

On the other hand, in December Schwarzkopf had decided to bring in joint surveillance target attack radar system (J-STARS), a joint Army-Air Force system that was clearly the greatest operational intelligence success of the war. J-STARS are sets of down-looking airborne radars carried in old Boeing 707s that are capable of tracking moving targets on the ground. It lets operational commanders look on the other side of the hill, both for purposes of targeting and responding to operational initiatives by the enemy. In the uncharacteristically bad weather that marked Desert Storm, J-STARS was essential both to read the battlefield and interdict retreating Iraqi units.

Stewart was also successful in linking the ARCENT intelligence community with other departmental and extradepartmental sources and in introducing new intelligence information distribution systems still in the developmental stage.[25] The support and direct involvement of the Army Intelligence Agency seems to have been exceptional.

Some problems could not be solved. A shortage of Arabic linguists was overcome partially by the use of Kuwaiti student volunteers, but there were never enough. Stewart was forced to create a special intelligence distribution communications network from developmental systems, and VII Corps had to borrow an unmanned aerial vehicle (UAV), while the Navy was using drones to adjust naval gunfire from its battleships. Investment in tactical and operational intelligence had not kept pace, or else maneuver commanders had not been prepared for the economies of scale with which they were forced to contend.

In light of the comparatively late arrival of intelligence units and a general officer G2, the potential contribution of intelligence was underestimated, particularly in view of the implications of the theater deception plan and the key role battle damage assessment (BDA) played in the synchronization of ground and air operations. On the other hand, delay in bringing in the 513th Military Intelligence (MI) Brigade was consistent with policy on minimum essential forces that obtained until November and the ARCENT commander's decision to delay introduction of echelon-above-corps units until the last minute to give priority to combat forces and, after December, essential logistics support. It would be hard to find something brought in that could have been left out of the flow in order to introduce the remainder of the 513th MI Brigade any sooner than was done. As it was, artillery units were still flowing in country on G-day, and a large number of HETs arrived only in time to evacuate units from Iraq. Unquestionably, the 513th did arrive in time, if only just.

There was no G2 present at the ARCENT commander's daily general officer meetings prior to Stewart's arrival to argue army issues from the standpoint of likely Iraqi responses and to represent the intelligence field for a place on the priority list. However, Yeosock believed that he benefited from the council of Brigadier General Jack Leide, the CENTCOM J2, whom he believed to be one of the best intelligence professionals in the business.[26] In short, Yeosock did not feel that he was short of good intelligence for the major decisions required of him under the circumstances. After December, Stewart was the right man in the right place to deal with the problems of the "unforgiving minute."

More characteristic of the role of ARCENT were the actions undertaken to wrestle with the problem of operational transport. Once the two corps were in theater, the Third Army had to oversee and harmonize their movement to operational assembly areas and the build-up of their respective logistic bases. Although General Pagonis, as 22d Support Command commander and deputy commander for logistics, was responsible for the executive effort, the anticipation of requirements and oversight of the execution remained Yeosock's responsibilities. When need be, he acted as a referee between consumers (the two corps commanders) and supplier (the SUPCOM commander).

As has been said before, operational art is conducted in the offensive by trucks, HETs, lowboys (another form of heavy equipment transport vehicle), other line-haul vehicles, and cargo and fuel carriers that are able to accompany fighting vehicles into an enemy's operational depths. In Europe, where the Army was designed to fight, an extensive highway infrastructure permitted heavy dependence on commercial line-haul vehicles and the superb German rail system. In the Iraqi desert, there was no road net to speak of, and rough terrain vehicles capable of carrying ammunition and fuel had to be found to make the large units employed capable of continuous movement to the enemy's operational depth (about 300-400 kilometers).

To deploy VII Corps to its assembly area east of King Khalid Military City (274 or 334 miles away, depending on the arrival port) and to redeploy the 1st Cavalry Division, the 24th Infantry Division, and 3d Armored Cavalry of XVIII Corps to the west of Wadi al Batin (330 to 375 miles away, depending on the unit), heavy equipment transporters and lowboys had to be found. (See figure 22.) Furthermore, none of these initiatives would be of any use at all if drivers could not be located for the vehicle trains. Yeosock invested his time and energies in December and January resolving these problems. The nature of the solutions, again, is instructive for those who would understand the role of the theater army.

The most sensitive problem had to do with the HETs required to move tanks (and the lowboys, which move only smaller-tracked vehicles). Based upon the arrival dates of tanks from Europe, the intention to complete the movements within two weeks of the onset of air operations, and various force modernization initiatives, ARCENT planners arrived at a requirement for 1,295 HETs against a supply of only 897 in the entire Army inventory.[27]

In late November and throughout December and January, Yeosock and his chief supplier, General Gordon Sullivan, the Army vice chief of staff, began the great HET hunt. Pagonis networked the logistics community, and CENTCOM approached the European allies through U.S. European Command.[28] On 14 January, there were only 461 HETs in theater, 335 from the host nation, 126 from U.S. sources. On 29 January, there were 653 including 100 Egyptian HETs. On 14 February, there were 759 HETs, including U.S. commercial and Italian models, compared to an expectation in December that 788

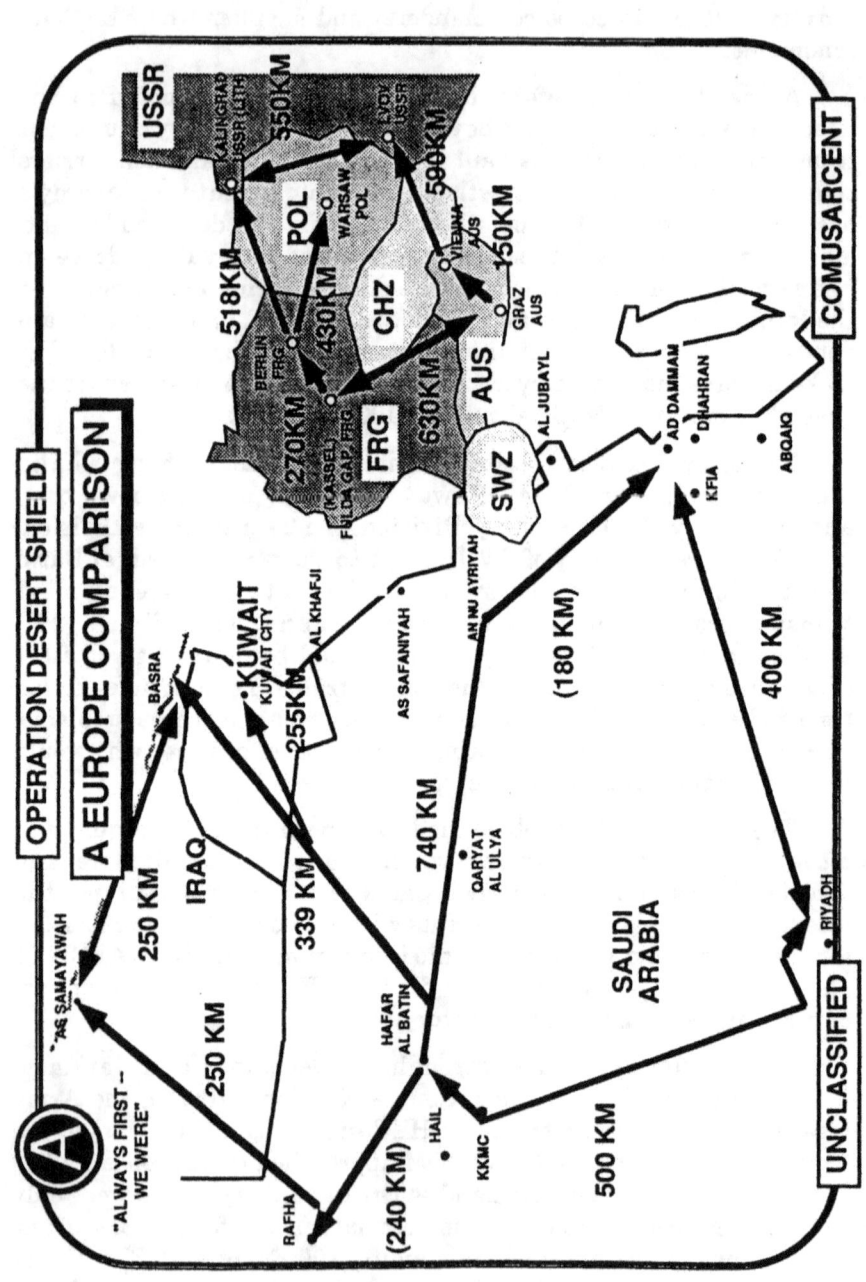

Figure 22.

would be in theater by 15 January.[29] The 1,295 requirement would be met only after Desert Storm, when a total of 1,404 HETs had been acquired from various sources.[30]

HETs were of sufficient importance that they gradually moved up the priority list in the ARCENT situation report until, on 7 December, they became the number-one equipment issue. Material-handling equipment was also considered a "war stopper."[31] The goal was to complete the movement to the tactical assembly areas and stock the two eastern logistic bases by 31 January. In December, it was clear that this was to take an extraordinary effort given the shortfall in trucks, the limitations in the road net, the distances involved, and the sheer scale of the problem.

Use of various line-haul assets became the ARCENT commander's principal command issue in December and January. Each day, following his morning operational update and general officers meeting, Yeosock would retreat to his office, where he would figure the progress on land movement to date. During the night, Colonel Bob Kliemon, the transportation officer in the ARCENT G4 office, provided information on vehicle availability. Colonel Dave Whaley, the commander of the 7th Transportation Group, would provide information about what was in the port requiring movement forward. In this way, Yeosock could manipulate the limited resources in hand and ensure that various problems—a poor run of HET tires, the need for repair parts, whatever it took to keep the flow going—were addressed at the highest levels of the Army.[32] Ultimately (12 January), he dispatched General Frix and the mobile CP to King Khalid Military City to provide overwatch of the various pieces for the great trek west. Yeosock's problem was far different from that of the planner who figures the requirements to do a job. His task was to take the "glass half-full" and make sure it met the demands of the situation at hand. And, of course, the people who had to live up to the expectations were the transportation managers of the 22d Support Command.

Besides centralized management of all aspects of the movement, Yeosock and Pagonis used what the former referred to as "work arounds," temporary expedients to compensate for shortages. The 1st Cavalry Division began moving to King Khalid Military City in late December in anticipation of the shift west. This move also reduced the surge load anticipated for mid-January when the VII Corps was to arrive at the same time the XVIII Corps was to begin its movement westward and the Support Command was to initiate the army logistics build-up west of the wadi. When the "Tiger Brigade" shifted north to join MARCENT in January (to replace the 1st U.K. Armored Division that came to VII Corps), it was sent overland rather than mounted on wheeled carriers. Repair parts were surged behind the brigade from the base at Dhahran to compensate for wear and tear on the vehicles. In similar fashion, two Bradley battalions of the 1st Armored Division self-deployed to the VII Corps assembly area.[33] Still, out on the MSR, a wheeled vehicle passed the MP at Hafar al Batin intersection about every fifteen seconds.

The forces in Saudi Arabia were heavily dependent upon host-nation vehicles and donated equipment from many nations to meet line-haul transportation needs. These vehicles were of limited use without American drivers or, in the case of vehicles driven by third-country nationals, "assistant drivers."[34] On 22 December, ARCENT laid out its requirements for drivers, and the 10th Personnel Command, the newly formed echelon-above-corps personnel manager, addressed itself to the task of obtaining no fewer than 7,444 soldiers to drive buses and trucks and to serve as "supercargoes" and back-up drivers on third country vehicles in case the civilian drivers decided not to come to the war.[35] To fill these requirements, the Army called up Reserve Component units and deployed them without vehicles. The Army accelerated training for new soldiers and even converted an air defense battalion (3/2d Air Defense Artillery) wholesale.[36] A number of highly trained light infantrymen went to war in the cab of a third-country line-haul truck.

The measure of the success was in the doing. By 9 February, the date of the briefing to the secretary of defense, SUPCOM had moved the two corps to their new assembly areas. It had stocked logistic bases that had not existed thirty days before with more than five days' rations—close to 100 percent of the forward fuel stockage objective (VII Corps' Log Base E was at 100 percent; XVIII Corps' Log Base C was at 73 percent) and ammunition (60 percent or better in the forward bases).[37]

The time required to complete the build-up past the 31st was a consequence of continued shortages in line-haul trucks, delays in ship arrivals, and the general constraints in the system. In the event, a line-haul truck took three days for a round trip—a day going, a day returning, and a day for maintenance and crew rest. Sometimes, the average was more like four days. That meant that two-thirds of the fleet was not productively engaged at any one time. Efficiency could be further reduced when maintenance availability declined. (The original SUPCOM plan had assumed only a 60 percent operational rate.) The delay in build-up was compensated for by the additional time involved in arriving at the 50 percent attrition of the Iraqi forces in the KTO. That, as it happened, was achieved as the troop build-up and force redeployment was coming to an end.

In addition to finding thousands of drivers, Personnel Command (PERSCOM) also established a replacement system that would provide trained squads, teams, and crews (with their combat systems) as unit replacements. PERSCOM also oversaw the normal individual replacement flow as well. Designated replacement battalion commanders were collected in theater against potential losses.[38] The scale of the medical system that backed up the combat forces and the investment in the replacement systems is indicative of an Army prepared for significant combat losses and another indication that, before 24 February, no one in authority expected an easy victory. About 13,580 beds were available in the ARCENT area of operations on G-day, backed up by facilities in Europe and CONUS.[39] The Army located a training team from the 7th Army Training Command in Europe at King Khalid Military City. This detachment set up a training program for the replacement squads, crews, and teams.[40] The presence of these basic combat units in Saudi Arabia represented a great cost to the total Army but reflected the corporate effort invested in victory.

The force modernization (the replacement of older systems with newer models) of Bradley and Abrams units that had begun before the dispatch of VII Corps continued. All units were not modernized before the offensive, however. Two armored battalions of the 1st Infantry were not upgunned (the 3d and 4th Battalions of the 37th Armor). And the 197th Infantry Brigade (Mechanized) (Separate) in the 24th Infantry Division attacked with infantry still in M113 armored personnel carriers rather than Bradley infantry fighting vehicles. In addition to combat vehicles, units swapped old commercial four-wheel-drive trucks for the ubiquitous high-mobility multipurpose wheeled vehicles (HMMWVs), the successor to World War II Jeeps.[41] Perhaps most important, by 23 February, in order to improve divisional off-road logistic mobility, 203 heavy expanded mobility tactical truck (HEMTT) fuelers and 435 HEMTT cargo trucks had been issued to ARCENT units, including the 1st Cavalry Division and "Tiger Brigade."[42] HEMTT fuelers were so important that significant air transport was dedicated to bringing in 269. Without the 100 HEMTT fuelers issued to the 24th Division, it is unlikely that the "Victory Division" would have made it to the Euphrates valley.

The principal addition to the Third Army was the VII Corps, designated to be the striking force for the coalition ground offensive.

The VII Corps started its preparation for Desert Storm in August 1990, although no one knew it at the time. Almost at once, following the Iraqi invasion, General Franks convened a small planning group in his headquarters "to get our heads in the game a little bit."[43]

Franks would command the largest armored force concentrated in a single attack in U.S. military history. He is not a typical cavalryman in appearance or demeanor. He is short, circumspect, and deliberate. A lot of U.S. service members are very likely alive today because of that circumspection. Franks is one of the few generals in the Army who wears a mustache, and he holds a Master of Philosophy degree in literature from Columbia University. He is a gentleman, a man of quiet firmness, extraordinary character, and self-discipline. Franks lost a leg in Vietnam (as did his G3, Colonel Stan Cherrie) while a staff officer in the 11th Armored Cavalry Regiment. He remained in the service, rising to command of the 11th Cavalry, the 1st Armored Division, and the VII Corps. He served between command tours as deputy commandant of the U.S. Army Command and General Staff College at Fort Leavenworth. In Desert Storm, he would move five heavy divisions against the Iraqi flank, maneuvering two of them and an armored cavalry regiment north, then east, in formation while retaining concentration—a maneuver reminiscent of another Frederick at a place called Leuthen.

At first, VII Corps' problem was to deploy various small formations and individuals from Europe to reinforce XVIII Corps, but Franks and his staff also speculated on the possibility of having to send larger elements, for example an armored division. Later, Franks would say he had been reminded, by the end of the cold war and the drawdown then in progress, of the transfer of European divisions to the Pacific in World War II following VE-Day. In addition, Franks had recognized the operational implications of the collapse of the Soviet bloc and had reoriented corps training to focus on movement to contact and attack from the march, in contrast with the European General Defense Plan scenario of linear forward defense that had dominated Army thinking since the fall of South Vietnam.[44]

When ordered to deploy the corps, Franks' earlier exploratory work proved invaluable. General Crosbie Saint, the commander of U.S. Army Europe, met with Franks on 4 November, even before the presidential deployment announcement, to decide on what units to deploy. Saint assumed responsibility for the deployment itself, thus freeing Franks and VII Corps to concentrate on their responsibilities in Saudi Arabia.[45]

It was decided that two armored divisions would be sent with the corps, as well as the corps troop package that included its armored cavalry regiment (the 2d Armored Cavalry). The decision was made, too, to take only units already modernized in favor of those still requiring new M1A1 tanks and M2 or M3 Bradleys. The 3d Armored Division from V Corps, the other U.S. Europe-based corps, was to be one of the divisions. VII Corps' own 1st Armored Division was the second. The 3d Armored Division was commanded by Major General Paul Funk. Coincidentally, Funk's son, who served as a captain in the Persian Gulf, was married to General Yeosock's daughter. The 1st Armored was commanded by Major General Ron Griffith. Later, the 1st Infantry Division, a Reforger unit from Fort Riley, Kansas, was added at Yeosock's request.[46] The 1st Infantry was commanded by Major General Tom Rhame.

Accommodation had to be made for units already in the process of deactivation and for certain NATO political sensitivities concerning reversion of U.S.-operated facilities to German control.[47] Saint and Franks elected to send a brigade package of the 3d Infantry Division (built around the 3d Brigade of the 3d Infantry) in lieu of one brigade of the 1st Armored. They also decided to replace the 1st Infantry Division (Forward), a brigade group of the 1st Infantry Division based in Germany, with V Corps' 2d Armored Division (Forward), another Europe-based brigade group of the U.S.-based 2d Armored Division.[48] The 1st Infantry Division (Forward), whose connection with its parent division was limited, was in an advanced stage of deactivation. Moreover, sending the 2d Armored Division (Forward) configured the 1st Infantry Division as an armored division, title notwithstanding. An armored battalion and air defense battalion of the 8th Infantry Division rounded out the 3d Armored Division.[49]

The 1st Infantry Division (Forward) went to Saudi Arabia to operate the ports that received the VII Corps, thus speeding the corps to the front. The men of the brigade were retained through the ground war as part of the potential replacement pool.[50]

In addition to forming the combat force, another task required coordination between U.S. European Command (USAREUR), Forces Command, and CENTCOM. The VII Corps support command had to be raised to a wartime strength suitable for an out-of-theater deployment. This involved an expansion of about 300 percent, largely by Reserve Component soldiers deployed by Forces Command from the United States. The VII Corps added 19,908 Reserve Component soldiers to its force structure.[51]

Deployment, of course, had to be in consonance with the Third Army plan. General Franks went to Saudi Arabia almost at once to meet with General Yeosock to discuss deployment and to conduct a reconnaissance. Before departing, Franks had received a call from Yeosock and General Pagonis to provide general guidance on preparing for the transfer of forces. Unlike XVIII Corps, which was involved in rapidly building a deterrent combat force, VII Corps could front-load sufficient engineers, command and control, and sustainment elements to prepare the corps assembly area for the inbound combat forces. Not surprisingly, Pagonis told Franks to bring all the HETs he could get his hands on.[52] An additional advantage enjoyed by VII Corps was the ability to talk to commanders already on the ground in advance of deployment. The corps made up a draft time-phased force deployment list, and Franks took it to Saudi Arabia for Yeosock's approval.[53]

Just as the 1st Infantry Division (Forward) was dispatched to handle inbound port operations for the corps, the 3d Infantry Division, one of the Army's proudest combat units, took responsibility for supporting port operations in the three ports used to depart Europe. The 3d also provided weapons and support personnel so the corps could conduct final predeployment training at the 7th Army Training Area at Grafenwöhr, Germany.[54] An Army that had prepared for reception of state-side Reforger units for war in NATO now reversed the process and moved divisions, regiments, brigades, and groups to the ports of Antwerp, Bremerhaven, and Rotterdam by train, barge, and road.[55] Some aviation units simply flew to ports in Italy. One of the unique features of Desert Shield-Desert Storm was that units in both CONUS and Europe moved to deployment ports on inland waterways by barge, not a normal way of doing business in either theater.

On 30 November, the ARCENT SITREP contained an entry concerning VII Corps that read: ". . . INITIALLY, THE CORPS WILL ESTABLISH A STRONG C2 AND LOGISTICAL CAPABILITY, DEPLOY A REINFORCED CAV REGT, AND PREPARE TO RECEIVE THE REMAINDER OF THE CORPS."[56]

By then, fifteen ships were en route to the ports. Of the corps equipment, 40 percent had departed the home station. XVIII Corps continued to modernize tanks and infantry units, and the 24th Division was conducting joint training with Saudi units.[57] XVIII Corps' 1st Corps Support Command (1st COSCOM) was completing its deployment, still playing catch-up from the earlier minimum essential force guidance. Meanwhile, the strength of Iraqi forces was estimated to have reached 3,790 tanks and 2,390 armored personnel carriers.[58]

By 15 December, as CENTCOM prepared to brief the secretary of defense, VII Corps could report forty-eight ships en route to the theater, four unloading, and two more due that day. Two days later, the 24th Division conducted a combined-arms live-fire exercise with a combined U.S.-Saudi force, the culmination of the corps' efforts at combined training.[59]

By the end of the year, the 2d Armored Cavalry Regiment, reinforced by the 210th Field Artillery Brigade, was screening the corps' assembly area west of the XVIII Corps, while the divisions prepared to receive their combat battalions. The 1st Cavalry Division was en route to assembly area Wendy, southwest of King Khalid Military City. At that time, 27 January, the last of VII Corps' equipment was expected.[60]

The new deployment was not without difficulties. To speed VII Corps to the theater, ships were loaded without regard to unit integrity. That meant a good bit of confusion existed, and sorting was necessary at the reception ports. The shortage of HETs led to clogged ports and concentrations of soldiers, who arrived by plane, then waited for up to three weeks for their equipment.[61] As late as 14 January, General Arnold observed to General Taylor at Forces Command that "Early deployment of combat units over CSS units and equipment continues to haunt us. MHE [materiel handling equipment] shipped and enroute will solve many of our problems. HETS, Low Boys & S.&Ps. continue to be well short of requirements. Backlog at the ports is considerable and growing."[62]

On 16 January, HET tires were identified as one of the highest-priority items, with 3,000 required immediately.[63] The estimate of Iraqi strength had reached 4,280 tanks and 2,880 armored personnel carriers. The next night the war began. (See figure 23.)

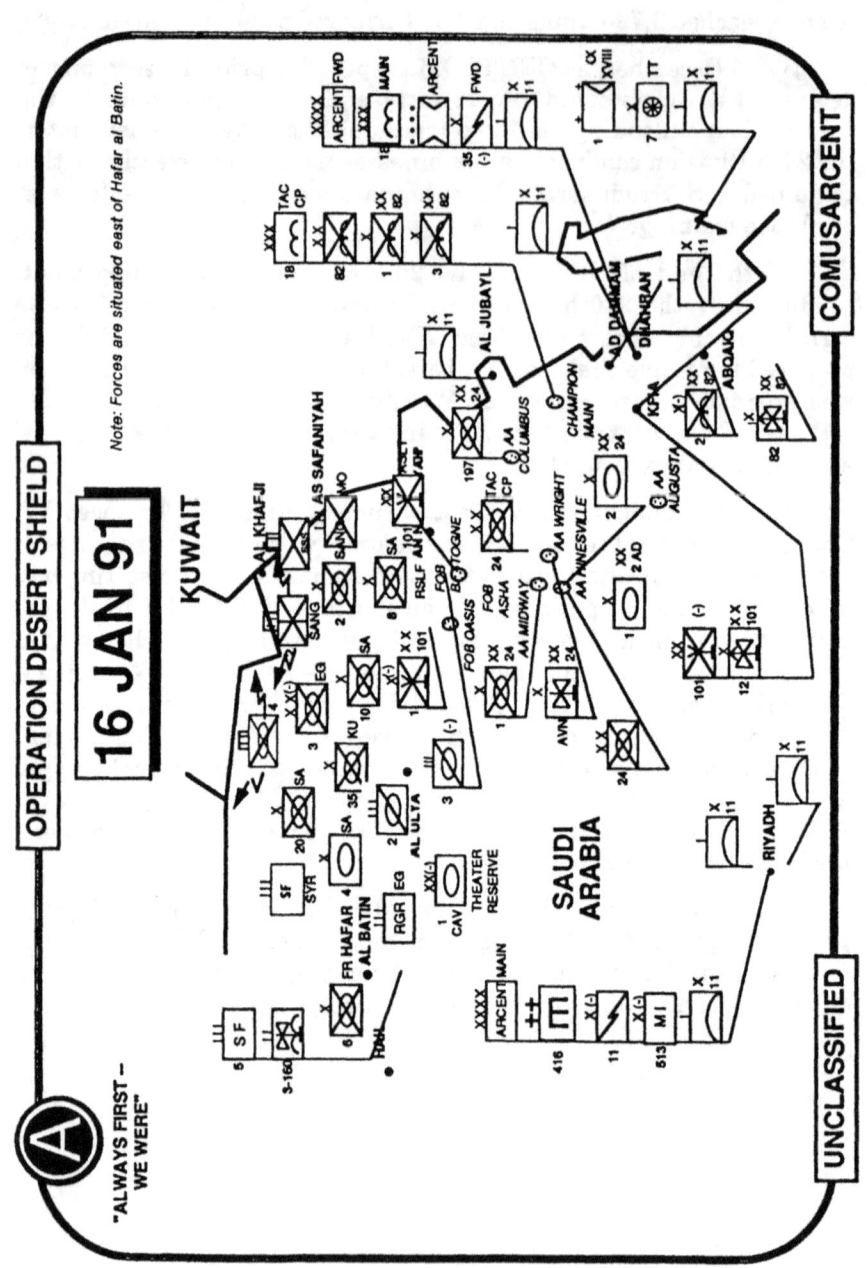

Figure 23. Allied deployments the day prior to the start of air operations

Notes

1. The British SAS had a good bit of trouble with winter weather conditions in Iraq and lost one soldier to hypothermia. See de la Billiere, *Storm Command*, 225, 239.

2. HQ, 22d Support Command, briefing titled, "Theater Logistics Concept," dated 27 December 1990, slide titled, "ARCENT Strength Projection," shows that the ARCENT target for 15 December to 15 January was 4,265 soldiers per day compared to 1,168 from 7 August to 6 December. General Pagonis compared the effort to Reforger in which only about 10,000 total soldiers were moved to the theater after a year's preparation. A transcript of General Pagonis' 27 December briefing prepared by 44th MHD, 4. A 27 December briefing was presented at the ARCENT MAPEX. The transcript reflects what General Pagonis said as he presented briefing slides. Hereafter, both documents will be referred to as HQ, 2d Support Command, briefing titled, "Theater Logistics Concept," dated 27 December 1990, with the transcript or slides indicated thereafter.

3. Interview with Colonel Jorgenson at HQ, ARCENT, 9 March 1991, 31. In fact, General Arnold had attended the armor school officer advanced course, had been a battalion and division staff officer, and a battalion commander in the 8th Infantry Division in Europe. He was not entirely innocent of heavy experience.

4. Colonel Jorgenson attributed this "demotion" to the CINC's refusal to talk to colonels. Interview with Colonel Jorgenson at HQ, ARCENT, 9 March 1991, 18. The explanation in the text was given the author by General Yeosock and is a more reasonable account.

5. De la Billiere, *Storm Command*, 42, 148–49.

6. Logistic support for enemy prisoners of war was largely provided by a Saudi contractor. Construction of facilities was done by the 416th Engineers, and custody and administration was in the hands of the 800th Military Police Command, which also had to do a good deal of the building.

7. The other two were global positioning systems and the 22d Support Command. HQ, ARCENT, Command Group, command briefing titled, "Theater Operations Desert Shield/Desert Storm," slide titled, "Commander's Keys to Success," dated 15 August 1991.

8. HQ, ARCENT, Command Group, Memorandum for Major General Taylor, ARCENT Rear, Subject: ARCENT Command SITREP as of COB 27 Oct (C+81), signed R. S. Frix, BG, USA.

9. Interview with Major General Steve Arnold, Eskan Village, 15 March 1991, 19. Description of parties as minicorps headquarters was a common metaphor in General Yeosock's explanations of his liaison parties.

10. On the special forces teams, see Dr. Richard W. Stewart, USASOC Command Historian, Roles and Missions of Special Operations in Desert Storm: An Initial Historical Summary. There are a number of after-action reports from ARCENT liaison parties. The quality of each is largely dependent upon the time remaining from redeployment to Riyadh and departure for CONUS. Interest was not always high. The best account concerning working with the Arab forces is that by Colonel

Daniel M. Ferezan, who was in charge of the team with the Egyptian Corps, Memorandum for Commander, Third U.S. Army, Attn: G3, APO NY 09772, Subject: Project 5/Liaison Team Golf After-Action Report, dated 31 March 1991. A testier report was prepared by Colonel Joseph D. Molinari, team chief to Joint Forces Command North, Subject: After-Action Report for the United States Liaison [sic], Advisory and Assistance Team to Joint Forces Command North during Operation Desert Shield-Storm, n.d. The teams were, by necessity, thrown together hurriedly at Fort Bragg, deployed to Saudi Arabia, and then sent almost at once to the field. Some seem to have taken being "jerked around" in this fashion better than others. The author attended the liaison officer after-action review in Kuwait City at Task Force Freedom in March 1991.

11. The author was in the ARCENT main CP when the matter was reported and discussed by CG and ARCENT staff. The unit was XVIII Corps.

12. Equipment is listed on a series of messages between ARCENT and CONUS (see for example, Message, 272015Z NOV 90, FM CDR XVIIIABNCORPS FT BRAGG NC//AFZQ-MS//, Subject: ARCENT Projects 5, 5A, and 9) and in a briefing titled, "ARCENT Communications Laydown," n.d.; and slide titled, "Field Army Liaison Team Commo Package (6 Required)." This briefing was prepared early in the planning process from notes on final sheet. See also liaison officer after-action reports.

13. Quoted in HQ, ARCENT, Command Group, undated memorandum written by Lieutenant Colonel Mike Kendall, titled, "CG Comments on the Context of ARCENT Operations." Memorandum will be retired with General Yeosock's personal papers to the Military History Institute, Carlisle Barracks, Pennsylvania.

14. Interview with Major General Steven Arnold, Eskan Village, 15 March 1991, 21–22.

15. Ibid. General Yeosock was entirely consistent in his view of the mobile CP and in the instructions he gave his staff and G6, Colonel Sutten. He intended to command from the main CP. Guidance is given in HQ, ARCENT, Command Group, Memorandum for Record, Subject: (Executive Officer's) Daily Memo, dated 2 January 1991, paragraph 4; and HQ, ARCENT, Command Group, Memorandum for Record, Subject: (Executive Officer's) Daily Memo, dated 29 January 1991, paragraph 5 (filed with General Yeosock's personal records at the Army Military History Institute); and interview with Colonel Jorgensen, 6, 16. Both General Yeosock and Colonel Sutten indicated to the author that command could have been shifted first to the Royal Saudi Land Forces Building within Riyadh had that been necessary before moving to the mobile CP.

16. Lieutenant Colonel Hentsch was a German General Staff officer who visited the front in August 1914 and is sometimes blamed for causing the Schlieffen Plan to be halted by way of his interpretation of the wishes of the High Command.

17. A briefing was prepared to align the relative responsibilities of both CPs by the G3 for presentation at the MAPEX in late December. Slides are titled, "USARCENT OPLAN 001—Desert Storm, Command and Control—Fwd," and "USARCENT OPLAN 001—Desert Storm, Command and Control—Main," all marked 122735D. According to Lieutenant Colonel Kendall, the CG's XO, General Yeosock did not allow the presentation. At the mobile CP, General Frix instructed the members, while the author was present, that there was only one "integrated staff" and the

mobile CP should think of itself in that way, each section as part of its parent division in the main CP.

18. Interview with Major General Steven Arnold, Eskan Village, 15 March 1991, 22–23. The author was in the mobile CP when General Frix announced General Waller's intent.

19. If General (Ret.) Donn Starry was the intellectual father of AirLand Battle—first as commandant of the Armor Center then as TRADOC commander following General DePuy—General (Ret.) Paul Gorman was the founder of the Army training system as a brigadier general of DePuy's TRADOC staff in the seventies. For the organization of TRADOC and the background on the two threads of TRADOC's approach to preparing for war, see Major Paul H. Herbert, *Deciding What Has to Be Done: General William E. DePuy and the 1976 Edition of FM 100-5*, Operations, Leavenworth Paper No. 16 (Fort Leavenworth, KS: Combat Studies Institute, 1988).

20. See interview with Colonel Carl F. Ernst, director, Battle Command Training Program, by W. Glenn Robertson in U.S. Army Combined Arms Command, 1990 Annual Command History, CAC History Office (Fort Leavenworth, Kansas), 297, et seq. Much of what follows is based on the author's observations as well as Colonel Ernst's interview.

21. Ernst interview, 335.

22. Message, 012359Z NOV 90, FM COMUSARCENT MAIN//AFRD-CS//, MSGID/SITREP/USARCENT MAING3//PERID/312400Z/TO:012400Z/ ASOF:012400Z, 8. Message, 012359Z DEC 90, FM COMUSARCENT MAIN// AFRD-CS//, MSGID/SITREP/USARCENT MAING3//PERID/302400Z/TO: 0102400Z/ASOF:012400Z, 11. Message, 152359Z JAN 91, FM COMUSARCENTMAIN//AFRD-DT//, MSGID/SITREP/USARCENT MAING3// PERID/142400Z/TO:1502400Z/ASOF:152400Z, 10. HQ, ARCENT, G3, ARCENT Morning Brief, Friday, 15 February 1991 (D+29), slide titled, "ARCENT Personnel Strength."

23. A complete report was returned to the Intelligence School for further analysis. The executive summary is by Brigadier General John F. Stewart, Jr., Operation Desert Storm: The Military Intelligence Story: A View from the G2, 3d U.S. Army (April 1991).

24. Interview with General Frederick Franks, by the Strategic Studies Institute, U.S. Army War College, Carlisle Barracks, Pennsylvania, at the Pentagon on 31 October 1991, 22. The author was present.

25. Stewart, *Operation DESERT STORM*, 12 et seq.

26. General Yeosock to author.

27. For the total number of Army HETs, Appendix R to Department of Defense, Office of the Secretary of Defense, Conduct of the Persian Gulf Conflict: A Final Report to Congress Pursuant to Title V of the Persian Gulf Conflict Supplemental Authorization and Personnel Benefits Act of 1991 (Public Law 102-25), January 1992 Final Coordinating Draft, R-G-64. For 1,295 figure, see HQ, 22d Support Command, briefing titled, "Theater Logistics Concept," dated 27 December 1990, slide titled, "Theater Heavy Lift Capability, Requirement to Move XVIII Corps."

Transcript of briefing makes it clear 1,295 was total figure for two corps notwithstanding title of slide. Ibid., 13-18.

28. General Pagonis in ibid. General Yeosock to author. ARCENT SITREP for 4 December requests CENTCOM intervention with EUCOM. Author's assumption is that ARCENT would not have asked were CENTCOM and EUCOM not dealing with the issue. Message, 042359Z DEC 90, FM COMUSARCENT MAIN//AFRD-CS//, MSGID/SITREP/USARCENT MAIN G3/PERID/032400Z/TO: 042400/ASOF:042400, 11-12.

29. HQ, ARCENT, SUPCOM (Prov) LOGSITREP #163, 152300CJAN91, 1. HQ, ARCENT, SUPCOM (Prov) LOGSITREP D+14 day 302300JAN91, 1. HQ, ARCENT, SUPCOM LOGSITREP D+30 152300FEB91, 1. Projection in December is in HQ, ARCENT, Command Group, briefing titled, "Sec Def Brief" (handwritten, no title slide), 15 December 1990, slide titled, "HET Status." These appear to be slides prepared for the commanding general to use during briefing the secretary of defense and chairman on 20 December. Numbers were soft as reference to December SITREPS will show.

30. Appendix R to Department of Defense, Office of the Secretary of Defense, Conduct of the Persian Gulf Conflict; A Final Report to Congress Pursuant to Title V of the Persian Gulf Conflict Supplemental Authorization and Personnel Benefits Act of 1991 (Public Law 102-25), January 1992 Final Coordinating Draft, R-G-64, lists total shipped. On 24 February, there were only 761 reported in theater. HQ, ARCENT, SUPCOM LOGSITREP D+39, 242300FEB91, 1.

31. Message, 072359Z DEC 90, FM COMUSARCENT MAIN//AFRD-CS//, MSGID/SITREP/USARCENT MAIN G3// PERID/062400/ TO:072400Z/ASOF:072400Z, 13. Paragraph 7 read: Our greatest need is transportation to move armored/mechanized forces great distances. HETs and like transportation is considered an integral and vital part of the force to be moved. It is not an add on. If adequate transportation is not shipped with the force, then the force will not be able to get to their tactical assembly areas on time. On Materiel Handling Equipment, see HQ, 22d Support Command, briefing titled, "Theater Logistics Concept," dated 27 December 1990, transcript, 4-5.

32. Lieutenant Colonel Mike Kendall, General Yeosock's XO, to author. HQ, ARCENT, Command Group, Memorandum for Record, Subject: (XO's) Daily Memo, 5 January 1991, dated 5 January 1991 and HQ, ARCENT, Command Group, Memorandum for Record, Subject: (XO's) Daily Memo, 16 January 1991, dated 16 January 1991. Daily Memos will be retired to the Army Military History Institute with General Yeosock's personal papers.

33. Message, 260300Z JAN 91, FM COMUSARCENT MAIN//DT//, MSGID/SITREP/USARCENT/D+9/JAN//, PERID/250300Z/TO:260300Z/ASOF:260300Z, 9.

34. The drivers issue was raised in 2 December ARCENT SITREP, Message, 022359Z DEC 90, FM COMUSARCENT MAIN//AFRD-CS//, MSGID/SITREP/USARCENT MAIN G3//PERID/302400Z/TO:012400Z/ASOF:012400Z, 13-14. See also, HQ, 22d Support Command, briefing titled, "Theater Logistics Concept," dated 27 December 1990, transcript, 17-18. HQ, 10th Personnel Command Command Report, Operation Desert Shield, 23 August 1990 to 16 January 1991, 19-20. General Yeosock tracked

influx of drivers in his morning briefings in late January and February, not without some confusion as to whether requirement was for 3,444, 4,000, or 7,444. The problem resulted from the fact that the second increment (4,000) was worked directly by COMUSARCENT and the vice chief to the bewilderment of their respective staff bookkeepers who finally ended up keeping two sets of books on both increments until the first was completely filled.

35. There were in fact two separate requests, one for 3,444 and one for 4,000, the latter made by General Yeosock in conversation with General Sullivan. It would appear that the first increment of 3,444 was received by 7 February and that 2,052 of the second increment of 4,000 would have arrived by 24 February to total 5,496. See slides titled, "Drivers Update in HQ, ARCENT, G3, ARCENT Morning Briefing, Saturday, 2 February 1991 (D+16)" and "HQ, ARCENT, G3, ARCENT Morning Briefing, Saturday, 23 February 1991 (D+37)." On 12 January, as the 15 January UN deadline approached, General Frix noted to General Taylor that host-nation drivers were starting to quit in large numbers. HQ, ARCENT, AFRD-DCG (122359Z January 1991), Memorandum for Major General Taylor, ARCENT Rear, Subject: ARCENT Command SITREP as of COB 12 Jan (C+158). After it became apparent that dire predictions about indiscriminate use of chemicals were not likely to prove correct, drivers came back, and, in some cases, even took their trucks into Iraq with the invasion forces.

36. HQ, 3d Battalion, 2d Air Defense Artillery Regiment, Memorandum for Major General Thomas H. Tait, Director Desert Storm Study Project, Subject: Study Project Team Visit. HQ, 702d Transportation Battalion (Provisional), Battalion Operations Diary, Saudi Arabia, 1990–91. The 702d was the Support Command unit responsible for direction of host-nation transportation.

37. HQ, ARCENT G4, ARCENT Morning Briefing Logistics Status slides for 9 February 1991. The stockage objective for the forward bases was five days' food and fuel.

38. HQ, 10th Personnel Command Command Report, Operation Desert Shield, 23 August 1990 to 16 January 1991, 17–29. After-action report implies issue only arose at MAPEX. When Army chief of staff was briefed on 24 December, he was asked for 116 tank crews, 120 Bradley crews, 18 AH-64 crews, and 24 UH-60 crews. HQ, ARCENT, Command Group, Chief of Staff U.S. Army Briefing, Monday, 24 December 1990 (C+139). The author flew to Saudi Arabia with a group of commanders being "prepositioned."

39. HQ, ARCENT, Command Group, command briefing titled, "Theater Operations Desert Shield/Desert Storm," dated 15 August 1991, slide titled, "Medical Force Structure-15 Feb 91."

40. HQ, 10th Personnel Command Command Report, Operation Desert Shield, 23 August 1990 to 16 January 1991, 29-1 to 31-7, contains relevant message traffic between chief of staff Army, DCSOPS, and Army MACOMS. Ibid., 17–18, addresses concept in broad terms.

41. In fact, the secretary of the Army was briefed on 14 March that of twenty-one M1A1 battalions requiring force modernization, seventeen had been completed. Eleven of thirteen M2A2/M3A2 Bradley battalions/squadrons were complete. HQ, ARCENT, G3 Force Modernization Branch, briefing titled, "ARCENT Force Modernization,"

dated 13 March 1991, slides titled, "M1A1" and "M2A2/M3A2." Briefing was given to Secretary of the Army Michael Stone on 14 April.

42. According to the final Title V Report, 1,343 HEMTTs were issued in excess of normal unit allowances. Department of Defense, Office of the Secretary of Defense, Conduct of the Persian Gulf War: Final Report to Congress Pursuant to Title V of the Persian Gulf Conflict Supplemental Authorization and Personnel Benefits Act of 1991 (Public Law 102-25), April 1992, Appendix T, Performance of Selected Weapon Systems, T-159. Numbers come from the ARCENT G3 files briefing slide titled, "Plus-Up HEMTT Distribution (as of 23 February 1991)."

43. Interview with General Frederick Franks at the Pentagon by the Strategic Studies Institute, U.S. Army War College, Carlisle Barracks, Pennsylvania, on 31 October 1991, 2.

44. Lieutenant Colonel Peter Kindsvatter, "VII Corps in the Gulf War: Deployment and Preparation for Desert Storm," *Military Review* 72 [sic] (January 1992), 4. Lieutenant Colonel Kindsvatter was VII Corps' historian during Operation Desert Storm.

45. Interview with General Frederick Franks at the Pentagon by the Strategic Studies Institute, U.S. Army War College, Carlisle Barracks, Pennsylvania, on 31 October 1991, 5–6, 8. Interview with Colonel Stan Cherrie at Fort Leavenworth, Kansas, 19 August 1991, 15.

46. Ibid. Reforger units were units committed to NATO's General Defense Plan but located in the United States. Each year during the cold war there was an annual exercise to rehearse the return of forces to Germany (Reforger).

47. Interview with Colonel Stan Cherrie at Fort Leavenworth, Kansas, 19 August 1991, 12–13. Interview of General Franks conducted in the Pentagon, Washington, D.C., by the Strategic Studies Institute, U.S. Army War College, Carlisle Barracks, Pennsylvania, on 31 October 1991, 5–7.

48. Two brigades of the 2d Armored served in the Persian Gulf, the 2d Armored Division (Forward) and the "Tiger Brigade." The division itself was in the process of deactivation at Fort Hood, Texas.

49. Interview of General Franks conducted in the Pentagon, Washington, D.C., by the Strategic Studies Institute, U.S. Army War College, Carlisle Barracks, Pennsylvania, on 31 October 1991, 5–7. The 1st Infantry Division was configured with three mechanized infantry battalions and six armored battalions. The 24th Infantry Division had five mechanized battalions and four armored battalions; the two U.S. armored divisions had four mechanized battalions and six armored battalions each. HQ, ARCENT, Command Group, command briefing titled, "Theater Operations Desert Shield/Desert Storm," dated 15 August 1991, slides titled, "Warfighting Command and Control VII Corps and XVIII Corps."

50. HQ, 1st Infantry Division (Forward), Desert Shield/Desert Storm After-Action Report: VII Corps Debarkation and Onward Movement, 30 May 1991.

51. Interview of General Franks conducted in the Pentagon, Washington, D.C., by the Strategic Studies Institute, U.S. Army War College, Carlisle Barracks, Pennsylvania, on 31 October 1991, 7.

52. Ibid., 10–11. Pagonis, *Moving Mountains*, 127.

53. Interview of General Franks, conducted in the Pentagon, Washington, D.C., by the Strategic Studies Institute, U.S. Army War College, Carlisle Barracks, Pennsylvania, on 31 October 1991, 7.

54. Ibid., 9.

55. Ports listed by Colonel Cherrie in interview with Colonel Stan Cherrie at Fort Leavenworth, Kansas, 19 August 1991, 22.

56. HQ, ARCENT, Message, 302359Z NOV 90, FM COMUSARCENT MAIN//AFRD-CS//MSGID/SITREP/USARCENT MAIN G3//PERID/292400Z/TO:302400Z/ASOF:302400Z, 3–4.

57. Ibid., 4.

58. HQ, ARCENT, Command Group, ARCENT UPDATE, C+115 (30 November 1990), slide titled, "Threat Summary, 30 Nov 90."

59. HQ, ARCENT, Message, 152359Z DEC 90, FM COMUSARCENT MAIN//AFRD-CS//MSGID/SITREP/USARCENT MAIN G3//PERID/142400Z/TO:152400Z/ASOF:152400Z, 4. HQ, ARCENT, Message, 172359Z DEC 90, FM COMUSARCENT MAIN//AFRD-CS//MSGID/SITREP/USARCENT MAIN G3//PERID/162400Z/TO:172400Z/ASOF:172400Z, 3, 5.

60. HQ, ARCENT, Message, 312359Z DEC 90, FM COMUSARCENT MAIN//AFRD-CS//MSGID/SITREP/USARCENT MAIN G3//PERID/302400Z/TO:312400Z/ASOF:312400Z, 14. HQ, ARCENT, Command Group, ARCENT UPDATE, C+146 (31 December 1990), slide titled, "Current Situation, 31 Dec 90."

61. Kindsvatter, "VII Corps in the Gulf War: Deployment and Preparation for Desert Storm," 9–11.

62. HQ, ARCENT, AFRD-DT (142359Z Jan 91), Memorandum for Major General Taylor, ARCENT Rear, Subject: ARCENT Command SITREP AS OF COB 14 Jan (C+160).

63. HQ, ARCENT, Message, 16312359Z JAN 91, FM COMUSARCENT MAIN//AFRD-DT//MSGID/SITREP/USARCENT MAIN G3//PERID/152400Z/TO:162400Z/ASOF:162400Z, 9.

6
Desert Storm: Air Power and Final Issues

It was one thing for the president to announce his intentions to create an offensive option in early November. It was quite another matter for him to build the national and international consensus to use it. Indeed, *The New York Times* lead editorial on 27 October pointed to the need for such an effort, observing that "The burden is on President Bush to show that a significant increase in American forces *will make less likely* their use in battle [emphasis added]."[1] In late October, Bush's personal popularity had been at an all-time low as he came through, and essentially lost, a bruising preelection budget battle with Congress.[2]

The political strategy selected by the president was to solve his international problem first, then use the prestige of international approval to influence the Congress. Theodore Draper and others have characterized this as a cynical ploy to permit presidential war making without congressional consent.[3] It was, in fact, nothing of the kind.

First of all, international approval was by no means assured, particularly since the acquiescence of China was required in the Security Council. Whether the president would have been willing to proceed without international sanction is not clear. If he failed to win support, he risked giving much aid to his congressional opponents—of whom there was no shortage in December and early January.

Second, Congress was neither dependent upon the approval of the president to raise the issue nor to vote on it, and no president to date has been willing to initiate a war in the face of a clear congressional mandate not to. Congress, it seems, was of two minds about how to proceed, but Senator Sam Nunn held hearings in December and a vote was taken soon after convening the new Congress in January.

Critics like Draper forget that Congress had been sensitized by its Vietnam experience and that the congressional decision to hold hearings—joined with a growing movement to hold a January debate and vote—demonstrated that Congress insisted on being part of the decision process if a course were set for war. There was nothing certain about the ultimate outcome when the president started building support for his two related, but essentially distinct, expressions of approval. The vote of the United Nations Security

Council on 29 November setting a 15 January deadline for Saddam to withdraw from Kuwait was most helpful. The vote was twelve to two, with China abstaining.[4]

Congressional hearings followed in December, but not without presidential opposition. The administration's inability to stop the hearings, indeed, its offer to hold discussions with Saddam in December (ultimately carried on to no evident gain in Geneva in January) is evidence of Congress' ability to make itself felt in these matters.[5] Congress finally voted to use force on 12 January following an impassioned and often eloquent debate. The congressional resolution, tantamount to a declaration of war, authorized "the use of United States Armed Forces pursuant to United Nations Security Council Resolution 678."[6] The Congressional resolution was passed by a vote of 52 to 47 in the Senate and 250 to 183 in the House—by no means a wide margin.

A *The New York Times-CBS News* poll published on 15 January showed the American people were almost evenly divided over the issue of war—47 percent for its initiation, 46 percent for additional use of sanctions.[7] The president did not wait long. On 16 January, he announced initiation of the Desert Storm campaign plan, beginning forty-two days of air operations against strategic targets in Iraq and operational targets in the Kuwait theater of operations. The first air attack of the war was conducted by Army AH-64s to destroy early warning radars in southern Iraq as part of a joint and combined air operation.[8] Soon afterwards, the president ordered a partial mobilization that authorized the retention of Reserve Component soldiers for up to a year.[9]

On the first morning of Operation Desert Storm, Third Army began moving west. (See figure 24.) The 1st Cavalry Division and 2d Brigade of the 101st Airborne Division had been placed under the tactical control of VII Corps on 12 January to provide for the security of the Hafar al Batin-King Khalid Military City area. The 2d Brigade of the 101st was located at Al Qaysumah. On the 17th, the 1st Cavalry Division moved north of the Tapline Road, just east of Wadi al Batin. That same day, the VII Corps fired its first shots in anger since World War II, when the corps' artillery fired Army tactical missiles (ATACMS) against Iraqi air defense sites as part of the joint suppression of the enemy's air defense.[10] Meanwhile, corps engineers overcame a major obstacle to movement on the friendly side of the border by pushing up large sand ramps to permit armored and wheeled vehicles to cross the east-west above-ground oil pipeline that paralleled the Tapline Road and whose continuous presence gave the road its name.[11]

Iraq was not slow to respond. On 18 January, seven Scud missiles fell on Israel, followed by one on Dhahran. The decision, taken during Internal Look, to make the 11th Air Defense Brigade a theater air defense asset now proved to have been wise indeed. Patriot missiles, by their rapid response and evident success in intercepting incoming Scuds, quickly restored confidence to those in the target areas, whatever the missiles' practical value in destroying Scud warheads. (See figure 25.)

As a military weapon, the Scud was tactically ineffective. Iraqi attacks on Israel, nonetheless, did have a significant impact; Scud attacks caused the diversion of a substantial number of tactical aircraft that otherwise would have been preparing the KTO. Instead, these aircraft attacked unproductive targets in western Iraq to reassure the government of Israel and keep that state out of the war. Even J-STARS (joint surveillance target attack radar system), upon which the coalition was dependent for early warnings of Iraqi spoiling attacks, was shifted to Scud hunting.[12] The diversion of political energy to keep Israel out of the war was also significant. Given the threat an Israeli attack on Iraq posed to coalition unity, these actions were understandable and probably unavoidable. Ultimately, British and U.S. special operations forces were committed to locating and calling down attacks on Iraqi mobile Scud launchers.[13]

U.S. leaders were fortunate that the only American military losses to Scud attacks occurred after the ground operations had begun. The incident, a strike on a troop billet in Dhahran that housed the Army Reserve's 14th Quartermaster Detachment, killed twenty-eight Americans and wounded ninety-eight more. It was the largest single incident of American losses of the war. One can only speculate on how well public support for the war would have stood up to such an event had it occurred on 19 January.

In the deployment of coalition forces, Third Army had to coordinate the movement of the Syrian forces eastward, out of what was now the Third Army sector. The Syrians were armed with Soviet equipment (as were the Iraqis) and, given Syria's ambivalence about joining the coalition offensive at that time, they were not entirely trusted. Great care was taken to ensure that they did not accidentally bump into U.S. forces moving west.[14]

The creation of an enemy prisoner of war holding capability also required the army commander's time. All of the logistic support for

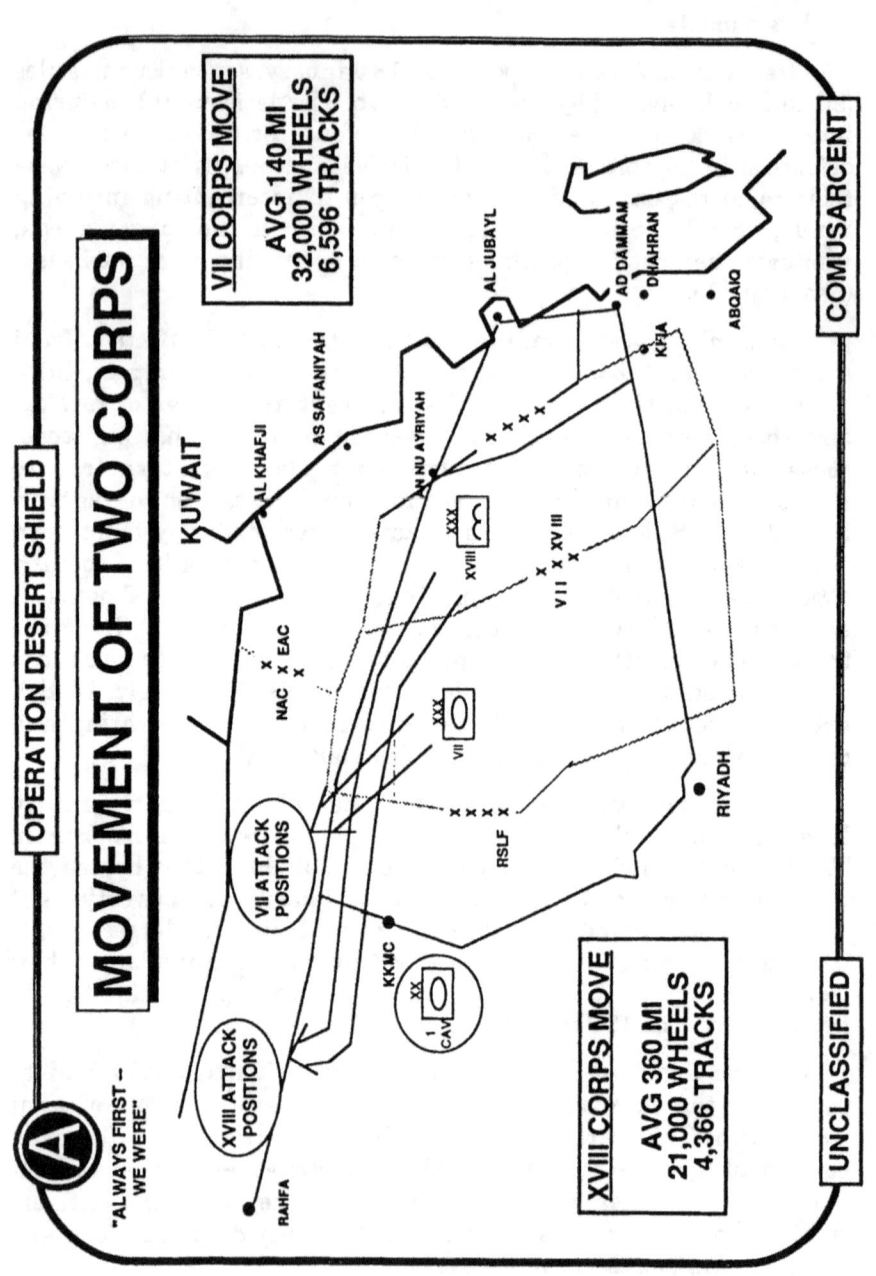

Figure 24.

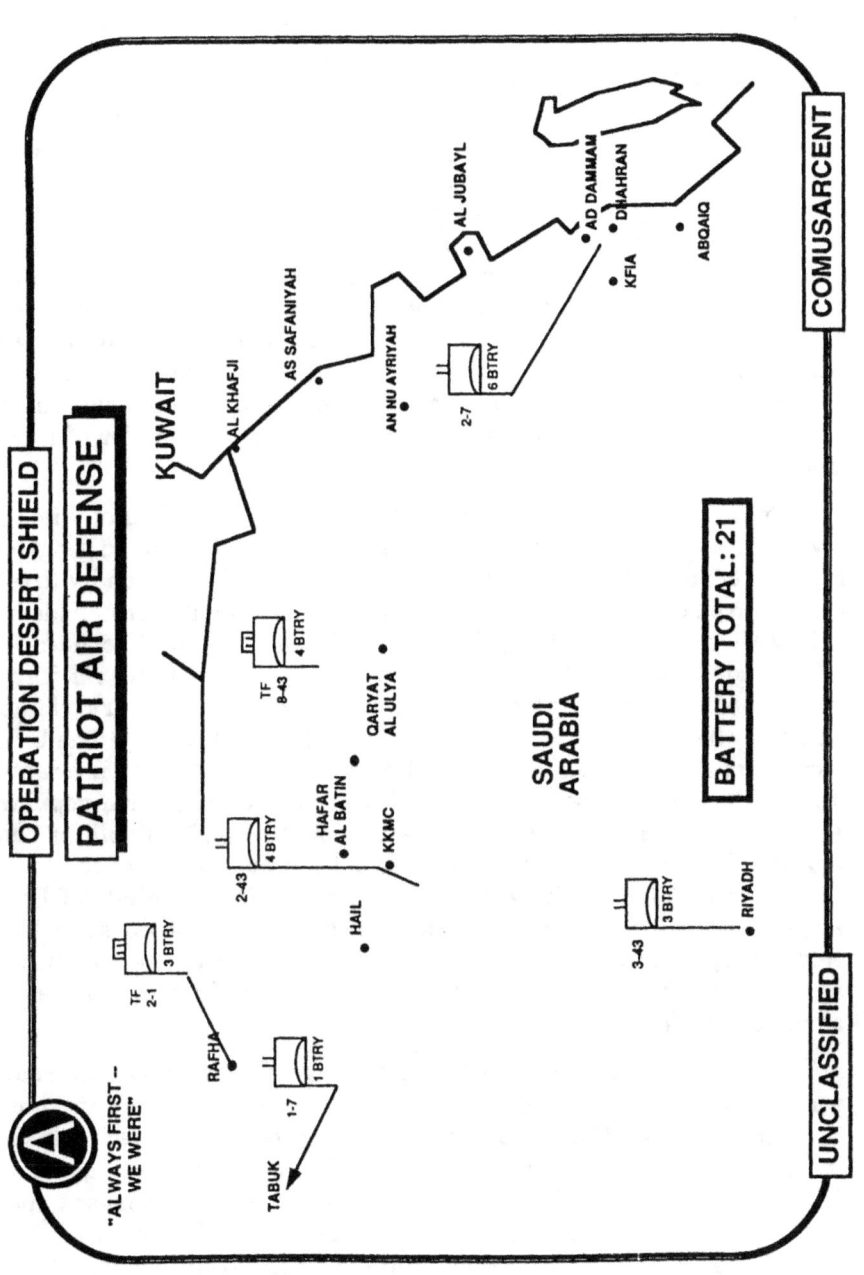

Figure 25.

this project, which amounted to feeding, clothing, and housing the population of a small city, was provided by a single Saudi contractor. Construction of the POW camps had to be accomplished by the 416th Engineers and the 800th Military Police Brigade, and that required a good bit of General Frix's attention from King Khalid Military City. General Yeosock was determined that U.S. enemy prisoner of war facilities should exceed international standards, and like everything else Third Army did, construction of adequate facilities and the securing of a fleet of buses for transporting prisoners were accomplished in a race against a growing demand. The first prisoners taken by Third Army troops were some Iraqi border police captured by the 3d Armored Cavalry Regiment in a skirmish on 22 January.[15] Also, about that time, Army psychological warfare teams, in coordination with the Air Force bombing schedule, began a sustained program of leaflet drops designed to encourage the surrender of Iraqi troops.

From January on, Third Army also spent a good deal of energy trying to solve the potential problem of fratricide, the killing or injuring of one's own forces by what is ironically called "friendly fire," a term given currency by a book concerning an incident of fratricide in a battalion commanded by General Schwarzkopf in Vietnam.[16] "Fratricide," according to historian Roger Spiller, "is the military version of an industrial accident."[17] Not new in war, fratricide generally has been accepted as part of the risk of soldiering.[18] The U.S. Army, nonetheless, became extraordinarily sensitive to such incidents during the period of post-Vietnam War recrimination, when popular American comedienne, Carol Burnett, took the serious role of the mother of a victim of fratricide in a television adaptation of the book about the incident in Schwarzkopf's battalion. In the minds of U.S. leaders, fratricide was elevated from the cost of doing business to "the worst thing we can do."[19] Concern about fratricide was so great that it had a direct and profound impact on the conduct of battle in southeastern Iraq.

The fundamental problem in the desert was that Army antiarmor systems could kill at ranges almost three times beyond those at which the target acquisition systems (visual sights) could discriminate between friendly and enemy systems. This problem was compounded in the desert because the general flatness of the terrain meant that there was little to get in the way of errant rounds.[20] The problem was complicated further because some items of coalition equipment—those manufactured in the Soviet Union, France, and the United States—were used by both coalition forces and the Iraqi Army. Thus, significant command attention was paid to getting a number of identification devices to the troops: reflective tape in inverted Vs, markings on helicopters (the Iraqis used a number of French models), and various emitting devices. Indeed, keeping a tight hand on vehicle and unit maneuver, as well as unit fire control, was an antifratricidal measure.

None of these efforts was 100 percent effective, and before the ground attack was launched, incidents of friendly air attack on misidentified ground vehicles, particularly at Khafji and later in the 1st Infantry Division, raised the level of concern to palpable dimensions. Just as continuous warnings about maneuver damage in NATO exercises in years past contributed to a U.S. proclivity to remain on roads and out of fields during the annual maneuvers, the concern for fratricide would introduce an element of caution into the conduct of the Gulf War that would slow and even stop operations of corps-sized forces. In spite of all efforts, of the 148 U.S. service members killed in action during the war, 35 died by "friendly fire." Of 467 wounded, 72 were hit by friendly fire.[21] These figures, of course, are as much or more a testament to the scale of the U.S. technological advantages over the Iraqis, both in killing *and* protective systems, as they are any indication of carelessness in the field. As a proportion of total casualties, the numbers look very high, but considering the total coalition fighting systems operative, the numbers are minuscule.

With the start of air operations, tension grew between the Air Force, which was concentrating its efforts on strategic and independent operational strikes, and the leadership of Third Army, which assumed that the ground attack would be the theater commander's principal means to achieve success and must, therefore, be given priority for direct employment of air assets. At its root, the argument was an old one, reflecting differing views of the role of air power in theater operations.

There were also problems over methods of battle damage assessment—that is, judging the extent of damage inflicted on Iraqi ground forces from the air—and others about the amount of air power to be dedicated to attacking specific targets nominated by Army tactical commanders. The interservice friction that characterized the period was a consequence, first of all, of locating control of all air forces at theater level. This was proper and inevitable given the relative scarcity of air assets and their wide range of maneuver and power of instant concentration. Air forces are the theater commander's most responsive form of combat power and the only form with theater-wide reach. But Army tactical doctrine and the experiences of senior Army leaders had created the expectation that air assets would be available to them in quantity. Moreover, heavy air attack of the enemy's first-line positions and, particularly, the artillery, which constituted the key to the Iraqi defensive system, was believed to be essential to success on the ground. Senior Army leaders failed to anticipate or understand their relative position in the competition for air assets or to divest themselves of service parochialism in the name of the jointness so applauded at war's end.

In January and early February, General Schwarzkopf ran the air war himself, with no one intervening between him and General Horner. Because Horner was also busy as joint force air component commander (JFACC), many believed the air war was being conducted by his principal subordinate, Brigadier General Buster Glosson, for his own amusement.[22] Glosson, unfortunately, got off to a bad start with the senior Army commanders at the ARCENT MAPEX and never regained their trust, becoming, perhaps, the most despised senior officer in theater to some Third Army commanders.[23] Glosson, unfortunately, appeared to be too glib in his assurances of Air Force support to an assembly of men highly concerned about the task before them. Colonel Joe Purvis, who was at CENTCOM throughout the war and is no mean judge of men, insists that Glosson was misunderstood by senior Army officers and was quite sincere in his promises of decisive support.[24] Glosson, of course, had to respond, first of all, to the orders of the theater commander. Thus, even if suspicions were true and Glosson was some sort of evil genius indifferent to Army requirements, Schwarzkopf permitted his actions and, indeed, was satisfied to have it that way.

Within the ground forces, this view of the conduct of the air war produced a great deal of angst, especially after 31 January—which was always seen as a sort of decision point on shifting the theater focus from air attack to a ground offensive as the principal military means of political suasion. This frustration came about not only because of a perceived need for air support to achieve assigned tactical and operational missions but because of the traditional way Army officers continue to view the dynamics of warfare.

The average senior officer in the U.S. Army is a prisoner of his own experience, which is almost entirely tactical—that is, focused on ground battle at division level and below. It is in battalions, brigades, and divisions that most Army officers gain their training and experience in war. In 1982, as part of the doctrinal revolution fostered by the Training and Doctrine Command, Field Manual (FM) 100-5, *Operations*, introduced the concept of operational art. Borrowed largely from the Soviet Army, though attributed generally to German practices in World War II, operational art involves the systematic use of tactical events to achieve strategic goals. Its innovation is the recognition that tactical success is not an end in itself but a means to a larger purpose in which tactical considerations must naturally be subordinated, though not necessarily sacrificed.

The consequence has been an Army whose rhetoric extolled jointness and high military art but which had a visceral belief in the relationship of arms and services best expressed by John Huston's vision in the movie *San Pietro*. *San Pietro* describes a bloody battle in Italy during World War II. At San Pietro, the Germans were in prepared positions. "No amount of artillery fire or aerial bombardment," Huston says, "could force them to withdraw."

> That was for the infantry to do; employing those weapons that confine and destroy life in narrow trenches, caves and fighting holes. It was up to the man with the rifle, the man under fire from all weapons, *the man whose way all our weapons, land, air, and sea, serve only to prepare* [emphasis added]. It was up to the foot soldier to attack a hidden enemy over ground that was sown with mines....[25]

The problem with this ethic, once generalized, is that it is only true on the battlefield in the tactical sense. It is the negation of jointness, defined as "attacking the right target at the right time with the right weapon,"[26] and the opposite of true operational art, which has long since become three dimensional.

A ground force is an operational and strategic instrument that destroys enemy forces and capabilities and occupies ground, generally to deny some advantage to the enemy. In a total war, the ground occupied may be the entire enemy state. AirLand battles are only a means to this end. Ground force objectives may be terrain- or force-oriented. The goal and unique capability of any ground force is the occupation or control of something. Air forces, because of their ubiquity, are capable of striking an enemy's strategic depths, without lengthy attritional battles and at relatively low cost. Therein lies their attractiveness. Unfortunately, they are also constrained by rational and legal limitations on the conduct of war that often limit their decisiveness as an arm acting by itself.

The concept of control from the air still seems elusive. In all wars to date, save in the one case where employment of atomic weapons (on an enemy unable to respond in kind) seemed warranted, there has been a point of diminishing return where air power alone was insufficient to bring about the strategic end state required. Ground forces have had to be committed to finish the job. In Desert Storm, Iraq proved remarkably resistant to air bombardment, and there was no indication Saddam was prepared to remove his occupying forces from Kuwait in response to air attack alone on targets in Iraq or on forces in Kuwait. Once again, it was ultimately up to the ground soldiers to seize that which the enemy's own infantry had occupied.

There was, thus, a tension between the importance of employing air power alone to achieve the valuable operational and strategic goals of which it is capable and using many of the same resources in a subordinate role in direct support of the ground forces in the achievement of their operational tasks. The Marine Corps force structure included high-performance air platforms. The Army's did not. The Army was dependent on the Air Force for the air component of AirLand Battle. Just as ground operations always seemed to be necessary—if not sufficient—for strategic success, significant air support was also necessary—if not sufficient—for tactical and operational success on the ground. Indeed, the idea of using deep fires, air and ground, simultaneous with close battle as a means of shaping future events was central to the concept of operational art. The control of such fires, especially those delivered by air, have remained a point of contention between Air Force and ground commanders. For years, it has been the central issue in interservice arguments over definitions of categories of air interdiction.[27]

Only the commander charged with achieving the strategic military objectives in the theater—only the theater commander in chief—was called upon by his position and responsibilities to accomplish the integration of the service arms. He had to be convinced that there were operational and strategic implications associated with any possible (ground) tactical failure. Or, put another way, he had to be assured there was the likelihood of a significant operational benefit as a return on the investment before he would commit his most responsive strategic and operational instrument (the air tool) to any tactical battle. Before committing tactical airplanes, he also had to be sure the ground force could not do the job in question with its own less expensive assets—attack helicopters, ATACMS, or multiple launch rockets.

In Operation Desert Storm, the theater campaign plan provided for a four-phase operation that was to begin with strategic bombardment, the gaining of air superiority, and preparation of the KTO for ground attack (the latter eventually came to mean isolating the KTO by destroying the bridges across the Euphrates and reducing Iraqi heavy forces by 50 percent, in the breach sites, even more). Only then would AirLand operations commence.[28] There was some hope that the first three phases might convince the Iraqis to give way and accept the UN resolutions concerning withdrawal from Kuwait.[29] Even if there was to be a ground attack, the deception plan required that much of the attrition effort focus on the Iraqi forces in Kuwait to convey the illusion of preparation for a main attack in the east. In addition, to ensure that the Northern Area Command (which faced strong Iraqi defenses) would attack successfully, ARCENT gave it a relatively high priority in the air effort.[30] Consequently, from D-day to early February, very little air power was invested in the tactical preparation of the corps' battlefield, a fact that became of primary importance to the corps and division commanders.

The situation became increasingly more frustrating as Army officers, who never doubted that a ground attack was a sine qua non to final success, saw most air assets employed against strategic or operational targets, especially the hunt for Scud launchers. They became increasingly concerned that they would be ordered into battle with their battlefield unprepared. By 1 February, a sort of consensus was achieved that about nine days of tactical preparation would be necessary for a successful ground attack. This would include destroying enemy artillery in range of the 1st Infantry Division breach site and fighting a counterreconnaissance battle to gain immediate tactical intelligence otherwise unavailable.[31] The difficulty was that no one knew when G-day (the start of the ground attack) would arrive, so no one knew if Schwarzkopf would reallocate his air assets in support of ground priorities in time to do what tactical commanders felt was important for their own success. Because Schwarzkopf saw any sort of questioning of his actions as an intrusion on his prerogatives and tended to react with intense anger when he felt challenged (particularly about the campaign plan), ground commanders were not likely to have much confidence in his sympathy with their needs. Instead, they turned increasingly to General Waller, since November Schwarzkopf's deputy, to mediate their needs with the CINC.[32]

These fundamental discontinuities were exacerbated by the lack of a mutually agreed-upon doctrine for air-ground coordination. Doctrine for air-ground integration is theater specific and generally (unless overruled by the CINC) the purview of the theater joint air component commander, in this case General Horner. A host of minor problems had to be resolved in theater, and their resolution increased Army suspicion of an air arm few took the trouble to understand. Among these issues were the question of whether AH-64s should be integrated in the air tasking order (they were not, unless they were part of a joint air attack plan) and whether ATACMS, with ranges of well over 100 kilometers, could be fired into an area in which air force planes were flying.

The air tasking order (ATO), which knit together all air missions flying on a particular day, was a lengthy document requiring about seventy-two hours lead time to prepare from the time a target was nominated until it was attacked. The ATO seemed unnecessarily rigid to ground commanders. Yet after the war, XVIII Corps' staff officers admitted that, within this rigidity, they were very successful in obtaining what they called opportunity CAS (close air support) or mission diversions by using various air-ground liaison systems: air liaison officers with the Army units, ground liaison officers with Air Force units, and the battlefield control element (BCE), an organization designed to provide for real-time Army-Air Force coordination.[33] A Third Army deep battle cell was formed at army headquarters only days prior to initiation of the air war.[34] This was the army-level staff agency where corps targets were consolidated and prioritized in accordance with the Third Army commander's priorities and then passed on to the Joint Targeting Board controlled by the Air Force. From the standpoint of officers of the lower headquarters, this Army staff agency was probably the source of some of the temporal rigidity and "unwarranted" subordination of tactical priorities that they believed they suffered. The Deep Battle Cell targeters ("targeteers") also reported later that they were generally successful in getting the Air Force to deviate from an air tasking order to pursue higher-value targets.[35] The source of friction, then, seems to have centered on the application of air power against numerous discrete and routine enemy positions on the desert floor and principally in the breach sites. These positions collectively threatened the success of the initial ground assault but individually could not compete with other theater-level priorities.

As much as Air Force action or inaction, the feedback to Army commanders was part of the problem. Because of the nature of the deception plan and the enemy communications posture (which avoided radio communication prior to the initiation of the ground attack), most target validation and battle damage assessment were based on means other than communications intercepts—a capability in which corps and divisions are strong. Therefore, target validation (accommodating movement of targets within the targeting cycle) had to be accomplished by Third Army with information moving both laterally to the Air Force and downward to the corps, the latter in such a way that it would be connected with targets nominated earlier against older information. This was often done inefficiently from the standpoint of the tactical commands, where target attack belongs to one staff agency and target "maintenance" to another. Moreover, simple feedback on targets attacked seems not to have been rapid or discrete enough to satisfy the Army briefing cycle. Hence, corps commanders were sometimes ill-informed about which of their targets were actually being hit.[36] Much of the frustration with this system was focused on the Air Force, notwithstanding that a good bit of the rigidity was in the Army targeting structure.

On the Air Force side, Army assessment of the damage inflicted on Iraqi forces by air attack (BDA—battle damage assessment) was not without its own confusions. The simple fact is that BDA is an art, largely subjective, and both services try to cloak this in what appear to be objective criteria. These, when they do not seem to be working, are changed. This naturally undermines mutual confidence in what is going on.[37] Assignment of authority for ground battle damage assessment to the Army is essential, since only the Army has both the expertise in what is important to ground warfare and the problem of ultimately having to live with the consequences of its errors. The lack of truly objective criteria, however, sometimes seems suspicious to airmen, who feel they are not getting credit for the good work they are doing at no small risk to their lives.

Both these cases, the BDA effort and the process of preattack target validation, were complicated by Schwarzkopf's proclivity to change his targeting focus within the ATO cycle. Because of the shortage of aerial and space-based observation platforms, operational reconnaissance, too, had to be projected days in advance to synchronize it with attack targeting. When the CINC shifted his focus from one enemy division to another, as he was wont to do, reconnaissance assets often could not respond in time. Hence, it was often impossible for the Army to present a timely target list to the Air Force operations cell, which then had to develop other means to ensure there was something on the ground to bomb at the grid submitted by some corps commander perhaps days before.[38] Poststrike analysis was also seldom rapid enough to respond.

On 5 February, General Arnold reported to the army commander that ARCENT was getting only 20 percent of the air support sorties it had requested. A revised target review process—an Army initiative that involved oversight by General Waller as the CINC's deputy—was supposed to start on the 7th. On the 8th, it seemed to be working, as VII Corps was scheduled to have its top eleven targets hit.[39] On the

11th, Arnold's cover note to the daily SITREP informed ARCENT units that the introduction of F-111s into the attack of ground targets was having a significant effect on attrition of the Republican Guard. On the 13th, however, the cover note reflected a falling off of delivered air support (31 percent accomplished versus 45 percent projected). That same day, General Yeosock expressed concern about the apparent shortfall and instructed Arnold to begin briefing Waller on the daily status of requests versus target attacks.40

Then, during the early morning hours of 14 February, Yeosock was hospitalized. He would not return to his headquarters until noon on the 23d, the day before the ground attack was launched. That morning (the 14th), the ARCENT SITREP that Arnold prepared, contained the following message:

> WE ARE CONCERNED THAT THE NUMBER OF AIRCRAFT SORTIES NOW APPORTIONED TO ARCENT IS INADEQUATE TO PROPERLY "SHAPE THE BATTLEFIELD" PRIOR TO OFFENSIVE OPERATIONS. AERIAL PREPARATION OF THE BATTLEFIELD IS ESSENTIAL TO FUTURE OPERATIONS, AND ARCENT WILL CONTINUE COORDINATION WITH ALCON TO EFFECT REALIGNMENT OF AIR APPORTIONMENT PRIORITIES.41

On the 16th, Arnold complained to General Frix, who had returned to the main CP in light of General Yeosock's illness, that the Air Force calculated their success in meeting Army requirements in accordance with targets attacked, not number of sorties flown—a process Arnold appeared to find disingenuous.42 The SITREP for the 17th again expressed Army dissatisfaction noting:

> ARMY NOMINATED TARGETS ON THE ATO ARE FREQUENTLY DIVERTED WITHOUT EXPLANATION, ARCENT CANNOT INFLUENCE THE SELECTION OF USAF TARGET BOXES, AND CAS HAS BEEN DELAYED FOR ANOTHER DAY. CORPS COMMANDERS ARE CONCERNED OVER THEIR INABILITY TO ATTRIT HIGH VALUE TARGETS . . . WHICH HAVE THE GREATEST POTENTIAL TO INFLICT FRIENDLY CASUALTIES.43

At the daily general officer meeting at army headquarters on 17 February, the G2 observed that artillery within range of the 1st Infantry Division breach site had not been destroyed. This concern was seconded by Arnold. That afternoon, Waller was appointed to command Third Army. He retained his authority for oversight of employment of air assets on behalf of the CINC. That night, Yeosock was flown to Germany for surgery. The following morning, the 18th, the ARCENT SITREP said:

> AIR SUPPORT RELATED ISSUES CONTINUE TO PLAGUE FINAL PREPARATION FOR OFFENSIVE OPERATIONS AND RAISE DOUBTS CONCERNING OUR ABILITY TO EFFECTIVELY SHAPE THE BATTLEFIELD PRIOR TO INITIATION OF THE GROUND CAMPAIGN. TOO FEW SORTIES ARE MADE AVAILABLE TO VII AND XVIII ABN CORPS. AND WHILE AIR SUPPORT MISSIONS ARE BEING FLOWN AGAINST 1ST ECHELON ENEMY DIVISIONS, ARMY NOMINATED TARGETS ARE NOT BEING SERVICED. EFFORTS MUST BE TAKEN NOW TO ALIGN THE OBJECTIVES OF THE AIR AND GROUND CAMPAIGNS AND ENSURE THE SUCCESS OF OUR FUTURE OPERATIONS.[44]

Whether because of the various complaints in the ARCENT SITREP or due to Waller's arrival as both targeting judge and army commander or simply because Schwarzkopf had decided it was time to shift his resources to preparation of the battlefield, there was an immediate change. That same day, Arnold announced that, on the 19th, Third Army would receive 432 sorties, the largest effort to date. The next SITREP would be fulsome in praise of Army and Air Force joint efforts, and the daily rate of 400+ sorties to ARCENT seems to have been maintained to G-day.

Still, procedures for allocation and control of close air support sorties (planes flown in direct support and under immediate control of ground commanders) remained a problem, with a resolution by Schwarzkopf only the night before G-day.[45] The issue here was General Horner's not unreasonable insistence that all air missions were to be dispatched against a target or a mission, not to be held on station in case something came up. In the end, procedures were established for air-interdiction diversions to satisfy immediate requests. The sheer volume of aircraft available (as well as periodic weather restrictions on flights) seems to have rendered the point null. Disputes about the meaning and positioning of the fire support coordination line, used to coordinate ground maneuver and independent air action, would continue to the cease-fire.

General Yeosock, too, seems to have gotten somewhat nervous about the focus of air support in late January and early February. He also seems to have taken a more cumulative than sequential view of the preparation of the theater of operations than did his corps commanders. That is, he worried more about the final picture than the daily box score. He also maintained a broader interservice perspective that recognized tradeoffs, such as those between immediate attack of targets protected by tactical air defense systems and mission availability on G-day. No doubt this viewpoint came from his close personal association and confidence in General Horner (a relationship not shared by his subordinates) and an intimate awareness of Schwarzkopf's propensity to become personally involved in targeting details about which the corps commanders were unaware. Finally, the critical fact is that coalition air power was overwhelming in its superiority and numbers. Once again, American forces were free to do things—like shift their forces in the face of an enemy and maneuver large, compact armored forces without fear of interference from the sky—because of the dominance of the air overhead. As was the case in Europe in World War II, for all the interservice friction, there was enough air power for everybody.

The first significant ground combat involving U.S. Army soldiers took place at the Iraqis' initiative while the concentration of Army forces west of Wadi al Batin was still under way. Elements of the Iraqi 5th Mechanized Division attacked the small Saudi border town of Khafji near the Persian Gulf. Many Americans who took their war news from CNN no doubt believed that Khafji was liberated by the Marines. Indeed, the Marines were repulsing other enemy probes to the west of Khafji at the same time and, in the press, all of these actions tended to get rolled together. In fact, Khafji was freed by King Abdul Aziz' 2d Saudi Army National Guard (SANG) Brigade, accompanied by American advisers from the Office of the Program Manager, Saudi Arabian National Guard (OPMSANG). The 2d Brigade, part of Joint Forces Command East, had over forty OPMSANG advisers, including the three- or four-man teams with each combined arms battalion.[46] They also had a Marine Corps air and naval gunfire liaison company (ANGLICO) team attached to provide air and naval gunfire support.

The battle of Khafji began about 2200 on 29 January when Iraqi armored forces crossed the Saudi-Kuwaiti border in the vicinity of the An Nuwaysib customs post and occupied the evacuated town of Khafji. Two Marine Corps reconnaissance teams were cut off within the town. They continued to evade capture and called in Marine air support and artillery fire throughout the battle.[47]

The recapture of Khafji began the following day. At 1600, the 2d SANG Brigade, defending the right flank of Joint Forces Command East's sector, ordered its 7th Combined Arms Battalion (CAB) to move quickly to Khafji.[48] In the words of one SANG adviser, the complete operations order to the 7th CAB was "Attack Khafji from the southwest to the northeast."[49] At 2300, the 7th Battalion and a Qatari tank company entered the town, failed to establish a foothold, and withdrew into a field west of the highway that was the main avenue of approach into Khafji. Outside the town and along the front, coalition air forces began to pound concentrations of enemy troops building up, apparently in support of the border incursions, thus isolating those Iraqis already inside Khafji and destroying the Iraqi capability to reinforce, withdraw, or exploit their initial success.

The following morning, now the 31st, the 2d Brigade attacked again with three combined arms battalions. By noon, the brigade's 8th CAB had linked up with the thirteen U.S. Marine observers. By 1900 the following night (1 February), the battle of Khafji was over, although clearing operations continued at various points for some days.[50]

The incident at Khafji was important for several reasons. First of all, it confirmed General Schwarzkopf's view that the Iraqis were not good at complex operations, and they were highly vulnerable to observation and air interdiction when they concentrated their forces to conduct tactical operations.[51] Second, the prominence given the Marine role in the affair at Khafji, as well as at the simultaneous incident at the As-Zabr police post west of the Al Wafrah oil fields in the heel of Kuwait, undoubtedly served to confirm the Iraqi belief that the U.S. focus remained in the east. Third, the aggressiveness of the SANG forces was reassuring to those in the coalition who wondered if the Saudis, who had never been tried in battle, would fight.[52] Again, in the words of an OPMSANG officer writing afterwards: "The troops attacked with a ferocity that surprised not only the Iraqis but several of our senior advisors that had extensive Viet Nam experience as well. An Iraqi officer was quoted as saying that they were shocked by the amount of fire and that [sic] fact that the bedouin were everywhere (not necessarily in anything resembling a coordinated attack, just everywhere)."[53] The ARCENT liaison officer (LNO) with Joint Forces Command East was also impressed, reporting: "Saudi soldiers are doing very well under fire. Almost too bold."[54] SANG casualties numbered fourteen dead and about forty wounded. The Saudis captured over 800 Iraqis and destroyed or captured more than 110 vehicles.[55]

Schwarzkopf's official appraisal was upbeat: "This performance in the first significant ground combat of the war demonstrates that U.S. and coalition forces can conduct ground and air operations together and in support of each other. The Saudi and Qatari forces performed extremely well in the successful execution of this combat in cities operation. They sent a quote coalition signal unquote to the Iraqis that was not missed."[56]

Marine forces involved in the attack on the As-Zabr police post suffered seven fatalities when a Maverick missile struck a Marine Corps light armored vehicle (LAV) (a wheeled armored fighting vehicle). According to a story published in the military history magazine, *Command*, from a first person account, the Marines lost a second LAV (with four more fatalities) to friendly ground fire. The highly publicized press account of fratricide was not lost on ARCENT decision makers and heightened concern about measures that would help lessen the possibility of repetition.[57]

Finally, as a footnote, the war's first U.S. female prisoner of war (POW) was captured at Khafji. Specialist Melissa Rathbun-Nealy, a truckdriver, and her male companion, Specialist David Lockett, missed their turn, drove north from the MSR into the fight at Khafji, and were captured by the occupying Iraqis.

After the battle of Khafji, while the air operations in the KTO approached their point of diminishing return politically and militarily, ARCENT planning polished off the remaining issues about the structure of the ground effort against the Republican Guard. Among the matters that had been deferred were the timing (sequence) of attack by Third Army units, the commitment of the theater reserve, and the preferred contingency plan for destruction of the Republican Guard. Two additional issues were threaded through the operational discussion of the closing weeks of preparation. The first was a proposal to shift the XVIII Corps' heavy force attack east to include the mission to capture the Al Busayyah base area (called Objective Purple), along with the derivative question of then transferring command of XVIII Corps' heavy forces to VII Corps for the final phase of the Third Army attack. The second matter involved a continued discussion of the necessity or desirability of an operational pause.

As mentioned earlier, the issue of the timing of the attack was driven by two considerations. The first was the desirability of initially fixing the Iraqi tactical reserves in Kuwait by attacking in the east, then following the second day with the main attack in the west. The driving issue within ARCENT, however, seems to have been the XVIII Corps' insistence that it was necessary to attack toward As Salman at least twenty-four hours prior to attacking with the 24th Infantry Division and 3d Armored Cavalry Regiment. This was argued in order to synchronize the flow of logistics through As Salman, to MSR Virginia, and then eastward to the armored forces on the corps' right flank. This would remain necessary until the engineers could create a direct supply route from south to north. Ultimately, a compromise was arrived at: the XVIII Corps' light forces—the 6th French Light

Armored Division, 82d Airborne Division, and 101st Airborne Division—would attack with Joint Forces Command East and MARCENT on G-day; and the XVIII Corps' heavy forces, VII Corps, and Joint Forces Command North would attack on G+1. This timing scheme also allowed Schwarzkopf to focus air support on MARCENT for G-day and then shift it to the heavy force attack on G+1.[58]

The value of this timing seems somewhat contradictory from the standpoint of deception. The attack in the east certainly supported the deception plan and reinforced particularly the idea of a main attack that sought to re-create an Inchon-like landing and double envelopment. On the other hand, the simultaneous attack in the far west would seem to have exerted a sort of counterforce on the Iraqi theater commander, at least with regard to the commitment of operational reserves. That would appear to support the thesis that the major consideration in timing the attack of the XVIII Corps was logistical necessity rather than operational cleverness, although the benefit with regard to employment of close air support should not be underestimated.

At the same time, the timing of the attack of XVIII Corps' heavy forces to coincide with VII Corps' and JFC North's offensive reflects the extent to which the logic of the situation had made the XVIII Corps' right wing a part of the ARCENT main effort as well as constituting a separate secondary attack blocking the Highway 8 avenue of escape. This same logic led to the discussion of alternatives to bring the 24th and 3d Armored Cavalry Regiment more closely into the main attack. The discussion turned on assigning the task of capturing the Iraqi logistics base at Al Busayyah to the 24th Division.[59] From the standpoint of XVIII Corps, this would open up maneuver room to its east (at the expense of VII Corps) and provide a line of communications behind the 24th Division once it turned down Highway 8. Because of the impact on VII Corps' maneuver room, the question that logically followed was whether it did not make equal sense, then, to attach the 24th to the VII Corps from that point forward in the attack—that is, give VII Corps responsibility for the entire wheel to the east from the Saudi border north to the Euphrates River and east to Basrah.[60]

Discussion of that question seems always to have run aground on the corps packaging that existed as a matter of the history of the deployment. The XVIII Corps had lived in the desert for some seven months already. It was certainly politically impossible to rotate them home just when the war looked like it was reaching its climax, so there was some need to find them something useful to do. Had the 24th

Division been attached to VII Corps, the XVIII Corps commander would have retained only the attack helicopters of the 101st Airborne Division capable of participation in the theater main effort. That would have been galling indeed for the XVIII Corps commander and his staff. Moreover, the VII Corps span of control was already large, four divisions, with the possibility of a fifth if the CINC released his theater reserve to ARCENT in time to get in the battle. So XVIII Corps continued to fight for more of the action, and the left flank unit of the great wheel remained in XVIII Corps, with its orientation principally to the north. Meanwhile, the bulk of the heavy forces and the mission of destroying the heart of the Republican Guard Forces Command went to VII Corps. Both General Yeosock and General Waller declined proposals to attach the 24th to the heavy corps (VII Corps), and XVIII Corps retained a sector of attack on the northern edge of the theater of operations, from the Euphrates southeast toward Basrah, in the final phase of the ground offensive.[61] Responsibility for coordinating the advance of XVIII Corps' heavy forces down the corridor, with the eastward movement of VII Corps, remained implicitly with the common higher headquarters—Third Army.

A second and related issue concerned the availability of the 1st Cavalry Division for the decisive battle with the Republican Guard. General Schwarzkopf had determined to retain a division reserve early on, and pressures from the members of the Joint Forces Command North for some assurance of support, if need be, tied the theater reserve division between the ARCENT effort and the ability to support the Egyptian Corps in Joint Forces Command North, should it run into difficulties. This had profound implications.

Yeosock's planners calculated that, if the 1st Cavalry Division was to arrive in time to take part in the anticipated battle, Schwarzkopf would have to release it by H-hour plus thirty-seven hours, given estimations of the flow of the attack and fixed factors of time and space.[62] Schwarzkopf brutally refused suggestions, which General Arnold persisted in making long after it would seem to have been politically wise, that he commit to such an action in advance.

Without this assurance and convinced of the need for three heavy divisions at the decisive point, General Franks fell back on counting on General Rhame's 1st Infantry Division to be the third.[63] That meant that General Rhame would have to conduct the breach, pass the 1st U.K. Armored Division through, disentangle his unit from the breach site, and catch up with the 1st and 3d Armored Divisions and 2d Armored Cavalry Regiment before the armored "fist" closed on the RGFC. To do that, the 1st Infantry Division's breach operation would have to be conducted quickly and the 1st U.K. passed through rapidly; otherwise, ensuring the arrival of the third division would be the principal brake on VII Corps' attack.

Attachment of the 24th Infantry Division to VII Corps, at some point, might have solved this problem but, first, the division had to link up with the 101st Airborne Division and ensure the security of the Highway 8 roadblock. There were significant Republican Guard forces already located along Highway 8, particularly the three Republican Guard infantry divisions (Nebuchadnessar, Al Faw, and Adnan). These might be reinforced by various heavy divisions, either from the north (outside the KTO) or east. Two active airfields, Tallil and Jalibah, also had to be dealt with. To have transferred the 24th a priori to VII Corps would have left the 101st Airborne Division alone on Highway 8 (or perhaps the 101st joined at some point by the 3d Armored Cavalry Regiment). General J. H. Binford Peay III, the commander of the 101st Airborne Division, was confident in his division's ability to execute this mission, but Schwarzkopf's initial objections to the As Samawah operations, as well as limits the distance of the initial air assault insertion placed on the operations, would seem to indicate that, elsewhere, such confidence in the division's abilities to sustain itself without heavy force reinforcement was lacking.[64]

For reasons addressed in earlier chapters, the Desert Storm order had not included a plan for the actual destruction of the Republican Guard Forces Command, perhaps because of the difficulty of predicting in advance where the RGFC might be located on the day of battle. Now, in conjunction with VII Corps, Third Army developed a set of contingency plans for destruction of the RGFC—plans that were contingent on the Iraqi reaction to the Third Army attack.[65] It is doubtful that Yeosock would have been inclined to select one plan over the other before he was able to observe how well the initial phase of the operation actually succeeded, as well as how the Iraqis behaved. General Waller, however, was not so disinclined. When he stepped in for Yeosock the week before the ground offensive, Waller selected a contingency plan that called for a coordinated attack on the Republican Guard and associated Iraqi heavy divisions by VII Corps and XVIII Corps, with XVIII Corps responsible for the destruction of the Hammurabi Armored Division, the RGFC unit closest to Basrah.[66]

When Yeosock returned on 23 February, he picked up just where he had been when he departed. He deferred the final decision on a destruction plan, making his decision contingent upon future battlefield conditions. On the 24th, he approved a revised contingency plan that provided for the VII Corps to destroy all Republican Guard heavy divisions (an entirely force-oriented mission), with XVIII Corps limited to conducting a supporting attack to cut Highway 8, fixing reinforcing divisions outside the KTO, and destroying the RGFC infantry divisions. The XVIII Corps was to be ready to continue the attack, on order, to seize Objective Anvil south of Basrah in order to block the retreat of the Hammurabi Division and to attack and destroy it.[67] At that time, the Hammurabi Division was still located in the VII Corps zone. The order to execute the revised contingency plan would not be issued until late afternoon on the 26th.[68]

This difference in view between Yeosock and Waller, again, reflects a difference between a Moltkean approach to operational command and the idea that the commander decides what he is going to do and forces the enemy to comply with his every intention. The more positivist view represented by Waller is perhaps more congenial to American Army officers, but Yeosock's Moktkean approach allows for the active independence of the enemy. The negative side of this style of leadership is that it often makes it difficult to resume positive control when immediate exploitation of an opportunity is called for.

The immediate cost of the Yeosock approach was that it left a certain ambiguity concerning the subdivision of the principal ARCENT mission—destruction of the Republican Guard Forces Command. Destruction of the RGFC was General Franks' explicit mission, *but only within an assigned zone of attack*,[69] a significant fact overlooked in postwar criticism of VII Corps by General Schwarzkopf.[70] Retention of the Highway 8 corridor as part of the XVIII Corps zone left responsibility for ensuring destruction of the RGFC with Third Army. Yeosock assigned the Hammurabi Division to XVIII Corps should that be required by the Hammurabi's withdrawal on Basrah. This is precisely what would happen.

At the same time, Franks, who was assigned the force-oriented mission of destruction of the RGFC *in zone,* was left with the assurance that he would have the three heavy divisions he believed he required for this task only if he succeeded in pulling the 1st Infantry Division out of the breach and getting it into the fight. He could count on neither the 1st Cavalry Division, which Schwarzkopf held, nor the 24th Infantry Division, which belonged to the other corps. He would behave accordingly. That would take time. Although ARCENT maintained no formal reserve, the XVIII Corps' heavy and airmobile forces were, by the nature of the operation, the reserve of last resort for the Third Army commander.

Yeosock's decentralized view of operational execution reflected his belief that large units, like corps, were not likely to be as responsive to rapid changes in direction or focus as were smaller tactical formations, divisions and below. This belief implied a more decentralized execution at the operational level, based upon seeking harmony in the long term. The more centralized approach anticipated by Waller demanded a closer and more active coordination of the actions of subordinate formations, which the more forceful and dynamic Waller clearly intended.

Yeosock outlined his vision of the battle the day before he was hospitalized. According to his executive officer's notes, the commander saw four stages for the offensive. These were to

> Cross the LD [line of departure] as fast as we can with as much as we can carry.
>
> Take on the RGFC a bn [battalion] or a bde [brigade] at a time; a war of attrition to deliberately destroy it.
>
> *Operational pause* to determine what is where and ignore that which does not matter.
>
> If he offers surrender, increase OPTEMPO and let NCA [national command authorities] decide.[71]

On 13 February, Yeosock directed that ARCENT units begin moving to their forward assembly areas the following day. General Arnold's daily memorandum reflected the start of cross-border operations.[72] These, however, were not the first hostile actions west of the wadi.

Most deliberate attacks are preceded by what is known as a reconnaissance-counterreconnaissance battle. This is a struggle carried on by the two opponents' reconnaissance elements for dominance of the intermediate zone between the main lines. Its purpose is to gain information for one's own side and to deny it to the enemy without bringing on a major engagement. Throughout February, at the level of tactical units (corps and below), there was such a contest between ARCENT and Iraqi forces in the area west of Wadi al Batin.

On 1 February, following the Iraqi attack at Khafji, XVIII Corps was building up its forces in the west of the ARCENT zone with its left flank in the vicinity of Rafah. VII Corps was forming around Hafar al Batin, with two armored divisions south of the Tapline Road and the 2d Armored Cavalry, 1st U.K. Armored Division, 1st Infantry Division, and 1st Cavalry Division(-) to the north of the MSR. As a further deception, a gap had been left between the two U.S. corps beyond the Iraqi western flank unit (the 48th Infantry Division), where Franks would send his enveloping attack. This area was patrolled only by aviation units. The "Tiger Brigade" was located in the east with MARCENT.

As units closed, they honed the specific skills they would need for their part of the attack. The 1st Infantry Division and 1st U.K. Armored Division practiced the critical breaching and passage of lines portion of the attack plan on which the VII Corps attack increasingly depended. Although there had been various small actions involving minor collisions (on 1 February, the ARCENT Provost Marshal Office (PMO) reported handling 154 prisoners of war to date), the Battle of Khafji changed the level of violence, and the two sides began to contest the no man's land between them. U.S. commanders feared an Iraqi spoiling attack, similar to Khafji, down Wadi al Batin. Such an attack would have threatened the most vulnerable and critical nodes of the U.S. concentration. Elsewhere in the Third Army sector, however, intelligence continued to report that most of the barren desert area in front of ARCENT, particularly that in front of XVIII Corps, was held only by scattered forces.

On 3 February, the 1st Infantry Division reported destroying an Iraqi armored bulldozer cutting a gap in the border berm that marked the boundary between Iraq and Saudi Arabia. Further reconnaissance revealed two more gaps. As a consequence, General Rhame reinforced the 1st Squadron, 4th Cavalry, which was his security force on the border, with a balanced (armor and mechanized infantry) task force and an artillery battalion, all under the command of Brigadier General Bill Carter, the assistant division commander. That same day, the French 6th Light Armored Division within XVIII Corps exchanged fire with an Iraqi patrol.[73]

On the 4th, VII Corps took responsibility for the Saudi border posts in its sector. The 1st Infantry Division destroyed an Iraqi radar on a transporter, and the U.S. Air Force destroyed a 1st Cavalry Division AN/TPS 25 radar with a Harm missile ten kilometers behind the fire support coordination line. Two U.S. soldiers were wounded.[74] Four Iraqis surrendered to the 1st Cavalry in what would become something of a daily farce—miserable enemy soldiers giving up to reporters, helicopter crews, or anyone else they could find.

On 8 February, with the final closure of XVIII Corps in their assembly areas in the west and 3d Armored Division in the port, Yeosock told his staff he considered his army now closed.[75] XVIII

Corps indicated it was ready to begin cross-border operations and reconnaissance in depth on order.

On the 10th, the 1st Infantry Division reported the Iraqis were infiltrating reconnaissance elements into the division's sector during darkness and conducting limited indirect fire—to no particular effect, it might be added. By the 11th, VII Corps reported taking a total of 113 prisoners.[76] On the 14th, cross-border operations were authorized by ARCENT Fragmentary Order (FRAGO) 036.[77] Instructions were generally permissive, requiring that ARCENT be notified twenty-four hours before operations were executed.

Three days later, VII Corps began moving into its forward assembly areas. Franks organized the movement of the two armored divisions and his cavalry regiment so these units would rehearse their movement to contact; that is, they would march west in tactical formation, then turn north to their forward assembly areas behind the 2d Armored Cavalry Regiment (ACR).[78] This movement actually began on the 15th with the forward (western) movement of the 2d Armored Cavalry followed by the 1st Armored Division, which had to cross in front of the 3d Armored to take its place on the outer flank of the corps. (See figure 26.) Both divisions had to cross the Saudi highway that ran from Riyadh to Hafar al Batin, an exercise that tried the diplomatic patience of both American and Saudi drivers. The 1st Infantry Division moved from the east of Hafar al Batin to the northwest toward its breaching zone.

On the 16th, the 3d Armored Division moved on line with the 1st Armored, and the 1st U.K. Armored Division moved to a forward assembly area between Hafar al Batin and the 1st Infantry Division (ID). (See figure 27.) On the 17th, the VII Corps "fist" maneuvered for the first time in formation to forward assembly areas north of the Tapline Road. (See figure 28.) The VII Corps was set. As a matter of reference, the 1st Brigade of the 3d Armored Division (AD) formed an armored oval twenty kilometers long from scouts to trains and ten kilometers wide from Vulcan to Vulcan.[79] Both divisions consisted of three brigades. One division in column (3d AD), one in a wedge—one up, two back (1st AD). Moving units of such size in formation across a barren plain was something no leader present had done, much less seen before. It was by no means as easy to do in the desert as it was to contemplate in the CINC's bunker in the Saudi capital, where individual vehicles, even units of hundreds or more, were subsumed in single counters on a map sheet. There was, in short, a wide gap between what the CINC had only to contemplate and what Franks and his commanders, Colonel Don Holder (2d ACR), Major General Ron

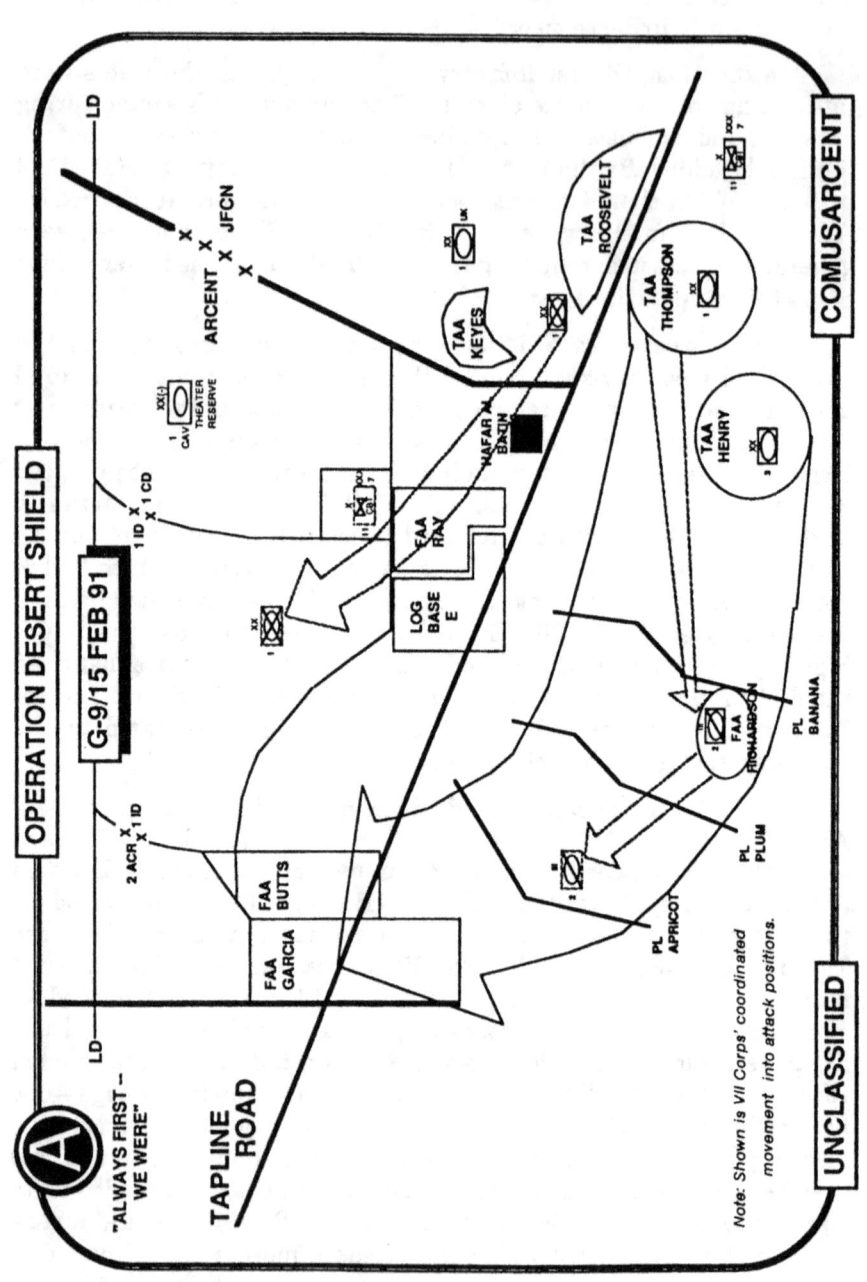

Figure 26.

Griffith (1st AD), and Major General Paul Funk (3d AD) had to do just to get to the Republican Guard.

On 15 February, Arnold had warned that "As we start cross border operations the greatest danger to our troops may well end up being safety."[80] A day later, two platoons of the 1st Infantry Division engaged each other leaving three soldiers wounded.[81]

On the 17th, the first fatal incident of fratricide among Army forces took place at 0110 when an AH-64 attack helicopter of the 1st Infantry Division, flown by the aviation battalion commander, misidentified two of the division's armored vehicles, killed two soldiers, and wounded six others.

The AH-64s had been responding to requests for fire from a unit on the ground that had been observing what it believed to be enemy vehicles. Earlier that night, a unit of the neighboring 1st Cavalry Division had also observed vehicles to their front, but because they could not positively identify them were denied permission to engage. About 2354 on the 16th, the 1st Cavalry unit (on the right) reported receiving two rounds in their direction about the same time that the 1st Division unit (on the left) reported firing on the vehicles they had observed. The operations officers of these adjacent units attempted to sort out the situation without success. The fatal incident followed shortly afterwards (170110), observed by the 1st Cavalry Division unit, which then withdrew behind the berm to avoid the possibility of further fratricide.[82]

The VII Corps' artillery and the 1st Infantry Division's artillery began heavy programs of artillery raids to attrit the Iraqi artillery in range of the breach site and to destroy enemy observation posts. The XVIII Corps did the same, although the desert in the west did not provide many worthwhile targets for the corps' guns. The heavy-light corps also began an aggressive program of armed aerial reconnaissances by its various aviation units. These proved to be lucrative prisoner hunts. Indeed, the corps would report on the 21st that one lesson learned was that the combination of psychological operations and attack helicopters had a great effect against Iraqi soldiers in sector. The most successful Army pre-G-day prisoner catch occurred on the 20th, when the 101st Aviation Brigade flew out to reconnoiter the site of the division's G-day air assault, engaged enemy bunkers, followed up with a PSYOP loudspeaker team, and took the mass surrender of 406 Iraqis.[83] An infantry battalion had to be brought into Iraq to accommodate all those wishing to surrender.

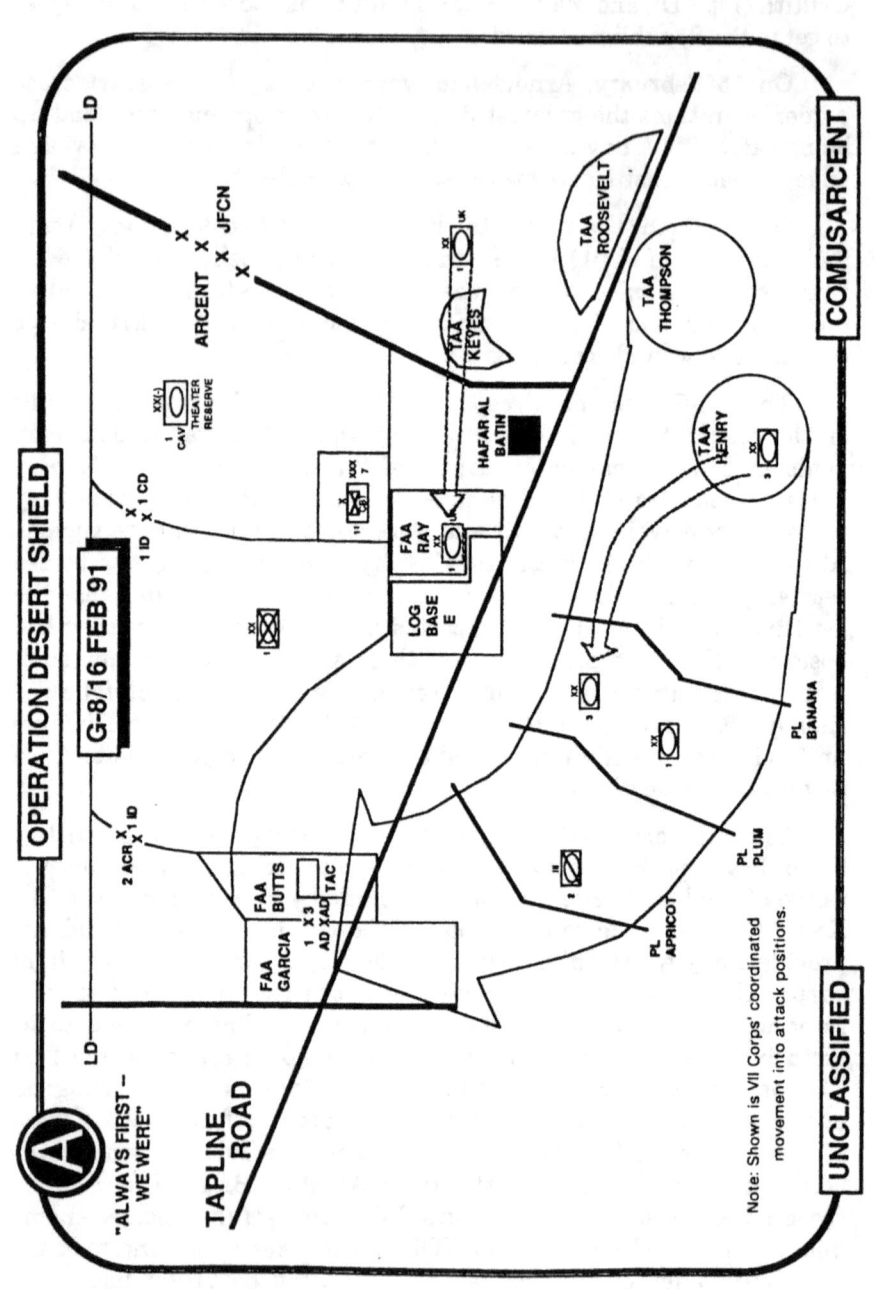

Figure 27.

203

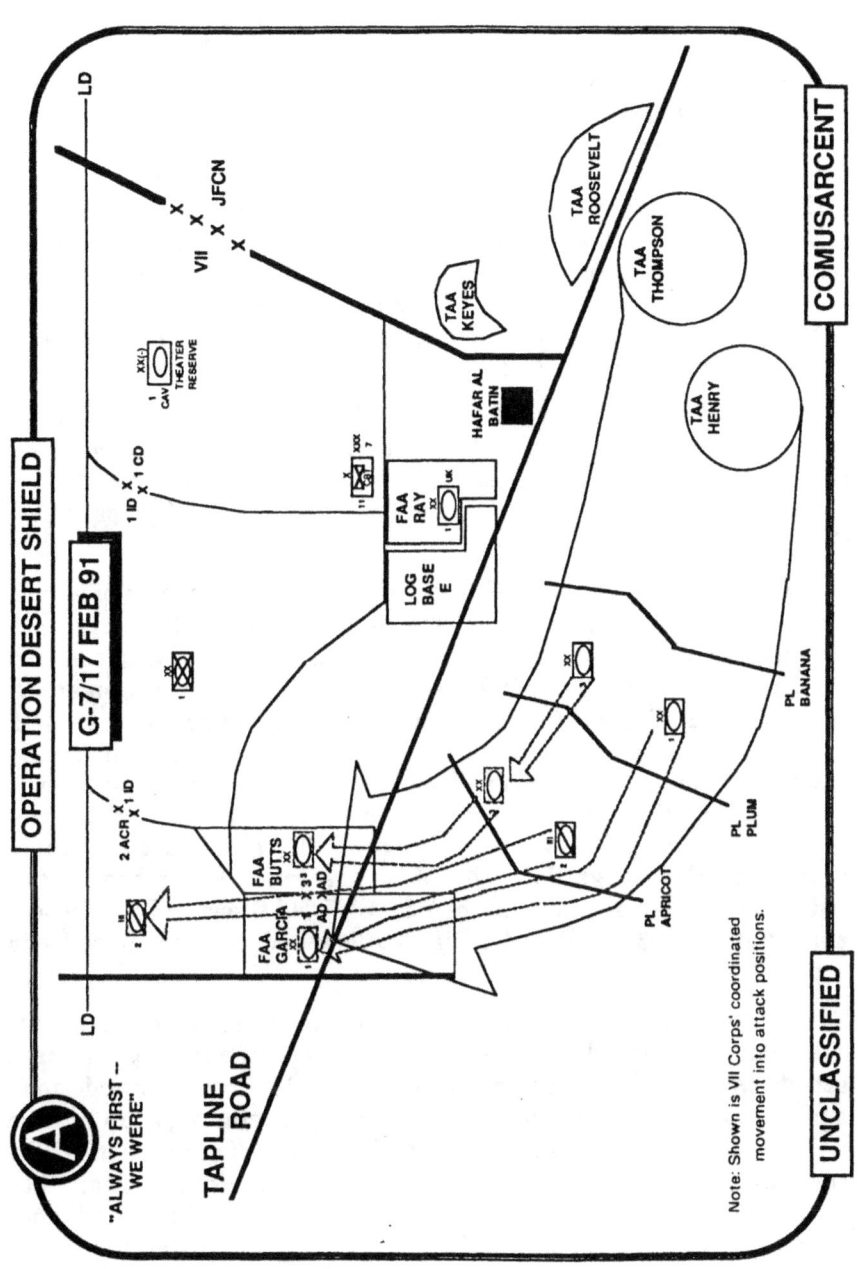

Figure 28.

It was not always that easy, however. As part of the ARCENT deception effort to lead the enemy to believe the ARCENT main attack would follow the Wadi al Batin approach along Kuwait's western border with Iraq, the 1st Cavalry Division (minus the Tiger Brigade), under the operational control of VII Corps prior to G-day, carried on an aggressive series of feints and demonstrations immediately to the west of the wadi in what the division called "The Battle of the Ruqi Pocket" (after a nearby Saudi border town).[84] On 20 February, during one of its reconnaissances in force, a unit of the 1st Cavalry Division (1st Battalion, 5th Cavalry) found itself under fire from dug-in Iraqis. Two Bradley's and one Vulcan air defense gun were lost, eight men were wounded, and two were killed.[85]

The following day, 21 February, ARCENT issued new, more restrictive guidance on the conduct of cross-border operations, requiring the corps to obtain authority of the ARCENT commander for operations of company size or larger.[86] Units were to be prepared for G-day at any time thereafter.

By the 23d, ARCENT had handled 972 enemy prisoners of war,[87] mostly from Iraqi front-line units whose function in the defensive scheme was to provide warning and die in place while buying time for the riposte of the Iraqi tactical reserves. The intelligence estimate in the ARCENT SITREP for the 20th noted that "Numerous reports indicate a serious morale problem as a direct result of coalition air attacks. . . . inadequate supply, disassociation with the Iraqi regime's policy toward Kuwait, poor training, and war weariness."[88] On the 21st, it reported, "The ability of the RGFC to conduct a theater counterattack is degraded,"[89] and as the ground war began, the ARCENT G2 assessed that "in the ARCENT/NAC sector, Iraq has lost approximately 53 percent of their artillery and 42 percent of their armor."[90]

These final preparations were played out against a political situation that seemed to some to offer the hope of avoiding a ground attack. On 11 February, Soviet envoy Yevgeni M. Primakov undertook a peace initiative to Baghdad that marked the beginning of an intense Soviet effort to broker a solution favorable to their former client.[91] On the 15th, Iraq made a qualified offer to withdraw from Kuwait that President Bush characterized as "a cruel hoax."[92] The Russians did not give up, however, and on the 17th, Iraqi foreign minister Tariq Aziz went to Moscow to meet with President Mikhail Gorbachev. The next day, Bush announced the military campaign would continue on schedule, and on the 20th, he told Gorbachev the Iraqi Army had four days to withdraw and accept UN sanctions.[93] On the 22d, the Soviet president announced a new peace proposal that Aziz accepted in Moscow. Bush and the coalition rejected the offer and ordered the Iraqis to begin an unconditional withdrawal in twenty-four hours or accept the consequences.[94] On the 23d, Iraq rejected the ultimatum, and the scene was set for the final acts of the war.

None of this diplomatic activity seems to have had any effect on the preparations for the ground attack, though the date for G-day oscilated (at G-3) from the 18th to the 21st, and some care was taken to ensure that prebattle activities were not irreversible. Selection of G-day was a matter of negotiation at echelons above ARCENT.[95]

General Waller commanded Third Army for the final week prior to G-day. At that time, there was no assurance that General Yeosock's health would permit his return to command and, as a result, there was some instability in concept. Waller, deputy theater commander since November, was a large man, as big as Schwarzkopf, with whom he had served in a number of earlier assignments. Waller was also as forceful as Schwarzkopf, but he lacked the hectoring tone or personal edge that so often accompanied the theater commander's impatience with subordinates. Waller was charismatic and firmly self-confident. As a lieutenant general and lately I Corps commander back in the United States, Waller was one of the Army's senior black general officers.

Waller's vision of the coming fight was somewhat different from Yeosock's. On the 18th, Waller shared his vision with his staff (as he did with the two corps commanders at their headquarters). The PERSCOM (Personnel Command) commander had estimated 20,000 casualties in the first five days. Waller observed that he expected a quick move to two key points, called Objective Collins (an area in the desert that served as the VII Corps pivot point east of al Busayyah) and Objective Gold (the Jalibah airfield), a principal 24th Infantry Division objective on Highway 8. Here, Waller expected the corps to rearm and refit while attracting enemy forces, then to turn east with the coordinated attack described earlier. He warned the staff that units should focus on safety and avoidance of fratricide (it was the day after the 1st Infantry Division's AH-64 incident).[96]

On the 19th, General Arnold anticipated a three- to four-week operation with three to four days to reach Orange and Collins, followed by a pause; three days of battle with the RGFC, again followed by another pause; and a deliberate mopping-up operation. The resilient and always pleasant G3 anticipated a commanders' huddle during each pause. That same night, Waller, who had been visiting the corps, directed his staff to caution his subordinate commanders not to conduct large-unit operations or take any irreversible actions, basically telling commanders: "Don't start a ground war."[97] All the renewed discussion of operational pauses seems to have taken hold. On the 20th, the VII Corps liaison officer informed the ARCENT commander's executive officer that, whereas VII Corps had not been planning a substantial pause, it now appeared they would conduct one (presumably on Objective Collins) to assess the enemy.[98]

In all this discussion of pauses, it is hard not to see the grey hand of the "SAMS Jedi Knights" and their often-scholastic approach to operations. Operational pauses, which are designed to avoid the sin of culmination, are one of the tricks of the trade that have received no small attention in the SAMS education, a sort of unwritten doctrinal construct. In theory, however, such pauses are spaced to follow achievements of major objectives—for much the same reasons infantry squads reorganize and redistribute ammunition after taking a tactical objective to compensate for the disorganizing effect of victory. In this sense, Yeosock's anticipation of a pause *after* the destruction of the Republican Guard would seem most appropriate.

After the fact, the intermediate halts otherwise proposed seem more like excessive caution, a desire to be safe and balanced at every step, a safety that would have its price in lost momentum. This must be judged, however, in light of the ARCENT commanders' preattack assessment of the enemy that remained highly pessimistic down to the launching of the ground attack—a pessimism encouraged, no doubt, by the various simulations run in the theater and in the United States that forecast heavy losses throughout.[99]

In the same way, the intricate maneuvers that called upon the 1st Infantry Division to breach, pass the 1st U.K. Armored Division to the east (not unlike a blocking back in football), then move into the slot behind the two armored divisions would also seem to bear the hallmark of the SAMS "red stripe"[100] fraternity, particularly when laid against expectations that the 1st ID could take severe losses in its first task. Yet if it took three heavy divisions to succeed in the main effort, as General Franks believed, where else was the third division to come from? There were no easy answers.[101]

On the 22d, the 2d Armored Cavalry reported its long-range surveillance teams in place to support the attack.[102] Waller's executive officer reported that the general had warned: "ARCENT must be able to stop the preparation for G-day for Iraq to demonstrate their good faith to comply with the UN resolutions and start again if they fail to comply. Must be able to still execute G-day of 24 February."[103]

On the night of the 23d, the 2d Armored Cavalry deployed two squadrons fifteen kilometers into Iraq to secure the engineers cutting the border berm. The 1st U.K. Armored Division located its reconnaissance elements with the 1st Infantry Division to mark lanes to the breach-site staging area, and the 101st Airborne Division inserted its long-range surveillance detachments and began final preattack aerial reconnaissance.[104] The preliminaries were over and the ground war was about to begin.

The ground offensive would be conducted more or less in accordance with the mission assigned by CENTCOM to ARCENT in January, as modified in the month following the publication of the Central Command order. Third Army was to conduct two corps attacks, "a supporting attack to block east-west LOCs along Highway 8 to isolate Iraqi forces in the Kuwait Theater of Operation" (with an on order mission to assist the main attack) and "the main attack with one U.S. corps attacking north *in zone* along the western Kuwait border to destroy Republican Guard forces."[105] As discussed above, the plan had been modified progressively, with increasing importance given the continuation of the attack by XVIII Corps beyond its initial rush to the Euphrates. (See map 7.)

The two corps were significantly different in composition, and their missions were fundamentally different in character. VII Corps, a homogeneous (though combined U.S.-U.K.) heavy corps, was assigned a "force oriented" mission, destruction of the RGFC in zone. The primary mission of XVIII Corps, a mixed medium-heavy-light force (U.S.-French), was terrain oriented and designed to block the Iraqi routes of withdrawal or reinforcement, then to fall in with its heavy forces on VII Corps' left and drive east toward Basrah. These tasks were fundamentally different, as were the formations to which they were assigned. The latter would require decentralized execution, the former something quite different indeed.

A force-oriented mission in the Iraqi desert implied battle as a process, a rolling fight, rather than as a discrete event. In light of anticipated force ratios, it demanded that the VII Corps commander conduct a highly controlled, carefully sequenced, and articulated attack by a force, at the outset, of eleven ground maneuver brigades (not counting the 1st Cavalry Division[-]), an armored cavalry regiment, seven attack helicopter battalions, and four supporting artillery brigades—all organized in four divisions with an armored cavalry regiment and aviation brigade under corps control.[106]

208

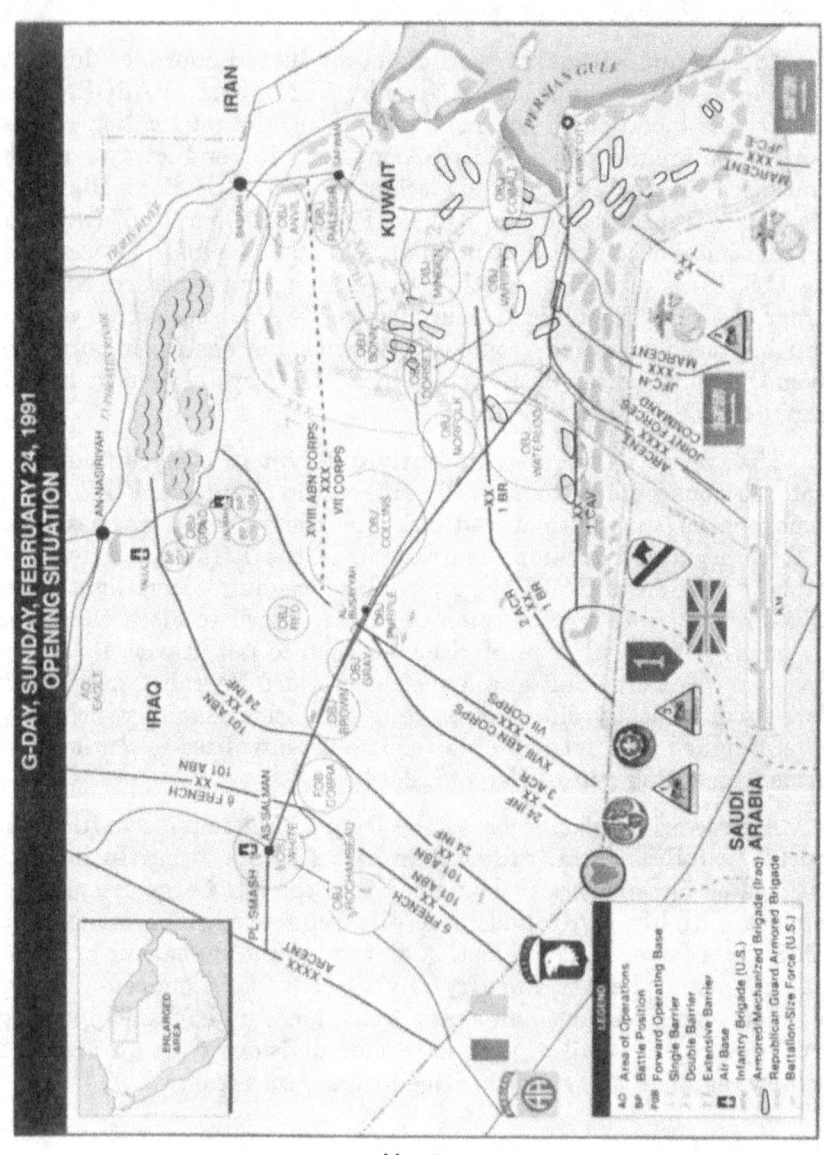

Map 7.

The XVIII Corps divisions, with more space in which to maneuver, would not require nearly the same control or coordination. To a great extent, each division would pursue a separate mission. The French 6th Light Armored would take As Salman, free MSR Virginia, and protect the ARCENT left flank. The 101st would launch its forces midway to the Euphrates the first day and form the first of several staging bases for its striking force of AH-64s and then follow up, as soon as possible, with another brigade of TOW (tactically tube-launched, optically tracked, wire-guided [missiles])-equipped air assault infantry to block Highway 8 until the 24th Infantry could cross the intervening desert and assume that task. Then, the 101st was to concentrate on advancing its AH-64 line to deep interdiction areas across the Euphrates to cut off escaping Iraqi forces that might flee north of the river on improvised or undamaged bridges. The 24th Division was to attack across an empty waste, day and night, to be the second division on the Euphrates, disrupting the enemy rear and, circumstances and time permitting, attacking down the highway to the southeast to assist in closing the KTO south of Basrah. The 82d Airborne Division would support the French and then clean up by-passed pockets of Iraqi soldiers left in the wake of the airborne division's more mobile sister units. The other heavy force, the 3d Armored Cavalry, would begin by maintaining contact with the VII Corps on the east and ultimately falling in as the fourth heavy brigade of the 24th Infantry Division. XVIII Corps' execution would be highly decentralized, and the corps headquarters would be involved primarily in sustaining the respective advances of its disparate forces.

Equally important to the corps commanders was the Third Army concept of operation. The order reads:

> As VII Corps finds and fixes the RGFC, COMUSARCENT will request from USCINCCENT the release of 1st CAV Division (-) as the theater reserve and attach 1st CAV Division (-) to VII Corps. VII Corps will be prepared to receive OPCON of the 24th Mech Division. VII Corps will then attack to destroy RGFC in zone. XVIII Corps will be prepared to attack RGFC in zone.[107]

The primary operational-level issue was going to be whether the 1st Cavalry Division(-) could be secured from the CINC's control in time to join the main battle, and if not, how the heavy forces of the XVIII Corps, whose first mission was to cut the Highway 8 escape route, would be brought into the decisive battle with the Republican Guard. The key element in attaining the 1st Cavalry's release was to gauge the reaction of the Iraqi tactical reserves, believed at that time to be the 12th Armored Division (later identified as the 52d Armored

Division),[108] to the ARCENT and Joint Forces Command North attacks. Whatever its number, that Iraqi unit's ability to resist the flanking movement of the 1st U.K. Armored Division was of particular concern. The Third Army assessment was that, once the 1st U.K. engaged the tactical reserve, it would, in effect, become the guarantee for the Egyptian Corps, toward which the British attack would converge. Third Army hoped that would trigger release of the 1st Cavalry Division, thus building the necessary "mass of maneuver" to close with and destroy the RGFC.[109] Schwarzkopf assigned CENTAF the responsibility for isolating the KTO by cutting lines of withdrawal across the Euphrates, thus denying the Iraqis exit or reinforcements.[110]

The Third Army's *Schwerpunkt*, its offensive center of gravity, was the VII Corps attack, scheduled for the morning of 25 February (G+1). Initially, the main effort of that attack, which in fact went in on the 24th and 25th, was the breaching operation conducted by the 1st Infantry Division (Mechanized) on the corps' eastern flank. As explained above, the penetration and breakout to be conducted by the 1st Infantry Division and the 1st U.K. Armored Division would set the pace of the entire VII Corps operation. After the British passed out of the breachhead to protect the corps' right flank (and at the same time relieved pressure in front of the Egyptian Corps), the focus and concentration of forces conducting the corps attack would shift west, to the iron fist of 2d ACR, 1st and 3d Armored Divisions, and whatever third heavy division ultimately became available.

General Franks envisioned conducting the phases of his operation using two very different operational styles. Indeed, he was to conduct two main attacks. With regard to the breach, his order said:

> The first phases of our operation will be maximum forces moving toward the RGFC with minimum casualties in minimum time. These phases will be deliberate and rehearsed. . . .
>
> The deliberate breach will be done with precision and synchronization resulting from precise targeting and continuous rehearsals.

The VII Corps order recognized explicitly that the second phase of the attack, the advance to defeat the RGFC, would be "METT-T [mission; enemy, terrain and weather and troops and time available] dependent and . . . [include] battles of movement and depth." "Once through the breach," the order continued,

> we will defeat forces to the east rapidly with an economy of force, and pass the point of main effort to the west of that action to destroy the Republican Guard Forces Command in a fast moving battle with zones of action and

agile forces attacking by fire, maneuver, and air. Combat service support must keep up because there will be no pause.[111]

Within the initial tactical operations, there were certain pacing events that had to be accomplished by the 1st Infantry Division's soldiers in fairly strict order. These were an advance to the main line of resistance, which included positioning five brigade equivalents of artillery forward to support the breaching operation;[112] the conduct of an artillery preparation; the breaching operation itself conducted by two maneuver brigades abreast; the clearing of an intermediate breachhead area to the range of direct fire systems (to Phase Line Colorado); the passage of the division's third brigade (in this case the 2d Armored Division Forward) while the breaching brigades rolled outward, so the sixty-kilometer final breachhead line (Phase Line New Jersey) would be held by three brigades abreast; then the passage of the British division with its supporting vehicles and its breakout into the Iraqi tactical depths to protect the corps' eastern flank and destroy if possible the enemy's principal tactical reserve, the Iraqi 12th (52d) Armored Division. Within all this, the advance of the gun line (five artillery brigades made up of thirteen field artillery cannon battalions and ten batteries of multiple launch rocket systems [MLRS]) through the breach had to be arranged in order that the artillery could range beyond the final breachhead line for the breakout and so that the general support artillery brigades would be repositioned to assume their new attachments as the corps shifted its center of gravity to the northwest. Speed in such a complex operation is relative, and, no doubt, it looked much easier to do from the confines of the Ministry of Defense basement, perhaps even from the offices of the Joint Chiefs of Staff in Washington, than it did in the desert on 24–25 February.

The VII Corps attack had been scheduled for G+1 in the original plan. Under that schedule, the 1st Infantry Division planned to accomplish on the 24th only the first part of its deliberate breach—closing the barrier belt. The 2d Armored Cavalry Regiment would screen forward on the western flank, while the 1st and 3d Armored Divisions positioned themselves to launch their enveloping maneuver the following day, simultaneously and in line with the 1st Infantry Division attack. In the dark desert night, punctuated by driving rain and blowing sand, soldiers awaited the dawn. (See figure 29.)

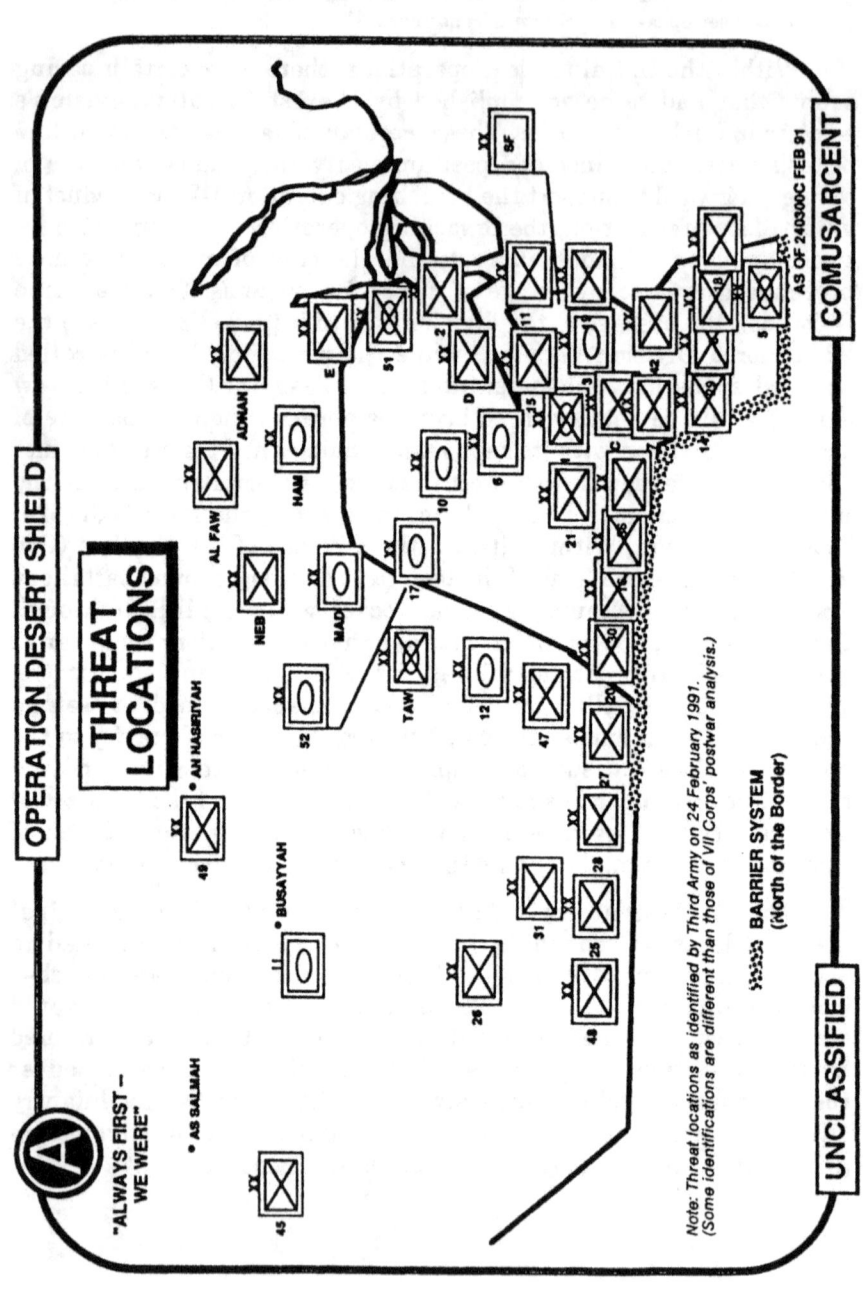

Figure 29.

Notes

1. "Escalation, 1990 Style," *The New York Times*, 27 October 1990, 22.

2. George Gallup, Jr., and Dr. Frank Newport, "Approval Ratings of Bush and Congress at New Lows," *The Gallup Poll Monthly* (October 1990): 34–35.

3. Theodore Draper, "The True History of the Gulf War," *New York Review of Books* 39, no. 3 (30 January 1992): 38–45. The Award-Winning Staff of *U.S. News & World Report* [Brian Duffey et al.], *Triumph Without Victory: The Unreported History of the Persian Gulf War* (New York: Times Books, 1992), viii, 414–15.

4. "U.N. Gives Iraq Until Jan. 15 to Retreat or Face Force: Hussein Says He Will Fight [headline]." Paul Lewis, "Warning by Council: Foreign Ministers Vote 12 to 2 for Resolution–China Abstains," *The New York Times*, 30 November 1990, 1.

5. *U.S. News & World Report, Triumph Without Victory*, 182, 184, 199 et seq.

6. "Authorization for Use of Military Force (Joint Congressional Resolution of January 12, 1991)," in Sifry and Cerf, *The Gulf War Reader*, 287–89.

7. Andrew Rosenthal, "Americans Don't Expect Short War," *The New York Times*, 15 January 1991, A11.

8. Sean D. Naylor, "Flight of Eagles," *The Army Times*, 22 July 1991, 12.

9. Concepts and Analysis Agency Document CAA-SR-91-18, HQDA After-Action Report (Desert Shield/Desert Storm), Appendix E: Chronology of Events, E-Chronology-52.

10. HQ, ARCENT, G3, Message, 180300Z JAN 91, FM COMUSARCENT MAIN//DT// MSGID/SITREP/USARCENT/001/JAN, PERID/170300Z/TO: 180300Z/ASOF:180300Z, 7–8.

11. HQ, ARCENT, Command Group, (Executive Officer's daily) Memorandum for Record, Subject: Daily Memo, 16 January 1991, dated 16 January 1991. (Executive Officer's memoranda will be retired with General Yeosock's private papers to the Military History Institute, Carlisle Barracks, Pennsylvania.)

12. Schwarzkopf, *Doesn't Take a Hero*, 416–21. Schwarzkopf states one-third of the strategic air was diverted to Scud hunt. Figures vary.

13. De la Billiere, *Storm Command*, 156, 191–92, 221–27, 235–49.

14. Comment based upon discussion in an ARCENT morning briefing at which the author was present and frequent mention in ARCENT SITREPs and executive officer daily memoranda during the period of the move. See report from 1st Cavalry Division on 22 January, for example, in HQ, ARCENT, G3, Message, 230300Z JAN 91, FM COMUSARCENT MAIN//DT// MSGID/SITREP/USARCENT/006/JAN, PERID/220300Z/TO:230300Z/ASOF:230300Z, 8.

15. HQ, ARCENT, G3, Message, 230300Z JAN 91, FM COMUSARCENT MAIN//DT// MSGID/SITREP/USARCENT/006/JAN,PERID/220300Z/TO:230300Z/A

SOF:230300Z, 10.

16. C. D. B. Bryan, *Friendly Fire* (New York: Bantam Books, 1977). Although Schwarzkopf's battalion was the unit involved, Schwarzkopf himself was not blamed for the incident that involved an artillery error. Indeed, the author of the book dealing with the incident clearly had nothing but the highest respect for then-Lieutenant Colonel Schwarzkopf and defends him at some length from charges made by the victim's parents.

17. Dr. Roger Spiller, Professor of Combined Arms Warfare, U.S. Army Command and General Staff College, to author.

18. For history of fratricide, see Lieutenant Colonel Charles R. Shrader, *Amicicide: The Problem of Friendly Fire in Modern War*, Research Survey No. 1 (Fort Leavenworth, KS: Combat Studies Institute, December 1982).

19. Comment by General John Yeosock, quoted in HQ, ARCENT, Command Group, Memorandum for Record, Subject: (Executive Officer's) Daily Memo, 18 January 1991, dated 18 January 1991. (Executive Officer's memoranda will be retired with General Yeosock's private papers to the Military History Institute, Carlisle Barracks, Pennsylvania.)

20. *The* Army report is summarized in Sean D. Naylor, "Friendly Fire: The Reckoning," *Army Times*, 26 August 1991, 4 and 6.

21. Statistical roll-up taken from ibid. Two incidents involved battalion commanders fighting their systems, as well as commanding their units. See Robert Johnson and Rick Wartzman, "Inquiry Sought on Army Account of Soldier's Death," *The Wall Street Journal*, 8 November 1991, A7; and Barton Gellman, "Felled by Friendly Fire," *The Washington Post National Weekly Edition*, 11–17 November 1991, 9–11.

22. See interview with Lieutenant General Calvin A. H. Waller by Brigadier General Timothy J. Groggin, et al., dated May 1991, 49–50, 60. General Waller's interview must be used with some care as he does not lack confidence speaking about some actions in theater about which he was obviously ill-informed, not the least the planning process prior to his arrival in November and the ARCENT order of battle during Desert Storm. He is, obviously, the best source on his own activities as deputy CINC. Interview with Brigadier General Steven Arnold at Eskan Village on 15 March 1991, 29–31. In the end, General Glossen was probably the victim of being a salesman prevented by conditions beyond his control (the CINC's desire to centralize control) from living up to his promises. The transcript of his briefing at the school house shows his remarks to be highly optimistic about air power available to ground commanders in light of what followed. Transcript of ARCENT MAPEX, tapes D and E in author's files.

23. A judgment by the author based upon comments made to him when discussing the friction over control of air support. Interestingly enough, General Yeosock is conspicuous by the extent of his confidence in the good intentions of the Air Force leaders, no doubt a consequence of his close association with General Horner. Author's discussions with General Yeosock and undated memorandum, Subject: CG Comments on the Context of ARCENT Operations, prepared by Lieutenant Colonel Mike Kendall. Memorandum will be retired with General Yeosock's personal papers. Memorandum reflects views expressed to author.

24. Colonel Joe Purvis to author.

25. Transcribed from film *San Pietro* by author.

26. Major Mark B. ("Buck") Rogers, USAF, Desert Storm Planner, CENTAF, quoted in Joint Publication 1, *Joint Warfare of the U.S. Armed Forces*, 11 November 1991, 68.

27. Generally the Air Force divides air support of the land battle in two categories: close air support (CAS), which is targeted and controlled by the Army, and air interdiction (AI), which is targeted and controlled by the Air Force. The Army argues for a subcategory called battlefield air interdiction (BAI), targeted by the Army and controlled by the Air Force. One of the best discussions is Lieutenant General Merrill A. McPeak, "TAC Air Missions and the Fire Support Coordination Line," *Air University Review* 36, no. 6 (September-October 1985): 65–72. McPeak was Air Force chief of staff during Desert Storm.

28. HQ, U.S. Central Command, Riyadh, Saudi Arabia, USCINCCENT OPLAN for Operation Desert Storm, dated 16 December 1990. The OPLAN provided for four phases, strategic air campaign, air supremacy in the KTO, battlefield preparation, and ground offensive. The issue, of course, was who would control the fires in Phase III, battlefield preparation. The ground commanders assumed they would. They were wrong, as it turned out. Until about G-8 (assumed), the CINC fought the air-attrition operation in the KTO with air alone. The order is silent about the need to refer to the secretary of defense and president for permission to initiate the ground offensive. It was this that constituted the major breakwater subdividing the third phase.

29. Waller interview, 2 May 1991, 51–53. General Schwarzkopf's centralization of the early air operations in the KTO is itself the best indication that this was the case.

30. Undated memorandum, Subject: CG Comments on the Context of ARCENT Operations, prepared by Lieutenant Colonel Mike Kendall. Memorandum will be retired with General Yeosock's personal papers. Colonel Daniel M. Ferezan, Memorandum for Commander, Third U.S. Army, Attn: G3, APO NY 09772, Subject: Project 5/Liaison Team Gulf After-Action Report, dated 31 March 1991. Colonel Ferezan describes the role of LNO parties.

31. HQ, ARCENT, Command Group, Memorandum for the Record, Subject: Notes from Huddle Meeting, 1 February 1991. Memorandum will be retired with General Yeosock's personal papers.

32. Waller interview, 2 May 1991, 58.

33. HQ, XVIII Airborne Corps, AFZA-GT-P (G3 Plans), Memorandum for Record, Subject: After-Action Brief for Operation Desert Storm, dated 8 July 1991, paragraph 12: "During the Air Campaign, we had great success in striking our priority targets. Although XVIII Airborne Corps was a supporting attack, we were able to keep our nominations visible to the Army and Air Force Targeteers. We took advantage of the SCUD-hunting effort and diverted air missions to achieve attacks against our targets."

34. HQ, ARCENT, G3, Deep Operations and Targeting Cell, After-Action Report, n.d., 2.

35. See interview with Lieutenant Colonel Bart J. Engram, ARCENT, G3 Deep Operations Cell, 27 March 1991, 2–3. Lieutenant Colonel Engram took a great deal of time at the end of the war to walk the air war down to the execution level with the Air Force wings that had supported ARCENT. His interview should be one of the primary sources in addressing Army-Air Force coordination.

36. HQ, VII Corps, Memorandum from AETSFA-FSE, Subject: Corps Fires After-Action Report, dated 15 March 1991, 5. Report states: "With hindsight, it appears that targets key to Corps plan were ultimately hit (222 targets)—over time—but not as fast as Corps expected. . . . Bottom line is that the effect of air delivered fires did clearly set the stage for minimum exploitation." Document is in VII Corps Archive, Corps Artillery Notebook, Combined Arms Research Library, Fort Leavenworth, Kansas.

37. The author attended ARCENT command briefings and observed the periodic revision of the formula for BDA to fit the existing cumulative estimate of strength remaining, which was derived from a variety of sources. This is good Kantian deductive reasoning (deciding what process *must* exist to produce the observable outcome), but it is bad science, failing to account for other possible hypotheses. In the end, the process in fact consisted of making a cumulative estimate and finding a way to explain how it got that way. That, of course, is probably the best that can be done, and if there is an error in the process, it is in the demand of maneuver commanders for something that cannot be delivered.

38. General Yeosock to author. The Air Force began using radar-equipped planes called "pointers" to scout forward and verify targets or locate alternatives for less-sophisticated A10s.

39. HQ, ARCENT, Command Group, (Executive Officer's) Daily Memo for 5 February 1991. CG comment: "Key issue is to have the air campaign start west of the Wadi. My mission. G3: Receiving a max of 20% of requested sorties." Assumed date for G-day (unofficial) was 21 February. HQ, ARCENT, Command Group (Executive Officer's) Daily Memo for 8 February 1991. (Executive Officer's Daily Memos will be filed with General Yeosock's papers at the Army Military History Institute, Carlisle Barracks, Pennsylvania.)

40. HQ, ARCENT, AFRD-DT, ARCENT Command SITREP D+25 (11 February 1991), Memorandum for Major General Taylor, ARCENT Rear, Subject: ARCENT SITREP. HQ, ARCENT, AFRD-DT, ARCENT Command SITREP D+27 (13 February 1991), Memorandum for Major General Taylor, ARCENT Rear, Subject: ARCENT SITREP. HQ, ARCENT, Command Group (Executive Officer's) Daily Memo for 13 February 1991. (Executive Officer's Daily Memos will be filed with General Yeosock's papers at the Army Military History Institute, Carlisle Barracks, Pennsylvania.)

41. Message, 140300Z FEB 91, FM COMUSARCENT MAIN//DT//, MSGID/SITREP/USARCENT/D+27/FEB//, PERID/130300Z/TO:140300Z/ASOF:140300Z, GENTEXT/COMMANDER'S EVALUATION/, 14.

42. HQ, ARCENT, Command Group, (Executive Officer's) Daily Memo for 16 February 1991. (Executive Officer's Daily Memos will be filed with General Yeosock's papers at the Army Military History Institute, Carlisle Barracks, Pennsylvania.)

43. Message, 170300Z FEB 91, FM COMUSARCENT MAIN//DT//, MSGID/SITREP/USARCENT/D+31/FEB//, PERID/160300Z/TO:170300Z/ASOF:170300Z, GENTEXT/COMMANDER'S EVALUATION/, 19, 43.

44. Message, 180300Z FEB 91, FM COMUSARCENT MAIN//DT//, MSGID/SITREP/USARCENT/D+32/FEB//, PERID/170300Z/TO:180300Z/ASOF:180300Z, GENTEXT/COMMANDER'S EVALUATION/, 17.

45. HQ, ARCENT, ARCENT Command SITREP D+37 (23 February 1991), AFRD-DT, Memorandum for Major General Taylor, ARCENT Rear, Subject: ARCENT SITREP. Another source for reading ARCENT G3's frustration is series of COMUSARCENT Planning Guidance messages that were dispatched daily to various addressees.

46. Letter to author from Office of the Program Manager (AMCPM-NGT-O), U.S. Army Program Manager, Saudi Arabian National Guard Modernization, dated 6 October 1991. The letter provided the author with an account of the battle, maps, and roster of OPMSANG members as well as other supporting documents.

47. "The Terrible Toll," *Newsweek, Commemorative Edition: America at War* (Spring-Summer 1991): 81–82. Typically, perhaps, the Marine Corps observers were interviewed on CNN upon linkup with relieving forces.

48. Letter to author from the Office of the Program Manager (AMCPM-NGT-O), U.S. Army Program Manager, Saudi Arabian National Guard Modernization, dated 6 October 1991.

49. Letter from Major Joe Pencoast (with PMSANG Support Group) to Dr. Roger Spiller, dated 21 February 1991.

50. CENTCOM reported Khafji was declared liberated at 311100Z. Message, 312115Z JAN 91, FM USCINCCENT, MSGID/SITREP/USCINCENT/175/JAN//, section 4 of 7, 2 (paragraph 2C(2)(A)). OPMSANG chronology gives end date/time as 011900 (C) February 1991: Letter to author from Office of the Program Manager (AMCPM-NGT-O), U.S. Army Program Manager, Saudi Arabian National Guard Modernization, dated 6 October 1991. Related missions would go on for some time.

51. Message, 012115Z FEB 91, FM USCINCCENT, MSGID/SITR EP/USCINCENT/176/FEB//, GENTEXT/COMMANDERS EVALUATION, FINAL SECTION OF 7, 3–4. Schwarzkopf's postwar comments on the conclusions he drew were in the transcript of the interview with David Frost, dated 22 March 1991, 16 (in possession of author). The ARCENT G2 estimate at the time was that the events indicated "that the Iraqi force is a disciplined one. It understands basic military maneuvers and can execute some relatively complex operations. However, we question the forces capability to control multiple division operations (perhaps with the exception of the RGFC) or to maintain momentum under well-executed fire."

Message, 010300Z FEB 91, FM COMUSARCENT MAIN//DT//, MSGID/SITREP/ USARCENT/D+15/FEB, 2. Schwarzkopf, *Doesn't Take a Hero*, 424–27.

52. Some Saudi detachments did fight in the Arab-Israeli wars in 1948 and 1973. See Chaim Herzog, *The Arab-Israeli Wars: War and Peace in the Middle East* (New York: Vintage Books, 1984), 23, 48, 94, 302; and Mohamed Heikal, *The Road to Ramadan* (New York: Quadrangle, 1975), 227.

53. Pancoast letter.

54. Quoted in HQ, ARCENT, Command Group, (Executive Officer's) Daily Memo, 1 February 1991. (Executive Officer's Daily Memos will be filed with General Yeosock's papers at the Army Military History Institute, Carlisle Barracks, Pennsylvania.)

55. HQ, U.S. Army Program Manager, Saudi Arabian National Guard Modernization AMCPM-NGT-O, Memorandum for Commander, U.S. Army Central Command, Riyadh, Saudi Arabia, Subject: Recommendation for the Valorous Unit Award, dated 30 April 1991. Proposed citation. Numbers are much larger than CENTCOM report for 1 February. The question probably involves a variation in the period covered and the normal difficulty with precision in such matters.

56. Message, 012115Z FEB 91, FM USCINCCENT, MSGID/ SITREP/ USCINCENT/176/FEB//, GENTEXT/COMMANDERS EVALUATION, FINAL SECTION OF 7, 3–4.

57. From the author's own observations as well as comments reflected in Executive Officer's Daily Memos throughout this period.

58. HQ, ARCENT, Command Group, (Executive Officer's) Daily Memo for 7 February 1991. (Executive Officer's Daily Memos will be filed with General Yeosock's papers at the Army Military History Institute, Carlisle Barracks, Pennsylvania.) Observation by Major General Arnold in HQ, CAC-T, Center for Army Lessons Learned, Fort Leavenworth, Kansas, Commander's Observations at the ARCENT AAR, DSSN112, 6.

59. HQ, ARCENT, Command Group (Executive Officer's) Daily Memos, 7 and 13 February 1991. (Executive Officer's Daily Memos will be filed with General Yeosock's papers at the Army Military History Institute, Carlisle Barracks, Pennsylvania.)

60. Ibid.

61. Ibid. Interview with Lieutenant General Calvin Waller by Brigadier General Timothy J. Groggin, et al., on 2 May 1991, 93. General Waller believed he had made the initial decision on this question. In fact, the issue was one of many revisits that were presented to him during his period of command in ARCENT. In an Army where commanders change with some frequency, no issue ever gets a final answer.

62. HQ, ARCENT, AFRD-DTP, Memorandum for USARCENT Historian, Colonel Swain, Subject: HQ, USARCENT, G3 Plans, Historical Narrative of Desert Shield, Desert Storm, Defense and Restoration of Kuwait, and Redeployment, dated 6 April 1991, 20–23.

63. Interview with General Frederick Franks at Fort Leavenworth, Kansas, 6 March 1992, 15–19. General Yeosock had expressed his intention to commit the 1st Cav to VII Corps if released by the CINC. The question for General Franks was when and where.

64. General Peay discussed this issue with the author when the latter visited the headquarters of the 101st Airborne in the field prior to G-day. Assessment of his confidence is author's own judgment based on this and other discussions.

65. HQ, ARCENT, AFRD-DTP, Memorandum for USARCENT Historian, Colonel Swain, Subject: HQ USARCENT, G3 Plans, Historical Narrative of Desert Shield, Desert Storm, Defense and Restoration of Kuwait, and Redeployment, dated 6 April 1991, 16–17.

66. Ibid. Appendix 8 to Annex N to COMUSARCENT OPLAN Desert Storm 001, 181300ZFEB91, Contingency Plan 1A: Destruction of RGFC (Phase IIID); Positional Defense in Place Template, and Change 1 to Appendix 8 to Annex N to COMUSARCENT OPLAN Desert Storm 001, 241900ZFEB91, Contingency Plan: Destruction of RGFC (Phase IIID); Positional Defense in Place Template COA6. This contingency plan is a metaphor for the way planning was done. The plan had a number of fathers in ARCENT and VII Corps, principally Major Kevin Reynolds, a BCTP augmentee to ARCENT G3, Major Dan Gilbert, an augmentee to G3 Plans at ARCENT, and Major Tom Goedkoop, VII Corps G3 Plans.

67. Change 1 to Appendix 8 to Annex N to COMUSARCENT OPLAN Desert Storm 001, 241900ZFEB91, Contingency Plan: Destruction of RGFC (Phase IIID); Positional Defense in Place Template COA6.

68. Message, 261500Z, FM CDRUSARCENT, Subject: FRAGO 058 to ARCENT OPORD 001 (Desert Storm) Destruction of the RGFC.

69. For the nonspecialist: The assignment of a zone of operations is a restrictive technique to prevent adjacent units from shooting or otherwise interfering with each other. Assignment of a zone of action to a commander gives him freedom of action within the area so designated but denies him attack or movement across the boundary without coordination and permission. Daring commanders have achieved notable success by ignoring boundaries, notably Rommel in World War I, but on other occasions, ignoring boundaries has led to incidents of fratricide and confusion. Coordination of action by adjacent units is the responsibility of their common higher headquarters.

70. Schwarzkopf's notorious criticism of Franks rests upon the premise that VII Corps had sole responsibility for destruction of the RGFC. This criticism ignores the territorial limits within which Franks operated, the role of Third Army and, coincidentally, his own responsibility for trying air interdiction into the ground offensive. Schwarzkopf, *Doesn't Take a Hero*, 450–78.

71. HQ, ARCENT, Command Group, (Executive Officer's) Daily Memo for 13 February 1991. (Executive Officer's Daily Memos will be filed with General Yeosock's papers at the Army Military History Institute, Carlisle Barracks, Pennsylvania.)

72. Ibid.

73. Message, 030300Z FEB 91, FM COMUSARCENT MAIN//DT//, MSGID/ SITREPUSARCENT/D+17/FEB//PERID/020300Z/TO:030300Z/ASOF:030300Z,9, 12.

74. Message, 040300Z FEB 91, FM COMUSARCENT MAIN//DT//, MSGID/SITREP/USARCENT/D+18/FEB//PERID/030300Z/TO:040300Z/ASOF:040 300Z, 10.

75. HQ, ARCENT, Command Group, (Executive Officer's) Daily Memo for 8 February 1991. (Executive Officer's Daily Memos will be filed with General Yeosock's papers at the Army Military History Institute, Carlisle Barracks, Pennsylvania.)

76. Message, 100300Z FEB 91, FM COMUSARCENT MAIN//DT//, MSGID/SITREP/USARCENT/D+24/FEB//PERID/090300Z/TO:100300Z/ASOF:100 300Z, 9. Message, 110300Z FEB 91, FM COMUSARCENT MAIN//DT//, MSGID/SITREP/USARCENT/D+24/FEB//PERID/100300Z/TO:110300Z/ASOF:110 300Z, 9.

77. Message, FM COMUSARCENT MAIN//G3//, Subject: FRAGO 036 to OPLAN Desert Storm 001: Cross Border Operations.

78. Lieutenant Colonel Peter S. Kindsvatter, "VII Corps in the Gulf War: Deployment and Preparation for *Desert Storm*," *Military Review* 72, no. 1 (January 1992): 15. HQ, ARCENT, Unclassified Desert Storm Command Briefing, dated 5 August 1991, shows movements on 15, 16, and 17 February.

79. HQ, 3d Armored Division, Overlay, Appendix 2 (Division Standard Movement to Contact Formation) to Annex C to 3AD OPORD 91-1 (Operation Desert Spear (Draft)), dated 22 January 1991. See also command briefing titled, "Vanguard Brigade (2d Brigade) 24th Infantry Division, Operation Desert Shield/Storm" (briefing has no date but about half the slides show 14 March date), slide titled, "Brigade Formation." The second brigade showed a formation of seventy kilometers in depth from reconnaissance line to support battalion and ten kilometers in width. The VII Corps G2/G3 log for 21-22 February indicates that the 1st Cavalry Division(-) (2 Brigades) was eighteen kilometers wide by twenty kilometers deep. HQ, VII Corps, G2-G3 Daily Staff Journal, 23 February, item 29 (1715). The 1st Armored Division's postwar briefing showed a division formation (division wedge) fifty to eighty kilometers deep by twenty to twenty-five kilometers wide. None of these are precise figures, but they do give an order of magnitude.

80. HQ, ARCENT, AFRD-DT, ARCENT Command SITREP D+29 (15 February 1991), Memorandum for Major General Taylor, ARCENT Rear.

81. HQ, ARCENT, Command Group, (Executive Officer's) Daily Memo for 16 February 1991. (Executive Officer's Daily Memos will be filed with General Yeosock's papers at the Army Military History Institute, Carlisle Barracks, Pennsylvania.)

82. Message, 180300Z FEB 91, FM COMUSARCENT MAIN//DT//, MSGID/SITREP/USARCENT/D+24/FEB//PERID/170300Z/TO:180300Z/ASOF:180 300Z, 12. Robert Johnson and Rick Wartzman, "Inquiry Sought on Army Account of Soldier's Deaths," *The Wall Street Journal*, 8 November 1991, A7. Robert Johnson and Caleb Solomon, "Gulf War Casualty: 'Friendly Fire' Downs the Soaring Career of a Gung-Ho Colonel," *The Wall Street Journal*, 10 September 1991, A1 and A8. On 1st Cavalry Division, see HQ, 1st Cavalry Division, *Battle of the Ruqi Pocket*, 7.

HQ, 1st Cavalry Division, DTAC, *Daily Staff Journal*, 16 and 17 February 1991, 10–12 (16th), 1–3 (17th). To imagine the sort of confusion that could exist in this situation, one should remember that, in conditions of darkness, there were elements of at least five separate units operating in a relatively small area and trying to control the situation—troops from two battalions of the 1st Cavalry Division (2-8 and 2-5 Cavalry) and three battalions of the 1st Infantry Division (1-4 Cavalry, 1-41 Infantry, and the 1st Aviation Battalion). The problem was compounded by occurring on a boundary between two divisions.

83. Message, 210300Z FEB 91, FM COMUSARCENT MAIN//DT//, MSGID/SITREP/USARCENT/D+35/FEB//PERID/200300Z/TO:210300Z/ASOF:210300Z, 12–13.

84. HQ, 1st Cavalry Division, paper and briefing titled, "1st Cavalry Division in the Battle of the Ruqi Pocket" (hereafter referred to as HQ, "1st Cavalry Division, Battle of the Ruqi Pocket").

85. Message, 210300Z FEB 91, FM COMUSARCENT MAIN//DT//, MSGID/SITREP/USARCENT/D+35/FEB//PERID/200300Z/TO:210300Z/ASOF:210300Z, 11. (ARCENT SITREP has a typo that indicates the incident took place on the 21st after issue of SITREP. The 1st Cavalry Division's records indicate the 20th.) "HQ, 1st Cavalry Division, Battle of the Ruqi Pocket," 9.

86. Message, 210500Z FEB 91, FM CDRARCENTMCP//G3//, Subject: FRAGO 043 to OPORD 001 (Desert Storm).

87. HQ, ARCENT, ARCENT Morning Brief, 23 February 1991 (D+37), slide titled, "EPW/CI Status and Location." Slide was prepared by ARCENT PMO Office for the daily briefing as of 222400Z February 1991.

88. Message, 200300Z FEB 91, FM COMUSARCENT MAIN//DT//, MSGID/SITREP/USARCENT/D+34/FEB//PERID/190300Z/TO:200300Z/ASOF:200300Z, 4.

89. Message, 210300Z FEB 91, FM COMUSARCENT MAIN//DT//, MSGID/SITREP/USARCENT/D+35/FEB//PERID/200300Z/TO:210300Z/ASOF:210300Z, 4–5.

90. Message, 240300Z FEB 91, FM COMUSARCENT MAIN//DT//, MSGID/SITREP/USARCENT/G-DAY/FEB//PERID/230300Z/TO:240300Z/ASOF:240300Z, 4.

91. Thomas L. Friedman, "Baker and Dole Disagreeing On Warning by Gorbachev," *The New York Times*, 11 February 1991, A13.

92. Rick Atkinson and Dan Balz, "Iraq Offers Conditional Withdrawal: Bush Rejects Proposal as 'Cruel Hoax,'" *The Washington Post*, 16 February 1991, A1, A12.

93. Serge Schmemann, "Gorbachev Gives Iraqi a Peace Proposal: Seeks a Pullout, Pledging Help Afterward," *The New York Times*, 19 February 1991, A1; and Paul Lewis, "U.S. and Britain Fault Soviet Plan: Allies Tell Moscow Iraq Must Agree to Pullout Deadline," *The New York Times*, 21 February 1991, A1.

94. Serge Schmemann, "7-Point Initiative: Moscow Proposal Omits Mention of Mideast Peace Conference," *The New York Times*, 22 February 1991, A1. Maureen Dowd, "Pressing Demands: U.S. Says New Proposal Fails to Meet Crucial U.N. Resolutions," *The New York Times*, 22 February 1991, A1. Andrew Rosenthal, "Ground War Vowed: Iraqis Say Ultimatum Is Shameful, but Show Signs of Wavering," *The New York Times*, 23 February 1991, A1.

95. Schwarzkopf's account is that he came under increasing pressure to advance the date of attack lest the Soviets should broker an Iraqi withdrawal that would allow Saddam's army to escape unpunished. Schwarzkopf, *Doesn't Take a Hero*, 440–45. De la Billiere, *Storm Command*, 278.

96. HQ, ARCENT, Command Group, (Executive Officer's) Daily Memo for 18 February 1991. (Executive Officer's Daily Memos will be filed with General Yeosock's papers at the Army Military History Institute, Carlisle Barracks, Pennsylvania.)

97. HQ, ARCENT, Command Group, (Executive Officer's) Daily Memo for 19 February 1991. (Executive Officer's Daily Memos will be filed with General Yeosock's papers at the Army Military History Institute, Carlisle Barracks, Pennsylvania.)

98. HQ, ARCENT, Command Group, (Executive Officer's) Daily Memo for 20 February 1991. (Executive Officer's Daily Memos will be filed with General Yeosock's papers at the Army Military History Institute, Carlisle Barracks, Pennsylvania.)

99. Aside from the PERSCOM commander's prediction of losses noted above, see James Blackwell's *Thunder in the Desert* (New York: Bantam Books, 1991), 106; and an exchange of letters from Colonel Trevor Depuy and Theodore C. Taylor in *Parameters* 22, no. 2 (Summer 1992): 96–98, for what civilian simulators were predicting. Certainly the prewar forecasting by attrition-based models, no less the military's uncritical fascination for such, should be shaken by this experience. Senator Edward M. Kennedy's estimate in the Senate debate of January 1991 was for 3,000 American casualties a week with 700 deaths. Kennedy's estimates are extrapolations from the Arab-Israeli wars and were not unreasonable. U.S. Congress, Senate, Senator Kennedy of Massachusetts speaking against war in the Persian Gulf, 102d Congress, 1st Sess., *Congressional Record* (10 January 1991), vol. 137, no. L, S127.

100. The red stripe on the trousers was the mark of the members of the German General Staff whose ideal SAMS presumes to emulate.

101. In a letter to the author, General Rhame wrote that corps estimates of losses for his division in the breaching operation were from 25 percent to 40 percent. Nonetheless, Rhame had sought the follow-on mission, sometimes in spite of reluctance by the corps to count on a division they expected to be seriously hurt penetrating the enemy defenses.

102. Message, 220300Z FEB 91, FM COMUSARCENT MAIN//DT//, MSGID/SITREP/USARCENT/D+36/FEB//PERID/210300Z/TO:220300Z/ASOF:220300Z, 10.

103. HQ, ARCENT, Command Group, (Executive Officer's) Daily Memo for 22 February 1991. (Executive Officer's Daily Memos will be filed with General Yeosock's papers at the Army Military History Institute, Carlisle Barracks, Pennsylvania.)

104. Message, 240300Z FEB 91, FM COMUSARCENT MAIN//DT//, MSGID/SITREP/USARCENT/G-DAY/FEB//PERID/230300Z/TO:240300Z/ASOF:240300Z, 10–12.

105. HQ, U.S. Central Command, Riyadh, Saudi Arabia, APO NY 09852, 16 December 1990, USCINCCENT OPLAN for Operation Desert Storm, 14 and 18.

106. HQ, U.S. Army Forces Central Command, Riyadh, Saudi Arabia, APO NY 09852, 5 January 1991, COMUSARCENT Operations Plan Desert Storm 001, 8, C-3, C-4.

107. Ibid., C-4.

108. The identification of Iraqi brigades was fairly accurate. There was less agreement on their divisional assignments. In this case, ARCENT continued to associate the armored brigades in tactical reserve behind the Iraqi front line with the 12th Armored Division. The VII Corps' postbattle analysis identifies it as the 52d. At this time, the VII Corps' analysis seems more convincing. For that reason, the author has adopted the device of using the VII Corps' reconstruction of the battlefield as the authoritative assessment. Where ARCENT addresses units under other identities, the ARCENT identification is followed by the VII Corps' assessment in parentheses (e.g., "... the 12th (52d) Armored Division" in the text refers to the brigades of the tactical reserve identified in ARCENT documents as the 12th Armored Division but found by VII Corps to be the 52d Armored Division). This device does not affect the content of the actions described, as the Iraqi brigade clusters fought as brigades, not coordinated divisions. The document accepted as authoritative is, HQ, VII Corps, Assistant Chief of Staff, G2, AETSCB memorandum, Subject: The 100 Hour Ground War: The Failed Iraqi Plan, dated 20 April 1991.

109. HQ, ARCENT, Command Group, (Executive Officer's) Daily Memo, 23 February 1991, 3. HQ, ARCENT, Command Group, (Executive Officer's) Daily Memo, 24 February 1991, 2. (Executive Officer's Daily Memos will be filed with General Yeosock's papers at the Army Military History Institute, Carlisle Barracks, Pennsylvania.)

110. HQ, U.S. Central Command, Riyadh, Saudi Arabia, APO NY 09852, 16 December 1990, USCINCCENT OPLAN for Operation Desert Storm, 15.

111. HQ, VII Corps, OPLAN 1990-2, Operation Desert Saber, 13 January 1991, 5–6.

112. There were actually two division artilleries, the 1st Infantry Division's and the 1st U.K. Armored and three artillery brigades, the 42d, 75th, and 142d (National Guard).

Lieutenant General John Yeosock, commanding general, U.S. Third Army

"Long ball hitters" at Fort McPherson awaiting movement to Saudi Arabia, December 1990. Kneeling are Maj. Clay Newman, Maj. Larry Pippin, Maj. Rich Halbleib, (unknown), Maj. Dan Gilbert, and (unknown). Standing are Maj. John Combs, Maj. Brad Smith, Maj. Bob Wegman, Maj. Tom Polmateen, Lt. Col. David Mock, Maj. Mark Wagner, Maj. Paul Hughes, (behind Wagner), and (rest unknown)

General Schwarzkopf and three of his planners: Lieutenant Colonel Greg Eckert, Major Dan Roh, and Colonel Purvis

Helicopter pilots had to learn to fly in the Saudi desert

Troops eating in austere desert conditions

Russia foreign minister, Eduard A. Shevardnadze, addressing the UN Security Council in the debate on the use of "all necessary means" to ensure Iraq's compliance with the UN resolution ordering it to withdraw from Kuwait by 15 January 1990

M1 tanks driving in column in the Saudi desert

A sand-table exercise conducted by the 1st Infantry Division just before the breaching operation

Soldiers from the 24th Infantry practicing a dismount from a Bradley tank

Lieutenant General Frederick M. Franks, commander of VII Corps, and his senior commanders: seated from left, Major General John Tilelli, Jr., 1st Cavalry Division; Major General Ronald H. Griffith, 1st Armored Division; Franks; Major General Tom Rhame, 1st Infantry Division; Major General Paul E. Funk, 3d Armored Division; and Major General Rupert Smith, U.K. 1st Armoured Division.

A 5th Special Forces trainer instructing Qatari soldiers before the ground phase of Desert Storm

Saudi heavy-equipment transporters carrying self-propelled artillery to tactical assembly area

Tanks being unloaded from HETs during the Gulf War

Tanks being unloaded from (HETs) during the Gulf War

Heavy equipment transporters (HETs) moving their cargoes of M1 tanks northwest along MSR Dodge

A 1st Cavalry Division MLRS counterbattery raid, 21 February 1991

Brigadier General John Tilelli (third from left) discusses a pre-G-day raid with his commanders and staff

Men from the 1st Infantry Division deployed along an Iraqi berm in late February

General Pagonis addressing 22d Support Command soldiers on the eve of the war

An M1 mine plow used in Desert Storm

An M1 tank refueling in the desert

U.S. Air Force A-10 "Warthog" tactical fighter

One of General Horner's targeting meetings

Abrams and Bradleys in a desert wedge formation

The 101st Airborne Division's soldiers waiting for Blackhawks to carry them 100 kilometers into Iraq on 24 February 1991

An unfinished oil trench that when filled and ignited with explosives was meant to fend off the coalition attack

Three Apache helicopters and one OH-58D scout helicopter from the 2d Squadron, 6th Cavalry Regiment, fly over a destroyed enemy tank in the Iraqi desert

Support colums such as this stretched hundreds of kilometers across the desert

Tankers from the 3d Infantry Division that supported the VII Corp on 27 February

General Schwarzkopf (center) with Lieutenant General Khalid bin Sultan (right), commander of the Arab forces during the war. General Calvin Waller, deputy CINC, is on Schwarzkopf's right, with Major General Robert Johnston, CENTCOM chief of staff, looking to the rear.

A G-day briefing in "Lucky Main" operations room at the school house on 24 February 1991

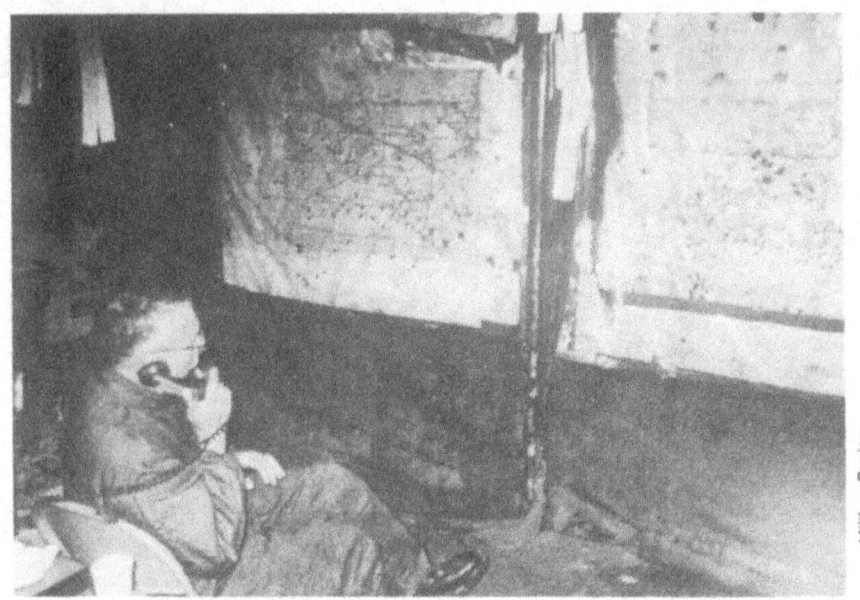

Following the battle with grease pencil on acetate, General Franks talks to his unit via telephone

General McCaffrey, commander, 24th Infantry Division, using his Blackhawk as a forward CP

Lt. Gen. Franks sketching out an idea in the sand relating to the double envelopment of Iraqi forces on 27 February. Watching is Lt. Col. David McKiernan.

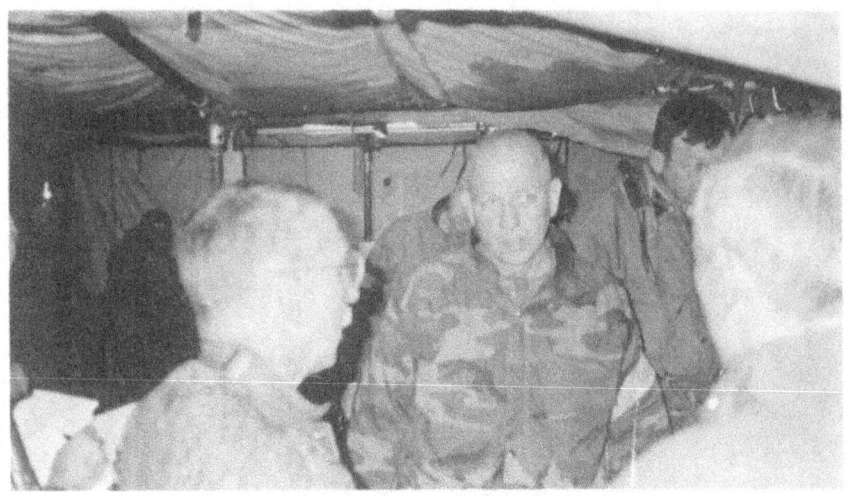

Lieutenant General Franks, VII commander, discusses the tactical situation with Major General Paul E. Funk, 3d Armored Division commander at the 3d AD TAC in Iraq, 0745 27 February 1991

Iraqi vehicles strewn along the roadside on the way from Kuwait City to Basrah

Destruction along the "Highway of Death," the road from Kuwait City to Basrah at the end of the Persian Gulf War

An M1 Abrams tank from the 24th Infantry Division, with turret traversed, during the attack into the Euphrates valley

Arab forces celebrating the Liberation of Kuwait City

General Schwarzkopf confronting Iraqi representatives with the coalitions's cease-fire demands

General Franks, center, with three fingers of the VII Corps armored fist on 6 March 1991: General Funk, 3d Armored: Rhame, 1st Infantry; and Griffith, 1st Armored

Secretary of the Army Michael Stone visiting Third Army headquaters at "Lucky Main." Shown on the front row, left to right: Brig. Gen. Monroe (G4); Brig. Gen. Sikora (PERSCOM commander); Brig. Gen. Stewart (G2); Brig. Gen. Arnold (G3); Lt. Gen. Yeosock; Secretary Stone; Maj. Gen. Mulchay (commander, 416th Engineer Command); Maj. Gen. Kelly (Defense Reconstruction Office); Brig. Gen. Taylor (PMSANG); Command Sergeant Major Smith; the G6/Signal Command commander, Col. Sutton is to Gen. Monroe's right rear; Col. John Jorgenson is in the second row between Yeosock and Stone.

Yeosock's "eyes and ears", Third Army's liaison officers: Lieutenant Colonel Gutwald, Colonel Molinari, Colonel Rock, Colonel Soriano, Colonel Petrie, Colonel Ferezon, and Colonel Nelson

Vehicles ready for shipment at the Port of Dammam

Victory parade for Desert Storm

7
Desert Storm: Battle

Two metaphors are suggested by the four days of concentrated ground attack that destroyed the forces of Saddam Hussein in southeastern Iraq and freed Kuwait. The first is that of J. F. C. Fuller's "Sea Warfare on Land":[1] the grand fleet maneuvering at sea, a picture of the disciplined movement in formation of great armored dreadnoughts (M1 Abrams tanks) and lethal but lightly armored battle cruisers (Bradley fighting vehicles) from which, as necessary, debouch B. H. Liddell Hart's "land-marines"[2] to clear trenches and built-up areas. Like destroyers and torpedo boats, Army attack helicopters concentrate rapidly and strike with deadly precision. Overhead, the skies, often dark and forbidding during the four-day ground operation, are clear of enemy planes and full of those of the coalition, striking both enemy concentrations and, increasingly, the retreating columns that clog the few routes out of the Kuwait–southeastern Iraq deathtrap. Behind the combat fleet toil the sea trains that carry the fuel and ammunition, in hundreds of thousands of tons, required to sustain the fighting fleet at range and to link it to its bases in the south.

The second metaphor is the relentless movement of the drill bit through the coal face. For though some of the first-line Iraqi forces did stand and fight, the Iraqi Army found itself no more effective in resistance than the coal vein that succumbs to the remorseless advance of the drill. Even when the Iraqis fought back, it did not matter in the context of the whole operation, and in the end, the American armed forces lost far fewer soldiers in the four-day ground battle than the Marine Corps did to a single terrorist bomb in Beirut in October 1983.

The enemy forces in the target area of the ground attack had been pounded by a sustained bombing effort that began within days of the initiation of hostilities on 17 January. At the same time, the theater of operations had been isolated by the attack of bridges over the Euphrates. A systematic attack of air defense systems in the KTO had rendered the Iraqi forces on the ground vulnerable to attack at will. Thus freed from interference and under the direction of General Schwarzkopf himself, coalition air forces had conducted an aerial campaign of attrition against Iraqi forces south of the Euphrates capable of interfering with planned operations.[3] (See figure 30.)

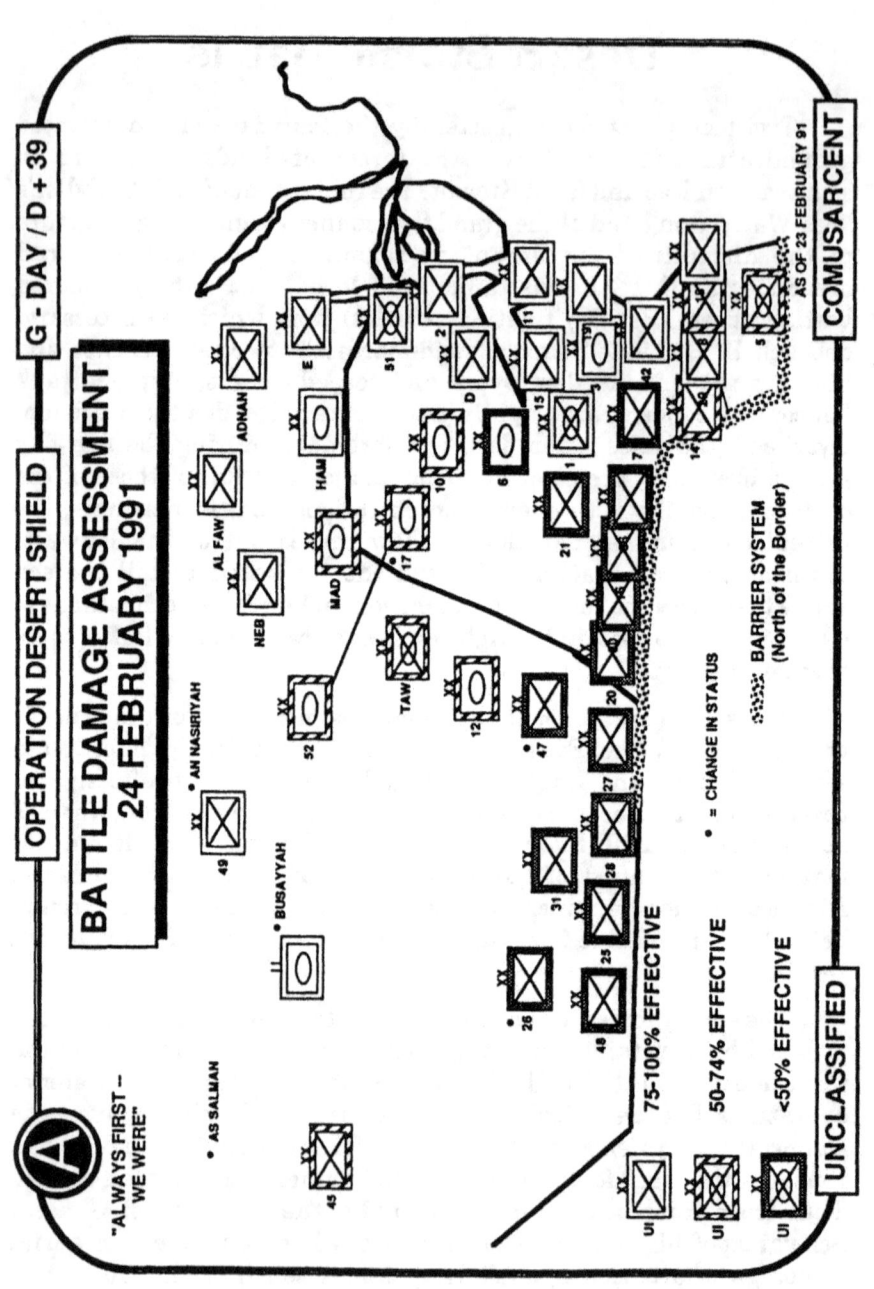

Figure 30.

One major element of AirLand Battle proved to be beyond the abilities of the Army and Air Forces engaged in Desert Storm. That was the execution of close interdiction by the Air Force in support of the Army's major operations, in particular the VII Corps' attack. The problems with this form of joint integration of forces had always been apparent. Indeed, the Air Force chief of staff, General Merrill McPeak, had addressed those problems years before.[4] Peacetime exercises, however, tended to gloss over them in the name of interservice comity.

Two structural issues were inherent in the problem of air-ground coordination. The first had to do with control. Air interdiction is controlled by the Air Force commander because it takes place beyond the range of ground systems. The Army talked of a category of aerial interdiction, battlefield air interdiction (BAI), that was to be flown to support the ground commander's scheme of maneuver. During the 1980s, the Air Force recognized BAI as a term addressing a subcategory of air interdiction but made no commitment to its place in the blue-suit hierarchy of targets. Air assets are allocated according to primary categories, and the air component commander decides what will be flown according to his priorities as a theater component commander. Because Air Force officers are not particularly knowledgeable about the conduct of ground operations, they are not inclined to allocate air assets to support ground maneuvers.

At the same time, the conduct of battlefield air interdiction assumes the ground commanders can locate their front line trace so their own forces are not attacked. The Army has long had a fire control measure, the fire support coordination line (FSCL), to accomplish this. The FSCL was intended to be a permissive fire measure; that is, the FSCL was supposed to be a line beyond which any force could fire without danger of hitting friendly maneuver forces. In Desert Storm, there were two problems with the FSCL concept. With the Army tactical missile system (ATACMS), the Army had a weapons system whose range permitted ground forces to fire beyond the FSCL, something the Air Force worried about given the density of planes in the airspace. And since ground forces were advancing, not withdrawing, the FSCL had to move with them. Senior ground commanders, who were dependent upon forward unit reporting through multiple command headquarters to stay informed, proved utterly incapable of reporting a reliable front line trace in a timely fashion. And, since the two services are, in fact, hierarchies joined at the top, which execute at the bottom, the information had to penetrate an Air Force operational information chain that took additional time for it to reach shooters thus causing systemic delays. The attack on British armored vehicles by U.S. Air Force planes was a consequence of the information chain's inability to relay this kind of data rapidly.[5]

Ultimately, CENTCOM took over the setting of the FSCL and used it as a boundary, assigning all terrain on one side to the ground commanders and all terrain and airspace on the other to the air component commander. In the words of the Third Army deep fires after-action report: "The end result, ironically, was that the high level of success attained on the ground frequently led to a loss of air support, since bombers could no longer execute their mission, and because the mission manager didn't have the necessary lead time to successfully divert the mission to another target."[6]

The result was that there was an area beyond the forward line of troops in which only Army aviation could operate and into which Air Force planes could operate only while under Army control (close air support). There, the decentralized organization of Army aviation may have prevented full use of this asset by preventing operational concentration of ARCENT's aviation assets in front of VII Corps when it closed with the Republican Guard. It was not possible to shift XVIII Corps' attack helicopter assets to VII Corps for the very practical reason that the helicopters' operating range was limited and tied to fuel pods on the ground in their rear. Army aviation units were not provided with the logistic redundance that permits flexible basing to allow response to fleeting opportunities. Ultimately, XVIII Corps' aviation brigades were committed to the control of the 101st Airborne Division northwest of Basrah. Even then, the 101st had difficulty accommodating the additional fuel requirements this entailed. The VII Corps would have been unable to sustain the XVIII Corps' attack helicopters without a major shifting of its resources across the Iraqi desert, and there is little reason to assume that this could have been accomplished easily or rapidly even if XVIII Corps had been willing to give up a major part of its combat power. That too was unlikely. In retrospect, the commitment of Army aviation beyond Basrah, where distinct water lines constituted the best available line of separation between the ground and air interdiction, was a poor solution. The Air Force capabilities, combining J-STARS observation with sophisticated attack tools, would seem likely to have been much more effective. VII Corps was unable to employ Air Force battlefield air interdiction as a blocking force in support of its maneuver units or maintain continuous interdiction with its own aviation brigade (the 11th). Indeed, because of its lack of control over the FSCL, it could not always interdict targets within range.[7]

The VII Corps attack on 24 February was less like the deep rapier thrusts of Guderian or Rommel and more like the "integral operations" dreamed of by the great von Schlieffen, in which the importance of individual battles was subordinated to the logic of "an integrated and continuous movement, war as uninterrupted forward motion,"[8] an inexorable advance of irresistible destructive power.

H-hour was 0400, 24 February. The weather on the border was mostly cloudy with rain showers of some violence in the early morning. Due to blowing sand, visibility decreased from crystal clarity at dawn to as little as 200 meters during the day. Patches of fog were also reported, and winds were from the southeast, gusting to twenty-five knots.[9] BMNT (beginning morning nautical twilight) was at 0531 the 24th; BENT (beginning evening nautical twilight) at 1824.[10]

The French 6th Light Armored Division, reinforced by a brigade of the 82d Airborne Division, was the main attack of the XVIII Corps. The French advanced at 0400 the morning of the 24th to "open the ball." Prior to the attack, the French had seized the lip of the escarpment that lies just across the Saudi border in Iraq. Their objective was to advance to As Salman (Objective White) to free the east-west lateral road, MSR Virginia, upon which the corps intended to accomplish the movement of the fuel and ammunition necessary to sustain the larger 24th Infantry Division (Mech) and the adjacent 3d Armored Cavalry Regiment attacks to the Euphrates valley (anticipated for G+1). This would be accomplished while the engineers opened more direct combat trails to the rear. The French confronted the largest enemy concentration in the southern half of the XVIII Corps sector and captured over 300 prisoners on G-day.

The elite 82d Airborne Division, perhaps the best light infantry in the U.S. Army and the first vital commitment of American prestige in August the previous year, was relegated, by the nature of desert warfare, to providing the French with additional infantry forces and then following its more mobile sister units, cleaning up and securing by-passed pockets of enemy resistance. This role was not particularly glamorous, and it did not get a lot of interest from CNN, but it was essential, and the soldiers of the 82d performed their tasks with characteristic discipline and good humor.[11]

Midway between the two flanks, the 101st Airborne Division, using its unique air mobility, inserted two brigades by air on the 24th and built up a forward operating base (FOB) Cobra halfway to the Euphrates. From there, the Euphrates River valley and Highway 8 could be interdicted the first night of the ground war by the division's attack helicopters. The air assault was unopposed, but an Iraqi battalion was located by troops of the 327th Infantry of the 1st Brigade. The Iraqi battalion, an element of the 49th Infantry Division, surrendered after coming under air and ground preparation fires.[12]

FOB Cobra permitted the launching of division and corps attack helicopters into the Euphrates valley eighty-five miles farther north. These movements were followed the next day (the 25th) by the division's third maneuver brigade. This cut that Iraqi line of withdrawal until a slower heavy ground force could cross the empty desert between the Saudi-Iraqi border and the enemy's principal line of retreat or reinforcement. The troopers of the 101st were on the river a full day before the arrival of the 24th Infantry Division and 3d Armored Cavalry. The range of their attack helicopters put enemy forces north and south of the river in jeopardy and, once the Iraqis broke, they could interdict Iraqis who escaped west out of Basrah.

The G-day air assault by the 101st to establish FOB Cobra was scheduled to begin simultaneously with the attack of the French 6th. The assault had to be delayed, however, until 0730 because of a fierce rainstorm followed by ground fog in the objective area.[13] A ground column, organized by the 1st Brigade under the command of the brigade executive officer, Lieutenant Colonel Jim McCarity, moved forward at 0700 and began arriving at FOB Cobra that afternoon. The combat element of the column consisted of thirty HMMWVs with TOWs, two artillery batteries, one infantry company, and two helicopter scout-attack teams. The column contained 2,000 soldiers in 700 vehicles and carried, among other things, 100,000 gallons of aviation fuel across a desert track called the Darb al Haj.[14] It was unopposed on its march to Cobra and was slowed only by the abysmal weather, which muddied the desert track.

The attack all across the theater front was enormously successful that morning, as the Iraqi infantry divisions, whose principal function had been to identify the location of the coalition main attack and to delay it until successively larger mobile reserves might be committed, declined the role of cannon fodder and surrendered in large numbers—not just to the forces of XVIII Corps but to the Marines breaching Iraqi defenses in the east and the attack by the Arab-Islamic Joint Forces Command East on the coast.

By 0840 on the 24th, Schwarzkopf, spurred by reports of Iraqi demolitions in Kuwait City, called Yeosock and asked his views on scrapping the plan's time schedule and attacking early with the heavy forces.[15] (See figure 31.) Yeosock first called his corps commanders and

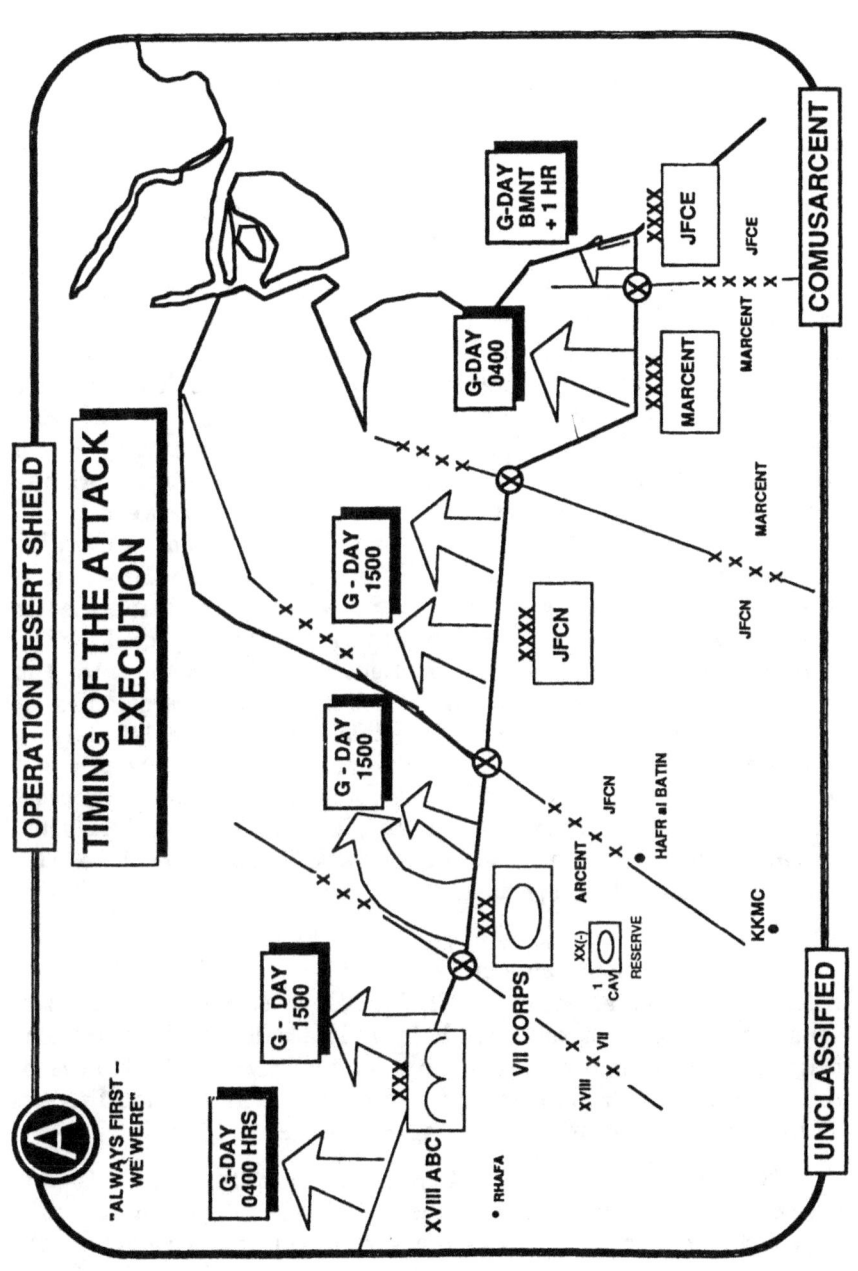

Figure 31.

then replied to Schwarzkopf that it was possible. The artillery of the 1st Infantry Division would be in position to begin VII Corps' breaching operation at 1230.[16] General Rhame wanted to begin the attack at 1300.[17] Schwarzkopf delayed the heavy force attack until 1500 so that the Arab-Islamic Joint Forces Command North could attack simultaneously with the Third Army's heavy forces. At 1430, the 1st Infantry Division fired its preparation, using the division artilleries of two divisions and three reinforcing brigades. At 1500, the breaching operation began. The "Great Wheel" was under way.

At Third Army, the G3 Plans section made up a final time line to project the battle now being joined through to the time of anticipated contact with the Republican Guard Forces Command. The chart is indicative of how the army commander saw the battle developing. It forecast the 24th Division seizing Objectives Brown, Gray, and Red and dominating MSR Virginia-Phase Line Smash by around H+35 (1500 on the 25th); the 1st U.K. Armored Division defeating a brigade of the Iraqi 12th (actually the 52d) Armored Division between H+35 and H+41 (1500–2100 on the 25th); and the 2d Armored Cavalry moving forward of Phase Line Smash at the same time. Based upon this success, Third Army anticipated Schwarzkopf releasing the 1st Cavalry Division in time to move by H+41. Yeosock expected the VII Corps to be prepared to close with the Republican Guard about 1500 on the 26th, with the 24th Division attacking a logistics complex at Juwarin at the same time. Based on this schedule, the 1st Cavalry Division would close into an assembly area north of the barrier belt (Lee) by 1900 that night (the 25th).[18] Using this measure of progress and a knowledge of events on the ground, Yeosock would feel the army was ahead of schedule for most of the attack.[19] Schwarzkopf, perhaps with urging from his superiors, would not share this view.[20] (See figure 32.)

The 1st Division scouts crossed the border at 0507 on the 24th, with the division's 1st and 2d Brigades crossing their lines of departure at 0545 en route to their final assault positions.[21] The brigades collected many Iraqi prisoners on the way, as did all forces for the remainder of the war and even thereafter. The division fired its artillery preparation at 1430 and began to breach at 1500.

The Iraqis had apparently slipped their 26th Infantry Division to the southwest to extend their defensive lines farther to the west than expected, but even so, the Iraqi forces were widely dispersed, and the barrier system proved inadequate. According to VII Corps' battlefield reconstruction (based largely on enemy prisoner of war [EPW] interviews), the brigades of the Iraqi division were stretched along the

233

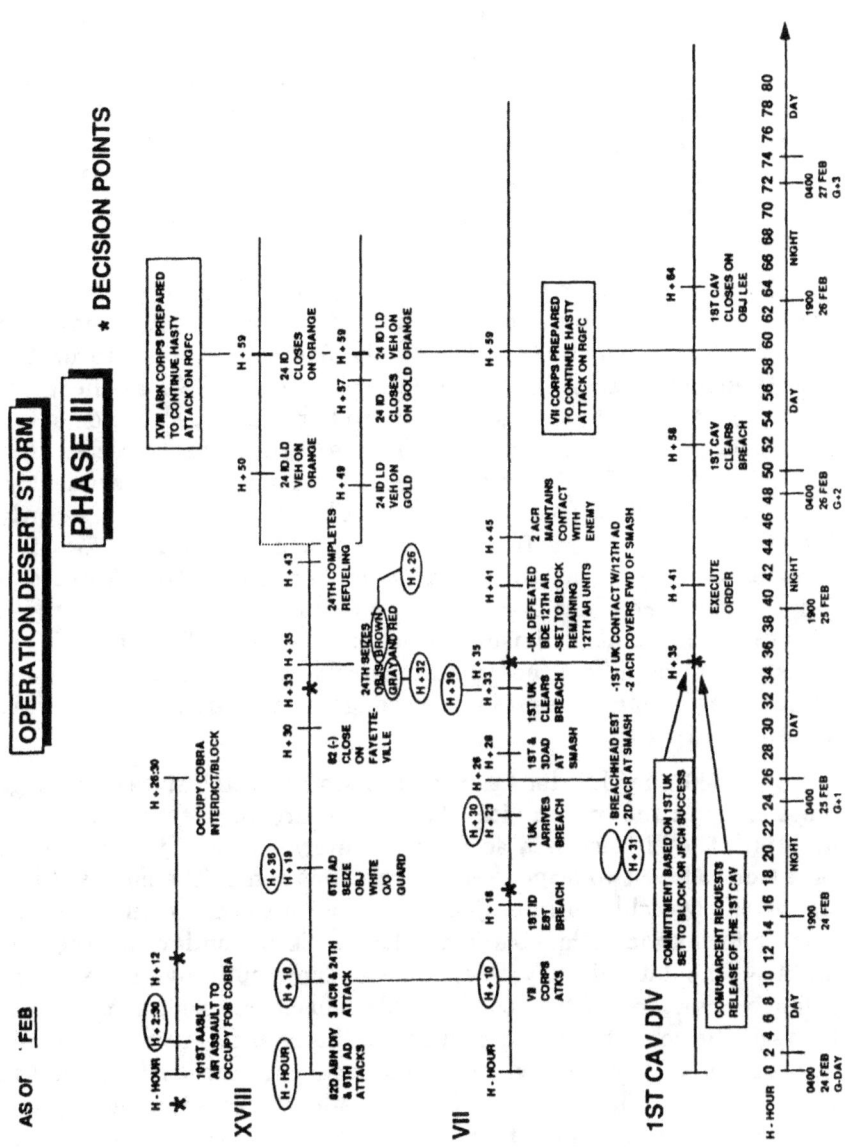

Figure 32. Third Army's final synchronization matrix

front and out of supporting distance from their reserve to the rear. The 26th was now to be overrun by the U.S. 1st Infantry Division and enveloped by the corps' iron fist. The corps' G2 report goes on to say of the adjacent (eastward) 48th Division's 807th Brigade (in front of the 1st ID) that "It is probably the unluckiest unit in the Iraqi army. Its soldiers have been under air attack for 39 straight days."[22] The 48th was reduced to about 50 percent from desertion, and its artillery was effectively silenced by the 1st Infantry Division's preparation and counterbattery fires. Nonetheless, the troops of the U.S. 1st Division did receive some scattered and ineffective artillery fire while passing the enemy barriers.

Both the Iraqis' (regular army) 12th and 52d Armored Divisions would begin repositioning the night of 24 February. The 12th moved to positions south of Al Busayyah, and the 52d shifted to shore up the first defensive echelon. The 52d (identified by ARCENT as the 12th) had suffered severe losses from the air and artillery preparation of the battlefield prior to G-day. Indeed, General Franks had directed that his staff make the 52d Armored Brigade "go away" and, consequently, it became known as the "go-away brigade." On G-day, it had only fifteen T-55 tanks and fifteen Russian-design infantry fighting vehicles (BMPs) remaining, the complement of two American companies.[23] One of the 52d Division's battalions would be destroyed with the 48th Infantry Division, which it supported. The remainder of its brigades would be attacked successively by the 1st U.K. Armored Division as it moved eastward through the Iraqi front-line rear areas.[24] (See map 8.)

By 1600, the U.S. 1st Infantry Division reported sixteen passage lanes clear at the breach site. By 1654, there were twenty-four. By nightfall, the division had secured its intermediate objective, Phase Line Colorado, a two-brigade semicircle that denied the enemy direct fire on the breachhead line. Franks met with the commanders of his leading formations, Rhame and Holder, to discuss options for the first night.[25] The 1st Infantry Division was now split by the enemy's defensive barriers. Its two lead brigades had cleared a number of lanes through the zone, but these still had to be proofed and marked, and exits and assembly areas within the breachhead, now in the dark, had to be organized. The division's third brigade, the 2d Armored Division (Forward) (a brigade-sized force) was still south of the defensive zone, as was the supporting artillery, four brigades worth (considering here the British division artillery as part of the parent division). The plan called for the third brigade to pass through the breach and attack straight ahead simultaneously as the two organic brigades rolled

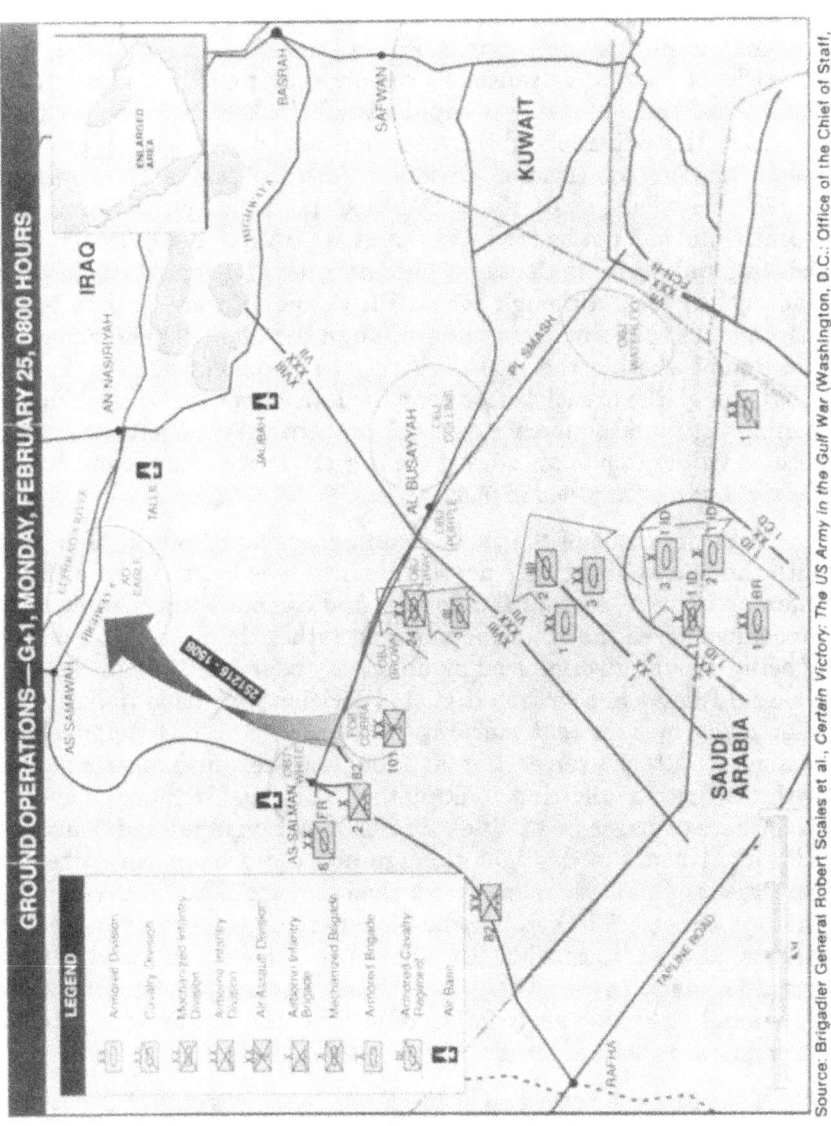

Map 8.

outward to clear the final breachhead line, New Jersey. Once set there, beyond indirect fire range, the 1st U.K. Armored Division would pass through the breach and out of the breachhead line to attack the Iraqi tactical reserves. But a great many vehicles, almost three division equivalents when one considers the artillery brigades, would have to move through the passage points before that could happen.

For his part, Rhame had serious reservations about committing the 2d Armored Division (Forward) into the passage of the breachhead area and executing the attack to Phase Line New Jersey in the dark. The risks of fratricide—caused by compressing three brigades into the small area and executing a rapid attack in the dark—were high. Further, the brigade's ability to conduct night operations was unknown. The 2d Armored Division (Forward) was a Europe-based brigade that had joined the U.S.-based 1st Infantry Division only recently and had not had the opportunity to train in night breaching at the National Training Center as had the other divisional brigades. The leading brigades, although set on PL Colorado, were still receiving sporadic fire that would continue through the night. There was also a question of whether the 1st U.K. Armored Division would be ready to pass through the breach before noon the following day. Colonel Holder, leading the flanking force, expressed concern that the left wing would become vulnerable to counterattack if it advanced into the open while the right wing remained in place.

The consensus of the three commanders was that, at this point, with the enemy's response not yet clear, it was better to hold the 1st Infantry in place, set on PL Colorado, and complete the opening of the breachhead area the following morning rather than accepting the risk of being caught disorganized by an enemy counterattack in the dark. General Rhame has written that this decision was made in light of an offer made by him that morning that the U.S. 1st Division should conduct its attack even earlier (at 1300) and then push straight ahead, with the British following, making their turn east without conducting a deliberate passage of lines out of a set bridgehead line. The additional hours of daylight thus gained could have permitted the movement of all three maneuver brigades of the U.S. 1st Division into the breachhead. That option had been rejected, however, leading Rhame, at least, to conclude that his superiors were satisfied with the progress made to date and that there was no pressure to accept additional risks this early in the offensive. The attack was, after all, fifteen hours ahead of schedule.[26]

That being the case and as the Egyptian Corps on VII Corps' right had not begun to breach the enemy positions to their front, Franks made the decision to keep the corps' scheme of maneuver synchronized. He had over 8,000 tracked vehicles and more than three times that many wheeled vehicles to move through the breach and the forty-kilometer gap beyond. He intended to do so without offering the enemy an opportunity to catch his force strung out and disorganized. He would not advance his left, the 2d Armored Cavalry Regiment and two armored divisions, until the British division, which would protect his right flank, was through the breach and into the attack. The 2d Armored Cavalry would hold its position roughly on line with PL Colorado and the two armored divisions north of the Iraqi-Saudi border, some thirty kilometers behind. Local actions to identify enemy elements and keep them off balance would continue through the night.

Franks also wanted the breachhead area cleared in daylight to provide for security for the fleet of vulnerable support vehicles. Besides, all three commanders knew the time would not be wasted in any event. There was plenty to do to prepare to continue the attack the next day. Four brigade equivalents of artillery would be passed into the breachhead before advancing the breachhead line or passing through the 1st U.K. Armored Division and various support forces for the forward brigades. The emphasis in the field that first night was on maintaining the concentration and balance of the attacking force and preparing for a deliberate passage of lines by the two-brigade British division on the following day. Even if the forward line of troops remained stationary, the passage lanes were active all night, as more and more combat power was moved north of the barrier belt. Attack helicopters worked forward of the ground maneuver forces all along the corps front throughout the night. Still, for all his earlier insistence, a pause had been imposed upon Franks by circumstances and by the decision to perform the breach job "with precision and synchronization," with an eye on the objective of hitting the RGFC with a "massed closed fist."

There was another indication, too, of the high sensitivity to the possibility of fratricide that night. As the 3d Armored Division advanced, it discovered an enemy unit between it and the 1st Infantry Division. Rather than risk an incident where the flank units of the two divisions might shoot at each other, Franks imposed a five-kilometer buffer zone between the units, notwithstanding the enemy within, and required the troops of the 3d Armored Division to withdraw from contact.[27]

On VII Corps' left, the 3d Armored Cavalry and the 24th Division, kept on their steady and generally unopposed advance to the Euphrates. The division was commanded by Major General Barry

McCaffrey, Third Army's most driven and perhaps most aggressive commander. McCaffrey was a genuine war hero who had been severely wounded in Vietnam. Now, his division, with its attachments, contained no less than 1,800 tracked vehicles, including 249 M-1A1 tanks, 218 Bradley fighting vehicles, and 843 older M-113 armored personnel carriers. It also had about 6,500 wheeled vehicles and ninety helicopters, eighteen of which were AH-64 Apaches. The division was supported by ninety 155-mm howitzers, twenty-four 8-inch howitzers, and thirty-six multiple launch rocket systems (MLRS).[28] The 24th stopped for fuel in early evening and then resumed the advance in order to be in position to launch attacks on its objectives along MSR Virginia-Phase Line Smash early the following morning.[29] In the center of the XVIII Corps zone, by the end of the day, the 101st Airborne had the bulk of two brigades, their direct support artillery, and a good bit of the support command at FOB Cobra.

The 1st Cavalry Division continued to conduct demonstrations in the Ruqi pocket during the 24th and 25th. These maneuvers appear to have been successful. The Iraqi concentration of forces in front of Wadi al Batin was substantial in contrast to the forces deployed farther west.

By the night of 24 February, both Schwarzkopf and Yeosock were well satisfied with the events of the day. At Third Army, Yeosock acquiesced in VII Corps' decision, reported by the ARCENT liaison officer, to hold the advance and concentrate on getting the 1st U.K. through. Looking toward the decisive battle with the RGFC, Yeosock instructed Arnold to examine using XVIII Corps to fix the Hammurabi Division before VII Corps attacked the Tawakalna and Medina Divisions; he also instructed Arnold to destroy the artillery of the RGFC infantry divisions (in the XVIII Corps' zone) by fire. Yeosock's executive officer, Lieutenant Colonel Mike Kendall, a laconic and unusually circumspect and precise infantry officer, recorded Yeosock's closing comment: "The intent, is to have XVIII Corps fix forces to allow VII Corps to maneuver against the RGFC divisions."[30] In his memoir, Schwarzkopf recollects: "That night, about twenty hours into the ground war, I went to bed contented."[31]

He did not remain so. A gap had begun to open between the tactical operations Franks was fighting in the field and the operation Schwarzkopf envisioned in the basement of the Ministry of Defense. The commander in chief had gone to bed anticipating continuous movement of the forward line of troops in VII Corps throughout the night—particularly of the armored fist. When he went to his map in the morning and found them still in place, he blew up and called

Yeosock.³² Yeosock, it seems, weathered the storm, explained the intentions for the day, and very likely—sympathetic with Franks' practical problems—underestimated the depth of the CINC's frustration. In the morning general officer meeting at Third Army, General Arnold reported to Yeosock that Schwarzkopf had imposed a limit of advance on the 24th Infantry Division (which would keep it from descending into the Euphrates valley). Arnold expected VII Corps to close on Objective Collins that day and continue with a hasty attack on the RGFC.³³

Yeosock instructed Arnold to tell VII Corps that the CINC's intent was "continuous progress, no lulls."³⁴ Otherwise, Franks was not made aware of Schwarzkopf's displeasure. Both Franks and Yeosock continued to believe that all was well as the VII Corps advance resumed at 0530 that morning, and reports of increasing contact came in through the day. Unfortunately, at the same time, a gap continued to exist between success reported (or anticipated) and that achieved as reflected on Schwarzkopf's briefing map. Another gap would open between the progress of the 24th Division, as it advanced relentlessly over extremely rough but largely empty terrain, and the supposedly slower progress of VII Corps' armored forces. This discrepancy would also become a source of irritation. During the 25th, while the CINC remained restless about the rate of operational success, Franks wrestled at the front with tactical possibilities in the sort of weather described most aptly by the British as "very dirty, indeed."

The ARCENT SITREP reported that morning (250300Z–0600 local) that the Iraqi 48th and 45th Infantry Divisions had been destroyed and that the VII and XVIII Corps had captured 3,000 prisoners. The G2 still expected the Iraqis, in extremis, to employ chemical weapons. Meanwhile, the anticipated time of passage for the 1st U.K. was given by Third Army as 0500Z (0800 local), with a completion time of 0900Z (1200 local). This proved to be very optimistic both as to start and completion times and, ultimately, quite wrong.³⁵

The error was introduced when the army liaison officer at the VII Corps tactical command post and a corps staff officer at the VII Corps main CP reported to the ARCENT mobile and main CPs respectively that passage would be completed by noon. Although the main CP was in receipt of a copy of the VII Corps FRAGO 138-91, which gave a start time of no later than 1200 local (which in fact was met) and a completion prior to the end of evening nautical twilight (which was not met), the duty officer at ARCENT seems to have continued to operate on the original misimpression—which was duly reported as indicated to CENTCOM.36 This sort of confusion should not be surprising in a scratch staff thrown together on short notice (both the VII Corps' staff officer and ARCENT LNO were augmentees); indeed, it is a characteristic example of the fog of war which, for all the Army's emphasis on training staff officers to value precise and correct information, has still not been removed. The problem of inaccurate staff reporting would later have painful consequences for both ARCENT and VII Corps.

The ARCENT SITREP also indicated that the French 6th Light Armored had taken its intermediate objective on the 24th (Objective Rochambeau) and would advance to As Salman on the 25th. The 101st reported that it had seized its forward operating base by 1039 on the 24th and had captured a battalion commander and his troops shortly thereafter. The division reported conducting limited air interdiction of Highway 8 during the night.37 Arnold's cover note on the ARCENT SITREP the morning of the 25th observed: "FOCUS today at Army HQ is on gaining early release of 1st CAV and on delivering a modified version of CONPLAN 6 (Destruction of the RGFC) to the Corps."38

On G-day, over to the right of the Arab-Islamic Joint Forces Command North, MARCENT had enjoyed significant success breaching what was supposed to have been an extraordinarily difficult barrier belt. At the last minute, MARCENT had decided to attack two divisions abreast.39 The Army's "Tiger Brigade," commanded by Colonel John B. Sylvester, under tactical command of the 2d Marine Division for Operation Desert Storm, followed the 6th Marines through the left-hand breach starting at 1530 and entered the surreal landscape of Kuwait, where the burning oil fires and darkness at noon seem to have reminded every observer of hell itself. On G-day, the "Tiger Brigade" suffered one man killed when a light Military Police vehicle struck a mine after dark. One M1 tank struck a mine in the breach and lost some road wheels. No one in the tank was injured, and the tank was back in action within a day.40

The Marines achieved their first day's objectives; in particular, the 1st Marine Division secured the Al Jabber airfield. The Marines would also repulse an attack by Iraqi armored forces advancing out of the smoke and haze of the Al Burgan oil fields on G+1 and then secure the Kuwait City International Airport and, with the "Tiger Brigade," cut the main Kuwait City-Basrah highway, thus completing an inner encirclement of Iraqi forces in southeastern Kuwait. Like the VII Corps, the Marine advance stopped at night on G-day.41

Finally, on G-day, the Joint Forces Command East attacked and advanced along the coast according to schedule.

The next day, 25 February (G+1), proved to be the most deadly single day of the war for U.S. forces. (See map 9.) The war's costliest incident took place far from the direct-fire battles of the Iraqi desert. It occurred in Dhahran. At 2036 (local time), the only Scud missile to do significant damage in the Arabian Peninsula fell on the warehouse sheltering, among others, the 14th Quartermaster Detachment, a Reserve Component unit from Pennsylvania, only recently arrived in country.[42] Twenty-eight soldiers were killed, and about one hundred were wounded. These losses were greater than those suffered by any combat division in the four days of ground battle.

Earlier on the 25th, however, successes had continued to pile up. The 101st Airborne Division inserted its 3d Brigade, commanded by Colonel Robert T. Clark, from its pre-G-day assembly area, all the way to the Euphrates valley, a distance of 155 miles (about 250 kilometers), thus cutting an Iraqi main line of withdrawal or reinforcement (though there was no evidence that the Iraqis intended to use it for either at this point). The 3d Brigade posed a threat just 145 miles from Baghdad.[43]

The 3d Brigade accelerated its insertion to try and beat the weather, which was worse on G+1 than it had been the day before. The operation actually began on G-day with a program of reconnaissance to ensure the insertion would be unopposed. Scouts looked over the landing zones and vicinity, first from the air, then with forces on the ground, including motorcycle scouts. The weather was so bad that even motorcycle troops were mired. The assault itself took place on the 25th.

About noon, the 3d Brigade placed its heavy equipment (two artillery batteries, three antitank companies [forty-eight TOWs], two mounted rifle companies, and some engineer troops) on the ground in an area short of the river called Landing Zone (LZ) Sand, then moved the column overland to Area of Operations (AO) Eagle along Highway 8, arriving in spite of all but impassable muddy desert tracks early on the 26th. An intermediate landing site had to be used for heavy equipment due to weight-distance limits on helicopters.

At 1508, the first light infantry troops moved into AO Eagle using sixty-six UH-60 Blackhawks. A second lift was grounded by weather at FOB Cobra until the following morning. However, at 1640 on the 25th, "Screaming Eagles" of the 101st were in the Euphrates valley, while the 24th Infantry Division was reforming to the south along

242

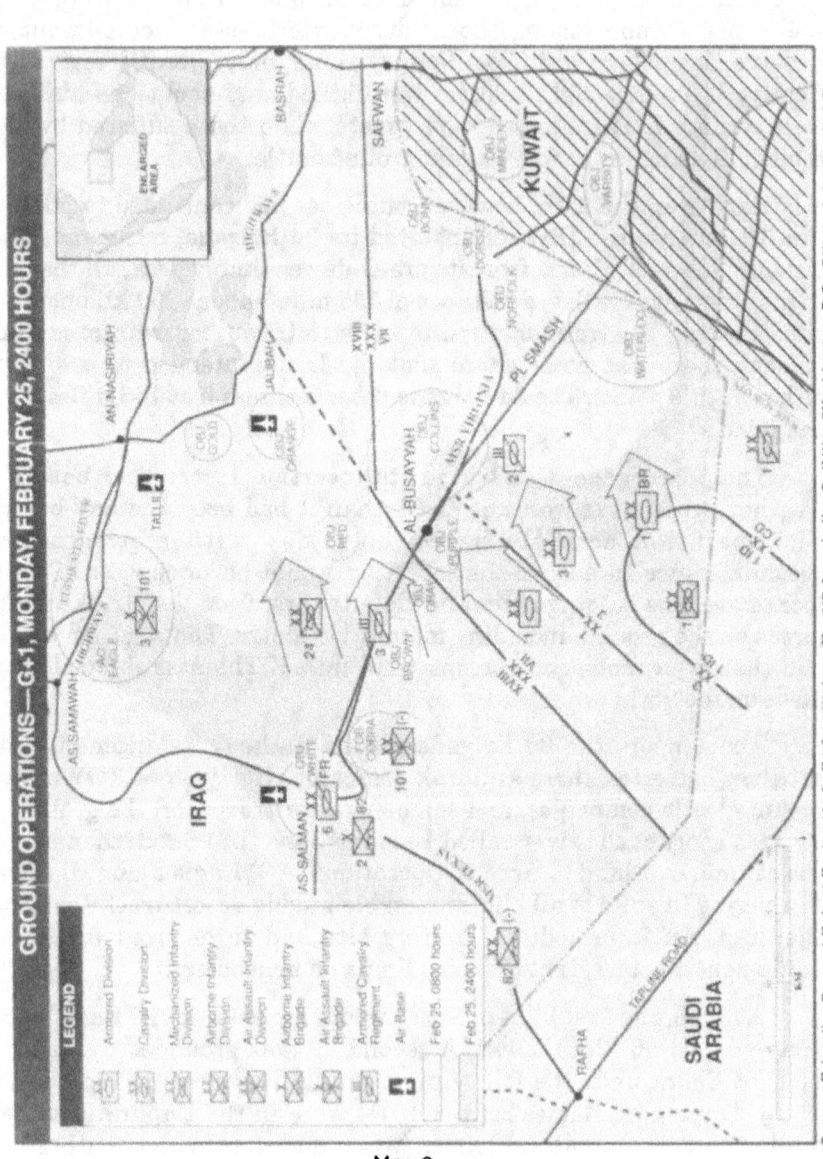

Map 9.

Phase Line Smash (MSR Virginia) to continue its advance to a linkup. By 2300, the highway was cut. Weather delayed the remainder of the personnel lifts until the following day.[44]

The 24th Division had crossed the line of departure on the 24th with three brigades abreast and then shifted into a "V" formation with the 197th Brigade on the left, the 2d Brigade on the right, and the 1st Brigade following the 2d. The division began its attacks on positions dominating MSR Virginia (Phase Line Smash) at 0300 on the 25th, when Colonel Ted Reid's 197th Infantry Brigade (Mechanized) (Separate), from Fort Benning, Georgia (deployed as the 24th Division's third brigade), attacked Objective Brown. The brigade objective, apparently an air defense site, was secured by 1004. At 0848, the 197th had linked up with the 101st Airborne Division on the heavy brigade's left flank.[45]

The other divisional units seized their objectives soon after. The 2d Brigade took Objective Grey on the MSR, and by 2150, the 1st Brigade, passing through the 2d, had seized Objective Red to protect the MSR to the north. The division then pulled its logistics tail in behind and began almost immediately to press on to the Euphrates.

The 197th Brigade prepared to continue the attack toward the Euphrates by 1600. By nightfall, engulfed in heavy rain, the 197th was 231 kilometers inside Iraq. After a second night's move, challenged by evil terrain and harsh weather, the 197th arrived in position to advance into the Euphrates valley the following day.[46] The limit of advance on the 24th Infantry Division had been lifted at 1800 the 25th.[47]

The French 6th Light Armored Division on the left flank attacked at first light (0530) on 25 February and secured the airfield at As Salman, thus opening MSR Virginia in the west. It would require another day to obtain the surrender of forces blockaded in the nearby town.

The success enjoyed in XVIII Corps and the speed with which the engineers laid down their combat trails behind the 24th Division led to the corps' decision not to establish its first intermediate logistics base (Oscar) in the vicinity of As Salman but to jump directly to Log Base Romeo farther east.[48] Meanwhile, the 24th Division, for the most part refueled and reorganized, again took up its relentless advance now oriented on Objective Gold, the enemy logistics complex at Juwarin in the Euphrates valley.[49] Its drive across empty but difficult terrain, in the face of abysmal weather and pitch darkness, opened a gap between

XVIII Corps and VII Corps that would be painfully apparent on briefing charts at CENTCOM and JCS.

On 25 February, the VII Corps "Wheel" moved inexorably onward. The Iraqis began to react to the U.S. attack by forming a defensive line, consisting of a brigade of the RGFC Adnan Infantry Division, the Tawakalna Mechanized Division, two brigades of the 12th Armored Division, the 37th and 50th Brigades—assembled from southwest to northeast to confront the VII Corps envelopment.[50] Although the defenders seem to have grasped what was happening operationally, to the extent they took counteractions against it, they lacked the means of intelligence acquisition to detect the "drill bit" before they found themselves confronted tactically with overwhelming armored killing power. In addition, forced to move about above ground, mobile reserves found themselves exposed anew to attack from the air by rotary and fixed-wing aircraft; they were thus subjected to further losses before they came into position to fight the direct-fire battle.

As Yeosock had predicted, the Iraqis could move, but they could not maneuver. U.S. divisions, too, did little actual battle maneuver, if by that one means the execution of complex positioning of brigades and battalions for relative advantage on the battlefield. In the U.S. case, the low level of maneuver reflected a lack of need rather than a lack of training. Divisions moved forward with two or three heavy brigades on line and simply overwhelmed the hapless Iraqis by superiority of combat power at each successive point. U.S. brigades might be relieved from the rear, but they tended to be employed straight ahead.

Because of the density of forces presented at any point of conflict and the skill with which U.S. commanders prepared their battlefields with fires, there is to date but one story of a unit, even as small as a company, that was repulsed by the resistance it confronted.[51] In the main, the Iraqis surrendered, or fought and were ground up. The Iraqi infantry surrendered in such numbers that prisoners proved to be an impediment to the advance, and many stories are told of Iraqis who were disarmed, provided with food and water, and waved on unaccompanied to the oncoming logistics elements in the rear.

On the VII Corps left, the 2d Armored Cavalry Regiment began its shift to an eastward track and uncovered the 1st Armored Division, which advanced north toward Objective Purple (Al Busayyah), an occupied logistics complex on the corps' left flank that constituted the outer corner of its multidivision turn.

The 1st AD was commanded by Major General Ron Griffith, quiet and systematic, perhaps the quintessential tanker, whose boxer's visage reminds one of another premier tanker, the late General Creighton Abrams. Griffith clearly believed in balance and concentration. The 1st Armored Division, "Old Ironsides," began its advance at 0630 the morning of the 25th from a position twenty-nine kilometers inside Iraq. That day, the division advanced behind its own cavalry (1st Squadron, 1st Cavalry) screen on a two-brigade front of about twenty to thirty kilometers. Helicopters screened forward of the ground troops and detected enemy positions.

The division destroyed the reserve brigade of the Iraqi 26th Division between 1300 and 1700 and continued on to Objective Purple. It advanced 144 kilometers in sixteen hours of maneuver and combat, a cumulative rate of 9 kilometers an hour.[52] While the ground elements fought with the Iraqi infantry and armored forces in front of them, the division's AH-64s went deep to begin attacking the forces to be fought in the next battle—the troops occupying Al Busayyah, a small desert town whose importance came from the Iraqi logistics site located there as well as from the XVIII Corps' desire for a track as an MSR to support follow-on actions of the 24th Infantry Division.

Because Al Busayyah was known to be an occupied, built-up area, Griffith decided to conduct a deliberate attack, preparing the objective by fire during the night of the 25th and 26th and then assaulting the next day rather than accepting the risk of heavy losses in a dismounted infantry attack in the dark. Griffith believed the logistics site was occupied by an Iraqi special forces battalion, an infantry battalion, and a tank company.[53] Al Busayyah had to be taken and cleared because its availability as an MSR would be compromised if occupying forces were left in place. Objective Purple would be taken the morning of the 26th during a continuous movement that would reorient the 1st Armored to the east as the left flank division of the corps' three-division maneuver mass.

The 2d Armored Cavalry, now in a movement to contact, oriented increasingly to the east in front of the 3d Armored Division and made its first contact with the Iraqi operational reserves at 0841 on the 25th. The 2d destroyed the defending brigade (the 50th Brigade of the 12th Armored Division) and moved on to the east until dark. The regiment, particularly the 3d Squadron, was in contact with enemy heavy forces, often in abysmal weather, from 0841 until 2100.[54] The regimental S2 estimated that the RGFC Tawakalna Division was located along the 65 Easting (a line of longitude), with a security zone of eight kilometers. The corps commander, visiting the regimental tactical operations center at 1530, ordered the regiment to maintain contact and fix the RGFC, locate their flanks, and be prepared to pass the 1st Infantry Division through. The decisive ground battle had begun.55

The 3d Armored Division followed the 2d Armored Cavalry and destroyed the various Iraqi units by-passed by the cavalry screen. At 1645 on the 25th, Franks visited the division command post and imparted his intentions for the attack against the RGFC shaping up for the 26th. According to notes from the 3d Armored Division commander's operational assistant, Major John Rosenberger, Franks called Yeosock to report on his situation and intentions and "stressed the importance of continuing the attack without pause given the lack of resistance encountered by 1st AD and 3d AD in zone." Franks indicated his intention was for the 1st AD to close with the RGFC Medina Armored Division, with the 3d AD to destroy the Tawakalna, then follow on by attacking what were believed to be the 52d and 17th Armored Divisions (actually the 12th and 10th). The U.S. 1st Infantry would pass through the 2d Armored Cavalry, and the corps would attack with three divisions abreast. The focus would be on the 1st and 3d Armored Divisions, which were clearly directed against the center of gravity of the RGFC, with the 1st ID on the right attacking parallel with the 1st and 3d Divisions toward Objective Norfolk and perhaps becoming an enveloping force if an opening developed.

These were instructions on a map. The manner of implementation became the subject of some disagreement between Major General Paul Funk, the 3d Armored Division commander, and the VII Corps staff once implementing orders began to be issued during the night. Specifically, Funk wanted more room to maneuver so he might attack with one brigade through a gap between the Medina and Tawakalna Divisions in front of him and then turn the brigade southeast behind the Iraqi line.56 In short, he wanted to maneuver within his zone rather than participate as part of a corps phalanx rolling east shoulder to shoulder. The pressure of time and the density of corps forces precluded the change. The 3d Armored Division responded and was attacking by 0755 with two brigades abreast and the third in reserve. Later, the reserve brigade would pass through the left-hand brigade, break through and, in conjunction with the division attack helicopters, destroy the forces in the Iraqi rear.

The 1st Infantry Division completed exploitation of its breach by 1100 on the 25th and passed the 1st U.K. Armored Division through, starting at 1200. The British would break out of the breachhead at 1500 and begin to fight their way through the Iraqi infantry divisions to the east almost at once.57 The passage of the British division, however, lasted until about 0200 into the morning of the 26th.

Thereafter, the 1st Infantry Division began to move north to fall in behind the 2d Armored Cavalry. After dark, the 1st Infantry Division passed through the regimental line and came abreast of the 1st and 3d Armored Divisions (the 3d had been uncovered by the regiment the night before) as they moved east in the great VII Corps three-division phalanx.

The notes and accounts within VII Corps and at Third Army make it clear that the gap was widening between Schwarzkopf's perception of what was necessary and his understanding of what was occurring in VII Corps. Much of the misunderstanding would seem to have been the result of imprecise use of language as the corps' intentions were passed through army to the theater headquarters; it was also the result of the inevitable tension between those who view war at the operational level and those whose primary focus is tactical. Franks was forward all day, everyday, visiting his commanders on the ground, taking the pulse of his forces, experiencing the weather and blowing dust or rain. Often the texture of the battle seems not to have worked its way to the theater commander far to the rear. Moreover, far from the battlefield, progress seems to have been equated only with movement.

Franks had talked about continuing without pause, yet, again, by 2100 on the 25th, the 1st Armored Division and 2d Armored Cavalry Regiment had stopped for the night, the former to prepare for a deliberate attack, the latter in a hasty defense to allow the corps to rebalance for the decisive attack the next day. From the tactical perspective, action continued. Combat did not stop. The 1st Armored Division attacked by air and artillery all night, enabling it to overrun its objective in the morning and continue on to its place on the left of the corps' wall of iron. For its part, 2d Cavalry was involved in repelling Iraqi attacks for much of the night.[58]

The picture being painted in the Ministry of Defense and, through there, to the Pentagon and perhaps the National Security Council seems to have been something else again. Operational-level warfare is largely perceived to be a matter of space and time. There were already reports of Iraqis fleeing the encirclement. Moreover, the Iraqi flight was quite visible to Schwarzkopf (and Yeosock for that matter) through the agency of J-STARS. J-STARS could indicate the build-up of a steady stream of vehicles up the road toward Basrah and beyond. It could not discriminate between a truck or a tank, of course, but the growing flight behind a deliberate blocking force was apparent. Whatever the Air Force had done to seal the KTO by cutting its bridges, it had not been enough to stop the Iraqi flight north out of Basrah entirely—nor would it be, as the ground attack progressed.

Schwarzkopf seems to have feared that the encirclement would not be fast enough to prevent the Iraqis from drawing off significant forces behind their covering line, and that the continuous attack from the air on fleeing units was not going to be destructive enough to do what needed to be done.

What Schwarzkopf did not seem to have considered was the logistic limits of the encircling forces, the U.S. 1st Armored Division and, ultimately, the 24th Infantry Division. (See figure 33.) Moreover, Schwarzkopf did not seem to be aware of the rather stark fact that increased speed, say at Objective Purple on the night of the 25th, would have been paid for in soldiers' blood—a cost Third Army commanders, from division through army, seemed to have been more reluctant to pay. Schwarzkopf either did not share this awareness, or else it was a price he found acceptable.

Yeosock and Arnold were aware of Schwarzkopf's general expectations; indeed, they had repeated them at their morning general officer conference. Arnold had then anticipated three battles for the 25th, one at Phase Line Smash (XVIII Corps), a second at Objective Purple (1st AD), and a third consequent to the reaction of the Iraqi 12th (really 52d Armored Division), the tactical reserve. Yeosock's guidance had been clear. The two corps were to continue as a movement to contact. "The CinC's intent," Yeosock said, "is continuous pressure, no lulls."[59] Clearly, in Yeosock's view, that was just what Franks was delivering.

In his memoir, Schwarzkopf writes that at about 2100 on the 25th, "Yeosock reported that while VII Corps columns were still unopposed, rain and sandstorms were slowing them down, and they were twenty miles short of Collins."[60] Schwarzkopf, who had just spoken directly to the president, indicates his disappointment at the report and the great frustration of General Waller, once more his deputy. Yet when Yeosock returned to his headquarters from the evening briefing at CENTCOM that night, he observed that Schwarzkopf was satisfied with the army's operational style, although he, Schwarzkopf, had expressed concern about the separation developing between the 24th Infantry Division and VII Corps (the 24th, whose Objective Grey was adjacent to Objective Purple, was dashing on by that night toward the Euphrates, while the 1st Armored Division waited until morning to cross Purple) and the fact that the weather for the 26th looked to be worse than it had been on the 24th or 25th.[61] The Third Army commander tried once more to obtain release of the theater reserve (1st Cavalry Division) that night and failed to do so. One can only observe that the effect of the rain and sandstorms, as well as enemy

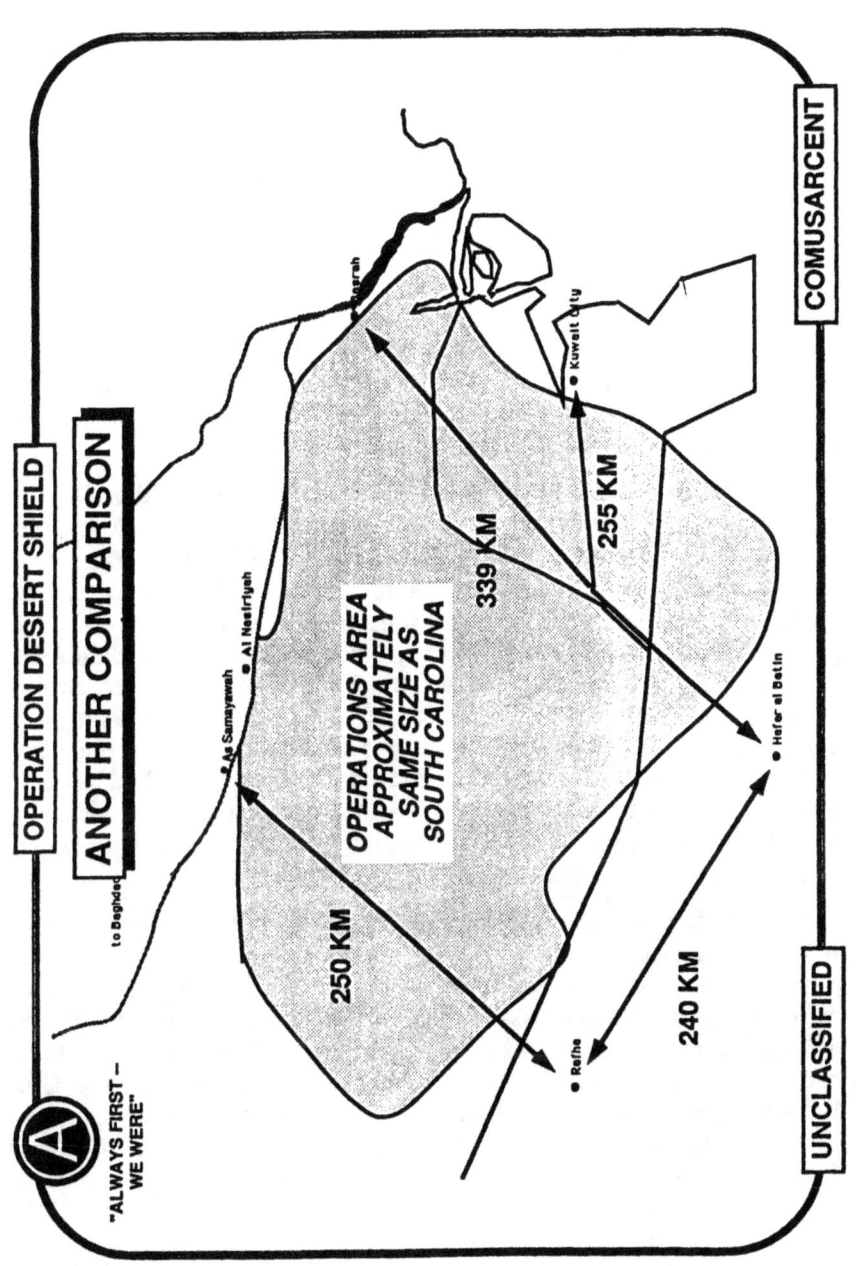

Figure 33.

resistance (for the corps was not unopposed), were more obscured when viewed from the Ministry of Defense basement than they were in the field. The CENTCOM commander was falling victim to the disease of "chateau generalship."

Yeosock's concerns for 26 February involved obtaining release of the 1st Cavalry Division, which the CINC continued to hold as reassurance for Joint Forces Command North and the Egyptians until the latter could complete their breach and breakout; setting a proper boundary to establish the terms for the two Army corps to destroy the RGFC; and bringing the two corps more or less on line by their securing of Objectives Orange and Collins (XVIII and VII Corps respectively) by early afternoon of the 26th.[62] From Yeosock's perspective, these actions were within what he understood to be the CINC's intent and within his own projected time lines. By morning, it would be clear that was not good enough for Schwarzkopf.

At 0135 on the 26th, Baghdad radio announced an Iraqi withdrawal from Kuwait.[63] President Bush responded quickly, first, through Press Secretary Marlin Fitzwater at 0630 on the 26th (local time was still 2230, the 25th in Washington) and then, later, on the morning of the 26th in Washington, with a brief (three-minute) personal statement. The thrust of the response was that Saddam's withdrawal was unsatisfactory without his corresponding acceptance of the various UN resolutions about abandoning any claim to Kuwait, payment of reparations, and release of prisoners.[64] Early morning intelligence reports indicated that, indeed, the Iraqi Army had begun a mass exodus led by III Corps in the east beginning at 2230 (local) on the 25th. There had been initial indications of withdrawal via J-STARS images as early as 0300 the 25th.[65]

At 0830 on the 26th, while the ARCENT staff was preparing for its routine morning update briefing, Yeosock was called to the phone for an urgent call from Schwarzkopf. (See map 10.) There are various colorful accounts in the press of the tenor of this call, most of which are supported by the circumstantial evidence and memories of staff officers in the vicinity.[66] The thrust of the business was that Schwarzkopf was dissatisfied with what he saw as the overly cautious and slow VII Corps offensive. This concern was shared by General Powell, far off in Washington, who compared VII Corps' progress unfavorably with that of the (as yet largely unopposed) 24th Division.[67] Lieutenant Colonel Kendall merely observed in his notes: "0840C: CINC called to prepare for more rapid OPTEMPO; 24 ID released from the limit of advance (PL Viking)."[68] Elsewhere he noted:

251

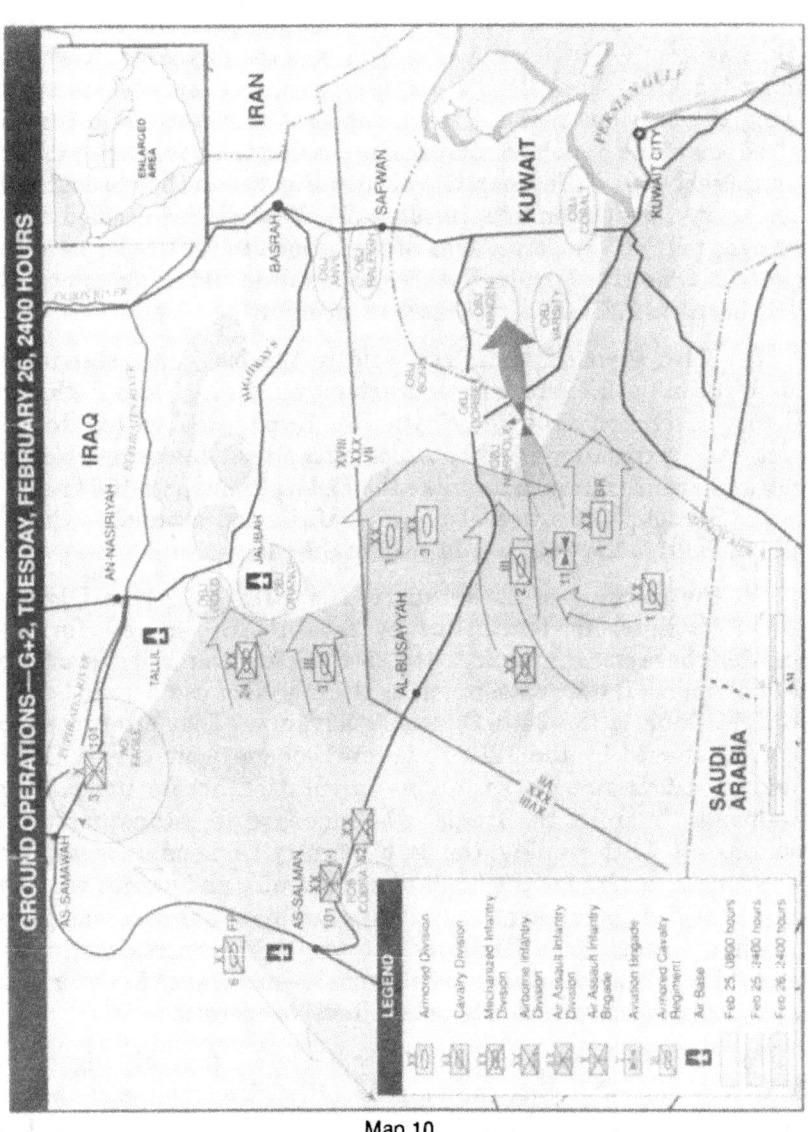

Map 10.

"CinC's guidance has changed from deliberate operations to a pursuit."[69]

Notwithstanding the withdrawal of the Iraqi III and IV Corps in the east, Iraqi operational reserves, much of the RGFC, and regular Iraqi Army armored and mechanized divisions were clearly under control and, as the Marines and 2d Armored Cavalry had learned on the 25th, prepared to fight to provide cover for the retreating forces.

For the VII Corps and Third Army commanders, the bitter irony in Schwarzkopf's call was that the 26th was the day when it was all coming together—the CINC's display of temper notwithstanding. During the previous night, Yeosock had set the battlefield for the destruction of the Republican Guard by issuing the boundaries for the advance eastward.[70] (See map 11.) Meanwhile, Franks had brought his three heavy divisions on line. Incidentally, Yeosock had decided not to turn over part of VII Corps' area of operations to XVIII Corps in the vicinity of Objective Purple. Rather, he required VII Corps to provide XVIII Corps an MSR through that area on order.[71]

The 24th Division would run wild in the Iraqi rear starting at midafternoon on 26 February and extending through the 27th. The "Victory" Division attacked down the Euphrates valley in two directions, overrunning the theater logistics site at Juwarin (Objective Gold) and, in an exercise not unlike the Federal Cavalry's 1863 raid on Brandy Station,[72] destroyed Iraqi aircraft on the ground at the air bases at Tallil in the west and Jalibah in the east.

On the morning of 27 February, the 101st Airborne Division showed its inherent flexibility by establishing a new forward operations base on the ground to the east, taking over a site secured by the 3d Armored Cavalry Regiment as the regiment came up to become the right flank of the 24th Division's advance. That afternoon, the 101st, reinforced by the 12th Aviation Brigade from XVIII Corps, would send four Apache battalions in rotation across the Haer al Hammar to interdict the Iraqis, who managed to escape northwest from Basrah. That evening, the 24th Infantry Division, now with the operational command of the 3d Armored Cavalry and formed with two heavy brigades and an armored cavalry regiment abreast, was poised to begin a descent down Highway 8 toward a line approximating the Rumayulah oil fields (and possibly beyond)—an advance foreshortened only by the political decision to cease offensive operations.

As for VII Corps, Franks had completed the shifting of his offensive center of gravity to his left on the 25th in spite of the foul weather. The corps had found the Republican Guard Forces Command

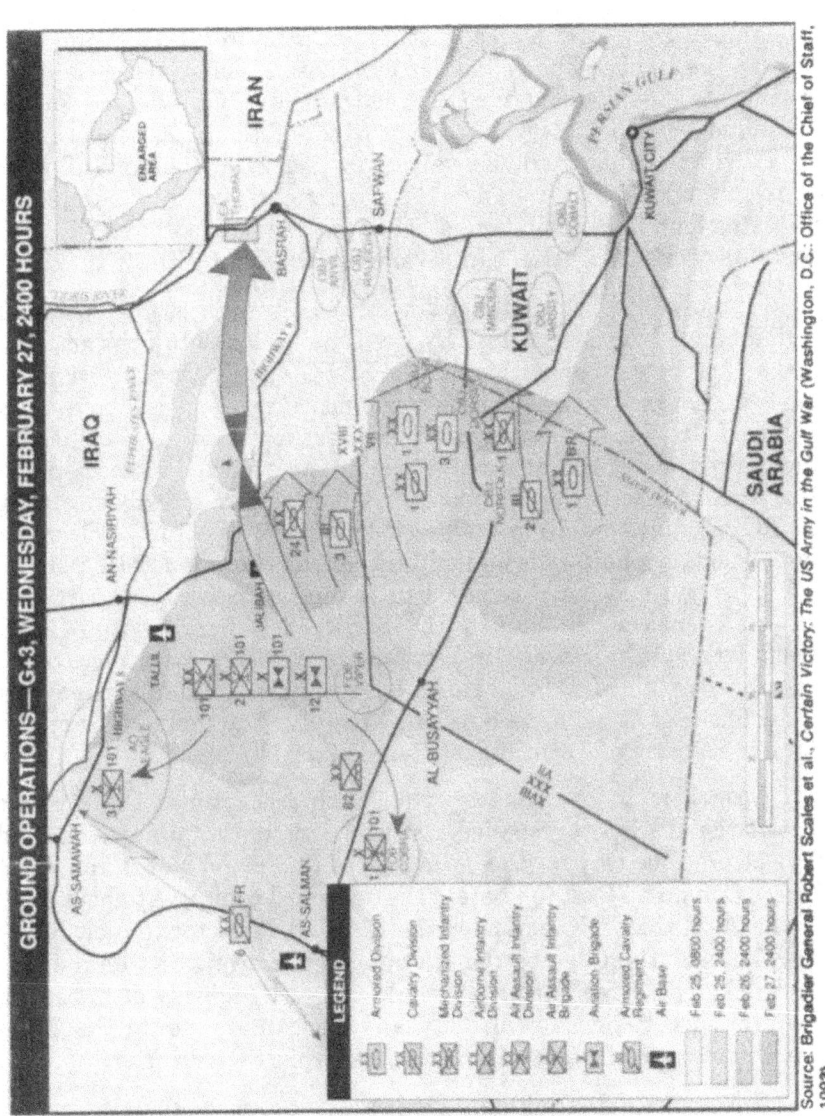

Map 11.

and, with or without the spur from the basement of the Ministry of Defense building, had begun execution of the second phase of its attack plan that evening. The plan would change in detail throughout the 26th, first, because of the sudden if late availability of the 1st Cavalry Division and, second, as the corps accommodated the changes inherent in the two-sided game of war.[73] The day would see the corps' "fist" roll east in what is known somewhat prosaically as a "relentless attack"— an eighteen-hour, continuous, disciplined, and unforgiving progress through the Iraqi defensive barrier by thousands of armored fighting systems. At 1354 that day, the CINC moved the ARCENT-Joint Forces Command North boundary south to provide additional maneuver room for VII Corps in northern Kuwait.[74] On the 27th, the 1st Infantry Division would break through on the corps' right, and Franks would be preparing for a final encirclement when the events associated with the cessation of offensive actions intervened on the night of the 27th–28th.

Franks called Schwarzkopf during the afternoon of the 26th and explained his true situation.[75] By the time he spoke to Schwarzkopf, Franks' troops were in battle with the RGFC, the 1st Cavalry Division had been released, and the pique of the morning seemed to have been assuaged. It seems, however, that Schwarzkopf continued to harbor uncertainty about the aggressiveness of the attack. In his memoir, Schwarzkopf asserts that Franks (whose forces were already engaging the RGFC) indicated an intention to turn his force south to clear his flank before beginning the main attack. Franks (to whom the assertion is a mystery) may have referred to using the terrain in northern Kuwait opened up for him by the earlier decision, and the CINC misunderstood the remark in consonance with the false picture he already entertained. While Franks quite rightly directed his energies to the business at hand, he now had a new flank to protect, the one in Riyadh. Schwarzkopf continued to fume in the bunker.[76]

Elsewhere in the theater, the Marines captured the Kuwait International Airport, repelled a second armored counterattack, and thus cleared the way for the Joint Forces Command North and Joint Forces Command East to liberate the despoiled capital. At about 1030 on the 26th, the CINC extended the MARCENT sector to include the Al Jahara-Mutla Ridge bottleneck outside of Kuwait City en route to Basrah.[77] The "Tiger Brigade" would cut the "highway of death" on the ground between Kuwait City and Basrah, as would the 1-4th Cavalry of the 1st Infantry Division, farther north, soon after.

Schwarzkopf finally released his theater reserve, the 1st Cavalry Division(-), at H+53 (at 0920 on the 26th), after the call to Yeosock and twelve hours later than ARCENT had estimated was necessary (based on time and distance) for the division to be available for the decisive attack.[78] The division passed through the 1st Infantry Division breach and raced north, arriving in time for a final attack on the 28th, which never occurred. Certainly, Schwarzkopf's reluctance to commit his own reserve until so late in the battle undermines any pretense of his to a superior vision or aggressiveness in anticipating the Iraqi collapse. Rather, his frustration seems to reflect both the consequences of being unable to keep up with a rapidly developing situation as well as he felt was necessary, and a new and largely political anxiety that Saddam might be able to save some face from the disaster that now confronted him. Yeosock's comments that day, reflected in Kendall's notes, indicate that Schwarzkopf was under pressure from Washington to destroy the RGFC more rapidly as pressure was growing at the United Nations to end the war. *The New York Times* attributed similar concerns to unnamed Bush administration officials.[79]

That night, presumably to reassure various higher authorities and perhaps educate them about the difficulty of the task being accomplished, the ARCENT SITREP went into some detail about conditions in the area of operations. The VII Corps' commander stated as his intent: "TO CONTINUE UNRELENTING ATTACK TO DESTROY THE RGFC AND CUT ESCAPE ROUTES." He noted the number of heavy brigades destroyed to date and the number of prisoners captured, pointing out that this had been done at an incredibly low cost in U.S. casualties. "CURRENT CONCERNS," the report continued, "ARE CENTERED ON WEATHER AND THE EFFECT HEAVY RAINS HAVE HAD ON THE SUPPLY ROUTES." The report indicated some of the measures required to keep the corps advance going, to include airlift of critical supplies of food, fuel, and ammunition.[80] The ARCENT commander noted as well:

> IMPRESSIVE SUCCESSES BY VII CORPS AND XVIII CORPS HAVE ALSO BEEN ACCOMPANIED BY THE CHALLENGES OF AN EXTREMELY RAPID OPERATIONAL TEMPO AND POOR WEATHER. RAIN, LOW CEILINGS, AND DENSE MORNING FOG HAVE LIMITED CAS AGAINST ENEMY ARTY AND ARMOR.
>
> RAIN HAS ALSO DEGRADED TRAFFICABILITY OF MSR'S AT A TIME WHEN RAPID TACTICAL ADVANCES HAVE EXTENDED SUPPLY LINES AND INCREASED SUSTAINMENT DEMANDS.[81]

Elsewhere, while the decisive action was taking place in VII Corps' area, high theater was occurring on the banks of the Euphrates in XVIII Corps' area of responsibility, and it was chiefly the doing of General McCaffrey's 24th Infantry Division. The XVIII Corps' FRAGO

66, issued at 1817 on the 25th, had directed the 24th Division to attack and seize Objective Gold, the theater logistics base at Juwarin. The division began its attack at 1400 on the 26th to seize battle positions in the river valley. The 1st and 2d Brigades fought their way to positions facing east toward Juwarin, while the 197th moved to a position facing Tallil (to the northwest). The 3d Armored Cavalry Regiment was placed under the operational control of the 24th Infantry Division at noon on the 26th and attacked on the right to seize Objective Tim, which was to become a new FOB Viper for the 101st Airborne Division's aviation units the following morning. The division fought through the night with the RGFC Nebuchadnessar Infantry Division and 26th Commando Brigade and reported seizure of Objectives Gold and Tim by 0330 on the 27th.[82]

At 2230 on the 26th, the 1st Brigade of the 24th Division, commanded by Colonel John LeMoyne, reported engaging tanks on HETs trying to move to the northwest. According to the ARCENT SITREP, fifty-four tanks on HETs were destroyed.[83] (For understandable reasons the destruction of anyone's HETs was the subject of some wry comments at ARCENT.) The following morning, the attack rolled on as the two organic brigades of the 24th conducted a deliberate attack on Jalibah airfield, which was reported secure by 1300. That afternoon, the 197th drove through the main gate of Tallil Air Base and down the strip destroying aircraft and various defensive installations before withdrawing.[84] The ARCENT LNO with XVIII Corps reported six helicopters and four fighters destroyed at Tallil and eight helicopters and ten fighters at Jalibah.[85] By early evening, the division was concentrated and refueling in anticipation of launching an attack down the Euphrates at 0400 the next morning.[86] The cost in friendly casualties to the division of over 26,000 (considering attachments) for Desert Storm was eight killed and thirty-six wounded in action, well below the permissible planning figure for CENTCOM of three companies per coalition brigade.[87] Over 5,000 prisoners were captured; over 360 armored fighting vehicles were destroyed.[88]

By 0730 on the 27th, the 3d Armored Cavalry Regiment had secured Objective Tim, and the 101st airlifted its 2d Brigade into the site to establish a new FOB Viper in the vicinity of Al Busayyah (north) airfield.[89] By 1400, Apaches from the 101st Aviation Brigade and the 12th Aviation Brigade were operating out of FOB Viper, attacking targets along the highway east of the 24th Division and in Engagement Area Thomas northwest of Basrah.[90] (See map 12.) This was an unanticipated mission, and it left the 101st interdicting Highway 8 in AO Eagle with one air assault infantry brigade, securing

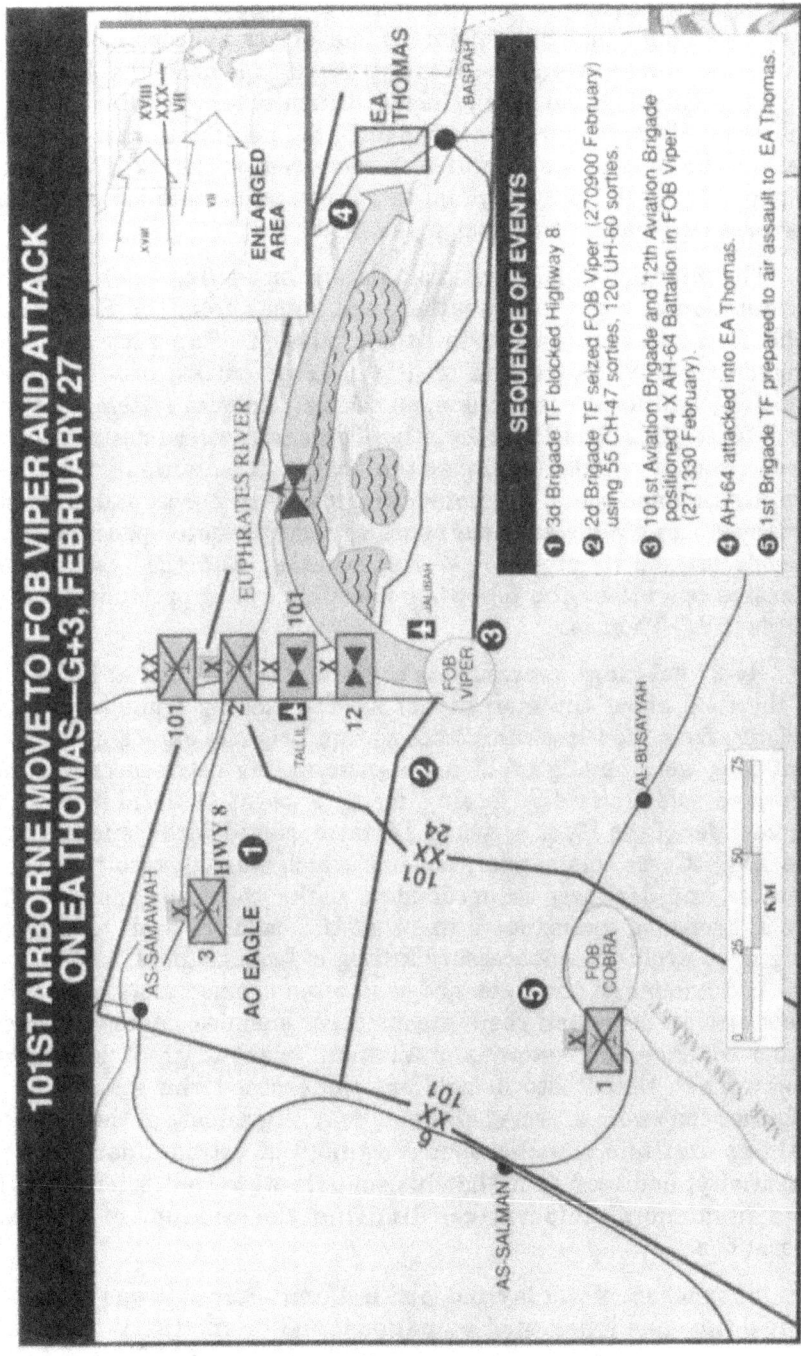

Map 12.

FOB Cobra with another (due to displace to Viper on the 28th), and the third providing a launching point for four attack helicopter battalions to interdict forces fleeing the KTO by two escape holes the Air Force had not been able to cut. The principal difficulty for the 101st involved aviation fuel, particularly since the corps did not immediately provide fuel for the long-range interdiction required of the 12th Aviation Brigade. The 101st provided fuel to get the immediate job done, and the corps replenished the division's stocks.[91]

The interdiction missions took place from 1430 to 1830 when the combination of night, bad weather, and smoke from the Kuwait oil fields forced the units to curtail their mission. The 12th Aviation Brigade reported destruction of fifteen Iraqi trucks, nine armored vehicles (significantly, no tanks), an SA-6 air defense system, and two air defense guns. The 101st Aviation Brigade reported destruction of three armored vehicles (again, no tanks), two ammunition trucks, and two air defense guns but noted that the Air Force had already destroyed many vehicles on the causeway escape route upon which the brigade focused its attention.[92] Bad weather and the cessation of offensive operations the following morning would preclude further efforts in AO Thomas.

By 27 February, concern was beginning to be raised at home and in the field about the morality of killing fleeing Iraqi soldiers.[93] Aviators from the 101st and 12th Aviation Brigades expressed concern that they were having problems discriminating between armed and unarmed soldiers in the fleeing mass, a point General Peay, the commander of the 101st Airborne Division, raised with General Luck, the XVIII Corps commander, but one which was not resolved before weather and darkness intervened to make the issue moot.[94] The general sense of commanders was that U.S. soldiers went to unusual lengths to avoid the unnecessary killing of Iraqi soldiers, who clearly had had enough of the fight and who often seemed more abused by their own leaders than their presumptive enemies. Moreover, most senior commanders, veterans of Vietnam, went to great lengths to ensure that Desert Storm soldiers understood the standards of behavior that were expected of them. Peay, a graduate of the Virginia Military Institute, a soft-spoken Virginian of extraordinary ethical sensitivity, had seen to it that his soldiers were well briefed on the legal and moral imperatives limiting the conduct of military operations.

But the face of war is cruel, and in Desert Storm, it was presented in real time and living color on national and international television. The vivid images carried in reports of the effects of U.S. bombing in

Baghdad, the Scud damage in Israel and Saudi Arabia, as well as the nature of the Iraqi flight, would lead to increased pressure on President Bush to find a way to stop the killing.[95]

The main attack was taking place in VII Corps. It began with the advance of the 2d Armored Cavalry Regiment and Third Armored Division the morning of the 26th and continued almost without pause until the evening of the 27th. The 1st Armored Division overran Objective Purple and continued east to fall in on the left of the 3d Armored Division on the afternoon of the 26th. The 1st Infantry Division passed through the 2d Armored Cavalry Division, fought through the Iraqis, and broke out on the corps' right center. The 1st U.K. continued its progress eastward and across Wadi al Batin, protecting the corps' right flank and opening the way for the Joint Forces Command North to attack toward Kuwait City.

In front of VII Corps, the enemy's heavy brigades were laid out in width and depth. The enemy front was such that the three heavy brigades of the much-abused RGFC Tawakalna Mechanized Division would face an armored division each. The Tawakalna was truly the most abused Iraqi formation. Schwarzkopf seems to have taken a special dislike to the Tawakalna and spent a good bit of his air effort on its attrition. Prebattle BDA (to the extent it can be relied upon) reported it one of the most reduced of enemy formations.[96] Now, it would fight the 1st and 3d Armored Divisions, the 2d Armored Cavalry Regiment, and the 1st Infantry Division—just about simultaneously.

The 1st Armored Division, on the corps' left, would also fight the RGFC Medina Armored Division, a brigade of the RGFC Adnan Infantry Division, and the remains of several regular Iraqi units. The U.S. 3d Armored Division would fight a brigade of the Tawakalna, the 10th Armored Division, and part of the 12th Armored Division. The U.S. 2d Armored Cavalry Regiment, which had already destroyed a brigade of the 12th Armored Division, would fight part of the Tawakalna and more of the 12th and be relieved the night of the 26th by the 1st Infantry Division, which would take over destruction of the Tawakalna, the 12th, and parts of the 10th Armored Divisions. Because the Iraqi battle array was breaking down, various units appeared at odd places on the battlefield, and reconstruction of the actions can only be approximate.[97]

The advance on the 26th was picked up first by the 2d Armored Cavalry Regiment, which had been in battle both the previous day and through much of the night of the 25th–26th. The regiment received the order from VII Corps implementing the contingency plan for destruction of the RGFC at 0522 that morning. The order directed the 2d ACR to advance to the east and fix the Tawakalna Mechanized Division, then to pass the 1st Infantry Division through to continue the attack.[98] First, the regiment had to uncover the 3d Armored Division to allow it to advance in the center of the corps' fist.

By 0620, the regiment was moving east. At 0713, it had its first confirmed contact with the covering force of the Tawakalna Division, which was apparently moving north.[99] By 0915, the weather had deteriorated severely. By afternoon, the 2d Armored Cavalry Regiment and most of VII Corps advanced toward the Republican Guard through a *Shamal,* a perverse mix of rain and blowing sand that can reduce visibility to next to nothing. VII Corps' battle with the RGFC was conditioned and, in some respects, favored by attacking out of this storm. For the most part, superior U.S. weapon optics allowed VII Corps' systems to see the enemy while remaining concealed from them.

After dealing with the covering force, the regiment had to be resupplied with ammunition by C-130 airdrops and with fuel and ammunition by CH-47 airdrops.[100] Franks, on his daily round forward, came to the regimental CP at 1250. He consulted with Colonel Holder and ordered the regiment east to fix the main body of the Tawakalna, then prepare to pass the 1st Infantry Division. About 1500, the regiment passed the line of departure with three squadrons abreast, made contact with the Tawakalna Division, and fought the six-hour battle named by the press as the "Battle of 73 Easting." At 2200 on the 26th, the 1st Infantry Division began passing through the regiment and picked up the fight within twenty minutes. The 2d ACR passed into the corps' reserve—for the remainder of the ground war as it happened. The regiment's fuel status was Red.[101]

The 3d Armored Division on the regiment's left began passing around the regiment at 0918 on the 26th. The division advanced with two brigades abreast, 2d Brigade on the north, adjacent to the 1st Armored Division, and 1st Brigade in the south, adjacent to the 2d Armored Cavalry Regiment. On the morning of the 27th, the 3d Brigade was passed through the 2d and continued the attack alongside the 1st until the division sector was pinched out during the evening of the 27th.

The 3d Armored Division fight was similar to that of the 2d Armored Cavalry Regiment and the 1st Infantry Division. After following the 2d Armored Cavalry Regiment north for two days, cleaning up the by-passed units left in the regiment's wake, the division began its turn east, then southeast, on the morning of the 26th. The 1st Brigade, commanded by Colonel Bill Nash, had been joined by the 2d Battalion, 29th Field Artillery, on the 25th as part of the corps' shifting of its center of gravity to the left. Throughout the 25th, the brigade moved north in a diamond formation at an approximate rate of advance of twelve mph. The 2d Battalion, 29th Field Artillery, had joined the brigade on the move. Two batteries of multiple launch rocket systems would join the column on the morning of the 26th, reinforcing further the fires available to the direct support artillery battalion (2d Battalion, 3d Field Artillery), already part of the brigade task force.[102] During the evening of the 25th, the brigade commander had received his warning order for the battle with the RGFC. It rained all night and visibility was poor the morning of the 26th when the brigade crossed the line of departure at 0530.[103]

The brigade drove east looking for the Tawakalna Division. It found one of its brigades about 1702, generally on the 72 Easting. The 3d Battalion, 5th Cavalry (a mechanized infantry task force, title notwithstanding), immediately moved three of its company teams on-line and, supported by artillery and A-10 close support aircraft, fought through a prepared defensive position. Task Force 4-32 Armor, in the north, also fought an engagement with enemy mechanized infantry from about 1920 until about 2000. The 4th Battalion, 34th Armor, in the south, engaged some miscellaneous enemy troops. Only the 3d Battalion, 5th Cavalry, remained in contact in the early morning hours.[104] At 0145 on the 27th, the 1st Brigade was told to change its direction more to the southeast and narrow the brigade front. At 0630, the brigade began moving forward by bounds. Prisoners surrendered in some numbers. At 0700, the 4th Battalion, 32d Armor, found a second defensive line and began to reduce it. By 0800, the task force had destroyed thirteen enemy tanks, sixteen BMPs, and fourteen other armored infantry carriers. Some 230 prisoners were taken.

The brigade continued on in this way throughout the day, attacking defensive areas, advancing between them with small meeting engagements along the way, and, when they were not actually attacking, taking prisoners in large numbers. The night of the 27th, the brigade passed into Kuwait, closing on its final objective in the early morning hours of the 28th.[105]

The 2d Brigade, in the north, had moved out at 0600 on the 26th and, like its southernmost peer, had advanced through indifferent resistance until about 1600. At that time, the brigade was preparing to refuel when it was ordered to continue the advance to maintain pressure on the RGFC. It engaged the same brigade of the Tawakalna

Division as its right-hand neighbor about 1630 and fought with it throughout the night until 1045 on the 27th. Then, the 3d Brigade passed through, while in contact with the enemy, and continued the divisional attack to the southeast alongside and beyond the 1st Brigade. The brigade crossed into Kuwait at 1658 on the 27th. The 2d Brigade estimated that it had destroyed twenty-seven enemy tanks and fourteen BMPs at the cost of two American soldiers killed and six others wounded. One of the killed was the victim of a misdirected U.S. dual-purpose ICM (improved conventional munition—an artillery round that disperses small, armor-penetrating bomblets above a target).[106] The division had advanced 225 kilometers in seventy-eight hours. It had fought and destroyed forces of the 29th Infantry Brigade and 9th Armored Brigade of the Tawakalna Division and elements of the 52d and 17th Armored Divisions. One Iraqi prisoner remarked to his captors: "You were like the wind. You come, blow and go away. You cannot shoot the wind."[107]

In one incident, where attacking through the *Shamal* had not worked to the U.S. advantage, A Troop, 4th Squadron, 7th Cavalry, of the 3d Armored Division—which was screening adjacent to the 2d Armored Cavalry Regiment on the south during the evening of the 26th—ran into an enemy position backed up with tanks and lost two killed, twelve wounded, and four Bradley fighting vehicles destroyed. The troop commander, believing because of the limited visibility that he was facing a force without tanks (unlike a regimental squadron, a divisional cavalry squadron has no organic heavy armor), he pressed his attack when first engaged. Perhaps because he deployed his platoons from column to line by splitting the following platoon sections around the forward platoon, left and right, the squadron's commander found disengagement unexpectedly complicated and confused. The troop was relieved by the tanks of the armored battalion task force following it, and the attack proceeded. For A Troop, the experience was both costly and traumatic. For the division, it was but a blip on the screen during a relentless advance.[108]

On the left of the 3d Armored Division and on the extreme left of the corps, the 1st Armored Division began its attack at 0630 the morning of the 26th—at Objective Purple. The attack passed through the objective and wheeled 90 degrees to the east, deploying three brigades abreast and attacking. "Old Ironsides" fought, in succession, a brigade of the ubiquitous Tawakalna Division, a brigade of the RGFC Adnan Infantry Division, and the RGFC Medina Division.[109] The division was in almost continuous combat over forty-eight hours and covered 115 kilometers from start to finish. Logistics, inhibited by the bad weather over roadless terrain, were beginning to restrict the wheeling corps. The 1st Armored Division required an infusion of fuel from the 3d Armored Division to maintain its advance.[110]

The 1st Armored Division's 3d Brigade (on the right) fought the northernmost brigade of the Tawakalna Division. The Tawakalna had been spotted first by an Air Force A-10 and attacked at 1624. The air attack was followed by division air scouts, who identified elements of the Tawakalna and 52d Armored Division. Ground scouts counted a total of fifty-two tanks. Thirty of these were then destroyed by artillery and AH-64 fire, after which, the 3d Brigade attacked through and destroyed the remaining twenty-two. At the same time, MLRS fire effectively neutralized a brigade of the Adnan Division, which apparently was the anchor of the Iraqi defensive line in the center of the division sector.[111]

During the night of the 26th–27th, a U.S. engineer unit that had been left behind during the division's advance was fired upon by a unit of the 3d Armored Cavalry Regiment coming up on the XVIII Corps right. A 1st Armored Division engineer was killed when misidentified by a cavalry squadron commander, who apparently ordered his gunner to fire across the corps boundary at what he took to be Iraqi infantry.[112] This incident is particularly important because it illustrates the difficulty of maintaining contact across unit boundaries, a problem that is even more difficult the higher the headquarters involved and the faster the forward units advance. In this case, the engineers, members of an attached unit, were far behind the advancing forward line of 1st Armored Division troops. It was night in the open desert, which by then was full of intermingled U.S. and Iraqi troops, some of the latter with hostile intent, some simply trying to escape. The squadron could not tell who was on its flank when they spotted the engineers.

While the 1st Armored Division disposed of the Tawakalna Division, its aviation elements and dedicated air support began to locate and fix the Medina Division. By 0810 on the 27th, the 1st and 2d Brigades of "Old Ironsides" would be engaging the Medina Armored Division in a battle that would last late into the night. The 3d Brigade would also join the battle within thirty minutes.

The ground maneuver battle was accompanied by a counterfire battle that engaged Iraqi artillery in both the VII and XVIII Corps sectors with Army tactical missiles and multiple launch rocket systems in combination with fire finder radar. The fight between the 2d Brigade of the 1st Armored Division and the 2d Brigade of the

Medina was the largest single armored engagement of the war. Sixty-one Iraqi tanks, thirty-four armored personnel carriers, and five air defense systems were destroyed in a single hour.[113] One hundred eighty-six Iraqi tanks, 127 armored personnel carriers, and thirty-eight artillery pieces were destroyed during the 27th at the cost of a single U.S. soldier. The 2d Brigade was commanded by Colonel Montgomery Meigs, namesake and direct descendant of the Union Army quartermaster general in the American Civil War.

In addition to the two RGFC divisions engaged, the 1st Armored Division overran elements of ten Iraqi regular army divisions, including the 12th, 17th, and 20th Armored Divisions—a measure of the confusion that existed in the Iraqi array by that time. During the 27th, the 1st Armored Division employed fifty-one air interdiction missions beyond the ground maneuver forces, six separate Apache company strikes, and significant artillery fire in support of the ground maneuver.[114]

For the entire four-day operation, the division claimed 418 tanks destroyed, 447 armored personnel carriers, 116 artillery pieces, 1,211 trucks, and 110 air defense systems. In addition, 2,234 prisoners were captured. The division lost only four killed—the two already mentioned and two others who were lost to enemy ordnance after the cessation of offensive actions.[115]

On the corps right, beginning at 2200 on the 26th, the 1st Infantry Division conducted an unrehearsed night passage of lines with the 2d Armored Cavalry Regiment then in contact with the enemy. A night passage of lines, dangerous enough under any circumstances, requires the following unit to approach the forward line in the dark, then to pass through its elements without being shot in the process. Passages of lines require a great deal of coordination even on a quiet sector. With troops in contact, they are very risky indeed, as soldiers' adrenalin is up, and men are prone to shoot first when unrecognized fighting vehicles come into view.

The 1st Infantry Division passed through the lines and carried on the fight with the Tawakalna's southern-most brigade and a brigade of the Iraqi 12th Armored Division. The division drove through the enemy's rear and into the open by 0430 the morning of the 27th. The 1st then refueled and began an exploitation by 1000 that would end that night with the division's cavalry squadron across the Kuwait City-Basrah highway and the division positioned for an envelopment of the RGFC's southern flank.[116] The 1st U.K. Armored Division, as it crossed into Kuwait and met the Joint Forces Command North and

MARCENT troops to the east, was also coming into position to cooperate in such a move, should circumstances require it.[117]

The "Tiger Brigade," on the MARCENT left flank, had advanced on 26 February to the Mutla Ridge, the only terrain feature astride the principal escape route from Kuwait City. The Iraqis had mined and fortified this ridge line, and the "Tiger Brigade" now attacked down the ridge, becoming the stopper in the bottle and finally closing off on the ground what was already known as the "Highway of Death" following an intense air interdiction. The 3d Battalion, 67th Armor, commanded by Lieutenant Colonel Doug Tystad, had to breach an Iraqi minefield to block the road, then seize an Iraqi-occupied Kuwaiti police post.[118] This attack was assigned to the task force's attached infantry company, C Company, 3d Battalion, 41st Infantry, commanded by Captain Mike Kershaw. The infantry dismounted and captured the police post after a room-to-room assault. During this fight, the task force's master gunner, Sergeant First Class Harold Witzke, became the second and final fatality suffered by the "Tiger Brigade" in its three-day adventure with the 2d Marine Division.

From the Mutla Ridge, the Fort Hood soldiers, remnants of a division being deactivated as part of the post-cold war reduction in force, blocked the retreat of numerous Iraqi units fleeing from southeastern Kuwait. Overall, the brigade reported destroying about 180 tanks, 135 APCs, thirty-six artillery pieces, and capturing 4,050 prisoners.[119]

The 1st Cavalry Division was up behind the 1st Armored Division by the close of the 27th, after a run north through the 1st Infantry Division breach and a race north and east. By evening on the 27th, it was ready to relieve the 1st Armored in the north to become part of a northern pincers in a double envelopment of the forces still outside Basrah in the VII Corps sector. The 24th Division was refueling during the early evening hours in anticipation of a final day's work that could lead to the outskirts of Basrah.[120] But events elsewhere were about to bring the "Great Wheel" to its conclusion.

Notes

1. Bvt. Colonel J. F. C. Fuller, "The Development of Sea Warfare on Land and Its Influence on Future Naval Operations," *Journal of the Royal United Service Institution* 65, no. 458 (May 1920): 281–98.

2. B. H. Liddell Hart, *Paris: Or the Future of War* (London: Kegan Paul, Trench, Trubner & Co., Ltd., 1925), 88. Liddell Hart used the term to differentiate mounted foot soldiers from the traditional infantry. According to his book *Thoughts on War* (London: Faber & Faber, 1944), 165, the term was coined in 1921.

3. See "Excerpts From Report by Schwarzkopf on the Fighting in the Persian Gulf," *The New York Times*, 31 January 1991, A12.

4. Lieutenant General Merrill A. McPeak, "TAC Air Missions and the Fire Support Coordination Line," *Air University Review* 36, no. 6 (September-October 1985): 65–72.

5. On 26 February, planes from the U.S. Air Force bombed two British Warrior vehicles, killing nine British soldiers and injuring eleven. According to General de la Billiere, reference to the need for a later inquiry into the circumstances of the incident led to a blowup by General Horner, whose pilots were responsible for the deaths. HQ, VII Corps, Corps Artillery, VII Corps Artillery memorandum, Subject: VII Corps Artillery Commander's Report, Operation Desert Storm, n.d., 3. Volume at Combined Arms Research Library, USACGSC, Fort Leavenworth, Kansas. De la Billiere, *Storm Command*, 291–96.

6. HQ, ARCENT, G3 (Deep Operations) (After-Action Report), March-April 1991, 10–11. Joint Lessons Learned Observation by Major Coombs, G3, Deep Operations, 1 March 1991 (JULLS Number 13265-29400 [00003]). Both documents are in possession of the author.

7. General Franks to author.

8. Arden Bucholz, *Moltke, Schlieffen and Prussian War Planning* (New York: Bing Publishing, 1991), 308. See, also, Michael Geyer, "German Strategy in the Age of Machine Warfare, 1914-1945," chapter 19 of *Makers of Modern Strategy from Machiavelli to the Nuclear Age*, ed. Peter Paret (Princeton, NJ: Princeton University Press, 1986), 532. That is not to say that commanders never had to dismount infantry. As will be indicated below, the 1st Armored Division conducted a deliberate attack on Objective Purple. The commander of the 7th U.K. Infantry Brigade writes that his brigade conducted six formal attacks the first thirty-six hours, in which infantry "debused" on four occasions, two at night. Brigadier P. A. J. Cordingley, "The Gulf War: Operating with Allies," *Journal of the Royal United Services Institute for Defence Studies* 137, no. 2 (April 1992): 19.

9. Except as otherwise noted, basic weather data is taken from HQ, VII Corps, G2 memorandum, Subject: The 100-Hour Ground War: The Failed Iraqi Plan, dated 20 April 1991, 90 and annex G-1-1. Various observations are taken from unit diaries. The nature of the weather in the battle area is not always apparent from official Air Force staff weather officer forecasts, though they are used for BMNT and EENT times. The weather in the battle area was different than that in Riyadh and even in

King Khalid Military City. On G-day, the author was in a helicopter flying over the forward area from 0300–0900. The pilot was forced to land during hours of darkness due to blinding rain showers. Early morning hours, from 0600, on the border were bright and clear, though intermittent showers could be severe locally and winds heavy enough to raise blinding dust. By 1500, the area had clouded over, and bad weather followed. Desert Storm was conducted in some of the worst weather experienced in southeastern Iraq for years.

10. Memorandum from G2/SWO, Subject: USARCENT Weather Forecast, dated 23 February 1991 (valid 23/1700–24/1700).

11. Comment made by Brigadier General Frank Akers to the author. The author's observation of troops in vicinity of Riyadh were the same.

12. Message, 241800C FEB 91, FROM: CDR 101ST ABN DIV (AASLT) [SITREP—no subject line used], Sequence Number: 200, 1. Untitled narrative prepared by Colonel James T. Hill, commanding 1st Brigade, 101st Airborne Division, on 2 March 1991. The 1st Brigade also prepared a detailed narrative, HQ, 1st Brigade, 101st Airborne Division (Air Assault), Memorandum for Division Historical Officer, Subject: TF 1-101, 327th Infantry Regiment, Historical Summary of Desert Rendezvous II: Offensive Operations Against Iraqi Forces, dated 14 June 1991.

13. HQ, 1st Brigade, 101st Airborne Division (Air Assault), Memorandum for Division Historical Officer, Subject: TF 1-101, 327th Infantry Regiment, Historical Summary of Desert Rendezvous II: Offensive Operations Against Iraqi Forces, dated 14 June 1991, 4.

14. Untitled narrative prepared by Colonel James T. Hill, commanding 1st Brigade, 101st Airborne Division on 2 March 1991, 1.

15. HQ, ARCENT, Command Group, (Executive Officer's) Daily Memo, 24 February 1991 (1315C), 4. (Executive Officer's Daily Memos will be filed with General Yeosock's papers at the Army Military History Institute, Carlisle Barracks, Pennsylvania.) Schwarzkopf, *Doesn't Take a Hero*, 451–53.

16. Interview with Major General Thomas Rhame, 26 July 1991, 4.

17. Ibid.

18. Slide titled, "Operation Desert Storm: Phase III (As of 24 Feb)," Operation Desert Storm Phase III Time Lines, Enclosure 24 to HQ, ARCENT, AFRD-DPT Memorandum for USARCENT Historian, Colonel Swain, Subject: HQ, USARCENT G3 Plans, Historical Narrative of Desert Shield, Desert Storm, Defense and Restoration of Kuwait, and Redeployment, vol. 3.

19. General Yeosock's expression to author later was "On schedule, under cost."

20. Tom Donnelly, "The General's War," *The Army Times*, 52d Year, no. 30, 24 February 1992, 8, 16–18.

21. HQ, 1st Infantry Division, Main Command Post, Daily Staff Journal dated 24 February 1991, items 15 and 17.

22. HQ, VII Corps, Assistant Chief of Staff, G2, AETSCB Memorandum, Subject: The 100-Hour Ground War: The Failed Iraqi Plan, dated 20 April 1992, 93.

23. Ibid., 96.

24. The Iraqi concept governing employment of the Republican Guard on the 24th is not clear, though there was some movement picked up by J-STARS.

25. Rhame interview, 6. Letter to author from General Rhame, dated 5 October 1992. For the 1st U.K. Armored Division's perspective, see Major General Rupert Smith, "The Gulf War: The Land Battle," in the *Journal of the Royal United Services Institute for Defence Studies* 137, no. 1: 1–5. See, also, Brigadier I. G. C. Durie, CBE, "1st Armored Division Artillery on Operation Granby," *Journal of the Royal Artillery* 18, no. 2 (September 1991): 16–29.

26. Letter from General Rhame to author, 5 October 1992.

27. HQ, VII Corps, Tactical Command Post, Daily Staff Journal for 24 February 1991, item 54. See, also, interview with Colonel Stan Cherrie, VII Corps G3, 29 August 1991, 36–37.

28. Major Jason K. Kamiya, A History of the 24th Mechanized Infantry Division Combat Team During Operation Desert Storm, "The Attack to Free Kuwait" (January through March 1991) (Fort Stewart, Georgia, n.d.), 7. This is a division summary of actions in the Persian Gulf. These numbers represent the organic division plus attachments provided by XVIII Corps from corps and echelon-above-corps troops.

29. See, for example, HQ, 197th Infantry Brigade (Mechanized) (Separate), AFVE-IN, Memorandum for Members of the Sledgehammer Brigade, Subject: Chronology of the 197th Infantry Brigade (M) (S) Participation in the Gulf War, dated 24 April 1991, 2–3. The 197th was the third brigade of the 24th Division for Desert Shield-Desert Storm.

30. HQ, ARCENT, Command Group, (Executive Officer's) Daily Memo, 24 February 1991 (242330C), 2. (Executive Officer's Daily Memos will be filed with General Yeosock's papers at the Army Military History Institute, Carlisle Barracks, Pennsylvania.)

31. Schwarzkopf, *Doesn't Take a Hero*, 455.

32. Ibid., 455–56.

33. HQ, ARCENT, Command Group, (Executive Officer's) Daily Memo, 25 February 1991 (1430C), 3. (Executive Officer's Daily Memos will be filed with General Yeosock's paper at the Army Military History Institute, Carlisle Barracks, Pennsylvania.) According to Lieutenant General Luck and the ARCENT AAR, the CINC called him directly about the limit of advance on the 24th and by-passed ARCENT. HQ, CAC-T, Fort Leavenworth, Kansas, Center for Army Lessons Learned, Commander's Observations at the ARCENT AAR, DSSN112, 7.

34. HQ, ARCENT, Command Group, (Executive Officer's) Daily Memo, 25 February 1991 (1430C), 3. (Executive Officer's Daily Memos will be filed with General Yeosock's papers at the Military History Institute, Carlisle Barracks,

Pennsylvania.)

35. HQ, ARCENT, Message, 250300Z FEB 91, FM COMUSARCENT MAIN//DT//, MSGID/SITREP/USARCENT/G+1/FEB//,PERID/240300Z/ TO :250300Z/ ASOF: 250300Z, 11.

36. Message, 250300Z FEB 91, FM COMUSARCENT MAIN/ /DT//MSGID/ SITREP/USARCENT//G+1/FEB, PERID/240300Z/TO:250300Z/ASOF:250300Z, 1–2, 10–11. Message FROM: CDR VII CORPS//CG//, Subject: Commander's SITREP (Combat) #38, Reporting Period: 232100Z to 242100Z FEB 91. HQ, VII Corps, TAC CP, FRAGO 138-91, DTG 24200C. ARCENT SPOT Report (from Mobile CP Logs), received by Major Ward, DTG242327C (note: three hours after FRAGO 138-91). Daily Staff Journal for 24 February, ARCENT Main CP, VII Corps Desk, item 29, 2330C, from Major Hanna (VII Corps). The ARCENT TAC had informed the main CP at 2220 that the 1st U.K. would be through the breach by 1200C, to begin possibly at 0800C.

37. Message, 250300Z FEB 91, FM COMUSARCENT MAIN/ /DT// MSGID/ SITREP/USARCENT/G+1/FEB, PERID/240300Z/TO: 250300Z/ASOF :250300Z, 12–14.

38. HQ, ARCENT, AFRD-DT, Memorandum for Major General Taylor, ARCENT Rear, Subject: ARCENT SITREP, 25 February 1992.

39. Lieutenant General Walter E. Boomer, USMC, "Special Trust and Confidence Among the Trail-Breakers," *The U.S. Naval Institute Proceedings* 117, no. 11 (November 1991): 49.

40. Colonel John Sylvester, "Report," as told on 6 March 1991 (provided to author by Colonel Sylvester), 2. The report is a transcript of an interview with Colonel Sylvester by a Marine Corps historical detachment, interview with Lieutenant Colonel Matthew S. Klimow, S3, 3d Battalion, 41st Infantry, at Fort Leavenworth, Kansas, 17 March 1992 (Tape 2), 14.

41. Klimow interview, 32.

42. Although losses to the 14th Quartermaster Detachment got most of the publicity due to its Reserve Component, community-based character, only thirteen of the twenty-eight dead were from the detachment. Nonetheless, the 14th suffered a 75 percent casualty rate. Rick Atkinson, *Crusade: The Untold Story of the Persian Gulf War* (Boston: Houghton Mifflin Company, 1993), 418–19.

43. Narration of Rakkasan (3d Brigade, 187th Infantry Regiment) Deployment and Participation in Desert Shield and Desert Storm (unsigned), 2–3. Narrative collection of 101st's historical officer.

44. Message, 251800C FEB 91, FROM: CDR 101ST ABN DIV (AASLT) [SITREP—no subject line used], Sequence Number: 201, 2. Narration of Rakkasan (3d Brigade, 187th Infantry Regiment) Deployment and Participation in Desert Shield and Desert Storm (unsigned), 3–4.

45. HQ, 197th Infantry Brigade (Mechanized) (Separate), AFVE-IN, Memorandum for Members of the Sledgehammer Brigade, Subject: Chronology of the 197th Infantry Brigade (M) Participation in the Gulf War, dated 24 April 1991, 3.

46. Ibid. See, also, HQ, 24th Infantry Division, briefing titled, "Operation Desert Storm Post-Attack Summary," dated 22 March 1991.

47. Message, 251517Z, FM CDR XVIII ABN CORPS//G3//, Subject: FRAGO 66 to OPLAN Desert Storm, 1.

48. Message, 270300Z FEB 91, FROM COMUSARCENT MAIN//DT//, MSGID/ SITREP/USARCENT/G+3/FEB/,PERID/260300Z/TO:270300Z/ASOF:270300Z, 13–14. HQ, 197th Infantry Brigade (Mechanized) (Separate), AFVE-IN, Memorandum for Members of the Sledgehammer Brigade, Subject: Chronology of the 197th Infantry Brigade (M) Participation in the Gulf War, dated 24 April 1991, 3–5. See, also, HQ, 24th Infantry Division, briefing titled, "Operation Desert Storm Post-Attack Summary," dated 22 March 1991.

49. Message, 252200Z, FROM CDRXVIIIABNCORPSFWD//G-3//, MSGID/ SITREP/XVIII ABN CORPS/025/FEB 91, PERID/FROM 242100Z FEB/TO 252100Z FEB/AS OF 251200Z FEB 91//, 4–5.

50. HQ, VII Corps, Assistant Chief of Staff, G2, AETSCB, Memorandum, Subject: The 100-Hour Ground War: The Failed Iraqi Plan, dated 20 April 1991, 109–10. See, also, Kindsvatter, "VII Corps in the Gulf War: Ground Offensive," 16–37. This essay contains diagrams that portray the enemy deployment throughout the ground war as VII Corps assessed it afterwards.

51. See "Stalking the Janus-Faced God of War: Two Small Units and the Different Battles They Fought," *U.S. News and World Report*, 20 January 1992, 52–54.

52. HQ, 1st Armored Division, AETS-KGC, Memorandum for Record, Subject: 1st Armored Division in Operation Desert Storm, dated 19 April 1992, 5–6. Memorandum contains graphics describing division actions.

53. Ibid., 6. See, also, 1st Armored Division Operations Briefing, slides titled, "Battle for Al Busayyah." ARCENT Commander's (Executive Officer's) Daily Memo indicates ARCENT was aware of the VII Corps' decision to conduct a deliberate vice hasty attack on Al Busayyah. At the VII Corps after-action review, discussion focused on the abysmal weather the night of the 25th–26th and the stiff resistance put up on the 26th following a night of preparation by fire. Some 451 EPWs were taken. ARCENT historian's Notes from Corps Commander's After-Action Review, 11 March 1991, 5. The VII Corps G2 battlefield reconstruction assesses the holding force as elements of the 806th Brigade, to include a commando unit. The post was site of the Iraqi VII Corps' rear command post. HQ, VII Corps, G2 memorandum, Subject: The 100-Hour Ground War: The Failed Iraqi Plan, dated 20 April 1992, 115–16.

54. Message, 260300 FEB 91, FROM COMUSARCENT MAIN//DT//, MSGID/SITREP/USARCENT/G+2/FEB//, PERID/250300Z/TO:260300Z/ASOF:260300Z, 10. HQ, 2ACR, Operation Desert Storm, 2ACR Operations Summary, 23 February–1 March 1991, 5–7.

55. HQ, 2ACR, Operation Desert Storm, 2ACR Operations Summary, 23 February—1 March 1991, 7.

56. Memorandum for Commanding General, 3d Armored Division, Subject: Battle Report: Operation Desert Spear, 24–28 February 1991, dated 2 March 1991, prepared by Major (P) John D. Rosenberger, Deputy G3, Operational Assistant to Major General Funk, 8–12. As for disagreement with VII Corps' staff, see interview with General Paul Funk, CG, Third Armored Division, by VII Corps historian at 3 AD Main, 4 April 1991, 21 and 23.

57. I. G. C. Durie, CBE, "1st Armored Division Artillery On Operation Granby," *Journal of the Royal Artillery* 118, no. 2 (September 1991): 25. At the VII Corps' AAR, the division commander, Major General Rupert Smith, noted that the defending divisions were organized in much greater depth than he had anticipated, hence he found himself having to sort out defending infantry before arriving at the tactical reserves. ARCENT historian's Notes from Corps Commander's After-Action Review, 11 March 1991, 3. This tended to slow the British clearance of the breachhead and delay by some hours the departure of the 1st Infantry Division for the next phase of the operation. See Rhame interview, 6–7.

58. The 2d Armored Cavalry battle has been written about in some detail. It first drew public attention through an extraordinary piece of journalism by Vince Crawley in *Stars and Stripes*, "Minute by Minute, Death by Death: One Unit's Battle Against the Republican Guard," *Stars and Stripes* 49, issue 327, 9 March 1991, 14–16. It has been further examined by a team headed by Colonel Michael D. Krause from the Center of Military History and Defense Advanced Research Projects Agency in a paper titled, "The Battle of 73 Easting, 26 February 1991: A Historical Introduction to a Simulation" (hereafter referred to as Krause, "Battle of 73 Easting"). See, also, Steve Vogel, "A Swift Kick: 2d ACR's Taming of the Guard," in *Army Times*, 5 August 1991, 10–61.

59. HQ, ARCENT, Command Group, Memorandum for Record, Subject: (Executive Officer's) Daily Memo, 25 February 1991 as of 251430C February 1991, 3. (Executive Officer's Daily Memos will be filed with General Yeosock's papers at the Army Military History Institute, Carlisle Barracks, Pennsylvania.)

60. Schwarzkopf, *Doesn't Take a Hero*, 460.

61. HQ, ARCENT, Command Group, (Executive Officer's) Daily Memo, 25 February 1991 (2335C), 2. (Executive Officer's Daily Memos will be filed with General Yeosock's papers at the Army Military History Institute, Carlisle Barracks, Pennsylvania.)

62. HQ, ARCENT, Command Group, Memorandum for Record, Subject: (Executive Officer's) Daily Memo, 25 February 1991, as of 252335 February 1991, 5. (Executive Officer's Daily Memos will be filed with General Yeosock's papers at the Army Military History Institute, Carlisle Barracks, Pennsylvania.)

63. Patrick E. Tyler, "Iraq Orders Troops to Leave Kuwait but U.S. Pursues Battlefield Gains: Heavy American Toll in Scud Attack: Administration Says Hussein Must Declare Pullout Himself," *The New York Times*, 26 February 1991, A1, A12.

64. Ibid.

65. Message, 260200Z (4 A.M. the 26th) FEB 91, FROM COMUSARCENT MAIN//CMO ARCENT//, [MSGID] ARCENT INTREP 70-91 AS OF 260200Z FEB 91. Message lists indicators "read" throughout the night. A paper prepared by the ARCENT G2, General John Stewart, on J-STARS performance, indicates that as early as 0300 local on the 25th, there were indications of an Iraqi withdrawal from Kuwait City. Appendix H to Joint Surveillance Target Attack Radar System (Joint STARS), Operation Desert Storm (ODS), Operational Evaluation Command (OEC) Summary Report, H-10. Appendix H is an extract from a book put together for Brigadier General Stewart, ARCENT G2, at the close of the ground campaign by members of the Army J-STARS operational detachment.

66. The source document seems to have been an article by Tom Donnelly of the *Army Times*, "The Generals' War: How Commanders Fought the Iraqis . . . and Among Themselves," *Army Times*, 2 March 1992, 8, 16, 18, and an editorial on page 27 of Peter Martin's TV coverage of the story appeared on *CBS Evening News* on 24 February 1992. Martin seems to have used Donnelly's article, then checked it against his sources. Schwarzkopf's own account is in *Doesn't Take a Hero*, 462–63.

67. Donnelly, "The Generals' War," 16. Schwarzkopf, *Doesn't Take a Hero*, 463.

68. HQ, ARCENT, Command Group, Memorandum for Record, Subject: (Executive Officer's) Daily Memo, 26 February 1991, 6. (Executive Officer's Daily Memos will be filed with General Yeosock's papers at the Army Military History Institute, Carlisle Barracks, Pennsylvania.)

69. Ibid., 5. In VII Corps G3 Ops log for 26 February, 1005 hours, item 19, "Re: ARCENT G3 [General Arnold] - CINC WANTS VII CORPS TO CONDUCT COORDINATED ATTACK TO DESTROY RGFC TONIGHT NLT BMNT 27 FEB."

70. Message, 251800Z FEB 91, FROM COMUSARCENT MAIN, SUBJECT: FRAGO 055 TO OPORD 001 DESERT STORM 001; BOUNDARY CHANGE BETWEEN VII CORPS AND XVIII ABN CORPS. The actual execute order would not be issued until the 26th at 1500Z (1800 local), but once boundaries were issued and objectives were clear to corps commanders, the FRAGO was an afterthought. Schwarzkopf flattered himself that his early morning tirade "had already galvanized Franks." In fact, like Schwarzkopf's knowledge of what was taking place on the battlefield, his tantrum was far behind events in the field.

71. Message, 251942Z FEB 91, FROM COMUSARCENT MAIN, SUBJECT: FRAGO 056 TO OPORD 001 DESERT STORM 001; BOUNDARY CHANGE BETWEEN VII CORPS AND XVIII ABN CORPS.

72. In 1863, just prior to the start of Lee's Gettysburg campaign, the Union Cavalry conducted a raid into the South that involved a raid on the heretofore markedly dominant Confederate Cavalry's encampment at Brandy Station. The raid was highly embarrassing to Confederate Cavalry commander, J. E. B. Stuart. Its effect was political and psychological.

73. See, for example, instructions issued by General Franks at 260725 in HQ, VII Corps, G3 OPS, Daily Staff Journal, 26 February 1991, item 13. Arrival of 1st Infantry Division and 1st Cavalry Division in battle zone as well as detailed management of the battle throughout the 26th and 27th would change the precise maneuvers employed.

74. Significant activities in HQ, ARCENT, Command Group, Memorandum for Record, Subject: (Executive Officer's) Daily Memo, 26 February 1991, 6. (Executive Officer's Daily Memos will be filed with General Yeosock's papers at the Army Military History Institute, Carlisle Barracks, Pennsylvania.) According to Lieutenant Colonel Kendall in a letter to the author (29 October 1992), the CINC's call concerning the boundary change was highly professional in tone, leading Yeosock to conclude the storm had blown over.

75. General Yeosock and General Franks have both told the author that General Yeosock concealed from General Franks the precise nature of General Schwarzkopf's ire, thus leading General Franks to say that he was not aware of General Schwarzkopf's comments until they appeared in the press. General Franks' public response appeared in the Reading, Pennsylvania, *Eagle Times*, 1 March 1992. The column was reprinted in the Department of Defense American Forces Information Services, Current News *Early Bird* for Tuesday, 3 March 1992, 2. The time of General Franks' call has been variously given as the evening of the 25th and morning of the 26th. Reference to General Franks' aide, Major Toby Martinez, confirms a time of 1600 the 26th, which would satisfy the requirement that it follow Schwarzkopf's call to Yeosock the morning of the 26th.

76. Schwarzkopf, *Doesn't Take a Hero*, 463. General Franks has been unable to account for the CINC's perception in discussions with the author. Another possible explanation has to do with a concept discussed at ARCENT that would have had the 1st U.K. open a line of communication by turning south and clearing Wadi al Batin, rather than continuing eastward as they ultimately did. See Brigadier I. G. C. Durie, CBE, "1st Armored Division Artillery on Operation Granby," *Journal of the Road Artillery* 118, no. 2 (September 1991): 27–28. This contingency was never executed.

77. Report from ARCENT LNO to JFC North in HQ, ARCENT, Command Group, Memorandum for Record, Subject: (Executive Officer's) Daily Memo, 26 February 1991, 3. (Executive Officer's Daily Memos will be filed with General Yeosock's papers at the Army Military History Institute, Carlisle Barracks, Pennsylvania.)

78. HQ, 1st Cavalry Division, DTAC, Daily Staff Journal, 26 February 1991, items 17 and 18, indicate General Waller called direct to the 1st Cavalry Division and instructed them to move. Lieutenant Colonel Kendall's (Executive Officer's) Daily Memo indicates the 0920 time.

79. Thomas L. Friedman, "The Rout Bush Wants: A Disorderly, Humiliating Iraqi Surrender Will End Hussein's Power, Officials Believe," *The New York Times*, 27 February 1991, A1, A21.

80. Message, FROM COMUSARCENT MAIN//DT//, MSGID/ SITREP/ USARCENT/G +3/FEB//, PERID/260300Z/TO:270300Z/ASOF:270300, 8, 13, 14.

81. Ibid., 15–16.

82. HQ, 24th Infantry Division (Mech), briefing titled, "Operation Desert Storm Post-Attack Summary," dated 22 March 1991.

83. Many of the divisional records for the period of the ground war were not made available to the author because they have been separated for the various investigations concerning the 24th Division that followed the cease-fire. Many of the

incidents therefore can only be tracked in reports recorded in higher headquarters. This incident was reflected in the ARCENT and XVIII Corps duty logs, the former on an ARCENT Spot Report form dated 262230C February 1991 (Mobile CP Journal Entry 99), the latter in XVIII Corps TAC Journal Sheet (FB Form 2768), dated 262205C February, Entry 23.

84. HQ, 197th Infantry Brigade (Mechanized) (Separate), AFVE-IN, Memorandum for Members of the Sledgehammer Brigade, Subject: Chronology of the 197th Infantry Brigade (M) Participation in the Gulf War, dated 24 April 1991, 8.

85. HQ, ARCENT, Command Group, Memorandum for Record, Subject: (Executive Officer's) Daily Memo, 27 February 1991, 5–6. (Executive Officer's Daily Memos will be filed with General Yeosock's papers at the Army Military History Institute, Carlisle Barracks, Pennsylvania.)

86. Message, 272200Z FEB 91, FROM CDRXVIIIABNCORPSFWD//G3//, MSGID/SITREP/XVIII ABN CORPS/027/FEB 91/, 4, 6.

87. HQ, 24th Infantry Division (Mech), briefing titled, "Operation Desert Storm Post-Attack Summary," dated 22 March 1991. CENTCOM planning limit is given in Department of Defense, Conduct of the Persian Gulf War, Final Report to Congress Pursuant to Title V of the Persian Gulf Conflict Supplemental Authorization and Personal Benefits Act of 1991 (Public Law 102-25), April 1992, 90.

88. HQ, 24th Infantry Division (Mech), briefing titled, "Operation Desert Storm Post-Attack Summary," dated 22 March 1991.

89. Message, FROM CDR 101ST ABN DIV (AASLT) (situation report), DTG 271800C FEB 91.

90. Ibid. HQ, 101st Aviation Brigade, AFZB-KF-CO, Memorandum for Commander, 101st Airborne Division (Air Assault), Subject: Executive Summary—Operation Desert Shield/Storm, dated 10 June 1991, 11.

91. HQ, XVIII Airborne Corps, TAC CP, Daily Staff Journal, 26 February 1991, Journal Entries 81, 82, 94. HQ, XVIII Airborne Corps, TAC CP, Daily Staff Journal, 27 February 1991, Journal Entries 6, 8, 12.

92. HQ, 101st Aviation Brigade, AFZB-KF-CO, Memorandum for Commander, 101st Airborne Division (Air Assault), Subject: Executive Summary—Operation Desert Shield/Storm, dated 10 June 1991, 11.

93. John H. Cushman, Jr., "War in the Gulf: A Defeat by Any Other Name: The Rules: Experts Back U.S. On Rules of War," 27 February 1991, A1. Schwarzkopf, *Doesn't Take a Hero*, 468.

94. General Peay to the author. The same issue was raised by pilots in the 3d AD. General Funk instructed them to concentrate on destruction of materiel and to allow the enemy soldiers to escape as they might. General Funk to author.

95. The question of the effect of such pressure and the administration's efforts to counter it remains to be written. See Steve Coll and William Branigin, "U.S. Scrambled to Shape View of 'Highway of Death,'" *The Washington Post*, 11 March 1991, A-1. Related articles are Randall Richard, "'Like Fish in a Barrel,' U.S. Pilots Say," *The*

Washington Post, 27 February 1991, A-28. R. W. Apple, "American and British Troops Gird for an Iraqi Last Stand," *The New York Times*, 27 February 1991, A1; and the editorial that day, "Beyond Fury, Cool Calculation" in *The New York Times*, 27 February 1991, A26, which seems to favor the approach the president ultimately took. On the 27th, the date the story of what came to be called the "Highway of Death" broke, *The New York Times* ran an article asserting the right to destroy retreating Iraqi formations. John H. Cushman, Jr., "Experts Back U.S. on Rules of War," *The New York Times*, 27 February 1991, A21.

96. HQ, ARCENT, briefing for Secretary of the Army Michael Stone, section titled, "Summary of the Battle," dated 13 March 1991. Briefing contains G2 slides, as of 1 February (D+15), that show the Tawakalna at 50–74 percent effectiveness, another for 14 February (D+23) showing Tawakalna at 50 percent or less, and a third for G-day showing it restored to 50–74 percent. Battle damage assessment was not the most precise business going on in the G2 world.

97. Principal reference is the VII Corps G2 Engagement Matrix, Tab F to HQ, VII Corps, Assistant Chief of Staff, G2, AETSCB, Memorandum, Subject: The 100-Hour Ground War: The Failed Iraqi Plan, dated 20 April 1991. See also Lieutenant Colonel Peter Kindsvatter, "VII Corps in the Gulf War: Ground Offensive," *Military Review* 72 (February 1992): 26, 29, 34.

98. 2d Armored Cavalry Regiment, Operation Desert Storm, 2ACR Operations Summary, 23 February–1 March 1991, 8. The written VII Corps FRAGO 141-91 had a date/time group of 261400C February 1991. By the time the FRAGO was issued, the attack was ongoing. The same is true of the ARCENT FRAGO 058, issued at 261500Z February 1991. Written orders tend to confirm the business was done electronically.

99. 2d Armored Cavalry Regiment, Operation Desert Storm, 2ACR Operations Summary, 23 February–1 March 1991, 9. Krause, "Battle of 73 Easting," 7.

100. 2d Armored Cavalry Regiment, Operation Desert Storm, 2ACR Operations Summary, 23 February–1 March 1991, 10.

101. Ibid., 11. Vince Crawley, "Minute by Minute, Death by Death: One Unit's Battle Against the Republican Guard," *Stars and Stripes* 49, issue 327, 9 March 1991, 14–16. Steve Vogel, "A Swift Kick: 2d ACR's Taming of the Guard," in *Army Times*, 5 August 1991, 10–61.

102. (Historical Overview, 1st Brigade, 3d Armored Division, in Operation Desert Storm) Activity/Event: Movement from Approximately 10 Kilometers North of the Line of Departure to Vicinity of Phase Line Saigon, Date/Time: 250001CFEB91 to 260630CFEB91, and Activity/Event: Movement from Vicinity Phase Line Saigon to Enemy Contact Approximately 262631CFEB91 PU 659104, Vicinity of Phase Line Tangerine, Date/Time: 260630CFEB91 to 270259CFEB91.

103. (Historical Overview, 1st Brigade, 3d Armored Division, in Operation Desert Storm) Activity/Event: Movement from Vicinity Phase Line Saigon to Enemy Contact Approximately 262631CFEB91 PU 659104, Vicinity of Phase Line Tangerine, Date/Time: 260630CFEB91 to 270259CFEB91.

104. Ibid.

105. (Historical Overview, 1st Brigade, 3d Armored Division, in Operation Desert Storm) Activity/Event: The RFCT (Ready First Combat Team) Continues the Attack Vicinity PL Bullet to Objective Minden, Date/Time: 270300CFEB91 to 280800CFEB91.

106. 2d Brigade, 3d Armored Division History (1st Edition), Operation Desert Shield, December 1990 through 27 February 1991 (262200C February 1992).

107. Quoted in 3d Armored Division, Task Force 5-5 Cav Summary of Events, Report Author: Captain Steven B. Wyman, Unit: Task Force 5-5 Cavalry, Third Armored Division, Activity/Event: Enemy contact of Task Force, Date/Time of Activity/Event: 271900CFEB91 to 272030CFEB91.

106. 3d Armored Division, Historical Report Format, Report/Author: Captain E. Allen Chandler, Jr., Unit: A Troop, 4/7th Cavalry, Activity/Event: Contact with Iraqi Tanks, Date/Time of Activity/Event: 26 February 1991. This same incident was described in "Stalking the Janus-Faced God of War: Two Small Units and the Different Battles They Fought," *U.S. News and World Report*, 20 January 1992, 52–54.

109. HQ, 1st Armored Division, Operation Desert Storm, AETS-KGC, Memorandum for Record, Subject: 1st Armored Division in Operation Desert Storm, 19 April 1991, paragraphs 8 and 9. Memorandum contains 1st Armored Division after-action briefing, as well as written narrative of operations.

110. Memorandum for Commander, 3d Armored Division, Attn: ACofS G3, Subject: Chronological History/Significant Events 16 March 1991, 19. HQ, 1st Armored Division, Operation Desert Storm, AETS-KGC, Memorandum for Record, Subject: 1st Armored Division in Operation Desert Storm, 19 April 1991, paragraph 9.

111. HQ, 1st Armored Division, Operation Desert Storm, AETS-KGC, Memorandum for Record, Subject: 1st Armored Division in Operation Desert Storm, 19 April 1991, paragraph 8. See, also, Kindsvatter, 31.

112. HQ, 1st Armored Division, Operation Desert Storm, AETS-KGC, Memorandum for Record, Subject: 1st Armored Division in Operation Desert Storm, 19 April 1991, paragraph 9. Barton Ballman, "Felled by Friendly Fire: But for Months, the Truth About an Army Corporal's Death Remained Buried," *The Washington Post National Weekly Edition*, 11–17 November 1991, 9–11, provides details of the incident. Ultimately the regimental, squadron, and troop commanders of the 3d Armored Cavalry Regiment units involved in this incident were censured by the commander, U.S. Forces Command, for the incident. Barton Gellman, "Army Reprimands 3 for Combat Death Despite Exoneration by Investigators, Officers Held Responsible for Error in 'Friendly Fire' Case in Iraq," *The Washington Post*, 4 June 1992, A5.

113. HQ, 1st Armored Division, Operation Desert Storm, AETS-KGC, Memorandum for Record, Subject: 1st Armored Division in Operation Desert Storm, 19 April 1991, paragraph 9. See, also, Erica E. Goode, "The Battle of Medina Ridge: A Desert Showdown Between the World's Mightiest Tanks," in *U.S. News and World Report*, 20 January 1992, 55–56. The Award-Winning Staff of *U.S. News and World Report*, *Triumph Without Victory: The Unreported History of the Persian Gulf War* (New York: Times Books, a division of Random House, Inc., 1991), 380–86.

114. 1st Armored Division Operations Briefing, slide titled, "Destruction of Madinah [sic] Armored Division (26–28 February 1991)."

115. HQ, 1st Armored Division, Operation Desert Storm, AETS-KGC, Memorandum for Record, Subject: 1st Armored Division in Operation Desert Storm, 19 April 1991, paragraph 11.

116. HQ, 1st Infantry Division (Mechanized), King Khalid Military City, Saudi Arabia, AFZN-CG, Subject: Memorandum for CG, VII (US) Corps, Subject: Operation Desert Shield and Desert Storm Command Report, 19 April 1991, 5.

117. Brigadier I. G. C. Durie, CBE, "1st Armored Division Artillery on Operation Granby," *Journal of the Royal Artillery* 118, no. 2 (September 1991), 25–28.

118. HQ, 1st "Tiger Brigade," 2d Armored Division, Actions of the 1st "Tiger Brigade," 2d Armored Division During Operation Desert Shield/Operation Desert Storm, 10 August 1990–1 March 1991, "Narrative," 6. Interview with Colonel John Sylvester titled, "Colonel John Sylvester Report," 6 March 1991 (provided to the author by Colonel Sylvester), 5–9.

119. The brigade after-action report lists different figures: 181/172 tanks, 148/126 APCs, 40/32 artillery pieces. HQ, 1st "Tiger" Brigade, 2d Armored Division, Actions of the 1st "Tiger Brigade," 2d Armored Division During Operation Desert Shield/Operation Desert Storm, 10 August 1990–1 March 1991, "Statistical Data."

120. HQ, 24th Infantry Division (M), 262230C February 1991, FRAGO 46 to 24th Infantry Division (M) OPLAN Desert Storm 91-3, PH VI. This document is the order for attack at 0535C (BMNT) the 27th. The order has an on-order mission to advance to Objective Anvil outside of Basrah.

8
Battle's End

Instead of a final, climactic battle on 28 February, offensive military operations came unraveled in the early morning hours. Based upon glowing reports of success from the field, President Bush stopped the relentless killing of Iraqi soldiers and called for cease-fire talks. The conclusion was not a clean fade to peace, either on the battlefield or in the headquarters. In spite of almost unprecedented success in the field, seeds of postwar controversy were planted in the high command and in American public opinion. The events at Safwan and later near a causeway across the Euphrates marshes are instructive about the difficulties of ending a war.

The conduct of military affairs in Southwest Asia was marked by the particularly smooth integration of political and military actions almost from the outset. Although the United States military response to Iraq's aggression suffered some initial growing pains, the more typical thread that ran throughout Operations Desert Shield and Desert Storm was the habit of following each key presidential announcement of political intention with a press conference by the secretary of defense and chairman of the Joint Chiefs of Staff in which political goals were translated into clear military objectives.

With the ubiquity of CNN, operational commanders in theater could receive this guidance immediately and react to it at once. That the Iraqis could also receive it probably added more to the desired effect of coercion (or was discounted by Saddam's paranoia as mere deception) than it exposed U.S. forces to any increased risk. The technique can also be seen as a means of reassuring allies and neutrals by letting them know publicly just what the United States was about. The practice was, therefore, instrumental in maintaining both the cohesion of the alliance and ensuring that forces in the field were aware of the national command authority's intentions.

All this broke down the night of 27 February. The result was confusion and disharmony and a major killing of Iraqi forces that had tried to flee the partial U.S. encirclement during the two days after the announcement of a "suspension of offensive combat actions." At that precise time, U.S. and Iraqi military leaders were supposed to have been discussing terms for a military cease-fire in the field. Iraqi forces in the Basrah pocket were permitted to depart to the north, through Basrah, and continued to do so with their equipment after the implementation of the cease-fire. This provided cause for postwar speculation, particularly since the forces escaping into Basrah later took part in suppressing local unrest there against Saddam's regime.[1]

What was absent was a clear and common vision of how U.S. forces should be distributed on the ground to facilitate the inevitable transfer of the conflict's focus and energies back to the political arena. Also lacking was a common concept of what action to take regarding those Iraqi forces, including elements of the Republican Guard, that had been driven back into Basrah and its environs. All this was missing, in part, no doubt, because the end of offensive actions came sooner than anticipated. It also reflects a fundamental weakness in a traditional U.S. view that the military and political conduct of war are separable at all but the highest levels. In this concept of civil-military relations, the soldier is given a mission and fights the war according to what is militarily correct—albeit within boundaries established by policy. He expects to be left alone to do his technical business of fighting until he has accomplished some gross military end that will enable the diplomats to arrive speedily at a resolution of the basic issues causing the war. The soldier then turns the conflict back to his political masters. Such a view in an age of instantaneous communications is, of course, not only misguided but dangerous in an army of a democracy.

The difficulty on 28 February was that it was not enough to ask if the president's military objectives had been accomplished. It also mattered politically how U.S. forces were postured when they stopped their offensive actions and what U.S. expectations were for the behavior of the Iraqi forces south of the Euphrates and Shatt al Arab, now effectively in the power of U.S. forces. The disposition of U.S. forces on the ground and their behavior toward the Iraqis with whom they were now intermingled were political more than military questions. Yet, in this case, clear military guidance did not follow the political declaration.

So events on the ground drifted, with field headquarters inventing their own interpretations of the situation. While most units drew in their lines and began to clear the area to their rear, the 24th Infantry Division, apparently on the initiative of its commander, continued to advance its main line of resistance slowly and deliberately until a major, one-sided killing took place two days after the "suspension" was announced by the president. Before that occurred, a clash took place between Schwarzkopf and the senior army commanders over selection and occupation of a site for cease-fire talks, a blowup that was occasioned by the confusion of the moment but which was rooted in the frustrations borne of military-philosophical differences that had become evident in the conduct of the ground war.

At 1800 on 27 February, the senior commanders in Third Army believed they had about one more day's war before them.[2] Although the 101st Airborne Division had a plan to land a brigade on Iraqi lines of retreat along the Shatt al Arab northwest of Basrah (Engagement Area Thomas) on the 28th, there had never been a serious plan at theater level to send ground forces north of the Euphrates River, nor was there any intent to get U.S. forces tied down in fighting in the built-up areas of Basrah. With the Iraqis broken and the armored fist of VII Corps moving forward, there would be no more terrain to cover after another day's fighting. The major Iraqi lines of retreat beyond the Euphrates appeared to be within the grasp of U.S. forces, and these were the focus of attention. Because Basrah, on the south side of the Euphrates and Shatt al Arab, provided a natural haven of sorts, the decision not to fight there was a potential problem. But as the day-and-night interdiction of various choke points by both the Air Force and 101st Airborne Division attack helicopters had already shown, the problem was not beyond solution.

How to transition from offensive operations to war termination was another problem. There was concern, at least in Third Army, that Saddam, driven north of the Euphrates, still might not yield. Meantime, there was the problem of destroying the remaining Republican Guard Forces Command heavy division still believed to be in the field, the Hammurabi Division, and those other remnants of the Iraqi armored forces still on the coalition side of Basrah.[3]

In VII Corps, General Franks and his G3, Colonel Stan Cherrie, had to adjust the corps' deployment to the diminishing maneuver space. The 3d Armored Division, in the left center of the corps, was being pinched out of the attack. The two men also wanted to get the 1st Cavalry Division, the one fresh division left, into the fight to relieve the now tiring 1st Armored. The 1st Cavalry Division was now following the 1st Armored Division but was unable to pass through because of the intensity of combat in which "Old Ironsides" was involved with the RGFC Medina Division. Both the 1st Armored Division and 1st Cavalry were up against the boundary with XVIII Corps in the north, so the relieving division had insufficient maneuver space to go around the corps' left. Franks considered requesting attachment of the 24th Division to VII Corps so that he could envelop the remaining Iraqi forces, particularly the Hammurabi Division. But he knew such a request would merely occasion an argument with the

XVIII Corps, so he dismissed the idea and requested additional maneuver space to the north instead.[4]

The friendly fire incident that claimed the life of the 1st Armored Division's engineer had already demonstrated that intercorps boundaries were difficult enough to deal with even when they were fairly clear in advance. They were not easily changed. So VII Corps' request for more maneuver room was not likely to be promptly answered. From the standpoint of the army commander, the advance of the 24th Division down the river valley, already scheduled to begin at 0400 the following morning, was going to solve the problem of the Hammurabi Division anyway—unless it withdrew into Basrah. Before a decision was made on the VII Corps request, however, other matters intervened.

In order to arrange the battlefield for a final attack on the morning of the 28th, Franks called his major subordinate commanders at 1800 on the 27th to fix their positions long enough to reorder the corps.[5] The 1st Infantry Division, which by now had broken through the Republican Guard mass of maneuver, was moving almost due east. The division was in a classic exploitation and pursuit aimed at Objective Denver, whose seizure would block the Kuwait City-Basrah highway. The 1st Division's cavalry squadron, the 1st Squadron, 4th Cavalry, was already astride that road south of Safwan, at the intersection with Highway 8 and the Basrah-Kuwait City highway, already blocked farther to the south by the "Tiger Brigade."[6] (See map 13.)

Pursuit at night was not so easy as clever critics would imagine. The division's 1st Brigade had entered a patch of broken ground—called by veterans "the Valley of the Boogers"—infested with Iraqi infantry. There, units became intermingled and the risk of fratricide rose in the dark. The division's 2d Brigade, on the left, missed the valley and sped on by. In the 1st Brigade, the soft-skin support vehicles of the 2d Battalion of the 34th Armor actually passed the unit's combat vehicles in the dark and found themselves on the battalion's objective when the sun rose—surrounded by Iraqi tanks and alone.[7] The men who passed through the "Valley of the Boogers," including the combative Tom Rhame, will not be convinced that pursuit through occupied broken ground in the dark is an easy task, even in the face of a broken enemy.

The corps commander's intent was that the 1st Division would resume the attack at 0500 the morning of the 28th and, on order, turn to the north to attack toward Basrah, either alone or in conjunction

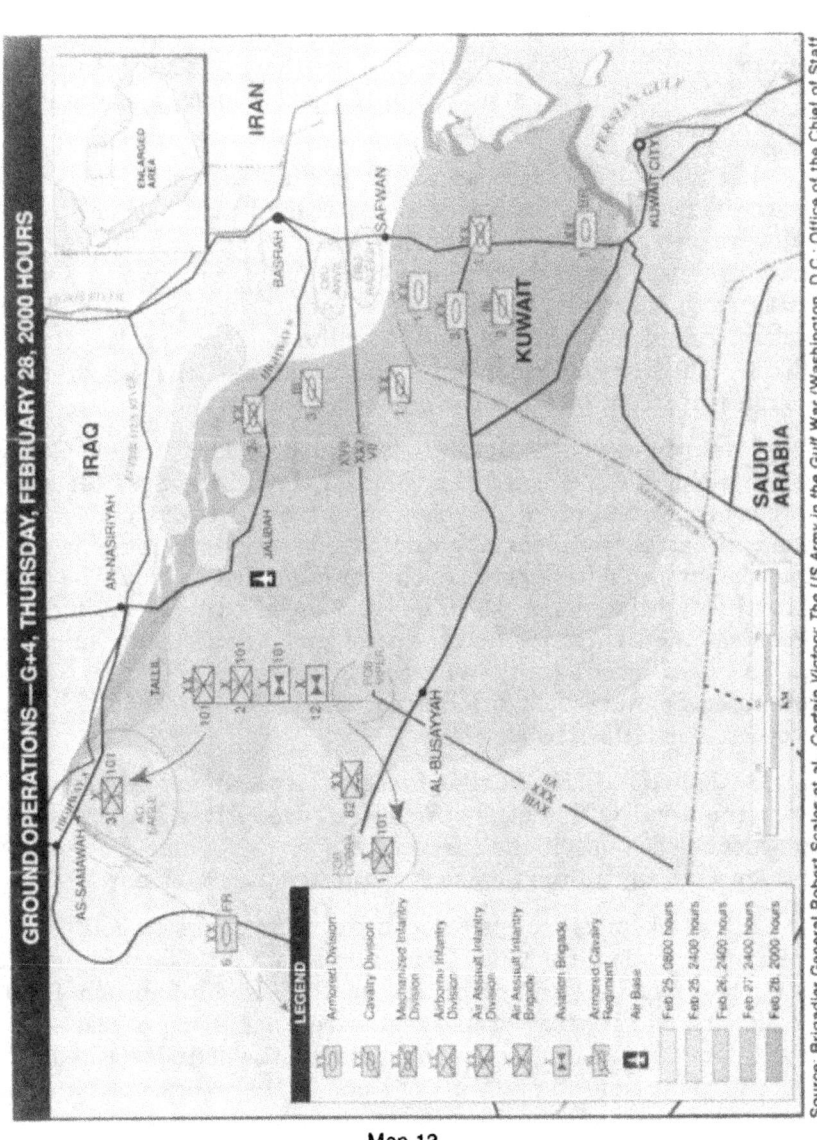

Map 13.

with the 1st U.K. Armored Division.[8] Though the VII Corps' staff journals record a call to that effect at about 2300 from the corps' G3, Colonel Cherrie, to the 1st Division's main CP, neither the division G3 nor division chief of staff have any memory of such a conversation. There is also no evidence of it in the available division staff journals. The division main CP had been left behind in the division's rapid advance and did not catch up until after the cessation of offensive actions. Its records for the period are incomplete. There is, consequently, insufficient documentary evidence to draw any firm conclusion about the fate of this message that, at 2300, was only an "on-order" mission that would require a subsequent execution order for implementation in any event.

The division's leaders were still looking eastward, toward the Basrah-Kuwait City highway and the coastal road beyond, as they quite properly would have in the absence of any order to the contrary. It is clear that Franks' intent for possible future actions had not been transmitted effectively to ensure it reached the one person whose full understanding was to be essential to the desired results, General Rhame. The division commander continued to focus his division's energies on execution of the last orders received.

Meanwhile, at 2100 (1300 Eastern Standard Time), General Schwarzkopf had conducted "The Mother of All Briefings."[9] It was, in fact, a declaration of victory. Although the CINC did indicate that armored battles were ongoing and that useful work remained to be done, he indicated in response to one question that he would be glad to stop the fighting when so ordered.[10] Interestingly enough, the *Washington Post* reported that the president "had seen only snippets of the televised briefing. . . ." According to the *Post*, General Powell recounted Schwarzkopf's briefing for the president. That led to the decision to halt the offensive.[11]

At 2230 (local), Schwarzkopf received a call from Powell speaking from the Oval Office of the White House. After indicating the president's wish to stop the offensive as soon as possible, Powell asked if there were any military reasons not to stop the attack now?[12]

Schwarzkopf called his component commanders to poll them on the same question. He called General Yeosock at 2300 and indicated that the "national command authority" (a euphemism for the president and secretary of defense) were considering a cease-fire at 0200Z (or 0500 local) the following morning, the 28th. He asked if that left sufficient time to get the word out to the troops on the cutting edge.[13] Yeosock informed the corps commanders and instructed the G3 to prepare an order to that effect.

Yeosock called Franks at VII Corps at 2310, the 27th, and indicated that the order was a warning order only, that the corps was authorized to use fires until 0500, that it should conduct no deep operations, and that the corps should be prepared to resume offensive operations on order. The emphasis was clearly on stopping the attacking forces in the field without exposing them, thereby, to enemy counterattack. The VII Corps wrote specific instructions for a cease-fire at 0500. By 0130 on the 28th, VII Corps forces had assumed postures of local security with an immediate mission of force protection.[14] Around 0200, ARCENT FRAGO 67 was published. Although it was titled "POTENTIAL TEMPORARY CEASE-FIRE," the content clearly seems to be an order for an 0500 temporary cease-fire. It was taken as such by both corps.[15]

Sometime between 2300 on the 27th and 0300 on the 28th, Powell called Schwarzkopf back and told the theater commander that the president intended to order the "cessation of offensive operations" for midnight Eastern Standard Time, 0800 local in Saudi Arabia: a 100-hour ground war. Negotiating a cease-fire would be left to the United Nations under whose authority the United States and the coalition acted. According to Schwarzkopf, Powell said that the conditions the president intended to set were to contain the stipulation that "Iraqis in the war zone must leave their equipment and walk north."[16] Schwarzkopf, at the urging of his chief of staff, Marine Corps Major General Robert Johnston, pointed out to the chairman that this would be impossible to enforce. "If we call this cease-fire," Schwarzkopf said, "we're going to see Republican Guard T-72s driving across pontoon bridges."[17] The decision in Washington was to accept that.

At 0300, Schwarzkopf called Yeosock to set the effective time for suspension of hostilities to 0800 local, three hours later than that noted earlier and announced to the corps in the ARCENT order.[18] The whole tone of the discussion at 0300 was in sharp contrast to that of Schwarzkopf's 2300 call. At 2300, the emphasis had been on force protection and separation of forces. Now, there seemed to be a frantic concern for inflicting the maximum possible damage on remaining enemy forces prior to the announced cessation of offensive actions five hours hence.[19] The goal was maximum destruction of enemy equipment. In addition, in discussing the arrangement of the battlefield at the "cessation," Schwarzkopf and Yeosock agreed to the assignment of a mission to secure a road junction just north of the Kuwaiti-Iraqi border near the town of Safwan.

At 0330, ARCENT published FRAGO 68, titled, "CONTINUE WITH OFFENSIVE OPERATIONS." This message changed the cease-fire time to 0800 and instructed subordinate commands to resume the offensive. The VII Corps was ordered to "attack in zone to destroy enemy armored vehicles and to seize the road junction vic. QU 622368 [north of Safwan]." The road junction was the sole terrain objective assigned by Third Army to VII Corps (though VII Corps had assigned terrain objectives to its divisions, e.g., Objective Denver).[20] Possession of the road junction would acquire wholly unanticipated importance within the next forty-eight hours. In light of later developments, and the importance Schwarzkopf places on the distinction, it is important to note as well that FRAGO 68 referred throughout to a cease-fire—four times in the coordinating instructions—specifically stating in the first subparagraph, "*cease-fire* commences 280500Z FEB 91 [emphasis added]."[21] Diplomatic distinctions did not carry very far from CENTCOM that night.

Franks' orders came by phone. The corps commander does not remember, and there is no evidence currently available to indicate whether he personally saw a copy of the written order before the "cessation of offensive actions," though it did get to the corps sometime that morning. The ARCENT liaison officer at the corps' main CP had a copy by 0455. He had received telephonic notice of its contents at 0350. The corps' TAC CP file contains a copy of the message without the dispatch time indicated. The corps' TAC CP file contains no cover sheet or date-time of receipt.[22]

Franks' actions that morning indicate that he did not fully understand that his mission with regard to the road junction in question was seizure rather than attack. In fact, the word most often used by VII Corps to address its actions later was "to interdict," not seize.[23] In light of the fact that VII Corps had been involved to this point in a force-oriented, rather than terrain-oriented, operation (no less that the 1st Infantry's Objective Denver would come close to accomplishing the same goal albeit fifteen or so miles to the south), such a misunderstanding is not surprising. This is particularly the case given the pressures of the moment (to restart a multidivision corps attack just believed halted). Viewed through the exhaustion of the leaders in the field, now beginning their fifth day of ground combat in abysmal weather, the orders themselves, to start again only to stop in five (or less) hours, must have been difficult to understand. By this point, Schwarzkopf seems like a man trying to drive an eighteen-wheeler truck with expectations of the responsiveness of a sports car. Not surprisingly, he did not get it—from either corps.

General Franks and Colonel Cherrie did try to move forces toward Safwan. Although the town would naturally have been in the sector of the 1st Armored Division, that division had just finished a long fight with two RGFC divisions and was still distant from the road junction. The 1st Infantry Division was closer, although a move to Safwan would require changing that division's boundary with the 1st Armored Division and changing the 1st Infantry Division's direction of attack (at least for some part of the division) by 90 degrees. By that time in the fight, the friction in the machine was simply too great to overcome in the time available.

At 0406, the VII Corps commander ordered his divisions to execute the missions assigned the night of the 27th with a line of departure time of 0600.[24] For the 1st Infantry Division, operating in ignorance of any instructions to the contrary, that meant continuing to attack to the east. The 11th Aviation Brigade was instructed to consider attacking the designated road junction with AH-64s. The choice of an aviation unit is consistent with the view that the mission was understood to be interdiction as opposed to seizure. The intention to launch the 11th Aviation Brigade against the road junction was reported to the 1st Infantry Division at 0502. In response, the 1st Infantry reported the location of their northernmost unit to corps at 0507 to avoid the possibility that the corps aviation unit would mistake them for retreating Iraqis. This concern led to cancellation of the 11th Brigade mission.[25]

At 0515, the corps added a new sector to the 1st Infantry Division zone. The intent was to form a small box, perpendicular to the current division orientation, that included the road junction and the northern extension of the Basrah-Kuwait City highway to the southern boundary of XVIII Corps, in which the 1st Infantry Division could take action against the road junction. This, too, seems to have been subject to confusion. The corps' journal records the instruction: "Danger 7 [General William Carter, the assistant division commander] given a sector 50 N/S grid line as western limit and 50 E/W grid line as their northern limit. Will go west of 50 N/S grid line [?]." The division staff journal reads, "Jayhawk 3 [Colonel Cherrie] told us to go out to 50 N/S grid line (Stay East of 50 N/S grid line)."[26] In the division journal, this message follows immediately an entry indicating that the division aviation unit had just been ordered to reconnoiter to the east of the division objective, to the coastal highway that intersected the Basrah-Kuwait City highway at the road junction in question to a point just short of the road junction itself.²⁷ General Carter has written that "the guidance from corps was to check the box east of the highway and interdict any escaping enemy—we found none—also to go north and look for enemy. . . . no mention was ever made in any order to seize the RJ [road junction] north of Safwan."²⁸ At 0520, the division was given priority in close air support.

While the 1st Infantry continued to report progress in their eastward movement, the corps evidently believed they were now oriented to the north. At 0533, the ARCENT mobile CP received a report from the VII Corps TAC that indicated that the 1st Infantry Division would be moving at 0530 to the road junction in question to establish a blocking position. This would not occur.²⁹ At 0555, the corps informed the 1st Armored Division on the left that the 1st Infantry Division was going to attack *to interdict* the highway and instructed the 1st Armored to clear all fires forward of Phase Line Kiwi (to the east) through the corps headquarters.³⁰

The 1st Infantry Division reported crossing its line of departure at 0545 and by 0615 reported closing on Objective Denver—its primary objective cutting the Basrah-Kuwait highway in the original sector. At 0626, the division declined additional aviation support (presumably from the 11th Aviation Brigade), believing, no doubt, that its own aviation brigade was equal to the reconnaissance-interdiction mission.³¹ There is no mention of the Safwan road junction as a specific terrain objective in messages to the 1st Division recorded in the corps' operations logs.

While all this was going on, the division commander was out of direct communications with his higher headquarters. General Rhame, who had been conducting an exploitation since breaking through the RGFC, commanded his division from a small command group built around two M1 tanks, in which he and his G3 were located with the forward brigades. Orders from the corps commander to the division commander had to be relayed through the division tactical command post.³² That is not to say that any error was introduced by the division TAC, rather to point out that conducting the sort of clarifying discussion that ensures fullness of understanding between commanders was not possible the morning of the 28th. Whatever was intended by ARCENT and the corps, the division focus remained to the east, getting across the Basrah-Kuwait highway south of Safwan (Objective Denver) in accordance with existing orders.

At 0500 on 28 February, Saudi time (2100, the 27th in Washington), while the commanders in the field attempted to restart their offensive, the president announced the "suspension of offensive combat operations" would occur at midnight Eastern Standard Time, 0800 in Baghdad.[33] In the desert, the ground offensive, once halted, was proving difficult to restart everywhere.

At 0723, a reported incident of fratricide (incorrectly reported it turned out) brought the action to a halt. The road to the designated road junction had been cut by troops of the 1st Infantry Division. The road junction, however, had not been occupied by ground forces, nor had Objective Anvil, an XVIII Corps objective dominating the same road complex farther north, been taken. The 24th Division only succeeded in firing an artillery preparation and launching attack helicopters toward the Basrah escape hatch. Initial reports to CENTCOM indicated the junction was secured when in fact it was not. The evidence of where the reports became garbled is inconclusive but would seem to have their origin in staff officers at corps or army failing to distinguish between an attack by aviation rather than an attack by ground troops, a significant difference.[34]

Immediate concern on the morning of the 28th, at all levels, was for locating all friendly forces and protecting the force from further losses. The status of the Safwan road junction at that point was a matter of detail, at least in ARCENT. Moreover, although it was clear by the morning of 1 March that the RGFC Hammurabi Division was in the Basrah pocket,[35] no move was made to prevent its withdrawal north of the river, something the coalition leadership could have ordered as a condition for continued suspension of offensive actions (in other words, a mutual freeze in place), and something the aviation assets of the CENTAF air armada, or even the 101st, could have enforced, as the latter had on the 27th when it interdicted area of operations (AO) Thomas.

Without such instructions, it was increasingly unlikely that the remaining Iraqi heavy forces would be destroyed, short of a willingness for the ground forces to engage in battle in the urban area of Basrah. And there is no evidence to date that the high command was willing to contemplate that at this point in the war. The fact was that, by the night of the 27th, the ARCENT attack was pushing the Iraqi heavy forces back on their remaining line of retreat as opposed to cutting them off from it. Of the forces on the ground, it appears that the 24th Division in the north (in XVIII Corps) was in the best position to cut the Iraqis off from Basrah. But the division had to negotiate the Rumayulah oil fields, which were then believed to be a greater obstacle than they turned out to be. In any event, the 24th had already slowed for refueling before resuming the attack—an attack not delivered due to the actions described above. The "Victory" Division had not intended to resume its advance until 0400 the following morning.[36] It did fire counterbattery fires throughout the night. The XVIII Corps, too, found getting off the mark difficult when the revised instructions arrived early on the morning of the 28th.

The VII Corps ground forces were effectively stopped in place by 0130 on the 28th. Although, strictly speaking, this anticipated the execution order from CENTCOM, the action must be viewed in light of the context in which these events occurred. The CINC's questions at 2300 indicated that the concern at the political level was for stopping the offensive and safeguarding U.S. forces. Schwarzkopf's speech made clear that the military objectives had largely been accomplished. Indeed, he would say as much in an interview with David Frost in March.[37] The Iraqi Army in Kuwait was clearly destroyed as a coherent force, whatever elements succeeded in withdrawing. The RGFC, if not annihilated, had suffered severe losses in manpower, equipment, and no doubt pride, and what remained intact was in full retreat and trapped between a water obstacle and a superior force, like Napoleon on the Berezina.

More Iraqis might have been killed, but it seems unlikely that any major formations would have been cut off. The destruction of an enemy army does not require killing every enemy soldier. This achievement is a moral as well as physical act and involves the imposition of will on a resisting opponent. That within days U.S. forces were able freely to impose an occupation of northern Iraq should be some evidence that the Iraqis knew themselves to be defeated and recognized the ability of the coalition forces to go where they pleased, at least on the Iraqi periphery. The hulks littering the battlefield were mute testament to the extent of their army's destruction. Indeed, VII Corps would destroy abandoned Iraqi equipment for the next eight weeks.[38]

The general objection, later, that some of the forces that did escape were used to defeat local insurrections, though correct, is another matter. The objection assumes significantly more could have been done to destroy those forces, but given the U.S. reluctance to fight inside Basrah, the case remains to be made. The argument mistakes the forces in the Kuwait theater of operations for the entire Iraqi Army. According to Schwarzkopf, much of the Republican Guard (presumably infantry divisions) had already fled north of the Euphrates.[39] Moreover, it is by no means clear that all the fleeing Iraqi soldiers took part on the government side of the insurrectionary activities. One cannot posit with assurance that, had the forces in the

Basrah pocket been destroyed, Saddam would not have triumphed against his domestic enemies anyway.

What Schwarzkopf seemed to be complaining about to Frost was being denied a few more hours to slaughter the fleeing Iraqis north of the Euphrates River, as if the hecatombs of southeastern Iraq were not adequate evidence of his victory.[40] Moreover, there seems to have been no impediment, if it had been felt necessary, to have ordered a freeze in place as the cost of the cessation and then to have placed the onus for its violation upon the enemy. In any event, such actions were the responsibility of Schwarzkopf and his superiors, not the men on the ground who were trying to figure out what a "suspension of offensive action," as opposed to a cease-fire, really meant.

The overthrow of the Iraqi government was never a coalition goal and, whatever its emotional preference, the United States was a partner in the coalition and supported the legitimacy of its endeavors.[41] The coalition goal, the liberation of Kuwait, had been achieved. There was no apparent or obvious successor to Saddam. It also seemed that little more was required to consolidate Saddam's Sunni power base in Baghdad than simultaneous risings of the Kurdish and Shiite minorities in northern and southern Iraq. Nor was anything more likely to discomfort America's Turkish and Saudi allies than the rebels' long-term success on their international borders.[42] Moreover, if U.S. forces were to be free to depart the theater soon, it was not in anyone's long-term interest to create a power vacuum in Baghdad that might require a prolonged U.S. presence. Unfortunately, the forces required to maintain a viable Iraqi state were also capable of continuing that state's more despicable methods of dealing with domestic political opponents. Debate over the consequences of the escape of some Iraqi units would follow later. During the night of 27–28 February, the chief consideration of commanders in the field was the safety of U.S. forces.

From the outset, U.S. operations were marked by a concern for casualties. Prewar simulations had indicated losses would be heavy, and for a variety of reasons, the military leadership did not look on that prospect with equanimity. Certainly commanders were conscious that they were responsible for the lives of their soldiers, who were not just cannon fodder but fellow citizens, the sons and daughters of the American people. They were also conscious that, in the volunteer Army built up over fifteen years, losses in men and materiel were largely irreplaceable. And as veterans of the Vietnam War and witnesses to the U.S. reaction to the losses in smaller incidents, like the Beirut bombing, U.S. leaders believed there was little tolerance for casualty reports on the home front, American or even Iraqi civilian ones. The public reaction to the bombing of the Baghdad bunker filled with civilians and the Scud attack on the U.S. billet in Dhahran only heightened this concern. In short, the Iraqi and American leaders were in some agreement as to the location of the U.S. moral center of gravity, and American political concern for avoiding unnecessary casualties was always present.

Throughout the war, concern for avoiding fratricide was especially high, increasingly so after Khafji and losses suffered during the counterreconnaissance battle prior to G-day. As the density of U.S. armored systems increased with the shrinkage of maneuver space, concern about the potential for fratricide became particularly acute.

When the initial instructions on the suspension of offensive operations went out at 2300 the night of the 27th, these emphasized the separation of forces and the protection of friendly units. Yeosock was conscious that orders to stop offensive operations would have to penetrate nine levels of command to be effective: from the CINC to ARCENT, the corps, divisions, brigades, battalions, companies, and finally to the men who issue all effective orders, the platoon leaders and sergeants on the firing line. That is rarely done quickly or cleanly, and now the soldiers and their leaders were at the end of four days of continuous advance and intermittent combat. It was likely recognition of these facts of military organization and human endurance that led the ARCENT and VII Corps commanders to assume, in the absence of other instructions, that the cease-fire would take effect at 0500 local, as originally indicated, and to issue orders for its execution early when no word came from CENTCOM. The alternative would have risked trying to get the word down the chain of command within a diminishing time period. Restarting an army halted after four days of battle was not likely to be accomplished in short order under any circumstances. Whatever the reason for the extension, the ground operations ended at 0800 on 28 February with Iraqi heavy forces still in the Basrah pocket undestroyed. The road junction in the vicinity of Safwan was unoccupied.

On the morning of the 28th, after the suspension of offensive actions, the first priority was organization of the battlefield. This was a particularly complex task, as armored warfare, especially in the desert, involves by-passing pockets of enemy forces. Armed forces of both armies were extensively intermingled, and because the communications systems of the Iraqi Army had been disrupted, it was not at all clear that the by-passed enemy would know of the new situation.

On the allied side, there were equal concerns for force protection and for establishing the continuity of coalition lines. Obtaining guidance on rules of engagement that squad leaders and soldiers could understand became an important issue. Initial guidance from the ARCENT commander was that continuity of friendly lines should be established. "If the Iraqis do not cooperate," he directed: "lay siege to them. Destroy them if they fire on us."[43] In a call to the commander of VII Corps at about 1200, Yeosock satisfied himself that this was being done. Following the daily component commanders meeting with Schwarzkopf at 1900, Yeosock instructed the G3 that the top priority was safety and security of the force.[44] (See map 14.)

At 2100, Yeosock received a call from Major General Robert B. Johnston, the CENTCOM chief of staff, who requested recommendations for a meeting site where the coalition commanders could hold cease-fire talks with the Iraqi military commanders. The ARCENT commander's desire was to hold such talks in Iraq and as far north as possible. He nominated three sites: Shaibah, near Basrah; Jalibah, on the Euphrates; and some point near the causeway across Lake Hammar and the Euphrates, one of the two remaining lines of retreat for the Iraqi forces (the other being the Basrah pocket). Shaibah was in Iraqi hands; Jalibah, occupied by U.S. forces; and the ground around the causeway, a no man's land that would be the site of a major engagement by the 24th Division on 2 March. Following these discussions, Yeosock believed the site would likely be Jalibah, and instructions were issued to the XVIII Corps to prepare the site.[45] He then left his office for his quarters. At 2345 (1545 Eastern Standard Time), the president announced the Iraqis had accepted the proposal to hold talks and the conditions required to do so. The time and place were not announced.[46]

Meanwhile, Schwarzkopf was trying to prepare a message for the chairman of the Joint Chiefs of Staff outlining his intentions for the cease-fire talks. The site was a key element and time was of the essence. Sometime after Yeosock arrived at his quarters, he called Schwarzkopf to inform him that Jalibah was not a good site because of the amount of unexploded ordnance spread around it. At that point, Safwan became the site of choice. This required recalling the message to the chairman and did not leave Schwarzkopf in the best humor. His temper would soon get worse.[47] Thus began, perhaps, the most painful and least creditable period for the Desert Storm high command, one

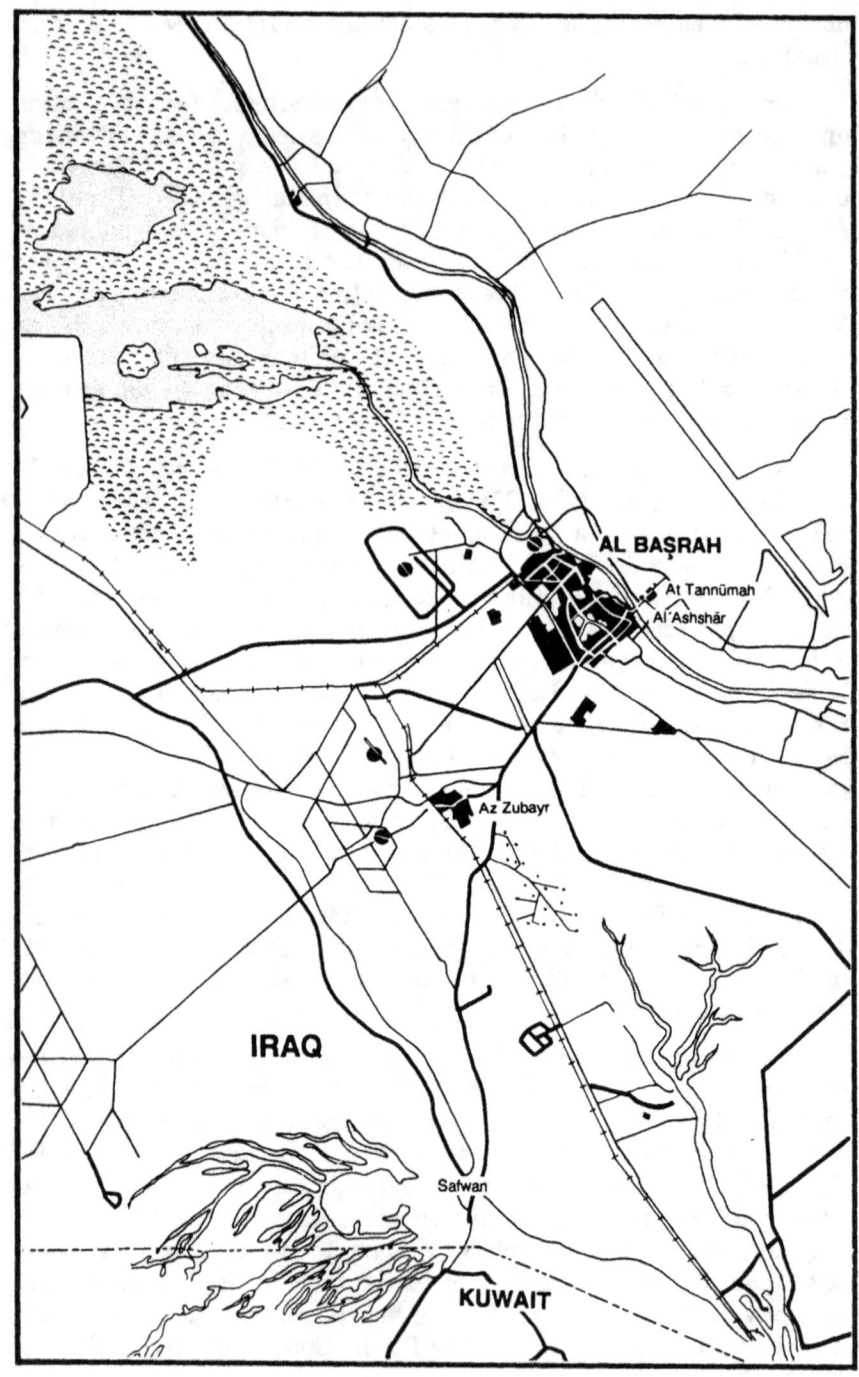

Map 14. Basrah

which, like most errors of the high command, would be redeemed by the soldiers on the ground.

Sometime thereafter but prior to midnight, ARCENT was informed that the meetings would be held at 0500Z (0800 local) on 2 March, near Safwan just north of the Iraqi-Kuwaiti border. ARCENT sent a warning order to VII Corps concerning the talks. The sites proposed included the road intersection that had been the sole terrain objective assigned VII Corps at the resumption of hostilities the night before; the airfield; and the old Iraqi custom post located nearby.[48] VII Corps was told to recommend a better site if they had one. The site was to be in Iraq, preferably with a large open building or series of buildings. Administrative requirements for the conduct of the meeting were also included.

Sometime after 0125 and prior to 0300, Yeosock called Franks and asked if the 1st Infantry Division could determine if the airfield near Safwan was secure for use as the conference site. This was the first time that the airfield itself had assumed any particular importance for the corps, and the duty log of the tactical command post reported that the "1st ID has not had eyes on airfield. Area in vicinity has extensive damage to personnel & equipment."[49] This report made its way up the chain of command and led to an explosion at CENTCOM.

Meanwhile, at 0308, Franks ordered the division to reconnoiter the site and *not to become decisively engaged*. This order was almost immediately modified (at 0320) in accordance with guidance from Yeosock, who ordered the search at first light. Yeosock had called General Rhame and General Carter direct, as he would regularly throughout the following day, to check on the status of what was being done. At 0430, Franks called Rhame and stated his intent. The tactical command post log records: "Intent is do not take any casualties. Unopposed move. No casualties. If you run into enemy forces, then stop and report to CG VII Corps." Interestingly enough, the VII Corps log indicates that Schwarzkopf's permission would be required to initiate hostilities.[50]

The tenor of the discussion among the senior officers is evident from the question posed Rhame by the corps commander. Franks asked Rhame "if the mission ever got to him to *interdict* road junction at QU 622370? If not, why not? Was there any traffic through that road junction? Did you have any eyes north of the northern limit from 1-4 Cav?"[51] Rhame had just gotten to sleep after 100 continuous hours of battle. His division had conducted the corps' main attack on G-day, advanced as corps reserve, passed through the 2d Armored Cavalry Regiment at night on the 26th while in contact, battled through the Iraqi armored screen, and finished as the eastern-most U.S. unit in Schwarzkopf's great wheel, situated across the major south-north line of retreat. He was now caught in a "Who shot John?" (meaningless blame fixing) exercise to appease an irate theater commander. Rhame was understandably nonplused.

At the other end of the chain of command, Schwarzkopf's dark side was in full control as he raged at Yeosock that his orders had been willfully disobeyed. In his memoir, Schwarzkopf complains not only about the misinformation that he unquestionably received but also about the importance of the entire complex to his control of by-passed Iraqi forces as well as a cache of Scuds nearby. Apparently, when he spoke to Yeosock (or perhaps because he did so at 0300) the morning of the 28th, a number of his concerns had not then been clear to the army commander. Schwarzkopf now required from the two commanders who had delivered the victory on the ground at an unbelievably low cost a written account of their actions with regard to failing to secure an obscure road junction in southeastern Iraq, the importance of which had apparently only become vital after offensive operations were halted by the CINC's commander in chief.[52]

In judging the conduct of events for the next fifteen hours, it is necessary to remember that the principals were all exhausted after the events of the preceding four days. Moreover, Yeosock, just returned, perhaps prematurely, from surgery in Germany, was visibly operating at less than his full physical powers. All three commanders were powerful men with heavy responsibilities. They now found themselves confronting the friction and fog of war in a most sensitive problem that seemed, at the time, to threaten the accomplishments of the past four days, achievements toward which they had invested the greatest part of their professional life and for which they had risked, and in some cases lost, the lives of their men. There was understandable fear that what seemed to be the success that would redeem the Army's post-Vietnam War reputation might now be compromised by a postoperational embarrassment sure to be blown up in the media. Implicit in Schwarzkopf's response was the threat of unwarranted public disgrace, a threat that weighed heavily on all concerned.

The units of the 1st Division upon which the task of securing the airfield and road junction fell were the 1st Squadron, 4th Cavalry, commanded by Lieutenant Colonel Robert Wilson, and the 2d Brigade, 1st Infantry Division, commanded by Colonel Anthony A. Moreno. Wilson received his mission from Rhame at 0240 the morning of 1

March at his position on the Basrah-Kuwait City road. The actual line of departure time was finally 0615. The squadron occupied the airfield unopposed but, while pushing north to secure the area, ran into an Iraqi unit, apparently an armored brigade of the Republican Guard Forces Command, in defensive positions.

About 0900, an Iraqi colonel arrived on the scene to ask why the Americans were in Iraq. The squadron officers—first, the troop commander of A Troop, Captain Ken Pope, then, the squadron commander—told the colonel he and his troops would have to leave the site. The colonel responded he could not do so without orders and departed to consult with his commanders. He returned at 1020 and stated that he still did not have orders to leave. He was told that either he had to leave or he would be attacked by coalition air forces. When General Carter arrived by helicopter at 1100 to see what was going on, the Iraqis had still not departed. The Iraqi commander finally relented and ordered his troops out of the area. By 1200, most of the Iraqis in the squadron sector were withdrawing toward Basrah.[53]

The division had ordered the 2d Brigade to join the cavalrymen at the airfield. That meant moving up the road to Basrah, through Safwan, a movement that proved more difficult than the clearing of the airfield. The brigade commander notified his task force commanders to prepare to move north to assist in securing the airfield and city of Safwan at about 0630 the morning of 1 March. Units started moving within thirty minutes. While most of the brigade moved overland, as had the cavalry squadron, the 4th Battalion, 5th Artillery, moved north up the road. At Safwan, they found their way blocked by an Iraqi infantry company from Tikrit, Saddam Hussein's home town. The Iraqis had no intention of moving and, indeed, indicated they would resist if the U.S. forces tried to move farther north.[54]

Colonel Moreno arrived at the site at 1100 and asked for a senior Iraqi officer to come speak to him. Two Iraqi generals and a civilian official arrived at about 1230 and read a prepared statement to Colonel Moreno. The statement indicated that Iraq wanted to meet in Geneva and asked who the United States would send as a representative. Moreno explained his mission was to secure the town and airfield for the negotiations. The Iraqis responded that they needed instructions from Baghdad and departed.[55] During the day, both General Carter and General Rhame would arrive to oversee what was being done, but Colonel Moreno would conduct all discussions with the Iraqis, largely to avoid requiring further delay should the Iraqis feel obliged to raise the rank of their "front man."[56]

While the contretemps took place in the vicinity of Safwan, the pressure continued on Third Army. Schwarzkopf had ordered Yeosock to destroy radars on a hill overlooking the airfield but, cognizant of the sensitivity of the situation on the ground, Yeosock decided to disobey that order. At 1045, he reported the situation as he knew it to General Waller, the deputy commander in chief, and requested new instructions. Waller also had orders from Schwarzkopf, who was sleeping, that he (Schwarzkopf) not be disturbed. Waller declined to disobey these orders.[57] At 1105, Yeosock called the CENTCOM chief of staff and repeated his request.

At 1115, Yeosock was informed that Brigadier General William Carter, the assistant division commander of the 1st Division, was en route to the airfield. Meanwhile, the Iraqis were observing the cessation of hostilities. At 1215, the ARCENT commander provided an update to the CINC. Schwarzkopf directed that the Iraqis were to withdraw from the area and instructed Yeosock to look for an alternative site in Iraq, in the XVIII Corps area. This was done soon after.[58]

At 1336, the CINC and ARCENT commanders again discussed the situation. Schwarzkopf's guidance was that, if the Iraqi brigade would not withdraw as requested, ARCENT was "to commit overwhelming force to surround him, use attack helicopters, talk to him, capture him if he refuses to withdraw. *If he attacks you, then return fire is permitted.*"[59] Schwarzkopf indicated to Yeosock that this was ordered by General Powell, who was upset that the road junction had not been taken, because the contrary had been reported to the White House. Moving the talks to an alternate site now was out of the question.

Schwarzkopf acknowledged the situation was delicate but insisted that the Iraqis had to be moved and, indeed, said he would move them himself if necessary. He reiterated that all this was to be done without firing a shot. Yeosock restated his mission to the CINC as he understood it: "My mission is to go into the Sawarah [sic] Airfield with overwhelming combat power; to surround the Iraqi forces and to have the Iraqi forces withdraw or be captured and to do so without the use of offensive operations."[60]

Yeosock passed the mission to Rhame, largely as indicated above. Rhame has indicated that, in discussing the mission, he was told to give the Iraqis an ultimatum to move or die by 1600. There was no doubt in his mind that the ultimatum was genuine.[61] At 1415, he instructed Colonel Moreno to tell the Iraqis that he would attack at 1600 if they had not moved.[62] Moreno repositioned his forces to constitute a visible threat and delivered the ultimatum when the Iraqi officials returned at 1500. The Iraqi commander requested a twenty-minute extension, which Moreno granted. At 1620, the 2d Brigade forces moved forward from two directions and occupied the town behind the withdrawing Iraqis.[63]

At 1650, Rhame reported to Yeosock that the airfield was secure with a five kilometer zone cleared around it. A cordon was being established along the access road, and the route from Kuwait was being cleared. Efforts now turned to setting up the negotiation site in accordance with the CINC's guidance.[64] The meeting was ultimately delayed until 3 March due to undisclosed "technical difficulties."[65]

The incident at Safwan that Yeosock referred to later as his greatest challenge in the war was essentially over by 1847 the night of 1 March. The 1st Squadron, 4th Cavalry, and 2d Brigade had achieved their mission by pluck and face, without losing lives, U.S. or Iraqi. Only the humiliation of defending their earlier actions in writing against the charge of willful disobedience remained for the corps and army commanders. This was done that night. Franks' response was delivered the following day.[66]

That night, after the evening CINC's conference, Yeosock brought back a list of tasks ARCENT would have to accomplish to support the cease-fire conference. He assembled his staff and personally worked through the night to see that the assigned and implied tasks were done. Among these was the drawing of a line of demarcation along which the forces could be separated. Yeosock established the line himself on a 1:50,000 map sheet that filled a wall in the ARCENT headquarters. He sent the proposed line to CENTCOM the following morning for use in the cease-fire talks. It would not take effect until after the meeting on 3 March, too late to avoid one more battle, brought on largely by the fog inherent in stopping armored warfare short.[67]

The incident at Safwan was the result not of willful disobedience but of bad reporting and the difficulty that higher headquarters had in determining just what "ground truth" looked like in detail even hours after the cessation of the offensive. Ironically, Schwarzkopf's scrupulous use of the chain of command, rather than calling division commanders directly (as he could have) to see what was really happening on the ground, probably added to the confusion and subsequent frustration. In the end, like the French soldiers in the novel *Paths of Glory*, the 1st Division was sent "to take with bayonets what a G.H.Q. ink-slinger already inadvertently captured at the point of his pen!"[68]

Events were indicative of the larger problem of friction in war. The heat of Schwarzkopf's response must be viewed not only in light of the immediate pressure on him to work out the details of the cease-fire talks—all of which required clearance from Washington—but also in the context of an estrangement between Central Command and ARCENT and VII Corps, at the root of which lay differing visions of armored warfare. The road junction near Safwan was not captured because at each echelon of command, from theater to division, the situation on the night of the 27th was understood differently. Because each commander understood the context differently, orders were misunderstood. And since orders were frequently passed orally, rather than in writing, execution depended on the understanding achieved, not necessarily on what was intended.

What was not getting transmitted was the commander's intent. At ARCENT, the commander had seen the CINC's press conference on CNN and understood the explanation of the chairman's questions in that light. At VII Corps, operations were slowed anyway as the corps prepared for the next day's attack, and given the apparent intent to stop the offensive, there seemed no immediate reason to begin new operations that were unlikely to be completed by 0500. The 1st Division was "in the clear," headed east, and the commander, in his tank near the lead brigades, was looking eastward not north to Basrah. That he received his instructions through a relay seems to have filtered out much of the commander's intent as well. Once halted and told to protect the force after four days of attack, the fighting units were unlikely to be postured, physically or psychologically, for immediate resumption of the offensive. Furthermore, the distinction between a cessation of hostilities and a cease-fire, which is so important at theater and national level, did not mean much at the level of company and platoon, where such things must ultimately be sorted out. Moreover, the requirement to obtain the CINC's permission before engaging Iraqis at Safwan only confirmed the view already spreading that there was a cease-fire, albeit a temporary one.

In an interesting commentary on fatigue that seems relevant to this experience, Douglas Southall Freeman notes that, during the American Civil War, "in the Army of Northern Virginia the men could stand almost anything for four days, but the fifth day in almost every instance they would crack." When judging the apparent unraveling of tight control on the night of 27–28 February by men who had had little rest for four days of movement and combat, one may well remember Freeman's warning: "Beware of the fifth day. . . ."[69] Interestingly enough, Major General Rupert Smith of the 1st U.K. Armored Division began issuing written, rather than oral, orders to avoid confusion due to fatigue on the part of sender and receiver.[70]

At higher headquarters in the early morning hours of the 28th, the road junction must have appeared very close. However, to reorient the thinking of the tactical commanders, especially given the fatigue of the moment, some indication of the value of holding that point should have been transmitted along with the mission. This does not seem to have been done. The obvious value of holding the point on the night of the 27th was that the road junction cut the Basrah-Kuwait highway and the coastal highway. But the first highway had already been cut, and as no large enemy presence on either road was evident when aviation forces were finally sent east and north, the tactical commander might have believed he had accomplished the ARCENT's intent. Moreover, had another site been selected for the cease-fire talks, in all probability no one would have given a second thought to the road junction, which had been assigned to VII Corps as an objective, or to the airfield and town, which never had.

The cessation of offensive actions lasted from 0800 (Saudi time) on 28 February until the morning of 3 March when the two sides met to establish the terms of a military cease-fire. The ambiguity of this situation also led to a major incident in the zone of the 24th Division on 2 March, an engagement in which the division, on the authority of the division commander, and in the name of force protection, advanced to close one of the Iraqi lines of withdrawal to the north side of the Euphrates River and, in the process, destroyed an Iraqi armored force moving to safety across the division's front.

At the declared cessation of offensive operations, the 24th Division reported it was deployed along Phase Line Axe, some twenty to thirty kilometers east of a causeway across Lake Hammar, which served as one of five Iraqi lines of withdrawal out of the ARCENT encirclement.[71] During the 28th, the division reported pushing out a security zone to Phase Line Knife, ten or so additional kilometers to the east of the division but still west of the causeway. The move was apparently made to secure the site of a downed 1st Division UH-60 helicopter in which ten U.S. service members had died.[72] That put the division's security element within ten kilometers of the causeway.

The Iraqi behavior at Safwan, treating with, rather than engaging, U.S. forces, demonstrated that some Iraqi forces in the north were aware of President Bush's declaration of a cessation of offensive operations. While waiting for the convening of cease-fire talks, the Iraqis continued to withdraw their forces in that area, where they were not cut off by coalition forces.[73]

Until the meeting at Safwan on the 3d, there was no agreed on line of separation between the forces nor any agreed on principles to prevent one side or the other from running into its enemy. Because the 24th Division sat astride Highway 8, which runs from Basrah to the northeast, south of the Euphrates, it blocked the only major alternate line of withdrawal available to the Iraqi forces in the Basrah pocket. Rules of engagement passed to the division by XVIII Corps on 1 March directed that

> Enemy personnel will not be allowed to depart KTO.
>
> They will be collected and processed as EPW.
>
> Commanders are authorized to take any measure necessary to protect installations, aircraft, units or personnel from enemy attack or *imminent attack*. Iraqi forces are still considered hostile. Wartime ROE are still in effect with the following exceptions.
>
> No offensive actions will be executed without prior approval of CDR XVIII ABN Corps
>
> If an enemy vehicle approaches with its turret turned opposite the direction of travel, the enemy vehicle will be considered indicating a non-hostile intent. If these conditions are not present, the vehicle will be considered having a hostile intent. *In either case*, all attempts will be made to allow the occupants of the vehicle to surrender before U.S. Forces will take hostile measures.
>
> Roadblocks are authorized to prevent the escape of enemy personnel and vehicles.[74]

The limitation on offensive actions would seem to imply that the prevention of escape was to be limited to those areas under friendly control. What constituted friendly control, however, was itself ambiguous.

Forces under command of the 24th Division had reported some minor incidents of combat after the announced cessation of offensive operations on the 28th. The 3d Armored Cavalry Regiment, acting under division command on the 28th, had been forced to fight its way forward to secure the site of the downed 1st Division helicopter. The regimental fight against an Iraqi tank company and artillery battery lasted from about 0930 to 1530 on the 28th. In another incident the same day, two bus loads of Iraqi soldiers drove into a roadblock established by the 2d Battalion, 7th Infantry. Soldiers in the first bus surrendered. Those in the second opened fire. U.S. soldiers returned the fire, killing six Iraqis, wounding seven, and taking nine prisoners.[75]

These actions were typical of events throughout the ARCENT sector, where isolated Iraqi forces ran into U.S. forces or resisted capture by U.S. units imposing order on the areas by-passed in the coalition advance. In many cases, captured Iraqis expressed surprise that coalition forces were even in southeastern Iraq. Still, CENTCOM expressed concern about the report that the two buses had been destroyed, asking if all occupants were male and why, and if only passengers in one bus had fired, why were the two destroyed.[76] The tenor of the questions indicates someone at higher headquarters expected greater than normal discrimination in the use of force in such matters. Against this, of course, was the guidance quoted above, not to let Iraqis get away.

The incident on 2 March was somewhat different, certainly in scale and also in the questions it appeared to raise about the extent to which the president's guidance to cease offensive operations was being observed by forces in the field. At 012207, the 24th Division reported to the corps' tactical operations center (TOC) that it was "moving forward in zone" to a line (QU15 N.S. line) short of the causeway road complex "looking for abandoned equipment." According to the entry in the corps' main log, the troops were to adhere to General Luck's guidance, which was to "Remind them not to get into a fight."[77] According to the division G3, Lieutenant Colonel Pat Lamar, the division believed it was adhering to guidance about clearing the division zone to the line of advance at the cease-fire because the division had reconnaissance elements beyond the causeway.[78] But 1st Brigade logs suggest, to the contrary, that division and brigade reconnaissance elements were moving into the causeway area the morning of the 2d. The order to the battalions of the 24th Division's 1st Brigade the morning of the 2d indicated that the brigade was to occupy the fifteen north-south grid line (west of the causeway) with platoon-size elements from each battalion task force, then pass the 2d Squadron, 4th Cavalry, screen line forward. The order addressed only the clearing of the area west of the fifteen north-south grid line. The order stressed safety and directed that "Approaching enemy who refuse to surrender will be killed." It also relayed the division commander's intent: "CG's INTENT: PROTECT FORCE, AWAIT RESULTS OF NEGOTIATIONS,

MAINTAIN CBT PWR, *DO NOT DRAW FIRE IF WE RESPOND TO FIRE DO SO WITH OVERWHELMING VIOLENCE* [emphasis added]."[79] As events developed it would prove difficult to advance (move east) and not draw fire.

At ARCENT, attention seems to have been focused on the location of the main line of resistance some distance to the west. ARCENT FRAGO 68 addressed destruction of "by-passed enemy equipment," and General Arnold had clarified the order to XVIII Corps, speaking of "going back" to destroy everything in the zone until 0800.[80]

According to the division's reports, the incident itself began at about 0720 when the 1st Brigade, 24th Division, on the left side of the division zone across Highway 8, observed forty Iraqi vehicles moving west into the division security zone.[81] Later, General McCaffrey would speculate that the column missed its right turn to bring it onto the causeway and blundered into the division there to the west.[82] The 1st Brigade's duty log indicates that the causeway was blocked and that the enemy column tried to turn back on itself, producing an apparently aimless milling around in front of the U.S. forces.[83]

At 0725, the divisional air cavalry was ordered to engage the Iraqi forces if the vehicles continued into the 24th's sector. At about 0800, the brigade attempted to "encourage the Iraqi forces to change direction and surrender. When U.S. troops were engaged by sagger and other direct fire weapons from trail enemy forces . . . ," the brigade returned the fire. According to a report submitted to ARCENT by Brigadier General Scott, the assistant division commander of the 24th, the action had opened at 0809 when the brigade reported that Iraqis had fired an RPG (rocket-propelled grenade) at them. At 0815, there were reports of T-72s moving west on heavy equipment transporters. At 0817, Task Force 2-7 Infantry reported receiving direct fire and, at 0821, destroying two T-72s.[84] At 0855, XVIII Corps reported to ARCENT that six T-72s, two T-55s, four BMPs, and two BRDMs had been destroyed by C Company, 2-7 Infantry.[85] The enemy was reported to have turned north.

After the first engagement, about 0925, McCaffrey concluded that the enemy intended to regain contact with division forces and, at 0940, ordered an AH-64 attack helicopter company to attack the enemy force. Later, a second attack helicopter company was committed. Using two infantry battalion task forces to block enemy forces moving west, an armored battalion task force, the 4-64th Armor, was maneuvered to the south (the rear of the enemy column moving north across the causeway) then swept north.[86] At 1407, a final damage assessment was received by ARCENT. It listed destruction of eighty-one Iraqi tanks, ninety-five armored personnel carriers, eight BRDMs, five artillery tubes, two BM21s, eleven FROG launchers, and twenty-three trucks.[87] The division moved its security zone forward another ten kilometers, far enough to control the causeway line of withdrawal.

The picture at company level was understandably a little different. C Company, 2d Battalion, 7th Infantry, was the company of the 24th Division, 1st Brigade, that was advancing down Highway 8 on 27 February on the division's left (northern) flank. The company commander, Captain Richard Averna, has indicated that he did not receive notice of revised rules of engagement until early the morning of 2 March.[88] From the morning of the 28th until around noon on 1 March, Captain Averna's company occupied a road block on Highway 8 around fifteen to twenty kilometers from the causeway exit. Around noon on 1 March, his battalion was ordered to advance and clear to their front. C Company advanced around noon and, from 1200 to 2100, fought a series of minor skirmishes in which they captured two tanks and destroyed a platoon of air defense 37-mm guns. The following morning (2 March), they were ordered to advance again. The rules of engagement now (for the first time, according to Averna) were that C Company was not to fire unless fired upon.[89]

C Company's advance began at 0530. Almost at once, one of the C Company platoons captured two T-72s and a BMP (Russian-design infantry fighting vehicle) parked along the road. Around 0615, the 3d Battalion, 7th Infantry, to the north reported a large number of vehicles moving along the road to the north across the causeway. The same movement was reported by C Company and D Company, 2d Battalion. The response by the commander of the 2d Battalion was to move forward to make contact but not to fire unless fired upon. Once the enemy was identified, the battalion commander denied a request to open fire. Then he permitted fire by artillery only, reportedly as a means to cause the Iraqis to surrender.[90]

While C Company waited for the artillery fire, the 3d Platoon ran into a squad-sized element of a BMP and a BMD in a defensive position with seven dismounted infantry. The Iraqis' dismounted infantry engaged with RPGs, and their armored carriers moved out to engage with SAGGER antitank weapons. With that, the 3d Platoon engaged and sent dismounted troops to seize the trench line. Two T-72 tanks, probably attracted by the developing engagement approached from the east rather than turning north along the causeway road. C Company massed its fires on the road junction of Highway 8 and the causeway access road. The artillery requested earlier finally arrived, and at the end of ten minutes, six T-72s, two T-55s, and ten BMPs were destroyed, principally by direct fire. Simultaneously, the companies to the north engaged the forces retreating over the causeway, and then attack helicopter units began to work the highway. At around 0930, C Company was ordered to capture the road junction and, supported by D Company, it did. Thereafter, the 64th Armor passed through and continued the attack to the north, killing whatever was left on the access road to the causeway. No U.S. losses were recorded in C Company that day.

The destruction of over 200 enemy vehicles, with a loss of only one U.S. tank (when an enemy tank next to it exploded) and one U.S. soldier wounded, was no small affair, and from the description given from the various reports, it is hard to resist the conclusion that the local division commander had done more than limit himself to defensive actions in the engagements in question. The facts are, however, that the rules of engagement passed to commanders for the period of cessation of offensive operations did not anticipate the situation that confronted the 24th Division—a threat of a collision with major enemy forces. There seems little question that the initial response by C Company was warranted, and the results of the C Company fight were not disproportional. The company was directly threatened, was fired upon, and took appropriate action.

It is the subsequent brigade attack on forces moving to the north that seems somewhat disproportional, but here one must keep in mind the position in which the commander on the ground found himself. He was confronted by a major enemy formation moving close enough to his own lines that, by its size and proximity, it represented a clear *potential* threat. Moreover, he had been fired upon by one force already, and he could only guess at the intentions of the main body in front of him. The choice he had to make was to await events and risk subjecting his force to a coordinated attack or preempt the threat by using his superior mobility and tactical vision of the battlefield. Once begun, the attack was bound to run its course. The disproportional effects were not markedly different from those in every other engagement in Desert Storm and, once battle was joined, were probably inevitable unless extraordinary restraint was practiced.

In judging the choice made, it is well to remember the guidance provided by the ARCENT commander, guidance that presumably reflected that of the theater commander. The guidance from Yeosock was that "War is not over; we have suspended offensive operations pending talks. This is not a cease fire. Must be prepared to resume offensive operations. COMUSARCENT's first priority is the safety and security of the force."91 By that standard, the choice made by General McCaffrey at the causeway seems capable of justification.

The remaining question, then, involves the justification for the 24th Infantry Division's presence on the causeway at all. Was this a defensive or offensive action? In fact, it was both. From the standpoint of the Iraqis firing at Captain Averna's Bradleys, it was the Iraqis who were defending themselves against an immediate threat; Captain Averna's troops, by their advance, were being offensive. On the other hand, to protect a force on a mechanized battlefield, it is essential to maintain contact with the enemy or to restore contact if it has been lost. In that light, McCaffrey's action that led to the offensive against the Iraqi troops at the crossroad was defensive and the Iraqi advance to the west inherently hostile. Such questions on the battlefield are pure sophistry. This engagement was the consequence of the inherent difficulty of separating intermingled forces where no terms of reference have as yet been agreed upon or dictated. The situation was highly unstable, and the weaker side paid the price for the ambiguity.

In his magisterial work on Clausewitz' treatise, *On War*, the late Professor Raymond Aron conducted a lengthy discourse on the identification by Hans Delbrück of two forms of strategy in Clausewitz' writings. These are (1) a strategy of annihilation (*Vernichtungsstrategie*) or overthrow (*Niederwerfesstrategie*) and (2) a strategy of attrition (or exhaustion) (*Ermattungsstrategie*).92 These strategies differ not only in the nature of the military objectives each requires but also in the kind of process that provides for the resolution of the political issues that caused the conflicts to begin with. In the first case, resolution comes about as a result of the acceptance, by one side, of the dictated terms of the other—because the former has no other recourse. In the latter, resolution is produced by negotiations based upon an economic calculation that the cost of doing otherwise would be excessive.93

In the Gulf War, the national strategy was one of attrition or exhaustion carried out by political and economic means. Within this comprehensive strategy, military operations played a significant part and, in so far as freeing Kuwait, they were decisive. The military overthrow of Iraq was never contemplated by the coalition, although Saddam's conduct of the war left his country extraordinarily dependent on the coalition's lack of extreme intent for its continued survival after 28 February. By locating most of his army in Kuwait, Saddam made it his stake in the contest, and no doubt to his surprise, he lost his wager to a military operational strategy of annihilation. Nonetheless, because of the nature of the national and coalition strategy, the final resolution of the conflict did not come with the destruction of the Iraqi Army. Indeed, as of this writing, the economic blockade continues, and Iraqi compliance with the United Nations' resolutions is negotiated in council chambers, on CNN, and in parking lots outside Iraqi nuclear facilities.

Of the two events that have been the subject of this chapter, the first, the incidents at Safwan, are simply indicative of confusion and haste. The Iraqis appeared to have had better control over their forces around Safwan than the allies expected and, with that control, the possibility of unintended conflict was probably less than it appeared. Of course, there was no way for the combatants to know that, and as the issue was made highly personal by Schwarzkopf, Safwan probably remains the more painful of the two.

The paradox is that the events of 2 March at the causeway seem to have raised so little concern at the time, locally or politically. Later, someone was concerned enough about them that an investigation was conducted by the Army, but nothing visible seems to have come of it, perhaps because the ambiguity of the instructions to the forces on the ground would have made any disciplinary action highly dubious. In retrospect, the act may well have added to the pressure on the Iraqis to comply with the proffered cease-fire terms. In short, the destruction of the Iraqi column may have met the coalition needs of the moment.

It is reasonable to believe that the information about the initiation of the action on 2 March, which came to the division commander by radio from troops in contact, may not have been precise in addressing the circumstances under which the combat began or was effectively ended before the sweep north of the 64th Armored. Experience tells one it probably was not. Moreover, a judgment by Captain Averna that most of the killing was done by the two-battalion fixing force in a very short time may also be correct. One can continue to be troubled, however, with the fact that most of the Iraqis killed seem to have been headed north or simply milling around—and not into the defender's lines, notwithstanding that some of their number quite clearly seem to have initiated the combat by opening fire when U.S. forces approached their position. Given that the Iraqi position had been fifteen or so kilometers beyond the 24th Division's front lines (taken as the main line of resistance, at any rate) at 0800 on the 28th when the president announced cessation of offensive operations and that only a small number of Iraqis seem to have acted with hostility that morning, the outcome remains somewhat disturbing. The above situation, however, may be irrelevant from the perspective of the men on the ground. With the events described, the conduct of the war passed from the battlefield to the council chambers.

Notes

1. "The Award Winning Staff of U.S. News and World Report," *Triumph Without Victory: The Unreported History of the Persian Gulf War* (New York: Times Books, a division of Random House, 1992), 399–406. The precise term used by the president was "suspension of offensive combat operations." Text is in "Kuwait Is Liberated: Military Objectives Are Met, Bush Says," from the Associated Press in *The Washington Post*, 28 February 1991, A27, A34. The president was clear that the "suspension was not yet a cease-fire."

2. Yeosock told Schwarzkopf he needed twenty-four hours to finish the RGFC in response to a question from the CINC on the afternoon of the 27th. Schwarzkopf, *Doesn't Take a Hero*, 467.

3. HQ, ARCENT, Command Group, (Executive Officer's) Daily Memo, 27 February 1991. On the issue of concern for a mechanism for war termination, the author was present at a meeting between General Yeosock and Generals Franks, McCaffrey, and Griffith in early February when General Franks raised this issue. Lieutenant Colonel Mike Kendall, General Yeosock's executive officer, indicated this was an issue the night of the 27th in comments to the author upon review of this chapter.

4. Interview with General Frederick Franks at Fort Leavenworth, Kansas, 6 March 1992, 26–39.

5. Daily Staff Journal, VII Corps TAC CP, 27 February 1991, entry 51 (an attachment with corps commander's instructions to divisions). Daily Staff Journal, VII Corps Main CP, at 1846 on 27 February 1991, item 38. Handwritten note, "VII Corps Update," 271940C, February 1991, note is account of VII Corps LNO Report to ARCENT Main CP. HQ, ARCENT, Command Group, (Executive Officer's) Daily Memo, 27 February 1991, 4. HQ, VII Corps TAC CP, Fact Sheet, Issue: To Provide Information on ARCENT Mission to Interdict Basrah-Kuwait City Highway and Seize Road Junction at QU 662368 Prior to 280800C February 1991.

6. Rhame interview, 26 July 1991, 15. Diagram 8, HQ, 1st Squadron, 4th Cavalry, Narrative History, 7 March 1991. Diagram 14 to HQ, 1st Squadron, 4th Cavalry, Memorandum for Record, Subject: 1-4 Cavalry History for Operation Desert Storm, dated 27 March 1991, an enclosure to HQ, ARCENT, Memorandum thru Awards Board, U.S. Army Forces Central Command, Subject: Recommendation for Award of Valorous Unit Award for 1st Squadron, 4th Cavalry, 1st Infantry Division, n.d.

7. Colonel Greg Fontenot to the author. Fontenot commanded the 2d Battalion of the 34th Armor. His vehicles became intermingled with those of Lieutenant Colonel Pat Ritter's 1/34th in the "valley." Fontenot asked for permission to halt long enough to sort out the confusion about the time the whole allied offensive was closed down at about 2200 by the events described below.

8. Daily Staff Journal, VII Corps Main CP, at 2300 on 27 February 1991, item 52. Daily Staff Journal, VII Corps TAC CP, at 2316 on 27 February 1991, item 48. Both journals, kept in two locations, reflect this conversation. HQ, VII Corps TAC CP, Fact Sheet. Discussion of possible combined 1st ID-1st U.K. attack to the north along Basrah-Kuwait City highway, Colonel Stan Cherrie to author.

9. CENTCOM news briefing, General H. Norman Schwarzkopf, USA, Riyadh, Saudi Arabia, Wednesday, 27 February 1991–1:00 P.M. EST.

10. Ibid., 16.

11. Ann Devroy and Dan Balz, "Bush Relaxes Effort to Abase Saddam," *The Washington Post*, 28 February 1991, A27 et seq.

12. Schwarzkopf, *Doesn't Take a Hero*, 468–71. Colonel Joseph Purvis to the author. Colonel Purvis was in the CENTCOM Operations Center when the call came in from General Powell to General Schwarzkopf. According to *The Washington Post* chronology, the president's briefing was at 1430 Washington time, 2230 in Saudi Arabia.

13. HQ, ARCENT, Command Group, (Executive Officer's) Daily Memo, 27 February 1991, 7. The precise timing anticipated remains an issue (see below).

14. Ibid. Daily Staff Journal, VII Corps TAC CP, 27 February 1991, item 51 and attachment. HQ, VII Corps TAC CP, Fact Sheet.

15. Message, 270920Z FEB 91, FM COMUSARCENT MCP//G3 OPS//, Subject: FRAGO 67 to ARCENT OPORD (Desert Storm 001), Potential Temporary Cease-Fire. Date-time group is incorrect. Dispatch time appears from various logs to have been around 2300–2400 local.

16. Schwarzkopf, *Doesn't Take a Hero*, 470–72.

17. Ibid., 472.

18. HQ, ARCENT, Command Group, (Executive Officer's) Daily Memo, 28 February 1991, 5.

19. Lieutenant Colonel Michael Kendall to author. This change of tone was also remarked on by Colonel Cherrie with regard to instructions from ARCENT to VII Corps.

20. Message, 280030Z FEB 91, FROM COMUSARCENT, Subject: FRAGO 068 to ARCENT OPORD (Desert Storm 001), Continue with Offensive Operations.

21. Message, 280030Z FEB 91, FM COMUSARCENTMAIN, Subject: FRAGO 068 to ARCENT OPORD (Desert Storm 001), Continue with Offensive Operations.

22. VII Corps TAC CP Logs are held at the USACGSC Combined Arms Research Library, Fort Leavenworth, Kansas.

23. HQ, VII Corps TAC CP, Fact Sheet, Issue: To Provide Information on ARCENT Mission to Interdict Basrah-Kuwait City Highway. This is also the word used in the VII Corps Daily Staff Journal in a message to the 1st Armored Division at 0555 the morning of the 28th, and it is consistent with the actions taken by VII Corps to conclude that the mission as understood was interdiction, not seizure.

24. Daily Staff Journal, VII Corps Main CP, at 0406 on 28 February 1991, item 6.

25. HQ, 11th Aviation Brigade, Memorandum for Commander VII (U.S.) Corps, Subject: Executive Summary to After-Action Report, 11th Aviation Brigade, Operation

Desert Storm, dated 18 March 1991, 2. Daily Staff Journal, 1st Infantry Division TAC CP, at 0502 and 0510 on 28 February 1991, items 18 and 20.

26. Daily Staff Journal, VII Corps TAC CP, at 0515 on 28 February, item 11. Daily Staff Journal, 1st Infantry Division TAC CP, at 0511 on 28 February, item 20. See comments by Colonel Terry Bullington, 1st ID G3, on confusion in order, transmission in Rhame interview, 26 July 1991, 27–28, 37.

27. Ibid., 0510, item 19.

28. Note on draft manuscript written by Brigadier General Bill Carter.

29. Message Form #18, 28 February 1991, attached to Daily Staff Journal, ARCENT Mobile CP, 28 February 1991. Message was logged in at 0858.

30. Daily Staff Journal, VII Corps TAC CP, at 0520 and 0555 on 28 February 1991, items 14 and 16.

31. Ibid., 0602, 0615, and 0626, items 17, 20, and 22.

32. Rhame interview, 26 July 1991, 31, 36. Daily Staff Journal, 1st Infantry Division TAC CP, at 0510 on 28 February 1991, item 20, reflects the mission to the aviation unit to reconnoiter the road to the north. At 0645, item 34 reflects execution of the mission.

33. Andrew Rosenthal, "Military Aims Met: Firing Ending After 100 Hours of Ground War, President Declares," *The New York Times*, 28 February 1991, A1.

34. Reported friendly fire incident is in Daily Staff Journal, VII Corps TAC CP, at 0724 and 0741 on 28 February 1991, items 29 and 34. HQ, ARCENT, Command Group, (Executive Officer's) Daily Memo, 28 February 1991, 1, indicates that on the morning of the 28th, the ARCENT Main CP believed the road junction had been occupied. The VII Corps Main CP, Message file, Unit Locations, 281000C February 1991, does not indicate any ground unit near the road junction. HQ, ARCENT, briefing slides, "ARCENT Update, G+5 (28 February)," slide titled, "Combat Unit Locations," as of 281200C February 1991 shows the 1st ID well south of the junction. These slides were prepared daily in the ARCENT Command Group for the CINC's daily component commanders' briefing. That same morning, the author asked at the mobile CP if the road complex in question had been occupied by either corps and was told it had not. Rather, both corps had sent aviation units only into the area in question. The incorrect report is reproduced in Schwarzkopf, *Doesn't Take a Hero*, 473, as a chapter header. The report in fact relates the final objectives, that of XVIII Corps, far beyond the 24th's capabilities from a standing start (which never took place) the morning of the 28th, given cessation at 0800.

35. Message, 010300Z MAR 91, FM COMUSARCENT MAIN//DT//, MSGID/ SITREP/ USARCENT/G+5/MAR//,PERID/280300Z/TO:010300Z/ASOF:010300Z,1–2.

36. HQ, ARCENT, Command Group, (Executive Officer's) Daily Memo, 27 February 1991, 6. HQ, ARCENT, Command Group, (Executive Officer's) Daily Memo, 28 February 1991, 3.

37. Schwarzkopf, *Doesn't Take a Hero*, 469–70. Transcript of Schwarzkopf interview with David Frost, dated 22 March 1991, 22. The text of the transcript reads: ". . . he

and I discussed have we accomplished our military objectives. The campaign objectives. And the answer was yes. There was no question about the fact that the campaign objectives that we established for ourselves were accomplished. The enemy was being kicked out of Kuwait, was going to be gone from Kuwait, that we had destroyed the Republican guard [sic] as a militarily effective force." It was Schwarzkopf's discussion of what constituted destruction (which generally followed the line above) that led to the controversy in the press. Ibid. "General's Account of Gulf War's End Disputed by Bush," *The New York Times*, 28 March 1991, 1.

38. The VII Corps formed a special headquarters to document destruction of enemy materiel to include plotting hulks on map. TF Demo reported 619 tanks, 685 APCs, 865 artillery and air defense weapons, and over 4,000 other vehicles destroyed prior to the corps' withdrawal into Kuwait and Saudi Arabia. HQ, 7th Engineer Brigade, AETS-EB (840), Memorandum for Commander, VII Corps, Attn: Military History, Subject: Command Report-Operation Desert Shield and Desert Storm, 9 April 1991, paragraph 10, page 3.

39. Schwarzkopf in Frost interview, 23.

40. Ibid. Colonel Doug Craft who worked in the CENTCOM Operations Center has related, however, that according to his memory of the events of that night, the CINC and the NCA were both concerned about "wanton destruction" of the fleeing forces. Interview with Colonel Douglas Craft at the Army War College, 19 April 1991, 19. Provided to the author by Colonel Craft.

41. This is made clear by the UN resolution providing a basis for the cease-fire talks passed on 2 March. The resolution affirms "the commitment of all member states to the territorial integrity of Iraq and Kuwait" and the intention "of the member states cooperating under paragraph 2 of Security Council Resolution 678 (1990) to bring their military presence in Iraq to an end as soon as possible consistent with achieving the objective of the resolution." "Text of Measure Approved by the Council in 11-1 Vote," *The New York Times*, 3 March 1991.

42. A well-informed, contrary view is in Laurie Mylroie, "How We Helped Saddam Survive," *Commentary* 92, no. 1 (July 1991): 15-18.

43. Lieutenant Colonel John M. Kendall, Memorandum for Colonel Swain, Subject: Chronology for 27 February-1 March 1991, dated 19 September 1991, 3. Lieutenant Colonel Kendall was General Yeosock's executive officer. He kept notes of all CG's meetings and at request of the author reviewed his notes for the dates in question and provided a summary in this memorandum. Guidance from ARCENT Main CP to XVIII Corps was: "... if Iraqi units enter our area then we are authorized to attempt to get them to surrender. If they don't we are authorized to use force to stop them and force them to surrender. We were specifically concerned with Highway 8. Same applies since it is in our sector." HQ, XVIII Corps, G3, FM Form 2768, CTOC Journal Sheet, DTG received 2045 28 February 1991, journal entry no. 70. The question which remains is what exactly constitutes "our area."

44. Kendall, Memorandum for Colonel Swain, Subject: Chronology for 27 February-1 March 1991, dated 19 September 1991, 3.

45. Ibid., 3-4. The XVIII Corps logs show that from 010045 March to 010400 March, the corps was involved in preparing to host the cease-fire talks at Jalibah. At 0400, they

were told to stand down on that. From noon on the 1st until the end of the meeting on the 3d, the 24th ID was on standby with a site on Highway 8, well inside the division sector west of the causeway.

46. Andrew Rosenthal, "Allied Generals and Iraqis to Meet Soon on Cease-Fire: Bush Stresses P.O.W. Return," *The New York Times*, 2 March 1991, 1. "The Persian Gulf War: Excerpts of the President's News Conference," *The Washington Post*, 2 March 1991, A12.

47. Memorandum for Record, Subject: Colonel Doug Craft's Memory of the Period 271800C to 281800C at CENTCOM HQ, prepared by author based on phone conversation. Interview with Colonel Douglas Craft at the Army War College, 19 April 1991, 10-12. Provided to the author by Colonel Craft. The public story is in the *Army Times*, "The General's War: How Commanders Fought the Iraqis . . . and Among Themselves," by Tom Donnelly, 8, 16-17. Schwarzkopf's account in Schwarzkopf, *Doesn't Take a Hero*, 473-78.

48. Message, 010010Z, FROM COMUSARCENT, SUBJECT: WARNORD NEGOTIATION SUPPORT. Message, 010315Z, FROM COMUSARCENT, Subject: FRAGO 070 to OPORD Desert Storm 001, Negotiation Support.

49. Daily Staff Journal, VII Corps TAC CP, no time given, 1 March 1991, item 3; 0125, item 2. Within item 3 is a note concerning a message from General Franks at 0308.

50. Ibid.

51. Ibid.

52. Testimony as to General Schwarzkopf's frame of mind has come largely from discussions by the author with staff officers who were witness, in one way or the other, to the events in question. There has been a marked reluctance by direct participants to discuss these events. However, given knowledge of the witnesses and General Schwarzkopf's reputation in the Army, as well as having personal knowledge of his temper when crossed, the author feels no compunction in accepting these accounts on face value. The content of the discussion is reproduced from notes in a Memorandum for Record, Subject: Situation at the Safwan Airfield, dated 1 March 1991, prepared by Lieutenant Colonel John M. Kendall at General Yeosock's direction. This memorandum will be retired with General Yeosock's personal files at the Military History Institute, U.S. Army War College, Carlisle Barracks, Pennsylvania.

53. An account of the actions of the 1st Squadron, 4th Cavalry, is in HQ, 1st Squadron, 4th Cavalry, Memorandum for Record, Subject: 1-4 Cav, 1st ID(M) Narrative History of Operation Desert Storm, 24 January-1 March 1991, dated 7 March 1991. See also Steve Coll, "Talks, Site Remind Iraqis Who Won," *The Washington Post*, 4 March 1991, A-1, et seq. Note from Brigadier General Bill Carter on draft manuscript.

54. HQ, 3-37 Armor, History of Task Force 3-37 Armor, Operation Desert Storm, 8.

55. Copy of handwritten note by Colonel Moreno. Jim Tice, "Taking a Town by Shooting the Breeze," *Army Times*, 26 August 1991, 18.

56. Rhame interview, 26 July 1991, 45. Note from General Carter.

57. Memorandum for Record, Subject: Situation at the Safwan Airfield, dated 10 March 1991, 1.

58. Ibid., 2–3.

59. Ibid., 4.

60. Ibid.

61. Rhame interview, 26 July 1991, 25–27.

62. Note by Colonel Moreno. Tice, "Taking a Town by Shooting the Breeze."

63. Ibid. HQ, 3-37 Armor, History of Task Force 3-37 Armor, Operation Desert Storm. Memorandum for Record, Subject: Situation at the Safwan Airfield, dated 10 March 1991, 3–6.

64. Memorandum for Record, Subject: Situation at the Safwan Airfield, dated 10 March 1991, 6.

65. Ann Devroy and Guy Gugliotta, "Cease-Fire Talks Delayed by 'Technical Details,'" *The Washington Post*, 2 March 1991, A1.

66. Interview with Colonel Cherrie. Comments by Lieutenant Colonel Mike Kendall to author.

67. HQ, ARCENT, AFRD-XO, Subject: Taskers in Support of Negotiations Meeting, dated 1 March 1991, and comments by Lieutenant Colonel Kendall, the author. There were twenty items to be accomplished.

68. Humphrey Cobb, *Paths of Glory* (Athens: University of Georgia Press, 1987), 21.

69. Douglas Southall Freeman, "Morale in the Army of Northern Virginia," in *Douglas Southall Freeman on Leadership*, ed. Stuart W. Smith (Newport, RI: Naval War College Press, 1990), 71.

70. De la Billiere, *Storm Command*, 297–98.

71. Message, 281800C, FROM COMMANDER 24TH INF DIV, TO COMMANDER XVIII ABN CORPS, Subject: Combat Operation Summary, Period, 271800C FEB 91–281800 CFEB 91, 2.

72. Message, 1100Z [sic, actually 011800Z], FROM COMMANDER 24TH INF DIV, TO COMMANDER XVIII ABN CORPS, Subject: Combat Operation Summary, 2. HQ, ARCENT, Command Group, (Executive Officer's) Daily Memo, 28 February 1991, 1. Routes of withdrawal are listed in the intelligence portion of Message, 020300Z MARCH 1991, FM COMUSARCENT MAIN, TO AIG1173, MSGID, SITREP, USARCENT, G+6 MAR, 1–2. A report at 1400 to ARCENT LNO with XVIII Corps indicates the same dispositions in the north along the causeway. HQ, ARCENT, G3 Main CP, ARCENT Spot Report No. 06015, journal entry F-15.

73. Message, 020300 MARCH 1991, FM COMUSARCENT MAIN, TO AIG1173, MSGID, SITREP, USARCENT, G+6 MAR, 1-2.

74. Message, 011120Z, FM CDRXVIIIABNCORPS, Subject: FRAGO #79 to XVIII Abn Corps OPORD Desert Storm, 4.

75. Message, 282330C FEB 91, FM CDR, 3RD ACR, TO CDR, XVIII ABN CORPS, Subject: Commander Daily SITREP (As of 282315C FEB 91), 1. HQ, ARCENT, Command Group, (Executive Officer's) Daily Memo, 28 February 1991, 4 (LNO report of 3 ACR fight). Message, 281800, FROM COMMANDER 24TH INF DIV, TO COMMANDER XVIII ABN CORPS, Subject: Combat Operation Summary, 2 (2-7 Inf affair).

76. HQ, XVIII Corps TAC CP, FB Form 2768, Message Form/CTOC Journal Sheet, DTG 010455C FEB 91, journal entry no. 50. Form passes question from corps main CP to corps TAC. Message indicates CENTCOM called direct to corps main CP.

77. HQ, XVIII Corps TAC CP, FB Form 2768, Message Form/CTOC Journal Sheet, DTG 012207 MAR 91, journal entry no. 16.

78. Memorandum of interview with Lieutenant Colonel Pat Lamar at Fort McPherson, Georgia, 16 December 1991.

79. HQ, 1st Brigade, 24th Infantry Division, Spot Report File, specifically FRAGO DTG 020011C March 1991, VOCO Bde Cdr to All Units, journal entry no. 15, 16, and various other early morning spot reports for the 2d. Quotation is taken from VOCO.

80. HQ, ARCENT, Message, 280300Z FEB 91, FROM HQ ARCENT MAIN//, Subject: FRAGO 068 to ARCENT OPORD (Desert Storm 001), Continue with Offensive Operations. HQ, XVIII Corps TAC CP, FB Form 2768, Message Form/CTOC Journal Sheet, DTG 280320C FEB 91, journal entry no. 39. This sheet records guidance from General Luck to the TAC CP. It is offered only to demonstrate that ARCENT and XVIII Corps seem to have been thinking mainly in terms of moving backwards in zone, not forwards.

81. There are a number of accounts of the 24th Division fight on 2 March. The ARCENT commander's executive officer wrote a memorandum providing an account of the incident as it was reported to ARCENT, Memorandum for Record, Subject: 24 ID Engagement, 2 March 1991, an attachment to HQ, ARCENT, Command Group, (Executive Officer's) Daily Memo, 2 March 1991. The incident is laid out briefly in Message, 021800Z MAR 91, FM COMMANDER 24TH INF DIV (M) TO COMMANDER XVIII ABN CORPS, Subject: Combat Operation Summary, Period, 011800C MAR 91–021800 MAR 91, 2-3; and in Message, 030300Z MAR 91, FM COMUSARCENT MAIN, TO AIG 11743, MSGID, SITREP, USARCENT, G+7 MAR, 15-16. General McCaffrey testified before Senator Nunn's Senate Armed Services Committee on 9 May 1991. Draft transcript of a briefing from Major General Barry R. McCaffrey, USA, Commanding General, 24th Infantry Division (Mechanized), and Members of the 24th Infantry Division on the Conduct of Ground Operations in Their Tactical Area of Responsibility During Operation Desert Shield/Storm, 42–44.

82. Testimony of General McCaffrey before the Senate Armed Forces Committee on 9 May 1991, 42.

83. HQ, 1st Brigade, 24th Infantry Division, Duty Summary (notes by duty officer) (012029–021722 Mar 91), entries for 0802–0807.

84. Message, 021800Z MAR 91, FM COMMANDER 24TH INF DIV (M) TO COMMANDER XVIII ABN CORPS, Subject: Combat Operations Summary, Period, 011800C MAR 91–021800C MAR 91, 2. General Scott's reports are summarized in Memorandum for Record, Subject: 24th ID Engagement, 2 March 1991, 1–2. The numbers of tanks destroyed vary, no doubt friction in the reporting system.

85. Memorandum for Record, Subject: 24th ID Engagement, 2 March 1991, 2.

86. Ibid., 1–2. Message, 021800Z MAR 91, FM COMMANDER 24TH INF DIV (M) TO COMMANDER XVIII ABN CORPS, Subject: Combat Operation Summary, Period, 011800C MAR 91–021800C MAR 91, 2–3.

87. Memorandum for Record, Subject: 24th ID Engagement, 2 March 1991, 2. The 24th Division operational report lists, only thirty-one tanks destroyed. This is inconsistent with all other accounts.

88. Interview with Captain Richard B. Averna, at Fort Leavenworth, Kansas, on 27 November 1991. Captain Averna was a student in the Combined Arms and Services Staff School at the time of the interview. The following account comes from that interview except where noted.

89. Ibid., 8.

90. See command account above, HQ, 1st Brigade, 24th Infantry Division, Spot Report File, and HQ, 1st Brigade, 24th Infantry Division, Duty Summary (notes by duty officer) (012029–021722 Mar 91).

91. Message, 020300Z MAR 91, FM COMUSARCENT MAIN, TO AIG 11743, MSGID, SITREP, USARCENT, G+6 MAR, 14.

92. Raymond Aron, *Clausewitz: Philosopher of War*, trans. Christine Booker and Norman Stone (London: Routledge & Kegan Paul, 1983), 70.

93. Ibid., 76.

9
Conclusions: "A Famous Victory?"

Following Iraqi acceptance of the military cease-fire in the field on 3 March, Third Army and its assigned forces became responsible for three different and often conflicting missions: to occupy southeastern Iraq until a United Nations permanent cease-fire was effected; to provide emergency support to Kuwait until relieved by a Department of Defense Reconstruction Assistance Office; and to begin redeployment of U.S. Army forces immediately, in keeping with the commitment Secretary of Defense Cheney made to the king of Saudi Arabia on 6 August 1990. As General Yeosock observed, these missions required ARCENT to go in three different directions at once, and they were complicated even further when civil unrest produced massive numbers of displaced persons in northern Iraq along the Turkish border and around Basrah. These refugees had to be supported, at least with the means of life, and arrangements had to be made to turn them over to a protecting power. (See figure 34.)

The United States committed relief forces to northern Iraq under control of the U.S. European Command. Third Army was tasked to support this effort, Operation Provide Comfort, by providing resources and even redirecting the movement of some units from the Desert Storm redeployment to Turkey and northern Iraq. Meanwhile, U.S. troop strength in Saudi Arabia dropped rapidly each day. Upon the departure of General Schwarzkopf in April, Yeosock became CENTCOM's deputy commander in chief until his own departure on 12 May. General Pagonis then remained in Saudi Arabia to see to the evacuation of remaining U.S. personnel and equipment. Iraqi forces in the Basrah pocket were allowed to withdraw north of the Euphrates River following the cease-fire. U.S. forces did not become involved in the popular uprising against the Baghdad regime that raged in Basrah in early March.

President Bush laid down U.S. objectives for the postwar settlement in his address to the joint session of Congress on 7 March.[1] These provided for a shared responsibility for regional security, the control of Iraq's access to weapons of mass destruction, a commitment to leave no residual ground force in the area, but to conduct joint military exercises, the maintenance of a naval presence, and a search for new opportunities for peace. Related to this were seven military objectives: (1) defend and rebuild Kuwait; (2) orient, support, and hand off a demilitarized zone to a United Nations Command; (3) protect and

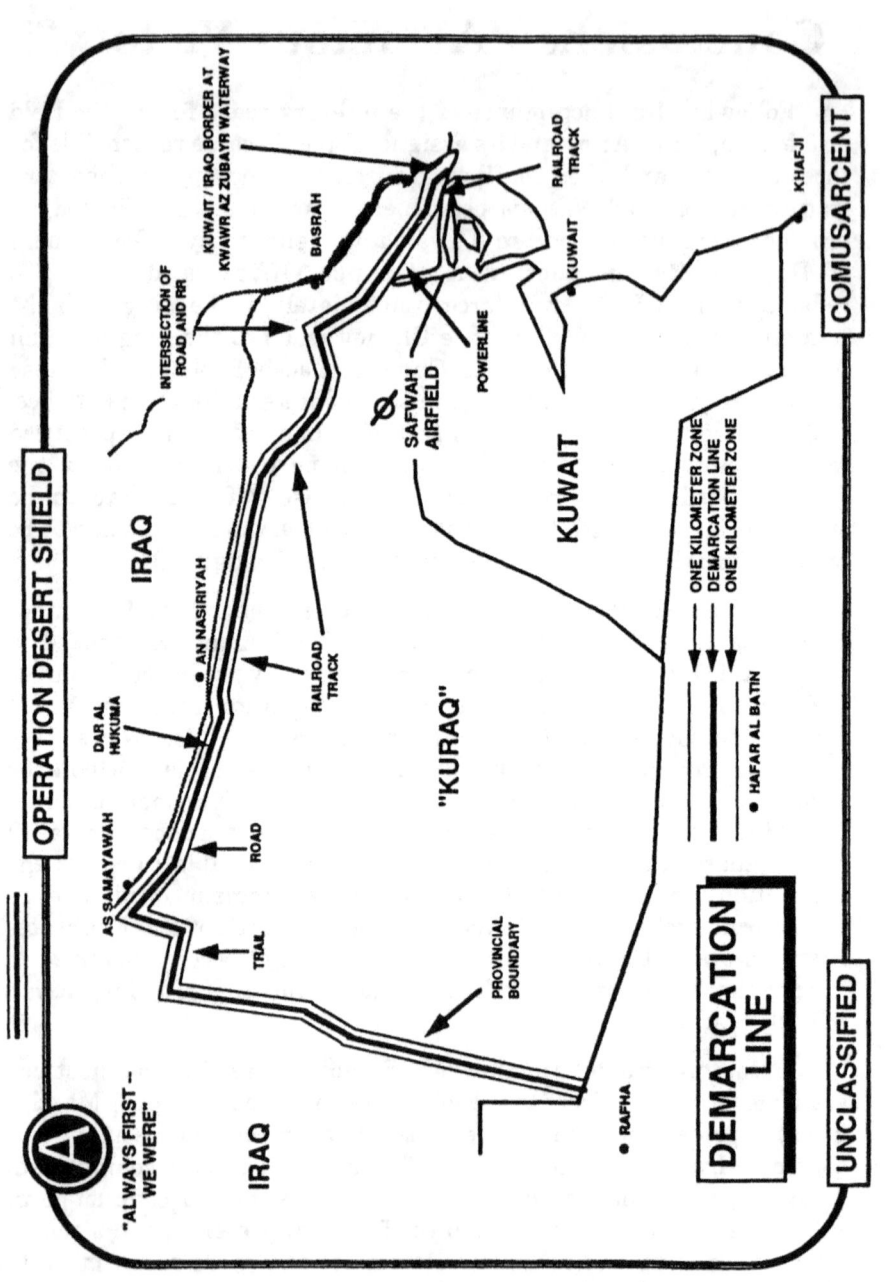

Figure 34.

support displaced civilians, ultimately to turn their care over to our regional allies; (4) leave some residual force in Kuwait temporarily; (5) conduct redeployment; (6) prepare equipment left behind in the region; and (7) capture the experience of Desert Shield-Desert Storm.[2]

To provide for emergency aid to Kuwait, Yeosock established an army task force, Task Force Freedom, under command of his deputy, Major General Bob Frix, using the mobile CP, "Lucky Wheels," as task force headquarters. The mobile CP left King Khalid Military City almost immediately after the cessation of offensive actions and moved to Kuwait City, first, to the international airport, then, to some Kuwaiti administrative offices. Task Force Freedom was a command and control element whose mission was to "ensure unity of effort in the restoration and reconstruction of Kuwait and provide for the transition of responsibility to the Secretary of the Army."[3] For Kuwaiti reconstruction, the Army secretary was to act as the executive agent of the secretary of defense. The secretary formed a special office, the U.S. Defense Reconstruction Assistance Office, to accomplish that effort under direction of Major General Patrick Kelly, an Army engineer.

Task Force Freedom saw to the process of damage assessment, provision of emergency services, explosive ordnance disposal (EOD) (necessary to clear mines and booby traps), disposition of civil affairs support, and contracting required to get the reconstruction effort on its feet. Its mission was short-term—to provide emergency support only. The principal elements of the task force were the 352d Civil Affairs Command,[4] a forward element of the 22d Support Command, and various specialist organizations: EOD detachments; military police; and medical, signal, and intelligence units. In occupied Iraq, VII and XVIII Corps were responsible for the requisite civil affairs duties and the destruction of war materiel left in place by the retreating Iraqi Army.[5] Third Army was also responsible for the repatriation of Iraqi prisoners in U.S. hands. This was done through the Saudi military.

The United States ultimately transferred 20,989 Iraqi refugees to the Saudis for long-term care and protection. Yeosock turned over the mission in the demilitarized zone to the United Nations Command on 6 May and removed the last U.S. soldier from southeastern Iraq on 9 May. The redeployment was conducted as rapidly as possible by bringing heavy equipment to central maintenance areas, cleaning and securing it, and turning it over to the 22d Support Command for movement based upon availability of shipping. Personnel were redeployed much faster by air, beginning on 10 March when Third Army stood at a strength of 298,293 soldiers. On 8 June, ARCENT had reached a state of 24,000 soldiers and dropped to 15,300 by 1 August, a year from the start of the crisis.

Yeosock and his headquarters departed for Fort McPherson, Georgia, on 12 May, after a somewhat longer absence than the general had expected when called by Schwarzkopf the previous August. A residual American presence was retained for a time in Kuwait and Saudi Arabia, principally to evacuate the American equipment and guarantee the security of the emirate. Some additional air defense units were deployed later to protect various Saudi sites when Iraq tried to stonewall UN cease-fire monitors. A year later, no end had been declared to Operation Desert Storm, and the naval and economic isolation of Iraq continued.

The commanders of Desert Storm dispersed back to the Army. Schwarzkopf was welcomed back to Florida by Mickey Mouse and to the United States by a joint session of Congress. He attended parades, signed a multimillion dollar book contract, retired, and went on the high-dollar speaking circuit—seldom, it seems, feeling obliged to recognize the assistance he may have received from his senior assistants in obtaining his triumph. Lieutenant General Yeosock returned to his duties as Deputy Commander in Chief, Forces Command, and Commander, Third Army. He retired from the Army in July 1992 and remained in the Atlanta area. Lieutenant General Gary Luck returned to Fort Bragg and continued as commander of XVIII Airborne Corps. He was later promoted to full general and appointed U.S. commander in chief in Korea.

The VII Corps returned to Germany. The "Jay Hawk" corps was deactivated in the spring of 1992 but not before Lieutenant General Frederick Franks was given a fourth star and appointed Commander, U.S. Army Training and Doctrine Command. As TRADOC commander, Franks paid particular attention to incorporating the lessons of Desert Storm into Army doctrine and focusing attention on what he called "battle command" and "battle space," the essential tasks and horizons of tactical commanders.

Lieutenant General William ("Gus") Pagonis, who had received his third star in theater in recognition of his accomplishments, remained in Saudi Arabia commanding ARCENT Forward. He subsequently was appointed to command the 21st Support Command in Europe. From there, he retired from the Army to direct logistic operations for Sears Roebuck, and Company. Lieutenant General Calvin Waller, the deputy commander in chief, and Major General Paul Schwartz, the chief of C3IC, both returned to Fort Lewis,

Washington, from whence they had been called to the Middle East, Waller as I Corps commander, Schwartz as his deputy. Both retired within the year.

Major Generals J. H. Binford Peay III, commander of the 101st Airborne Division; Ron Griffith, commander of the 1st Armored Division; and Barry McCaffrey, commander of the 24th Infantry Division, were promoted to lieutenant general, McCaffrey after an additional year as commander of the 24th Division. Peay became Army deputy chief of staff for operations and, then, after being promoted to full general, vice chief of staff of the Army. Griffith was appointed the Army inspector general. McCaffrey was first the special assistant to the chairman of the Joint Chiefs of Staff, then J3 (operations), after which he, like Peay, received his fourth star and was sent to Panama as Commander in Chief, U.S. Southern Command. Major General Paul Funk, who had commanded the 3d Armored Division, was posted to the Joint Staff for a year and then to the Armor Center as commandant.

Major General Tom Rhame took his 1st Infantry Division back to the United States. He soon quickly returned to Saudi Arabia to the U.S. Military Training Mission. After a year, he was joined by his old G3, Colonel Terry Bullington. Rhame was later promoted to lieutenant general and assigned to the Department of Defense to administer security assistance programs. The 1st Division's assistant division commander, Brigadier General Bill Carter, was first given command of the Army's National Training Center at Fort Irwin; after promotion to major general, he succeeded to command of the 1st Armored Division in Germany. Colonel Don Holder, commander of the 2d Armored Cavalry Regiment in VII Corps, was promoted to brigadier general and posted to a NATO staff. He was later promoted to major general and command of the 3d Infantry Division. Major General Johnnie Johnson, who commanded the first division deployed, the 82d Airborne, was promoted to lieutenant general and given command of First Army. Major General John Tilelli returned to Fort Hood, Texas, with his 1st Cavalry Division and then became first assistant deputy chief of staff for operations at Department of the Army, then, as lieutenant general, the deputy chief of staff of operations. Major General Pete Taylor, the multihatted chief of staff of Forces Command, was promoted to lieutenant general and given command of III Corps at Fort Hood. He was succeeded at III Corps by General Funk.

The Third Army headquarters returned almost immediately to its prewar strength, notwithstanding the need to man a cell in General Pagonis' Saudi establishment. Major General Frix remained as deputy commander. Later, he was transferred to Sixth Army in the same role. Major General Steve Arnold received a well-deserved appointment as commander of the Army's 10th Mountain Division. In the next two years, he would take his division to Miami, Florida, to provide hurricane relief, and to Somalia to participate in the peace-keeping operation, Restore Hope. In 1994, after a tour at Department of the Army, Arnold assumed command of Third Army.

Brigadier General John Stewart was promoted to major general and became deputy chief of staff for intelligence for U.S. Army, Europe, and then commandant of the Intelligence School. Brigadier General Jim Monroe, the stalwart ARCENT G4, finally was able to take up the appointment at Tank Automotive Command in Detroit, to which he had been on his way in August 1990. He, too, would be promoted to major general, become deputy commander of Tank Automotive Command, then, commandant of the Ordnance Center and its school.

Within a year, Third Army would turn over almost all of its "proprietary" colonels and lieutenant colonels. Most would retire. Colonel Joe Purvis, who had headed Schwarzkopf's "Jedi Knights," returned to his assignment in Hawaii, no longer an anonymous colonel. He retired within two years to build houses in Florida.

General Gordon Sullivan who, as vice chief of staff, was the constant presence with the senior officers in Desert Storm, became chief of staff of the Army following the retirement of General Carl Vuono in the summer of 1991. Sullivan, whose daily phone calls to Army general officers in the desert were frequent and always encouraging, took as his task the maintenance of the service's core values and purposes during a period of dramatic reduction. A deeply sensitive and patriotic soldier, Sullivan sought during his tenure as chief to infuse the nation's senior service with his optimism and sense of the obligations of service in "America's Army."

General Crosbie Saint, the Army's premier tanker, had missed the biggest armored war of his career and retired as commander in chief of USAREUR in July 1992. Fate is not always kind.

Reflections on Desert Storm

Wars, particularly limited and coalition wars, are seldom entirely satisfactory to any one participant. As a member of a coalition, a state is not a free agent but must be willing to give way to the sensitivities of its allies, not just for reasons of noblesse oblige but for pragmatic considerations. In a coalition, one has goals of one's own, the accomplishment of which depend upon the cooperation of others whose own purposes may be compatible but by no means identical. Limited wars, in their turn, rarely make the enemy disappear, and though some behavior or status may be changed, the underlying issues that caused the war in the first place are generally submerged rather than resolved by the outcome. Great battles and campaigns have a way of being disappointing in their aftermath, hence little Peterkin's question: "But what good came of it at last?" To which Robert Southey has Old Kaspar reply: "Why that I cannot tell. . . . But 'twas a famous victory."[6] This seems to be the current fate of the victory of Desert Storm after the debris of the parades have been cleared up and the thousands of citizen-soldiers who answered the nation's call in 1990 have returned to their workaday lives.

But one ought not to let defeat be torn from the jaws of victory simply because that victory took place in a world where success is rarely complete or perfect. Desert Shield-Desert Storm was a famous victory, and if, like the Battle of Blenheim of which Southey wrote, it failed to return perpetual peace to the region in which it occurred, it is difficult not to believe the world is better off because there was a rapid and effective response to Saddam Hussein's seizure of Kuwait.

Desert Storm prevented Iraq's potential seizure of a disproportionate amount of the developed world's oil supply. Also, Saddam Hussein's Iraq does not stand at the brink of becoming a nuclear power, and Iraq's sustained defiance in the face of continued diplomatic and economic isolation surely vitiates any remaining faith that military action could have been dispensed with. In short, the region, if not the world, seems a safer place because Desert Storm was successful.

Still, new and dangerous problems have replaced the old. These, most sadly, have proved less susceptible to the Desert Storm solution. At least one, that in Somalia, was in a single armed engagement about as costly as the four-day Desert Storm ground offensive. The battle in Mogadishu on 3 October 1993 produced two Congressional Medals of Honor and ended in a rapid withdrawal of U.S. forces. The experience in Somalia underlines a suspicion about the limited value of conventional military forces in circumstances of civic collapse. The case of North Korea has been no less resistant to the Desert Storm solution. The world's last Stalinist regime has replaced Iraq as the principal pathologically hostile power threatening the strategic balance in a region deemed vital to U.S. interests. But the risks involved with miscalculation are greater than they were in the Persian Gulf, and to date, the U.S. response has been measured to say the least. U.S. memories of the Korean War are not such as to encourage hasty action in any event, Desert Storm notwithstanding.

One could draw any number of insights from the experience of the Gulf War. Here, I shall offer those having to do with the structure of war, the implications of technology, the significance of generalship, and the apparent implications for concepts of war in whatever new world order emerges. Many of these insights are based upon a supposition, quite possibly to be proven wrong in the end, that the "new world order" will not be an era of global superpowers but a global system of regions. In some regions, there may be dominant but not hegemonic powers, where, if local allies can be had, an external power or an alliance capable of projecting military power may play a balancing role to further or protect national interests. Without a new ideological divide, such alliances will be ad hoc. Wars will seldom involve the overthrow of a contending power, because the intervening powers or alliances will seldom have the will to reorder the region once the immediate problem is solved or to accept the consequences of leaving a power vacuum that might be filled by an even worse successor. If this set of assumptions is true, then Desert Shield-Desert Storm will serve as a significant signpost. If, instead, a new cold war emerges or if the United States is forced to become involved in inchoate communal wars such as those in the Balkans, these lessons will have no more utility than those of the Franco-Prussian War had for the men of 1914.

The structure of war discussed in this book has involved principally four levels of activity: (1) what B. H. Liddell Hart called grand strategy; (2) what might be called theater strategy; (3) operational art as defined in the Army's FM 100-5, *Operations* (1986); and (4) J. F. C. Fuller's (or Jomini's) grand tactics. These levels encompass the activities of the executive branch of government, the theater commander, the component or army headquarters, and the operations of the major ground maneuver forces, the corps. In the actions of each, there are classic theoretical principles or concepts that found reconfirmation in the world in 1990–91.

Perhaps no more complete success was achieved in the Persian Gulf War than that in the field of grand strategy. Liddell Hart wrote that the role of grand strategy is "to coordinate and direct all the resources of a nation towards the attainment of the political object of the war—the goal defined by national policy."[7] It is grand strategy that provides the context and sets the limits within which the military must operate, and in this, President George Bush, Secretary of State James Baker, and Secretary of Defense Richard Cheney proved themselves masters of their trade. It is hard to think of a war in which diplomatic and military actions have been better harmonized. The administration was able to simplify greatly the ambiguity within which the soldier operated. It did so by isolating Iraq and branding it as an outlaw state, by calling into existence a global and regional alliance in which, nonetheless, there were only two dominant members, and by achieving the mandate of the United Nations without tying military actions to that body.

The president allocated more than sufficient means and provided clear guidance as to what he wanted done militarily. It was he who decided when military operations would begin and when they would end, consistent with the requirements of policy, coalition politics, and the safety of the forces involved. Ultimately, it was the balance maintained between the military and diplomatic fields that ensured the conditions at the end of the war would be significantly better than those that might have obtained had it never been fought. That is the true measure of acceptability for the decision to commit political questions to resolution by the sword.

Within this general proposition, there are a number of observations that might be made. First of all, there is the revalidation of Clausewitz' critical distinction between real war and, for want of a better term, "ideal" war. The Army had always tended to underestimate the possibility of a land war in the Persian Gulf because it was clear that major land forces could not be dispatched there in time to stop an aggressor already on the spot. This reasoning was sound. It took almost three months before the Army had a significant force capable of undertaking sustained operations should they be required. By then, Kuwait was lost, and indeed, in August 1990, the operation, viewed in strictly military terms, seemed highly risky if Saddam did have designs on Saudi oil fields.

But Clausewitz pointed out over a century ago that enemies were not unknown to each other. "From the enemy's character, from his intentions, the state of his affairs and his general situation, each side, using the *laws of probability*, forms an estimate of its opponent's likely course and acts accordingly."[8] In August 1990, the problem was no longer abstract but practical, an estimate could be made, the risk gauged, and action taken based upon that assessment. "When war is no longer a theoretical affair, but a series of actions obeying its own peculiar laws," wrote Clausewitz, "reality supplies the data from which we can deduce the unknown that lies ahead."[9]

Saddam, driven by economic, historical, and geographical imperatives, likely set out merely to seize a province.[10] Whatever his intentions, which were only subject to informed supposition or judgment, he then posed a threat to global economics, the regional balance of power, and the territorial integrity of Saudi Arabia. There was risk in the short term for President Bush if he intervened, but its dimensions were knowable or at least calculable. Similarly, there were risks for Saddam Hussein in the long run, and his loss, no less than the American president's success, reminds us that in any probability of success, there is a possibility of failure. To rephrase Bernard Brodie only slightly, nations do not go to war because they think war is safe. They go to war because they think they will win. In this, they are often mistaken.[11]

The second grand strategic observation one might make of the Persian Gulf War lies in the recognition by the Bush administration that there are significant limits on the utility of a state's military power as a means to resolve international problems, even when one is the world's only remaining superpower. Unmatched military might is not useful if it cannot be brought to bear and if its use is deemed to be illegitimate by the rest of the world. In short, a sole superpower has an inherent obligation not to bring against itself the combined opposition of the rest of the world, rather as democratic Athens did in the Peloponnesian War.[12]

The willing participation of Saudi Arabia in any U.S. military actions was absolutely essential to the achievement of U.S. goals. First of all, Saudi Arabia provided the base from which a land and aerial attack could be launched. Second, and no less vital, the participation of the Saudi king, with his religious as well as political stature in the Arab world, went far, indeed, toward legitimizing the U.S. coalition efforts against a major leader in the Arab world. One need only look at the position in which the king of Jordan found himself, with the support for Saddam in his streets, to recognize the importance of this Saudi contribution and of the concomitant obligation of U.S. forces not to take any action that would rebound on their hosts, either by exceeding the UN mandate or remaining in the peninsula beyond their welcome.

These were matters of high policy in which Schwarzkopf, as well as the Third Army commander, found themselves involved continuously. Even the commander of the 7th U.K. Armored Brigade, the first British commitment to Desert Shield, wrote of his own diplomatic burden upon arriving in the peninsula.[13] Judgments about the decision to end the war when the president did, to stop military action short of requiring the removal of Saddam Hussein, to accommodate Saudi cultural norms, and to depart rapidly without complaint can be made only in light of these limits. The lesson for the future is that even sole superpowers cannot have things their own way in a world they can influence but not dominate. Saudi Arabia is still a long way from the port of Savannah.

An effective U.S. theater strategy was indispensable in the Gulf War. By theater strategy is meant the purposeful integration of military resources in the theater of war to achieve the military objectives set by the president and his secretary of defense. This integration is achieved largely by concept, structure, and process: concept in providing a clear design for the combined actions of the forces deployed; structure by establishment of a command and control organization capable of achieving the concept; and process in development of a common plan for all forces to serve as the basis of all subsequent actions. In this, General H. Norman Schwarzkopf gets very high marks indeed.

As commander in chief, Schwarzkopf had two essential tasks, one political, one military. The political task was to create, where none existed, a reasonably effective military coalition, first to defend Saudi Arabia, then to free Kuwait. His military task as U.S. unified commander was to harmonize the activities of U.S. forces in such a way that each contributed its own unique form of power to a synergistic whole. He also had to develop a unified plan of operations and see to a reasonably harmonious execution of that plan to achieve the assigned military objectives at the least cost to the American people. It is clear that Schwarzkopf succeeded in both roles. While he was aided greatly by his component commanders, each in their own sphere, there is no question that it was the CINC himself upon whom the greatest burden for allied and joint service cooperation ultimately fell. Given his normal lack of patience, the coalition task, carried out over many months of intense pressure, clearly called for expenditure of vast reserves of self-discipline that seem never to have failed him when dealing with allies.

The theater strategy varied as the mission evolved. Initially, U.S. military action consisted of a naval blockade to isolate Iraq from external support by sea, with overland commerce also closed off by the diplomatic encirclement achieved through the United Nations—Jordan excepted. To back up this blockade and to increase pressure on Iraq to depart Kuwait voluntarily, air and ground forces were sent to Saudi Arabia, lest the desert kingdom's role as a principal coalition member provoke Iraq into extending its offensive farther south. The dynamic process of introducing various types of U.S. forces in the force deployment process was the practical manifestation of this part of theater strategy. What often looked at the corps level as interference in their deployment was, in fact, Schwarzkopf and his component commanders manipulating the deployment flow as they became aware of new requirements or local capabilities that permitted substitution of one capability for another.

As part of the deterrent strategy in the peninsula, Schwarzkopf quickly built up an unanswerable offensive air plan that required change only in scale and detail once an air-ground offensive option was developed to free Kuwait. For the defensive phase of the Gulf War (Desert Shield), a defensive ground force was constructed and placed into positions behind the Gulf Cooperation Council forces already facing the Iraqis. Required to develop an offensive strategy to free Kuwait, Schwarzkopf was able to build on his original air concept to add an offensive ground component and to harmonize the two while the naval blockade continued. The CINC's ability to rise above his own service biases and to adopt a theater offensive plan centered on an aerial campaign of attrition—upon which ground operations were contingent and to which they were clearly secondary—indicates a technical grasp of the military art.

The organization of the command by departmental components, instead of creating a unified or joint ground component command comparable to the joint air component, does not appear to have had a significant effect on the outcome. It was unlikely that a single unified high command was politically desirable, given very legitimate Saudi sensitivities. In that case, forming a joint task force headquarters to provide a single ground component for U.S. land forces (over Army and Marine Corps elements), separated by the Joint Forces Command North into two simultaneous but largely distinct operations, does not seem likely to have added much but an additional senior headquarters between the CINC and his troops.

Schwarzkopf is said by General Waller, his deputy, to have referred to him (Waller) as his "Bradley," and Waller speaks of his role as ground component commander as deputy commander in chief.[14] The analogy is both historically and organizationally inapt. In North Africa, Bradley went forward to be Eisenhower's eyes and ears and was quickly coopted by Patton. In France, Bradley was a major subordinate commander, and Eisenhower, like Schwarzkopf, was ground component commander with other components and Allied forces subordinated to his command. Schwarzkopf was ground component commander by default and that seems to have been no more inappropriate in his case than it was in Eisenhower's. Schwarzkopf was already unable to exercise close executive supervision over forces in the field through his unified headquarters—and unable by temperament to leave execution entirely to his senior subordinates. The utility of another organizational model is questionable under the circumstances as they obtained in Saudi Arabia, though some second order adjustments, such as an earlier appointment of a joint targeting board under the deputy CINC to assist the CINC in coordinating air and ground offensives, might have been useful.

The process of conducting theater strategy consists of the practical combination of immediate decisions and long-term campaign planning, both carried out over time, which gives shape and substance to the theater commander's strategic concepts. Because of the lack of technical depth in a joint headquarters, the planning process became centered in the components very early on. Viewed in the large, the entire process evolved very much as JCS Publication 1, *Joint Warfare of the U.S. Armed Forces*, anticipates: "Campaign planning is done in crisis or conflict (once the actual threat, national guidance, and available resources become evident), but the basis and framework for successful campaigns is laid by peacetime analysis, planning and exercises."[15]

Internal Look was the culmination of peacetime analysis, planning, and exercise. Desert Shield was an initial response to one set of practical circumstances and missions that built upon Internal Look. Desert Storm was another response to yet another set of circumstances and missions, which, in turn, built upon Desert Shield. At the end of the day, the coalition high command had integrated the forces of a very disparate set of allies into a potent, indeed, irresistible offensive force.

Planning for the final offensive was a multimonth, multiechelon, iterative process—not a series of events where a higher plan was received, and then the next lower plan written, and so on down to the lowest platoon. Indeed, such a process would have been unrealistic given the need to balance and rebalance the desirable against the possible. That the best way to attack the Iraqi array was through the Iraqi desert was obvious. The real issue was to figure out how far west forces could go and how they were going to get there, as well as how that movement was to relate to the air operations upon which any ground offensive was seen to be dependent. The planning process was punctuated by a series of events, guidance given, planning sessions, discussions, and back-briefings in which the entire command structure worked out their understanding of Schwarzkopf's concept, then filled in the details appropriate to each level.

From theater strategy, one descends in planning to operational art. Operational art is "the employment of military forces to attain strategic goals in a theater of war or theater of operations through the design, organization, and conduct of campaigns and major operations."[16] The last major action of the CINC in the realm of theater strategy was the assignment of theater objectives, the identification of decisive objectives, and their assignment to components. Campaign planning then consisted of working out the ways and means for the accomplishment of these objectives.

In campaign planning, it is not the final document that is important. It is the process itself that matters. In the television program, Gwynne Dwyer's War: A Commentary, prepared by the National Film Board of Canada, Israeli General Dan Lanner responded to a question from Dwyer in this way:

> "Well, in my opinion, a battle never works. It never works according to plan. . . . the plan is only a common base for changes. Everybody should know the plan so you can change easily. But the modern battle is very fluid and you have to make your decisions very fast and mostly not according to the original plan."
>
> "But," Dwyer replied, "at least everybody knows where you're coming from."
>
> "And," Lanner shot back, "where you're going to, more or less."[17]

It is this idea of a plan as a point of reference rather than a blueprint for execution that is often lost sight of in the training of American officers—this, and the idea of planning as a process rather than an event. In Desert Storm it was both. The joint and component plans for Desert Storm were published at about the same time.

The great lesson of the operational art for Desert Storm has nothing to do with the metaphysics of selecting "centers of gravity"—so popular a concept with graduates of the School of Advanced Military Studies—nor with the insight that it was better for ground forces to go around than through the Iraqi array, which was obvious (although, in the event, the Air Force may have rendered the distinction moot). Rather, it is in the extent to which logistics dominates the operational offensive. The U.S. Army has been spared this inconvenience by forty years of sitting on the inter-German border. J. F. C. Fuller had pointed out this reality in his biography of U.S. Grant, written in the 1930s. According to Fuller, Grant "realized that as tactics are based on strategy, in its turn strategy is based on administration; that is, if action depends on movement, movement depends on supply."[18]

The issue for the operational commanders was never whether to go around. The question was to determine how far one could go around with sizable forces dependent on a sea of fuel and a mountain of supplies to sustain any type of offensive. The operational artist was not the philosopher of war who recognized what needed to be done; he was the technician of war who knew how to do it with what was available. In the end, the theater campaign design did produce the disruption of the enemy land force before the launching of the ground attack, but it did so principally by attrition from the air, not maneuver on the ground—though the flank attack by VII Corps certainly added to the dislocation of the enemy. Like Schlieffen's great plan, the ground attack was "a rolling offensive once begun, a series of loosely related but independent battles" that, in their aggregate, destroyed the Iraqi Army in the KTO.[19]

The most serious breakdown in the smooth functioning of the chain of command occurred between the theater commander and one of his tactical subordinates, that is, between General Schwarzkopf and Lieutenant General Franks. As General Bernard Trainor has pointed out most perceptively,[20] Franks, the tactical commander, was fully involved in the conduct of an approach to contact at a time when the theater commander began to demand a pursuit. Operational demand and tactical reality were at odds. Franks was on the battlefield. He was absorbed in the messy business of combat, which was accompanied as always by confusion, incomplete information, danger, and abysmal weather. Schwarzkopf could watch hundreds of enemy vehicles fleeing north in real time, as though on a TV screen, and talk to the Pentagon as if it were around the corner. It was Yeosock's task, however, at Third Army to reconcile the conflicting views, either to get Franks to move faster or to explain tactical realities to the CINC. (And, finally, Yeosock could have pointed out that, in the joint air component, Schwarzkopf had a splendid tool for interdicting the enemy's withdrawal.)

Yeosock might have prevailed upon Franks to accept the risk of keeping the two armored divisions and armored cavalry regiment in motion the night of 24-25 February, although it is unlikely that the speed of the 1st Division's breaching operation and the subsequent 1st U.K.'s passage of lines could have been increased materially. That *might* have brought the 1st Armored Division to Al Busayyah in time to take the town in daylight, thus obviating the need for the second pause. If it did not, Yeosock might have insisted that the division carry the town in the dark. That, almost certainly, would have risked more casualties from friendly fire and might not have saved any time since forces making dismounted night attacks ordinarily require a good bit of reorganization when daylight comes. The division could have continued the advance a brigade short, of course, but that would have hurt it when it met the Republican Guard soon after. The first action would have entailed a risk that was more uncertain the night of the 24th than it is today, and the latter might have produced no gain at all.

Yeosock did none of these things. Indeed, his concept of command and his relationship with Schwarzkopf had much to do with his actions. Yeosock was unlikely to second-guess the tactical commander on the ground. His whole understanding of operational command was evident in his phrase about "unencumbering" the corps commanders. Schwarzkopf's rages, which Yeosock took for granted as irrational rather than specific, were simply one more distraction from which he could "unencumber" General Franks. That he did not convince the CINC that his intentions were being implemented as rapidly as possible does not seem to have been clear to Yeosock until the morning of the 26th. Rather, he seems throughout to have been confident that, in the end, it was all going to work itself out. Implicit in all this was a difference of view about how many lives this marginal gain was worth.

Yeosock's Moltkean approach to operational command and his dependence on his corps commanders also contributed to the gap that developed between the 24th Division and the eastward movement of the VII Corps. In retrospect, Yeosock might have intervened to get General Luck to swing the 24th Infantry Division eastward earlier. Instead of allowing the "Victory" Division brigades to run up and down airfields, he might have prevailed upon the XVIII Corps commander to advance the division attack east on Highway 8 by as much as twelve hours. Whether the logistics system (particularly fuel resupply) could have responded had that been ordered, remains to be proven. In any event, Luck seems to have been as disinterested in stopping General McCaffrey's moment of high theater as was Yeosock. It was difficult at the time not to see the airfield attacks as highly productive.

It cannot be disputed, however, that there was a breakdown between perceived operational imperatives and tactical realities. It is equally indisputable that it was Yeosock's place to mediate between the two. This was a human as well as a technical problem, and it is at least clear that the human part was unsuccessful, whatever the technical choices of the moment.

The major criticism of the conduct of the campaign, in retrospect, has a great deal to do with aesthetics and little to do with practical matters. One senior officer at Third Army put the matter this way: "It was my only chance to take part in a battle of Cannae and we failed to bring it off."[21] What he referred to was the failure to close the encirclement outside of Basrah because of the cessation of offensive operations the morning of 28 February. The details of this question have already been examined. It is appropriate here to add only two additional observations. The first is that even Cannae was not so perfect a victory as mythology would indicate.[22] More to the point, Cannae did not end the Punic War. In the end, Hannibal and Carthage were defeated.

Kuwait is free. The Iraqis in the Basrah pocket were allowed to go by default, or on purpose, not through any efforts of their own but because the coalition's goals were deemed to have been achieved. To decide, after the fact, that this "release" was a mistake is interesting, but not particularly practical, given that the efficiency of the operation can only be judged correctly in light of the goals and knowledge of circumstances that existed at the time. To close the pocket on the ground would have required that the 24th Infantry Division move even faster than it did, not likely given that it was commanded by a driven man to begin with (and that Basrah was far from the line of departure). It would have required also a willingness to accept the casualties likely to result if infantry were put into Basrah. Landing an air assault brigade in AO Thomas also looks good in retrospect, but at the time, it involved a good bit of risk because of uncommitted and escaping Iraqi forces. Finally, it is hard to envision a defeat more nearly total than that imposed south of the Euphrates. Such yearning after the perfect is simply moonshine!

That is not to say that the execution of the campaign might not have been done with more speed and more aggressiveness, and that gets to the heart of the conflict between Schwarzkopf and his Army commanders. This, in turn, involves what Jomini and Fuller refer to as grand tactics, essentially the employment of large forces on the battlefield.[23]

The VII Corps' attack was, by design, deliberate and cautious during its first two days, clearly designed for evading risk of any early disorganization while the corps won maneuver room. The cost of that care was obviously paid in time. The reason for this has to do with the state of mind of the Army commanders themselves. To a man, they expected high casualties from the ground operation. They had been assured of as much by various simulations and pundits since August

1990, and disposed to believe computer printouts, they prepared accordingly. Only Schwarzkopf seems to have anticipated the disorganizing effect of massive attrition and technological overmatch, and he too showed caution at the outset and later retained for too long a theater reserve of two heavy brigades and worried about the huge 24th Infantry Division getting out on a limb on the Euphrates. The Army needs to reconsider the credibility of simulations that depend principally on Mr. Lanchester's equations and neglect the moral factors of war, even though they are far less predictable.

Far more worrying is the idea that has taken hold in the late twentieth century that one can make war without suffering losses from enemy action or fratricide. There can be no question that concern for fratricide constituted a major operational obstacle—slowing the operations in the breach, delaying the attack on Objective Purple, and stopping the renewed VII Corps attack entirely the morning of the 28th. Congressman Les Aspin's Committee on Armed Services reported after the war that, "In planning Operation Desert Storm, minimizing allied and civilian casualties was *the highest priority* [emphasis added]."[24]

While minimizing casualties is certainly an important human concern, it can produce a terrible inhibiting effect when it becomes *the most important* consideration. As British historian Cyril Falls observes, "It is remarkable how many people exert themselves and go through contortions to prove that battles and wars are won by any means except that by which they are most commonly won, which is by fighting."[25] Fighting inevitably carries with it loss of life and limb, and American commanders seemed extraordinarily sensitive to that fact.

Napoleon wrote that the "first object which a general who gives battle should consider is the glory and honor of his arms; the safety and conservation of his men is but secondary; but it is also true that in audacity and obstinacy will be found the safety and conservation of his men."[26] But, of course, Napoleon ruined his army and his state and ended on a distant island. Sir Michael Howard, in the midst of the Gulf coalition's air campaign, warned that

> However skillful may be American statesmanship, however successful the allied armed forces in the field, if American public opinion is so horrified by the sight of slaughter that it ceases to be supportive of the whole enterprise, Saddam Hussein might still not lose the war. In this, as in so much else, the Clausewitzian analysis remains starkly relevant.[27]

In the Gulf War, this unwillingness to recognize the connection between risk and battle losses probably had little practical effect on an outcome that was, in retrospect, fairly certain. Yet it is an unwillingness deeply ingrained in our Army and trained by peacetime safety measures (valid in their own context) and no doubt by the memory among many officers of the effect of Walter Cronkite's weekly loss reports during the war in Vietnam. The fear this concern raises remains as a significant American weakness, and this fact must not be overlooked in the satisfaction with the results of this war. An imperative for low losses is a very weak reed upon which to build a combat doctrine, as weak perhaps as a total disregard for casualties.

George Patton wrote to his son in August 1944, "I have used one principle in these operations . . . and that is to—'fill the unforgiving minute with sixty seconds worth of distance run.' That is the whole art of war, and when you get to be a general, remember it!"[28] This is a much different approach from being "ahead of schedule and under budget." But Patton was fighting a total war (and not the first battle) and enjoyed strong public backing and involvement. Desert Storm, as Sir Michael seems to warn, for all its vocal public support, lacked—or was perceived to lack—that depth of public feeling necessary to bear heavy losses. Rightly or wrongly, the ground attack of Operation Desert Storm reflected more Montgomery-like concern for a tidy battlefield and balanced attack than pursuit of the "unforgiving minute." A major cause of the friction between the CINC and his field commanders was his greater willingness to risk a higher butcher's bill for greater speed in attack. Such judgments are highly subjective, largely individual, and very contingent in their effect. (Section 28 of the first chapter of Book I of Clausewitz' *On War*, with its reference to a "remarkable trinity," remains a good theoretical guide in relation to this problem. It provides, however, no easy answers.)[29]

Schwarzkopf's postwar obloquy of Franks was highly overstated.[30] Franks' mission may have been destruction of the Republican Guard, but Yeosock *and Waller*, with the CINC's knowledge and implicit approval, kept VII Corps within boundaries that limited its mission to "destruction in zone." If any Republican Guard troops in that zone escaped destruction, they did so by moving out of it, something it is not at all clear Franks could have influenced given his inability to affect deep-air interdiction. The partial escape of the Hammurabi Division would seem to be the responsibility of Third Army, which controlled the entire Army zone, *and the CINC himself*, since Schwarzkopf reserved responsibility for integration of the Army and joint Air Force components. Moreover, the escape of the greater part of Iraqi heavy forces from the Basrah pocket occurred either in the face of J-STARS observation and Air Force interdiction beyond the fire support coordination line or after the truce talks with the Iraqis on 2 March, in which Schwarzkopf played a far more active role than the commanders of Third Army or VII Corps. Both of the above were a theater responsibility (Schwarzkopf's). Bridges out of Basrah, not road junctions at Safwan, were the route to a safe haven.

Two years after the Gulf War. in a talk at Fort Leavenworth, Franks listed the principles he believes should govern a commander in battle: getting the entire organization in the fight, maintaining a "balanced stance," dealing face-to-face with subordinates, paying attention to logistics, and reinforcing success.[31] (See figure 35.) These same principles guided the actions of VII Corps during Operation Desert Storm.

There is certainly a lesson from this war about technology, and it is that a clear technological advantage is a very nice thing to have. One U.S. division commander has observed that "we could have beat them with their equipment," and perhaps he is correct. The fact is, the U.S. military did not have to, and the war, no doubt, has given many the idea that technology is the answer to everything. Indeed, a dangerous consequence of the war may be that it seems to have reversed Michael Howard's contention that "technology may have made war more terrible, or any rate, more terrible for more people, but it has for this very reason made it less attractive and less likely ..."[32]

It was, of course, the very one-sided nature of the technologies in question that made this difference. Looked at from the other side, it has since become clear that the "surgical air strikes" in Baghdad were surgical only if one's standard is a comparison to the effect of the ordnance dropped by a flight of B-17s over Germany in World War II. As George Ball observed before the air war, ". . . if the medical profession adopted the standards of the Air Force, any patient seeking an appendectomy might well have his heart and brain removed, while his appendix remained intact."[33] At least, with precision munitions, the patient's appendix would now be gone, too. *The New York Review of Books* quotes one postwar survey: "Baghdad, . . . where some four million people lived, is a city essentially unmarked, a body with its skin basically intact, with every main bone broken and with its joints and tendons cut . . . . The health system is collapsing. There are no phones and no electricity and no petrol and only a people reduced to daily improvisations and scroungings."[34]

PLANNING IS NOT FIGHTING

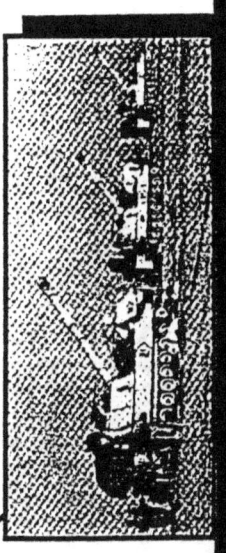

PLANNING ...

- FOCUS ON THE ENEMY YOU FACE
- ASK: HOW CAN I BEST HURT THE ENEMY?
- LISTEN TO YOUR OWN ORDERS; HOLD BRIEFBACKS AND REHEARSALS AT ALL LEVELS
- KEEP SIMPLICITY IN THE PLAN
- KNOW YOUR JOB AS WELL AS YOUR SOLDIERS KNOW THEIRS
- ASK: WHAT'S THE WORST THAT CAN HAPPEN?
- FOCUS INTEL: PIR x 6
- ESTABLISH THE POINT OF MAIN EFFORT
- BE PREPARED TO BE SUCCESSFUL

...FIGHTING

- GET ENTIRE ORGANIZATION INTO THE FIGHT
- REUSE COMBAT ASSETS
- SHIFT POINTS OF MAIN EFFORT
- KEEP A RESERVE; CONTINUALLY REINFORCE
- STAY IN A BALANCED STANCE
- MAINTAIN FACE-TO-FACE WITH SUBORDINATES; GIVE ORDERS IN SOLDIER'S TERMS
- FORGET LOGISTICS AND YOU WILL LOSE
- *REINFORCE SUCCESS*

WHERE TOMORROW'S VICTORIES BEGIN

Figure 35.

A United Nations' report of 22 March 1991 states that "The recent conflict has wrought near-apocalyptic results upon the infrastructure of what had been, until January 1991, a rather highly urbanized and mechanized society. Now, most means of modern life support have been destroyed or rendered tenuous."[35] In short, war is still war, and technological advantage looks to cheapen war only for the side that has it.

The extraordinarily low casualty figures for attacking American ground forces were also the result of an advantage purchased by sustained investment in technology and training—an investment that seems to have been a wise one. A ground war today, without that advantage, could be something different, indeed—especially if the enemy's materiel was on a par with our own.

Generalship was also a significant facet of the Gulf War. As Napoleon said:

> The personality of the general is indispensable; he is the head, he is the all, of an army. The Gauls were not conquered by the Roman legions, but by Caesar. It was not before the Carthaginian soldiers that Rome was made to tremble, but before Hannibal. It was not the Macedonian phalanx which penetrated to India, but Alexander. It was not the French Army which reached the Weser and the Inn, it was Turenne. Prussia was not defended for seven years against the three most formidable European Powers by the Prussian soldiers, but by Frederick the Great.[36]

Undoubtedly the theater of war in the Arabian Peninsula was dominated by the personality of General Schwarzkopf. No act taken had meaning except in reference to his mercurial and unforgiving personality. But the habit of killing messengers has a cost. Messengers stop telling the king what he ought to hear. The unwillingness of senior Army commanders to question the sending of the 24th Division away from the main attack is but one example. The lack of a common view between the Third Army commanders and the CINC on the likely enemy resistance, along with the need for haste in exploitation, are others.

To a great extent, communication had broken down because of Schwarzkopf's arbitrary treatment of those he relied upon to act as an extension of his will. The high command of Desert Storm was no Nelsonian band of brothers who could be advised only that "no man will do too far wrong who lays his ship beside that of the enemy" and then be left to execute the commander in chief's plan.

Schwarzkopf's great shortcoming was his inability to take an elevated view of the battlefield, to recognize and accept the presence of friction in execution and "noise" in the information system.[37] Increasingly behind events, he could neither influence nor understand the limitations on the maneuver of massive armored forces in the field. Nor was he willing to leave the tactical execution to the man on the spot, who was capable of seeing and feeling the forces present in the iron fist of VII Corps. "Iron will power," Clausewitz says, "can overcome this friction; it pulverizes every obstacle, but of course it wears down the machine as well."[38]

The net effect of the theater commander's personality on the force he commanded was largely negative. General Waller's position was, therefore, essential, precisely because he was not afraid of the CINC, and he was willing to be the messenger. Because Waller was approachable, he also became the mediator between Schwarzkopf and his subordinates. But then, while critiquing Schwarzkopf's method, one must remember that, to paraphrase the other "great helmsman," war is not a tea party.

General officers, and Schwarzkopf had a handful of them, are powerful men who have risen in a competitive bureaucracy, seldom entirely by selfless service. Many are not unaccustomed, when their proposals are not accepted, to going around their boss to sponsors in their service departments. If Schwarzkopf was to be master in his own house, he needed to preserve a certain distance. Eisenhower, after all, did not have to maintain his position in an environment where every division commander (no less countless staff officers) could telephone friends in the Pentagon or around the Army daily, or where other commanders in chief with good ideas could simply pick up the phone and call "to help out." There was a good deal of networking, not always to the detriment of the effort, for it meant that the collective minds of an institution were brought to bear in a way not heretofore possible. At the same time, for all the mutual kind words immediately after the war, Schwarzkopf was the recipient of a good deal more "help" from the national security adviser and the chairman of the JCS—or those who claimed to speak in their names—than he might have wished.[39] Still, one must note the difference between Schwarzkopf's treatment of his subordinates and the way Eisenhower and Marshall treated Bradley after the miscalculation of the Ardennes. The contrast is especially significant given Schwarzkopf's own definition of character.

Army generals in Southwest Asia stand out by virtue of their executive abilities, their determination to succeed with the resources made available to them, and their ability to find expedients to get around shortfalls and difficulties. They were not all gentlemen, but they were all determined and effective.

Operation Desert Storm was a transitional war in which forces raised and trained to fight on the Central Front in Europe against a great power were, instead, deployed to the open desert to fight a local tyrant with more technology than he knew how to use. What does this war have to say to the Army of the twenty-first century?

First of all, it suggests that operational command and control is not analogous to tactical command and control. This conclusion was at the core of Yeosock's frequent observations that nine echelons separated him and the fighting platoons. Indeed, his whole method of command was a matter of "direction" rather than control. It is because of the distance from the fighting line and the difficulty of getting precise and accurate information that operational command requires more anticipation. Fewer decisions are better. Planning horizons are more distant. At the same time, it is clear that the means exist today for jumping the chain of command in order to obtain information needed immediately to exploit an opportunity rapidly. The Army, however, has not figured out how best to utilize this means while respecting the chain of command necessary for articulated operation. It is also clear that even with clear transmission of words across the ether, miscommunication can and will still take place between the operators of two telephone handsets.

Strategically, Desert Shield showed the importance to the United States of air and maritime superiority and the ability to exploit them. Without air and maritime superiority, the Army would not have gotten to the war. Because of the shortage of roll-on, roll-off ships, the deployment of armored forces took longer than the distance alone warranted.

At the theater-strategic level, at least in the desert, air forces have become the arm of rapid maneuver and deep attack, armies the fixing force. However, if air power proved vital, indeed decisive, in this war—operationally and tactically—the enemy was not defeated until his depleted army was destroyed by men on the ground and until air power was provided with exposed ground targets by its terrestrial "beaters." Massive air power was necessary, even critical to success. It was not sufficient alone.

Aside from the positive (offensive) contribution of air supremacy, ARCENT could not have made war in the way that it did without it. The concentrations of armored formations and the vast accumulations of fuel, parts, and ammunition required to project a force into the enemy depths, represent a significant vulnerability if they cannot be protected from enemy attack from the air. All the talk about nonlinear warfare, war with discontinuous fronts, does not affect the simple fact that mechanized armies rely more than ever on materiel to stay in the field, and an armored Army must be based, and to a great extent tethered somewhere. It cannot operate like a fleet at sea.

Desert Storm showed that a different kind of Army is required for operational offensives from that required for forward defense in Europe. Operational warfare is made with wheeled vehicles, and the U.S. Army simply did not have enough of them, at least in theater. Desert Storm also showed that in mechanized warfare, the large manpower-intensive army has not gone away, it has simply moved its personnel from the battle line into shops and dumps and into specialties that make the machines more effective. Finally, the Gulf War demonstrated again that prewar investment in people, training, and good equipment pays off in blood saved on the battlefield.

Finally, this war was marked by three important, even decisive, conditions that may not repeat themselves in future contingencies. First, this part of the Persian Gulf was well endowed with exactly the sort of infrastructure that could compensate for the allies' own shortcomings in the strategic projection of heavy forces. In this regard, at least, Saudi Arabia was a "mature" theater of operations. Second, the global balance was such that there were no other strategic distractions; the theater of operations could enjoy the full support of the entire American military. Finally, as Count Alfred von Schlieffen wrote in his classic *Cannae*, "A complete battle of Cannae is rarely met in history. For its achievement, a Hannibal is needed on one side, and a Terrentius Varro, on the other, both cooperating for the attainment of the great objective." Whether or not there was a Hannibal on the allied side, there was certainly a Terrentius Varro in Baghdad.[40]

Notes

1. "Transcript of President Bush's Address on End of the Gulf War," *The New York Times*, 7 March 1991, A8.

2. HQ, ARCENT, Command Briefing Operation Desert Storm, dated 15 August 1991, slide titled, "Military Objectives."

3. Ibid. Slides titled, "Task Force Freedom" and "TF Freedom Mission."

4. HQ, 352d Civil Affairs Command, AFKA-ACDM-CG, Memorandum for COMUSARCENT, Subject: Combined Civil Affairs Task Force (CCATF) After-Action Report (AAR), Operations Desert Shield/Storm. The report is an excellent overview of civil affairs problems from the standpoint of the civil affairs specialists. A slightly different point of view is in HQ, ARCENT, G3 (AFRD-DTP), Memorandum for USARCENT Historian, Colonel Swain, Subject: HQ USARCENT G3 Plans, Historical Narrative of Desert Shield, Desert Storm, Defense and Restoration of Kuwait, and Redeployment.

5. Lieutenant Colonel Peter S. Kindsvatter, "VII Corps in the Gulf War: Post Cease-Fire Operations," *Military Review* 72 (June 1992): 2–19.

6. Robert Southey, "The Battle of Blenheim," in *The Oxford Book of War Poetry*, ed. Jon Stallworthy (Oxford: Oxford University Press, 1984), 66.

7. B. H. Liddell Hart, *The Decisive Wars of History* (London: G. Bell & Son, Ltd., 1929), 150–51. This is the operative consequence of Clausewitz' observation that "war itself does not suspend political intercourse or change it into something entirely different. In essentials that intercourse continues, irrespective of the means it employs." Carl von Clausewitz, *On War*, ed. and trans. Michael Howard and Peter Paret (Princeton, NJ: Princeton University Press, 1976), 605. Similarly, Raymond Aron wrote: "The distinction between diplomacy and [military] strategy is an entirely relative one. These two terms are complementary aspects of the single act of policy—the act of conducting relations with other states so as to further the 'national interests.' " Raymond Aron, *Peace and War: A Theory of International Relations*, trans. Richard Howard and Annette Baker Fox (New York: Doubleday & Co., 1966), 24.

8. Clausewitz, *On War*, 80.

9. Ibid.

10. Saddam's behavior seems to indicate as much, particularly his involvement in Kuwait City, which delayed any move farther south had that been his intention. Some have called this an error on his part. It is, of course, an error only if he intended to move south. The stockage of great quantities of materiel in southeast Iraq does not indicate intention either. Military men, in general, overensure when they can. U.S. forces set a sixty-day stockage level for munitions for a war they expected to last no more than two weeks.

11. Bernard Brodie, *Strategy in the Missile Age* (Princeton, NJ: Princeton University Press, 1965), 224.

12. Aron, *Peace and War*, 25; and Thucydides, *The Peloponnesian War*, trans. Rex Warner (Harmondsworth, England: Penguin Books, 1972), 49.

13. Brigadier P. A. J. Cordingley, "The Gulf War: Operating with Allies," Journal of the *Royal United Services Institute for Defence Studies* 137, no. 2 (April 1992): 18.

14. Interview with Lieutenant General Calvin Waller by Brigadier General Timothy Grogan at Fort Lewis, Washington, 2 May 1991, 126–27.

15. Joint Publication 1, *Joint Warfare of the US Armed Forces*, 11 November 1991, 46.

16. FM 100-5, *Operations*, May 1986, 10.

17. In Gwynne Dwyer, *War: A Commentary by Gwynne Dwyer*, Episode 1, "The Road to Total War," National Film Board of Canada, 1985.

18. J. F. C. Fuller, *The Generalship of Ulysses S. Grant* (Bloomington: Indiana University Press, 1977), 214.

19. Arden Bucholz, *Moltke, Schlieffen and Prussian War Planning* (New York: Bing Publishing, 1991), 242. Quotation refers, of course, to Schlieffen's ideas, not the Gulf War.

20. Lieutenant General Bernard E. Trainor, U.S. Marine Corps, Retired, "Schwarzkopf and His Generals," in *U.S. Naval Institute Proceedings* 20, no. 6 (June 1994): 47.

21. To the author.

22. Livy, *The War with Hannibal, Book XXI–XXX of The History of Rome From Its Foundation*, trans. Aubrey De Selincourt (Harmondsworth, England: Penguin Books, 1965), 149; and Polybius, *The Rise of the Roman Empire*, trans. Ian Scott-Kilvert (Harmondsworth, England: Penguin Books, 1979), 274.

23. Jomini, *The Art of War*, trans. Captain G. H. Mendell and Lieutenant W. P. Craighill (Philadelphia: J. B. Lippincott & Co., 1862—Greenwood Press reprint, n.d.), 62; and J. F. C. Fuller, *The Foundations of the Science of War* (London: Hutchinson & Co., Ltd., 1925), 107. Liddell Hart attributes the term to Guibert in *The Ghost of Napoleon* (New Haven, CT: Yale University Press, 1933), 81.

24. U.S. House of Representatives, Committee on Armed Services, Washington, D.C., 30 March 1992, *Defense for a New Era: Lessons of the Persian Gulf*, 88–89.

25. Cyril Falls, quoted in T. Harry Williams, "The Military Leadership of North and South," in *Why the North Won the Civil War*, ed. David Donald (New York: Collier Books, 1960), 34.

26. Napoleon, Maxim No. XV, in *The Military Maxims of Napoleon*, trans. Lieutenant General Sir George C. D. Auguilar (New York: Macmillan Publishing Co., 1987).

27. Sir Michael Howard, "Clausewitz: Man of the Year," *The New York Times*, 28 January 1991, A23.

28. Letter George S. Patton, Jr., to son George, 21 August 1944, ed. Martin Blumenson, *The Patton Papers, 1940–1945*, vol. 2 (Boston: Houghton Mifflin Co., 1974), 523.

29. Section 28 addresses Clausewitz' "remarkable trinity."

30. Schwarzkopf, *Doesn't Take a Hero*, 383, 433, 455–56, 461–63, 475–76.

31. Slide in possession of author.

32. Michael Howard, "War and Technology," *Journal of the Royal United Services Institute for Defence Studies* 132 (December 1987): 21.

33. George W. Ball, "The Gulf Crisis," *The New York Review of Books* (6 December 1990): 12.

34. Richard Reed of UN Children's Fund, quoted by Samir al-Khahl, "Iraq and Its Future," *The New York Review of Books* 38, no. 7 (11 April 1991): 10.

35. "Excerpts from U.N. Report on Need for Humanitarian Assistance in Iraq," *The New York Times*, 23 March 1991, A5.

36. Fuller, *Foundations of the Science of War*, 127.

37. See Alan Beyerchen, "Clausewitz, Nonlinearity, and the Unpredictability of War," *International Security* 17, no. 3 (Winter 1992–93): 59–90.

38. Carl von Clausewitz, *On War*, 119.

39. Schwarzkopf, *Doesn't Take a Hero*, 315, 321–28, 326–27, 359–62, 368, 386–87, 418, 440–45. See comment by de la Billiere, *Storm Command*, 103.

40. General Field Marshal, Count Alfred von Schlieffen, *Cannae* (Fort Leavenworth, KS: The Command and General Staff School Press, 1936), 238. The final conclusions are repeated from the operational narrative the author prepared for the commander, ARCENT, in July 1991. At this writing, the author continues to believe they are appropriate.

Appendix A

Command and Control, ARCENT, February 1991

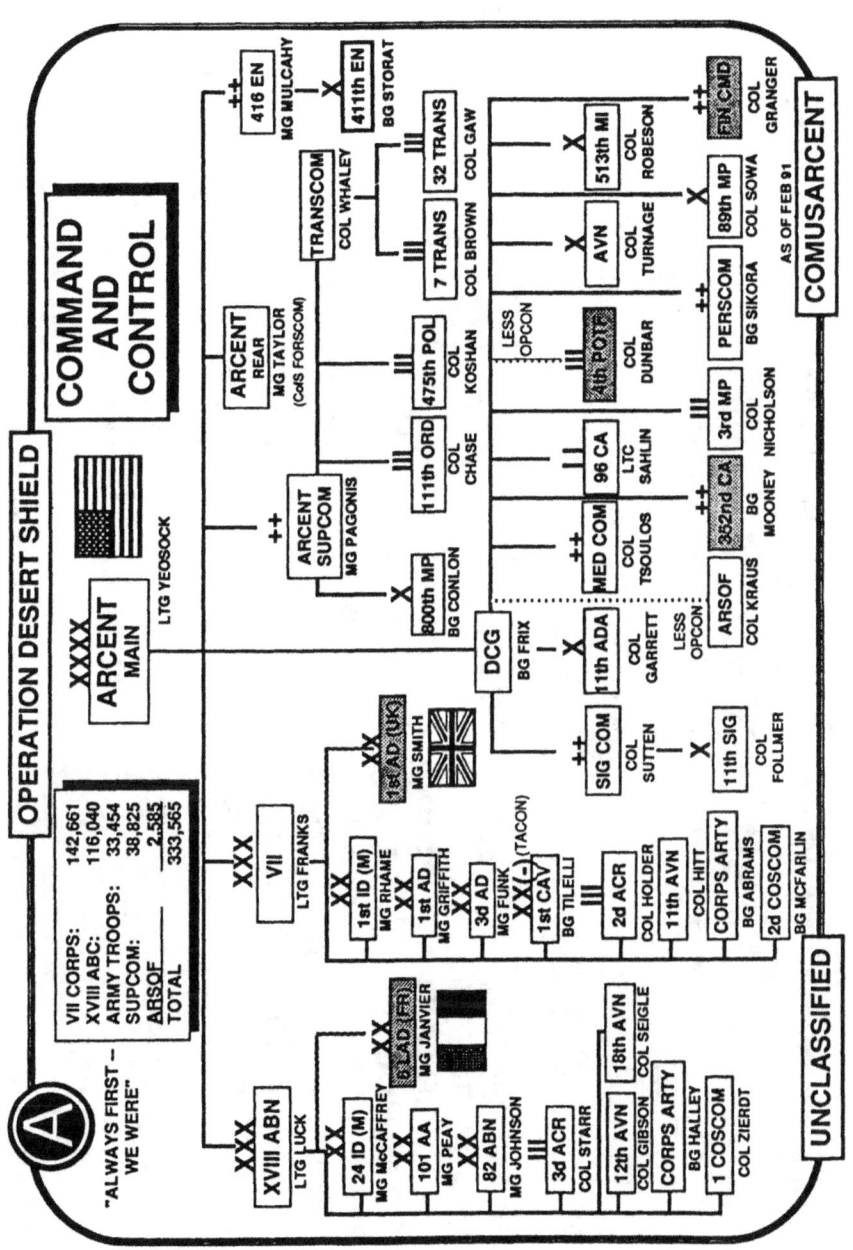

Appendix B
Task Organization, Operation Desert Shield, 5 March 1991

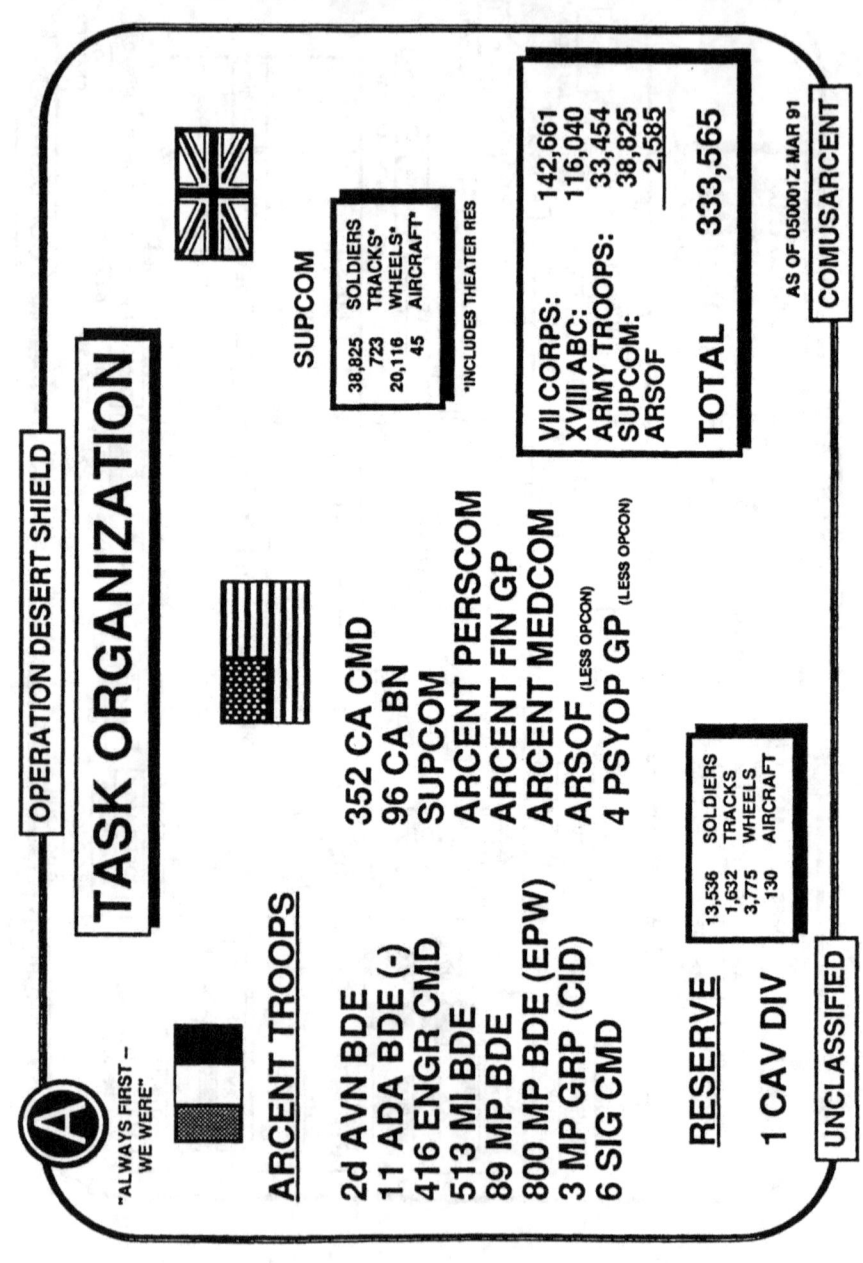

Appendix C
Warfighting Command and Control, XVIII Airborne Corps

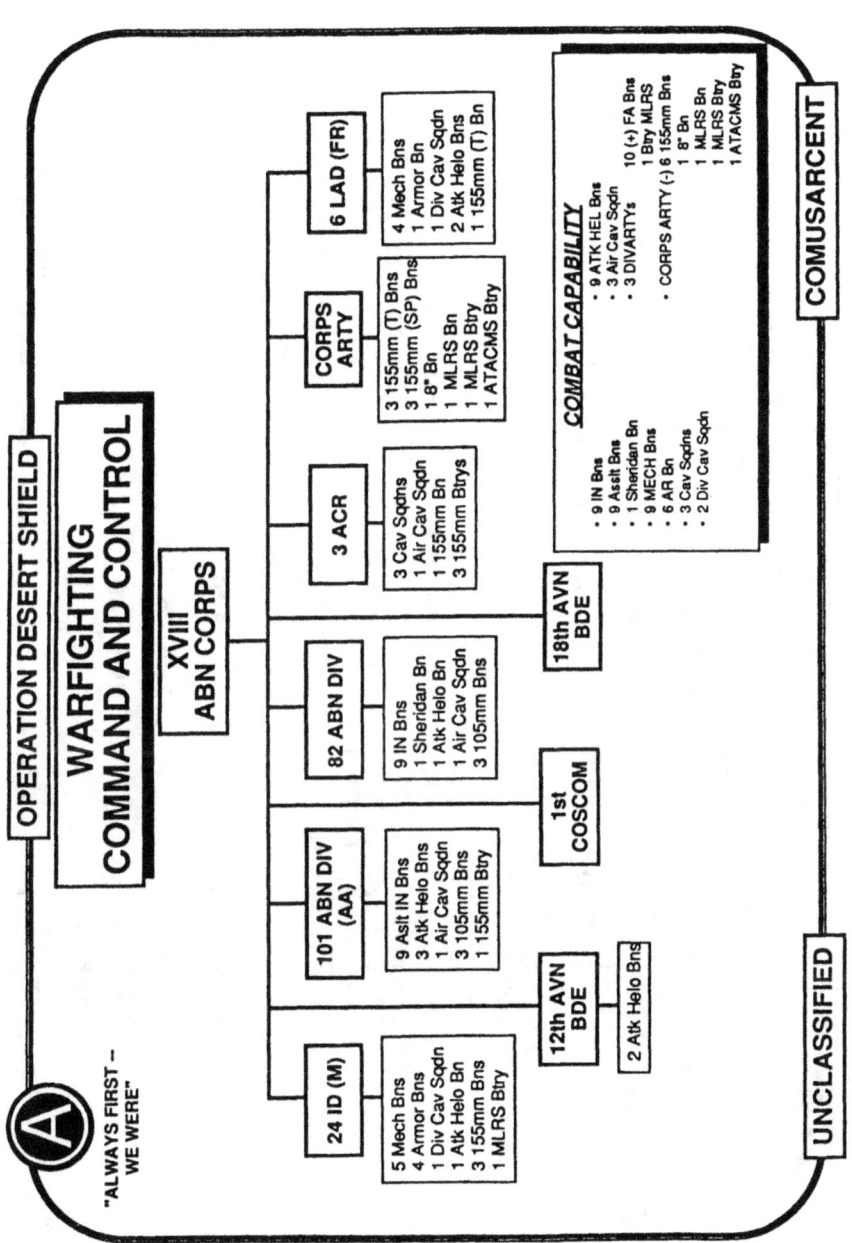

Appendix D

The XVIII Airborne Corps' Task Organization, 5 March 1991

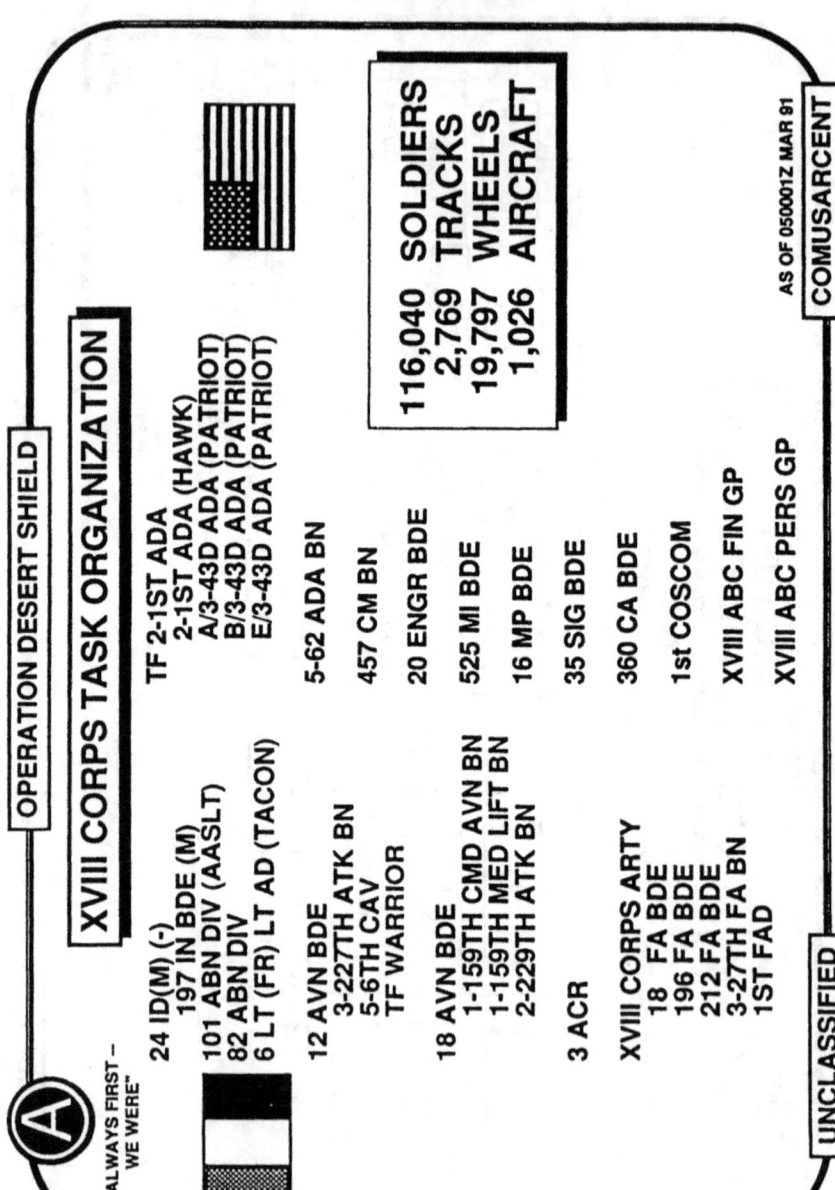

OPERATION DESERT SHIELD

XVIII CORPS TASK ORGANIZATION

116,040 SOLDIERS
2,769 TRACKS
19,797 WHEELS
1,026 AIRCRAFT

24 ID(M) (-)
 197 IN BDE (M)
101 ABN DIV (AASLT)
82 ABN DIV
6 LT (FR) LT AD (TACON)

TF 2-1ST ADA
 2-1ST ADA (HAWK)
 A/3-43D ADA (PATRIOT)
 B/3-43D ADA (PATRIOT)
 E/3-43D ADA (PATRIOT)

5-62 ADA BN

457 CM BN

20 ENGR BDE

525 MI BDE

16 MP BDE

35 SIG BDE

360 CA BDE

1st COSCOM

XVIII ABC FIN GP

XVIII ABC PERS GP

12 AVN BDE
 3-227TH ATK BN
 5-6TH CAV
 TF WARRIOR

18 AVN BDE
 1-159TH CMD AVN BN
 1-159TH MED LIFT BN
 2-229TH ATK BN

3 ACR

XVIII CORPS ARTY
 18 FA BDE
 196 FA BDE
 212 FA BDE
 3-27TH FA BN
 1ST FAD

"ALWAYS FIRST — WE WERE"

AS OF 050001Z MAR 91
COMUSARCENT

UNCLASSIFIED

Appendix E
Warfighting Command and Control, VII Corps

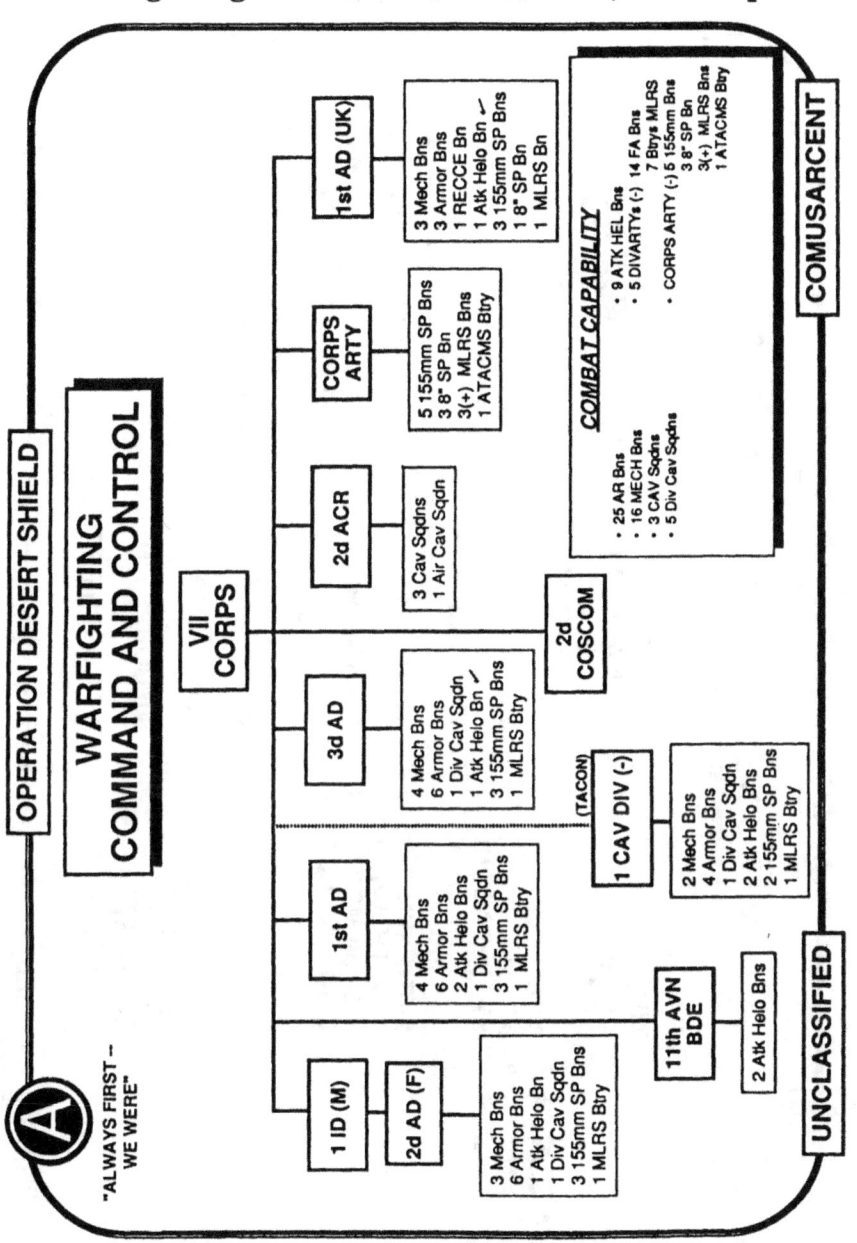

Appendix F
The VII Corps' Task Organization, 5 March 1991

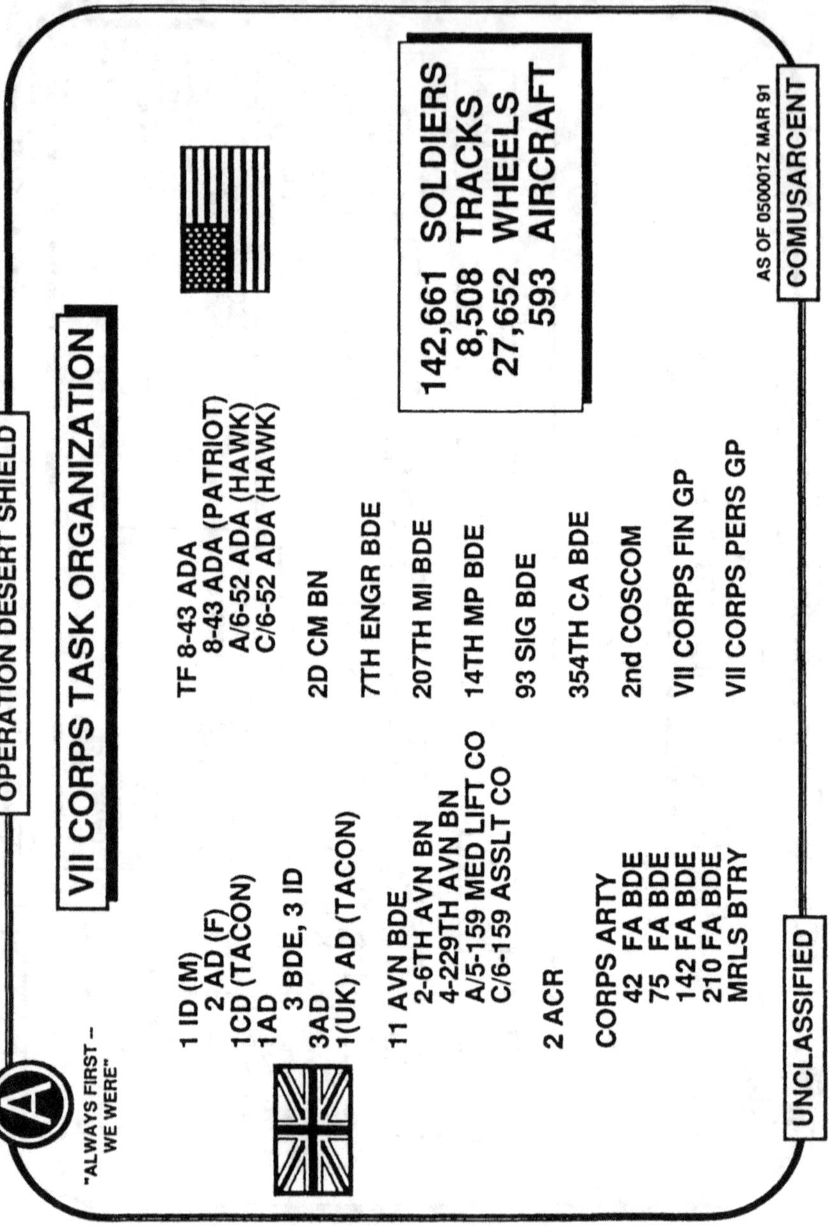

OPERATION DESERT SHIELD

VII CORPS TASK ORGANIZATION

"ALWAYS FIRST — WE WERE"

1 ID (M)
2 AD (F)
1CD (TACON)
1AD
  3 BDE, 3 ID
3AD
1(UK) AD (TACON)

11 AVN BDE
  2-6TH AVN BN
  4-229TH AVN BN
  A/5-159 MED LIFT CO
  C/6-159 ASSLT CO

2 ACR

CORPS ARTY
  42 FA BDE
  75 FA BDE
  142 FA BDE
  210 FA BDE
  MRLS BTRY

TF 8-43 ADA
  8-43 ADA (PATRIOT)
  A/6-52 ADA (HAWK)
  C/6-52 ADA (HAWK)

2D CM BN

7TH ENGR BDE

207TH MI BDE

14TH MP BDE

93 SIG BDE

354TH CA BDE

2nd COSCOM

VII CORPS FIN GP

VII CORPS PERS GP

142,661 SOLDIERS
8,508 TRACKS
27,652 WHEELS
593 AIRCRAFT

AS OF 050001Z MAR 91
COMUSARCENT

UNCLASSIFIED

Appendix G
Current Combat Capability, 24 February 1991

OPERATION DESERT SHIELD

CURRENT COMBAT CAPABILITY

OUR MISSION IS TO ATTACK TO DESTROY THE REPUBLICAN GUARDS FORCES COMMAND.

ATTACK WITH:

- 25 Mech Bns
- 31 Armor Bns
- 6 Cav Sqdns
- 7 Div Cav Sqdns
- 18 Bns of Infantry
- 1 Sheridan Bn
- 18 Attack Helicopter Bns
- 4 Air Cav Sqdn
- 9(-) DIVARTYs w/ 8 Btrys of MLRS
- 2 Corps Arty (-) w/ 3 155mm Bns (T), 8 155mm Bns (SP), 5 8" SP Bns, 4(+) Bns MLRS, & 2 ATACMS Btrys
- 21 Patriot Btrys linked to AWACS

ANTI-ARMOR CAPABILITY

M1A1	1650
M1	116
CHIEFTAIN	117
AMX30B2	44
M551	56
BFV/CFV	1583
AMX10RC	96
AH64	257
AH1S/F	141
TOW	549
HOT (FRENCH)	84
• TOTAL	**4693**

"ALWAYS FIRST – WE WERE"

AS OF 24 FEB 91

COMUSARCENT

UNCLASSIFIED

Appendix H
Chronology

16 Jul 90	ARCENT OPLAN 1002-90 (draft) (Defense of Saudi Arabia) published
2 Aug 90	Iraq invades Kuwait (0140Z)
	UN Security Council Resolution 660 condemns invasion and calls for withdrawal of Iraqi troops
	United States imposes an embargo on Iraq, deploys USAF tanker squadrons, moves USS *Independence* battle group toward Persian Gulf
4 Aug 90	General John Yeosock, commander, Third Army, is summoned to MacDill Air Force Base by General Schwarzkopf
5 Aug 90	Secretary of defense party flies to Saudi Arabia meeting with King Fahd
6 Aug 90	Saudi king requests U.S. forces in defense of kingdom
7 Aug 90	President Bush orders deployment of military forces and Operation Desert Shield begins
8 Aug 90	President announces deployment and U.S. national objectives
	ARCENT advanced command and control element arrives in Saudi Arabia
9 Aug 90	The XVIII Corps advanced CP and first units of 82d Airborne Division arrive in theater
10 Aug 90	CENTCOM OPORD issued
12 Aug 90	The 82d Airborne Division establishes advanced base at Al Jubayl
	President orders Navy to enforce embargo
13 Aug 90	First ships carrying the 24th Infantry Division depart from Savannah
14 Aug 90	Division-ready brigade of 82d Airborne Division completes deployment

5 Aug 90	Secretary of defense requests president to call selected Reserve forces to active duty
18 Aug 90	U.S. Navy fires first shots enforcing the blockade
19 Aug 90	Iraqis observed building barriers on Saudi border with Kuwait
22 Aug 90	President informs Congress that he is invoking his authority to call-up selected Reserves
	ARCENT OPORD 1 Desert Shield published
25 Aug 90	UN Security Council Resolution 665 authorizes use of force to enforce sanctions on Iraq
27 Aug 90	First ship carrying 24th Infantry Division arrives in theater
28 Aug 90	MARCENT assumes security of Al Jubayl
7 Sep 90	Brigadier General Steven Arnold arrives to be G3, Third Army
14 Sep 90	Schwarzkopf orders Third Army to plan for defense of Riyadh
16 Sep 90	"Jedi Knights" arrive at CENTCOM
25 Sep 90	The 24th Infantry Division closes
5 Oct 90	The 1st Cavalry Division begins to arrive
7 Oct 90	The 101st Airborne Division completes deployment
11 Oct 90	CENTCOM chief of staff and party brief President Bush on one-corps plan
14 Oct 90	The 3d Armored Cavalry Regiment completes deployment
17 Oct 90	The Third Army commander and British theater commander (General de Billiere) briefed for first time on offensive planning
22–23 Oct 90	Chairman of the Joint Chiefs of Staff briefed on one- and two-corps options
24 Oct 90	CINC's planning group placed under Third Army's supervision
25 Oct 90	1st Cavalry Division completes deployment

	Secretary of defense begins talking about additional force build-up in Saudi Arabia
30 Oct 90	The XVIII Corps reports closure in Saudi Arabia
4 Nov 90	General Saint and General Franks select Europe-based brigades for deployment with VII Corps
6 Nov 90	Saudi king and U.S. secretary of state agree to coalition command plan
8 Nov 90	President Bush announces offensive option and doubling of forces in peninsula
14 Nov 90	Schwarzkopf briefs subordinate commanders on his campaign plan
29 Nov 90	UN Security Council sets deadline for Iraqi withdrawal
30 Nov 90	The XVIII Corps briefs corps plan to ARCENT commander
7 Dec 90	The VII Corps commander briefs corps plan to ARCENT commander
20 Dec 90	Secretary of defense and chairman of the Joint Chiefs of Staff briefed on offensive plans
23–28 Dec 90	Movement exercise at Support Command in Dhahran
27–30 Dec 90	Third Army MAPEX at Eskan Village
28 Dec 90	Movement briefing for CINC. General Pagonis "signs his contract"
30 Dec 90	Syrians announce they are unwilling to attack Iraq
8 Jan 91	Schwarzkopf approves Third Army plan
12 Jan 91	"Lucky Wheels" deploys to KKMC
17 Jan 91	Air operations begin against Iraq
18 Jan 91	First Scud missiles fired at Israel and Saudi Arabia by Iraq
29 Jan 91	Iraqi attack at Khafji (counterattack lasts to 1 Feb)
1 Feb 91	Commander's huddle at KKMC
4 Feb 91	The VII Corps takes responsibilty for border in attack sector

8 Feb 91	Third Army commander reports force closed
9 Feb 91	Final briefing to secretary of defense and chairman, Joint Chiefs of Staff
13 Feb 91	Third Army directs movement into forward assembly areas
14 Feb 91	General Yeosock hospitalized
	Cross-border operations authorized
15 Feb 91	The VII Corps begins movement into attack positions
20 Feb 91	Battle of Ruqi pocket
	President Bush gives Iraqis four days to withdraw from Kuwait
22 Feb 91	President Gorbachev announces final Soviet peace proposal; Iraq accepts; United States does not
	United States gives Iraq twenty-four hours to begin withdrawal or accept consequences
23 Feb 91	Iraq rejects U.S.-Coalition ultimatum
	General Yeosock resumes command of Third Army
24 Feb 91	Ground attack begins
28 Feb 91	Cessation of offensive actions
2 Mar 91	The 24th Division's "Battle of the Causeway"
3 Mar 91	Cease-fire talks at Safwan
15 Mar 91	Ramadan begins

Glossary

-A-

ACCB	air cavalry combat brigade
ACR	armored cavalry regiment
AD	armored division
ANGLICO	air and naval gunfire liaison company
AO	area of operations
ARCENT	Army Central Command
ARTEP	Army Training and Evaluation Program
ATACMS	Army tactical missiles
ATO	air tasking order

-B-

BAI	battlefield air interdiction
BCE	battlefield control element
BCTP	Battle Command Training Program
BDA	battle damage assessment
BENT	beginning evening nautical twilight
BMD	Russian-design infantry fighting vehicle
BMNT	beginning morning tactical twilight

-C-

CAA	Concepts and Analysis Agency (Army)
CAB	combined arms battalion
C-day	force deployment date
CENTAF	Central Command Air Force
CENTAG	Central Army Group (NATO)
CENTCOM	Central Command
CEV	combat engineer vehicles
CINC	commander in chief
CONUS	continental United States
CONUSAs	stateside Army-level headquarters
CP	command post
C3IC	Coalition Coordination Communication Integration Center

-D-

DCG	deputy commanding general
DCSLOG	deputy chief of staff for logistics
DCSOPS	deputy chief of staff for operations
DFE	division force equivalent
DRAO	Defense Reconstruction Assistance Office

-E-

EPW	enemy prisoner of war
EST	Eastern Standard Time
EUCOM	European Command (U.S.)
Exercise Internal Look	A 1990 exercise based on an Iraqi threat to the Arabian peninsula

-F-

FOB	forward operating base
FORSCOM	Forces Command
FRAGO	fragmentary orders
FSCL	fire support coordination line
FSS	fast sealift ships

-G-

G-day	24 February, the beginning of the ground phase of the campaign
GPS	global positioning system

-H-

HEMTT	heavy expanded mobility tactical truck
HETs	heavy equipment transporters
HMMWV	high-mobility multipurpose wheeled vehicle

-I-

ICM	improved conventional munition
ID	infantry division

-J-

JFACC	joint force air component commander
J5	joint operations officer
J4	joint logistics staff officer
JSCAP	Joint Strategic Capability Plan
J-STARS	joint surveillance target attack radar system
Just Cause	U.S. military operations in Panama

-K-

KKMC	King Khalid Military City
KTO	Kuwaiti theater of operations

-L-

LAV	light armored vehicle
LNO	liaison officer
LORAN	long-range very-low-frequency navigation systems
LZ	landing zone

-M-

MACOM	major Army command
MAPEX	map exercise
MARCENT	Marine Central Command
MEB	Marine expeditionary brigade
MEDCOM	medical command
METT-T	mission, enemy, terrain and weather, and troops and time available
MI	military intelligence
MLRS	multiple launch rocket system
MPS	maritime prepositioning ships
MSR	main supply route

-N-

NAVCENT	Navy Central Command
NCA	national command authorities

-O-

Operation Urgent Fury	1983 U.S. invasion of Grenada
OPLAN	operations plan
OPMSANG	Office of the Program Manager, Saudi Army National Guard
OPORD	operations order

-P-

PERSCOM	Personnel Command
PL	phase line
PMO	provost marshal office
PMSANG	Program Manager, Saudi Army National Guard
POW	prisoner of war

-R-

REFORGER Exercises	return of forces to Europe exercises
RGFC	Republican Guard Forces Command
RPG	rocket-propelled grenade

-S-

SANG	Saudi Army National Guard
SAMS	School of Advanced Military Studies
SCUD	ballistic missile (enemy variety)
SITREP	situation report
SLUGR	small lightweight global positioning system
SOCCENT	Special Operations Command, Central
SOF	special operations forces
SOFA	Status of Forces Agreement
SUPCOM	Support Command

-T-

TAA	tactical assembly area
TAACOM	theater army area command
TAC (or tac)	tactical
TACSAT	tactical satellite
"Tiger Brigade"	1st Brigade, 2d Armored Division
TOC	tactical operations center
TOE	table of organization
TOW	tube-launched, optically tracked, wire-guided (missile)
TPFDD	time-phased force development data
TPFDL	time-phased force deployment list
TRADOC	Training and Doctrine Command
TRANSCOM	U.S. Transportation Command

-U-

UAV	unmanned aerial vehicle
USAREUR	U.S. Army Europe
USMTM	U.S. Military Training Mission

Bibliography

Notes on Sources

This study is not accompanied by a bibliography because, though the author has consulted them, for the most part this book has not been written from published sources. It has been written based upon personal observation, the study of documentary evidence, and personal interviews (where such have been useful to clarify points upon which other documents have been silent). The decision of the author not to become overly involved in published sources was more a consequence of the period in which he undertook his study than from any other factor. There has been no shortage of published accounts of the Gulf War, but there has been very much a lack of *documented* accounts upon which one might rely. Indeed, a sign of the maturing of the field will be the first history that *does not* depend on Bob Woodwards' instant narrative of the strategic direction of the war as a primary source (as found in *The Commanders* [New York: Simon and Schuster, 1991]).

The early accounts are not without value, but they suffer as a class from the haste in which they were written. Among these are James Blackwell's *Thunder in the Desert* (New York: Bantam Books, 1991) and James F. Dunnigan and Austin Bay's *From Shield to Storm* (New York: William Morrow, 1992). Colonel (Retired) Harry Summers' *On Strategy II: A Critical Analysis of the Gulf War* (New York: Dell Paperback, 1992) was more opportunistic and had as much to say about the author's well-known views on the Vietnam War as it did the war in the Persian Gulf. Indeed, Summers' book reflected no research base whatever. Among the better early books was the *U.S. News and World Report*'s, *Triumph Without Victory: The Unreputed History of the Persian Gulf War* (New York: Random House-Times Books, 1992). This work went a long way toward explaining the complexity of the air war to those innocent of the problems associated with it. Its account of the ground war suffered from the proximity of that magazine's "War Horse," Joe Galloway, to the 24th Division commander; Galloway misread the organization of the theater command structure. *Triumph Without Victory*, nonetheless, began the worthwhile task of portraying the war from the perspective of those who fought Desert Storm. It also started the ill-considered debate about whether or not the apparent success had been suitably complete. This theme was taken up by others, like Jeffrey Record, in *Hollow Victory: A Contrary View of the Gulf War* (Washington, D.C.: Brasseys [U.S.], 1993). Record's book, however, was at least internally consistent, whereas the *U.S. News'* conclusions seems an afterthought by an editor who had not read his own account before drawing sensational conclusions meant to hype his sales.

Among the best of the first wave of Gulf War books is Lawrence Freedman and Efraim Karsh's, *The Gulf Conflict 1990–1991: Diplomacy and War in the New World Order* (Princeton, NJ: Princeton University Press, 1991). Freedman and Karsh still rely heavily upon Woodward, but they benefited from their experience of working on a television documentary that brought them together with a number of knowledgeable second-level governmental officials from the Bush administration. They also profited from their knowledge of Middle East regional newspapers and Soviet affairs, which permitted them to form a more global vision of the events leading up to the war, no less the problems of maintaining the coalition.

General Schwarzkopf's autobiographical account (with Peter Petre), *It Doesn't Take a Hero* (New York: Linda Grey, Bantam, 1992), appeared after a year. This highly tendentious and self-serving account may be true to the theater commander's view of the events of the war (and his earlier career), but it certainly lacks the virtues of statesmanship or objectivity. A much better firsthand account was written by General Peter de la Billiere, *Storm Command* (London: Harper Collins, 1992), an account not generally available in the United States. De la Billiere, by contrast with Schwarzkopf, is disarmingly candid and his evaluation of the theater commander is both admiring and critical. It remains the best firsthand account of the operation of the high command. Lieutenant General William ("Gus") Pagonis, the Army Support Command commander (and the only battlefield elevation—to Lieutenant General—among the senior Army officers in theater), provides a short account of the significant logistic challenges of the war. Coauthored with Jeffrey L. Cruikshank, *Moving Mountains* (Boston, 1992) was published, interestingly enough, by the Harvard Business School Press. Only about half the book actually deals with the war, and that is none too informative—except that there is nothing else on the subject.

To date, the best journalistic account is Rick Atkinson's *Crusade: The Untold Story of the Persian Gulf War* (Boston: Houghton Mifflin, 1993). *Crusade* is exciting to read but suffers from its narrowness of focus. It begins with the start of the air combat and ignores for the most part the five and one-half month build-up that preceded it. Like most of its predecessors, it misses entirely the structure of the theater command by component. For those interested in war at the eyeball level, however, Atkinson is a splendid storyteller, and he was the first (de la Billiere aside) to really address the influence of personality on the events of the conflict. The U.S. Army put a team together at Fort Monroe, Virginia, to place the Army's institutional view of the war on the record, with particular attention to the efforts of those who actually did the fighting. Led by Brigadier General Bob Scales, the team produced a splendid book with excellent graphics and photographs titled *Certain Victory* (Washington, D.C.: Office of the Chief of Staff, U.S. Army, 1993). Finally, the Office of the Secretary of Defense assembled a massive and multivolume compendia in a report to Congress: *The Conduct of the Persian Gulf War, Final Report to Congress Pursuant to Title V of the Persian Gulf Conflict Supplemental Authorization and Personnel Benefits Act of 1991 (Public Law 102-25)*, issued in April 1993. To date, these books represent the field, with a number of other accounts addressing the role of air power and, particularly, the military relations, or lack of them, with the press.

For the most part, this present account has been based upon documentary sources assembled in the theater or upon return to the United States. The sources used are, with one exception, now housed in an archive run by the Combined Arms Command historian at Fort Leavenworth, Kansas. *The New York Times, The Washington Post,* and *Army Times* served as the newspapers of record. The one exception noted is the notes written for General Yeosock by Lieutenant Colonel Mike Kendall. These are deposited in Yeosock's papers at the Military History Institute, Carlisle Barracks, Pennsylvania.

Documentary sources consisted, first of all, of documents produced at the time of the events they have been used to explain or, second, they were deliberately created memoirs drawn up after the fact as part of the Army's own effort to document how it accomplished what it did in the Persian Gulf. In the latter case, as my great and respected friend Lieutenant Colonel Dave Mock has reminded me pointedly, the planning organizations are better represented than the operators. Planners have more time after combat begins to reflect and record their views than do the operators, who continue to work up to the date of final departure. There is, thus, an undeniable tilt toward crediting the planning actions and a corresponding neglect of the minutia associated with the conduct of daily operations without which no plans achieve life.

Two categories of contemporary (as opposed to retrospective) records have been used widely. These are the daily situation reports, through which the Third Army commander (or normally his staff officers) told various higher headquarters how they saw the world on any given day, and the collection of briefing slides the commander used to explain himself to his boss, the theater commander, both daily and for a variety of ad hoc purposes. The outsider can easily overlook the importance of briefing slides in an Army organization. They are the coin of dialog. Briefing slides summarize the affairs and arguments surrounding any issue. Staff officers spend a good bit of time finding the information they contain in a timely manner and, though one can sometimes doubt where the last significant digit may be on any particular slide, the information contained therein becomes reality for those who must decide. General Yeosock's personal staff maintained the slides he used in a disciplined and orderly fashion throughout the war and provided a complete set of the slides to the author. These have been of inestimable value, and their authors (especially Lieutenant Colonel Mat Kriwanek) are owed a large debt for their efforts.

The daily memoranda of the meetings the Army commander attended, prepared by Yeosock's executive officer, Lieutenant Colonel Mike Kendall, have also been an extraordinary source of information, particularly of the period after December 1990. Unit staff journals were generally indifferently kept and badly preserved. Most units made some effort to collect their operational records after the war, but initial consolidation efforts lacked energy. Many key records remain to be located. To energize the effort when it became clear that routine procedures were inadequate, General Frederick Franks, now Training and Doctrine Command commander, established a Gulf War Archive at Fort Leavenworth. Through his personal intervention and great effort, the VII Corps' after-action reports, including copies of key records, were sent to the archive to start the collection. Other record sets arrive daily, and the collection at Leavenworth is the most accessible and complete archive available to researchers who can meet clearance requirements or identify the records desired for declassification. The Combined Arms Command historian, Dr. Roddler Morris, and his staff have assembled and continue to build a number of finding aids to help in the identification of records for outside researchers.

Finally, a word about postwar accounts is called for. One of the primary sources for anyone interested in the actions of Third Army in the Gulf War is a set of narratives written and placed in large binders by the officers of the Third Army G3 Plans shop in the days after the war while they waited in Saudi Arabia for the return of the headquarters to the United States and their own dispersal back to the posts from which most had been drawn. This multivolume account covers all aspects of the planning process from the point of view of the majors and lieutenant colonels who did the spade work. They are clearly written and accompanied, in most cases, by the documents necessary to understand their subject matter.

The VII Corps' unit after-action reports represent the largest volume of records in the Gulf War Archive, and many such reports are quite good (though some are less informative). There is a large archive at Fort Bragg of XVIII Corps' records that remains to be fully culled and organized. Anyone who believed in 1990 that electronic media would replace paper records was overly optimistic, for the Army in the Persian Gulf moved on its paper and xeroxed or reprinted the most routine documents in hundreds of copies. Record copies may never be properly established, and much that remains on computer disks may ultimately be lost, but there will be, nonetheless, a mountain of documentary evidence to support the various services' official histories whenever they are begun. Hopefully, this account, which is inevitably part memoir and part documented narrative, will help them understand what they find.

www.ingramcontent.com/pod-product-compliance
Lightning Source LLC
Chambersburg PA
CBHW050158240426
43671CB00013B/2170